ALL OR NOTHING

ALL OR NOTHING

THE MEMOIRS OF A DRUMMER

STUART MEADOWS

BROWN DOG BOOKS

First published 2021

Published under licence by Brown Dog Books and
The Self-Publishing Partnership Ltd, 10b Greenway Farm, Bath Rd, Wick,
nr. Bath BS30 5RL

www.selfpublishingpartnership.co.uk

ISBN paperback book: 978-1-83952-316-8
ISBN hardback book: 978-1-83952-317-5
ISBN e-book: 978-1-83952-318-2

Cover design by Paul Davies
Internal design by Andrew Easton

Printed and bound in the UK

This book is printed on FSC certified paper

MIX
Paper from responsible sources
FSC® C013604
FSC
www.fsc.org

DEDICATION.

TO DAD FOR INTRODUCING ME TO THE WONDERFUL WORLD OF MUSIC.

TO GRANDAD FOR INTRODUCING ME TO THE IDEA OF PLAYING DRUMS.

TO MUM AND GEOFF FOR BUYING ME MY FIRST DRUMKIT.

TO ALL OF THE ABOVE FOR SUPPORTING ME THROUGH 'ALL OR NOTHING'.

Foreword

You have probably seen him around. He's hard to miss. Standing tall with his spiky black/white barnet, he is frequently visible in the crowd at punk shows. He is also often spotted at the same events sat down on a drum stool, bashing the living daylights out of the kit in front of him for the likes of 999, Conflict, Resistance 77, The Lurkers, English Dogs, March to the Grave…. there's quite a list.

Stoo's recollections were always going to make for an insightful and entertaining read for fans of the punk scene, but what greets you in the pages that follow is so much more. If you think you know Stoo, think again.

This is a brutally honest, at times shocking, and frequently unnerving account of his life. Punk rock chaos, misbehaviour, band bust-ups, and friendships are recalled with clarity, but that's only part of it. There is also a human story of an often troubled soul who has conquered demons aplenty and dragged himself back from the precipice to achieve musical ambitions beyond his dreams, and crucially, to find stability within himself to maintain his focus. Navigating a life full of pitfalls, narcotics and family troubles, to emerge battered, bruised, but ultimately triumphant, is a testimony to an inner strength we can all aspire to.

Importantly, All Or Nothing is a rare instance of music, specifically an unshakeable passion for punk rock, saving a life.

Redemption is real and here lies the tale of a man who has earned it. The hard way.

Phil Singleton

(February 2021)

CONTENTS

INTRODUCTION

March 2020

In the space of just a few weeks, it seems that the world is about to be sent reeling into a situation that it was ill prepared for. 'Social Distancing' is now the order of the day. As March began, I was looking at a schedule jam packed with dates all over the world – tours in America and Canada, gigs in Germany and Ireland, and festivals all over the UK. Then bang, everything comes to a halt automatically meaning that everybody – and I mean everybody – is affected. The music industry, for the first time ever, is stopped in its tracks. Promoters, club owners, doormen, bar staff, sound engineers, merch guys and printers and of course musicians are all forced to down tools and contemplate their futures as the very thing they love and feel passionate about is wrenched from their grasp.

But let's not be selfish here. Covid-19 has impacted upon everyone and everything. Every being on the planet has been somewhat affected, with poor souls even losing their lives due to the pandemic. Everything I have ever known has been turned upside down. My days have been turned into a Groundhog Day-like existence and believe me, for a person who is used to the everyday freedoms that I suppose we all take for granted, this is a bitter pill to swallow. I'm used to travelling. I'm used to rehearsing. I'm used to expelling the energy required to perform a whole succession of gigs whilst drumming.

For as long as I can remember, drumming has been my life. Something that I not only enjoy, but a way of life. Playing music is my exercise. Bashing out a full punk rock set is something akin to a full gym workout. It is my social life and I thrive off interaction with the punters and the camaraderie with the other band members I'm involved with; for me it is a positive and productive existence. It gives me a sense of pride and achievement. The getting home after I've done gigs with that pleasant feeling of satisfaction. THE BUZZ. Writing new songs from their embryonic stage to completion, getting in the studio to see our creations develop into a finished piece. Again, THE BUZZ. I am mindful that I have spent my years doing something that many others would love to do. Not just playing an instrument, but actually taking it further. Whilst writing this, I am not only submersed in the midst of the chaos caused by Corona virus, but I am in fact in the fortunate position of having a new album with 999 about to be released, but we will talk about that later. What I am saying is that the very thing that makes me tick, the thing that drives me, influences me and gives me purpose and makes me feel at one with myself has had to end. And although it won't be forever, I have come to the realisation that I have to be humble and ride it out until eventually this strange time passes. By the time you read this, hopefully these unprecedented circumstances will have moved on and some semblance of our previous lives will have resumed. Right, that's that over with. Let's roll!

If you are taking the time to read this book, I'd assume you must be a person not unlike myself, a fanatic of music. Primarily, that is how I would describe myself. The fact that I learned to play drums is a huge bonus as it has allowed me to delve deeper into the music scene with all of its trials, tribulations, benefits and pitfalls. You may yourself even be a musician reading this book and so you may be able to relate to a lot that has been written down here. And with that, you'll know more than anybody that there's two sides to being one of those supposedly artistic types. Musicians, myself included, are Jekyll and Hyde-type characters. For as much as we tend to be creative, charismatic, energetic and driven, we also bring a plethora of character defects to the table. More often than not though, you - the fans of the bands you worship and appreciate don't get to see that side of us. I count myself in with that, as one of the supposed bohemian types who, for one reason or another, comes across as one that people look up to, due to having an ability to pluck people out of any form of dull or boring 'normalness' for an hour or two, at a gig or even for the length of just a song or an album. You must remember one thing, though. And that is that we are flawed. I am flawed. And no doubt whilst reading this, you will be able to make those assumptions for yourself as you learn who I really am and the colourful journey I have thus far undertaken. I have got to this point in my life because of people, and let's be honest, we are all influenced by the people that we are involved with. Whether it be good or for bad, this is what makes us human and the music scene absolutely epitomises this.

Any of you who know me well know that I have played and still play with various bands. With this comes my interactions with various PEOPLE. And with that in mind, it just needs to be stated from myself that all of the individuals I have come across and worked with have my full respect, irrespective of whether we've had differences of opinion, musically or personally. For this story to be true, I need it to be known that I intend to share my experiences warts and all, and by doing so I suspect it will piss some people off. That's not my intention, but I intend to note things down just as I see and remember them. Rest assured I am aware that I, too, will also have pissed people off along the way. I love music. I loved music way before I learnt to play an instrument. I'm sure we can all remember hearing something, a song perhaps, a sound or a lyric when we were kids that triggered something inside. It's a feeling, not necessarily something that you can explain, but whatever it was it was bloody good. It was energising and uplifting. For me it took me away from myself. It still does, particularly when playing. For me, music is a release and if it's loud enough it gives me a buzz.

I first recall experiencing that feeling when I was a kid. My Dad was a music fan and used to play his 60s records via the radio or on one of his old record players or radiograms. One song that sticks out is *Run Away* by DEL SHANNON. I'm sure most of you will know it. Catchy as fuck lyrics and a great keyboard solo in the middle. *Tobacco Road* by the NASHVILLE TEENS was another one. That's an amazing song and to me still sounds raw and ahead of its time. There were snippets of the MONKEES' songs like *I'm A Believer* and the ROLLING STONES, *The Last Time,* with its distorted guitar intro etc. LITTLE RICHARD was another one. That bloke had such a powerful and amazing voice that I used to repeatedly play his singles *Babyface* and *Lucille* that my Dad gave to me just before my folks split up in 1978. These were some of my first little introductions to music and there would be many more to come. And so it was at around this time in the late 70s that one day I heard a song and it changed me forever. It was different from anything I'd heard before and at that time it was acquainted with a new form of music. Well, not necessarily a new form as such, but this song sounded different from anything I'd heard before, made all the more so by the vocal delivery. And so, this is where my story really begins…

PART 1.

1. BORN IN THE SUMMER OF LOVE

I was born on 4 May 1967 right slap bang in the middle of hippiedom and the summer of love. My Mum (Pamela Frances Burch) was 19, my Dad (Richard Meadows) 21. Mum was from Grantham and Dad was a city kid, born and raised in Nottingham. I came into the world at Nottingham City Hospital and my first address was in Nottingham, somewhere in the Hyson Green area but, to be honest, like with most people, I have little recollection of my first three years. I can remember my brother (James Ivan Meadows) coming into the world in 1970. My folks would have been like any other young couple who had a couple of sprogs to take care of. They would have struggled and just got on with it, having their fair share of ups and downs along the way. Apparently I was an unruly child and my Mum had to constantly keep her eye on me. I wasn't a shy kid and, if not kept in check, would just wander off and do my own thing. I didn't like going to bed when I was told and I always had an abundance of energy. But even from as early as aged 5 or 6, I became aware of music. At that point, it was pop music like the records previously mentioned and a myriad of others as my old man would always have the radio playing. Often Radio Luxembourg and occasionally Radio Caroline, I was hearing sounds that without realising it at the time, I connected with. I remember it that vividly it has to be so. I have a recollection of observing my Dad once drumming on the table with his hands. Looking back, he would have been a good drummer because I can remember being a little impressed by what he was doing. He looked quite a natural as he drummed in time to whatever the song was. Maybe rhythm is an inherent thing. There was, however, another person in my life who would later become a massive influence, steering me in the direction of drums and a musical vocation. We will get to that soon.

At the age of 6 in 1973 Mum, Dad, James my brother and I emigrated to Port Elizabeth in South Africa. When looking back on that time, of which we were there for just under three years, I remember a predominantly good time. It was certainly a stark contrast to England and the UK. I remember the sun and the sea, both of which I loved. I was never afraid of the sea and learned to swim out there. We had a Volkswagen Beetle and I can remember another, a Ford Escort. We had lots of barbeques or braais, as they are called over there. Once again, music was always in the air as my Dad always liked it on in the background. Still being a young family, as my folks would have been only in their mid- to late twenties, I can remember that we gravitated towards other young families from the UK. I suppose home being the UK gave everybody something to relate to. Outdoor get-togethers were arranged with lots of laughter, drinking of booze, barbeque food and music is something that I distinctly remember. I used to be sent off to school in my short trousers, a peaked cap, a blazer and a little case. Back then, I would go into the bush, the equivalent of the woods or wasteland in the UK, and find tortoises. I gathered a right collection of about 12 or 13 at one point – I even had one with only 3 legs.

I used to get in a bit of trouble too, as for some reason I enjoyed breaking glass. I remember breaking some windows of an old building and the police caught me. I was taken home and given a good hiding from my Dad. I started nicking sweets from shops, too. Luckily I never got caught but on one occasion I was with my brother James. Having him around was not something I needed when trying to nick some sweets, so I told him to go home and I'd bring him some back when I'd done. Anyway, I filled my pockets from this shop and made my way home, feeling really proud of myself that I'd got away without paying for these goodies, and as I approached home, James was waiting and as soon as he saw me he started shouting, 'Did you get me some sweets?' Well, that was it, my cover was blown as I had no money and my parents had not given me any, so they knew I'd stolen them. That was another good hiding and I was banished to my room. In some sense it was just kids' stuff, but I was starting to show signs of the unruly behaviour that I mentioned earlier. On the whole, I remember these three years in South Africa as happy ones but my Mum was missing England. I guess that is when I first acknowledged that not all was well within my parents' relationship. My Dad was enjoying life out there and was quite content in his job as a Supermarket Manager, whereas my Mum was hankering for home more and more. Mum basically said to Dad that we should go back home as she wasn't happy and that if it didn't work out back in the UK, we could always return to South Africa. Underneath though, Mum wasn't interested in ever living in Africa again. We returned to the UK in mid-1977.

We got back from South Africa, and what I can only describe as a dark cloud hung over us on our return. The weather was shit and I remember a slight mood of depression setting in as soon as we got back. For one, the weather makes all the difference, especially when you've been used to a very warm climate to all of a sudden being thrown back into an environment filled with grey skies and downpours of rain. On top of all that, England was in the middle of a recession so my Dad couldn't find any decent work and it just made him regret our relocation. Mum started working on the markets to bring in some money but Dad just really didn't want to know. His heart was not in it and, in short, serious cracks started to show in their relationship. Over the next 12 months, I saw and heard my parents' relationship deteriorate to the point where they decided to split up. I was only 9 years old and was left feeling quite confused.

Dad hung about and tried to get his shit together and I enjoyed spending time with him. He got a job as a milkman and I loved going out with him, getting up at the crack of dawn and helping him deliver his round. But as I say, his heart wasn't in being back in England and he was in fact yearning to get back to South Africa. Sometime in 1978 he left and returned to Port Elizabeth. I was absolutely gutted and, no doubt, so was James. Our Dad had gone. Not up the road or to another town or city, but to the other side of the world. To be honest, I felt somewhat betrayed, and over the coming years I started to resent him for clearing off so far away. Although I had these feelings towards him, two things came about that were to prove very positive from his ultimate departure. One, he left me all of his records and one of those old record players, and two, without realising it at the time, my Dad being in South Africa would play a significant part in saving my life years later. I was just 10 when Dad left, and aside from a brief visit when he returned to England in 1980, the next time I saw him was when I was 23 when he came to visit me in Lincoln prison where I was serving a 3-year stretch for a series of drug-dealing offences.

So my folks have split up and I am 10 years old. It was inevitable that my Mum was going to find herself another fella, which was totally natural I suppose, but I can't pretend that I was overly enamoured with the prospect of sharing my Mum with another stranger. I can't say that I went into myself or became insular, but to be honest I didn't get a lot of excitement from playing with my Action Man, and so as time progressed I was going out and getting into all sorts of scrapes. It's 1977 and I've been soaking up all of the records Dad had left me as well as taking in other music I heard at the time. ABBA, QUEEN, THE ELECTRIC LIGHT ORCHESTRA, BACCARA and BROTHERHOOD OF MAN. I know what you're thinking, 'Jesus Christ, where's he going with this?' but that is just what I can remember. Rock music hadn't struck a chord with me yet, but I do remember one of those K-TEL compilations that I acquired at the time and it had GOLDEN EARRING (*Radar Love*), MUD, NAZARETH and SUZI QUATRO. I thought they were great songs and still do to this day. So in a way, looking back, I became insular to the point that I started to develop an obsession with music. I was also starting to show certain character traits. If I get into something, whether it be a topic or a subject that interests me, then I jump into it 100%. I wasn't a particularly academic child by any stretch of the imagination, but I really liked English, Art and History. Anything else I wasn't interested in and was subsequently shit at. I did become quite a strong athlete and a good swimmer, and because I was good at these sports, I gave it my all. That innate ability and desire to push harder and into realms of obsession can also have a darker side, but you will see that come to light as we move on. By this time I am attending Huntingtower Primary School. I am not the happiest kid on the block but there were certainly a lot of kids worse off than me. I remember being in the classroom with a small group of kids, and a lad called Colin, who is now a taxi driver and who I still see about every so often, mentioned the name JOHNNY ROTTEN and then SID VICIOUS. I was struck to attention. These names to me sounded dark but at the same time colourful, dangerous and exciting. I obviously wanted to know more, and me being me with a nose for seeking out what I wanted, went on a hunt to find out more. It didn't take long and shortly thereafter I found the song that would change my world quite dramatically. That song was *Anarchy In The UK* by the SEX PISTOLS! BOOM! All the music I'd heard up to that point, and admittedly for a kid of 10 I'd not heard that much, but to hear that record was like a bomb going off. You can't put your finger on it or describe it, but anything I'd heard before that didn't compare to how this record made me feel. Hearing *Anarchy*, coupled with its just as good B side, *I Wanna Be Me*, energised me. At this time, I was going through a difficult phase as I was in a situation where my folks were gonna get divorced and my Mum was courting a new relationship with a bloke that I didn't like. It wasn't his fault, I just didn't like him. I had these mixed emotions of confusion, of being let down, of thinking somehow that the dissolution of my parents' relationship was somehow my fault. In short, I was having feelings of anger. And in 1977, that song had enough anger in it that I connected directly with it. Up to that point I'd been relatively unaffected by anything, as I suppose most kids are at that age. But with me approaching secondary school age, there was definitely a shift in my psyche due to the situation I found myself in. I loved my parents but I felt let down. This is how I saw it as a ten/eleven-year-old, although looking back now I understand that obviously sometimes these things just happen. So yeah, that record empowered me to the point where, at the time of hearing it, I became aware of the term used to describe it. PUNK or PUNK ROCK. To me that was like, 'Wow, does that mean there are more records like this out there?' With that, I was now on a quest to seek out this type of music and, being angry as I was, inflicting this wall of noise would go part of the way to showing my parents how angry I actually was. My parents, bless them, would be the ones who bore the brunt of this new-found interest. What amazes me, looking back, is the realisation that – and this is still something that happens today – if I'm interested in something or need to seek information relating to something, the topic of interest seems to find its way to me. Whether it be about history or the English language, or whatever. What I am looking for always seems to land at my feet just when I need it to. And so the same can be said about music.

2. PAMELA, WHAT IS THAT BOY LISTENING TO?

I started secondary school and I soon realised that I was going to struggle with certain aspects of my secondary education. If I could garner a little interest in a subject then there was a good chance that I could retain some of the information. However, after only a short time my schoolwork started to suffer. Not because I was backward or anything, but because I was easily side-tracked. I don't have the greatest attention span anyway, and I know I get distracted quite easily. My obsession with music started at around the same time that I started at secondary school and so with that my mind would be preoccupied henceforth. I embarked on a quest to find every record the SEX PISTOLS had released and find out every detail about them. On top of that, I wanted to know about other punk bands that were out there, and my, oh, my, I wasn't disappointed. Compilation albums were all the rage then and one in particular seemed to just fall in my lap (or searched me out). It was called 20 OF ANOTHER KIND with an amazing eye-catching cover of some spikey-haired female on the front. So whilst being too young to have caught these bands as they were making themselves known, I was getting an initiation into first wave punk from my bedroom and whatever little sound system I had at the time. For me the SEX PISTOLS' official releases were fantastic, including all of the single B-sides. For me, they were the kings and everybody else followed. To be honest, *Anarchy in the UK* is probably now my least favourite PISTOLS song but at the time it was seen as the record that started a musical revolution. Along with the 20 OF ANOTHER KIND compilation I remember another called CRIME OF THE CENTURY, which was a double album with a cover that was a piss-take of a SUPERTRAMP album with a similar cover. I found out about all of the current punk bands up to that point, two of which I would eventually play for and record with in later years. With the huge array of bands I was discovering at this period in time, my interest seemed to be causing some dismay to my elders. At the age of 12, believe it or not, I was now acquainted with a lot of the premier names on the punk rock scene. Some became household names and some were lesser known. You had the bands everybody knew, such as the PISTOLS, the CLASH, the DAMNED, the STRANGLERS and the JAM (who I was never a big fan of at the time but have since come to realise were fucking good songwriters). Then you had the likes of the X-RAY SPEX, SHAM 69, SLAUGHTER OF THE DOGS. And then the lesser known but no less good bands such as MENACE, THE RAPED, THE SUBURBAN STUDS… the list goes on. I'm just giving you an idea here as the list of bands I could name would take up pages and pages, but you get the picture. All of this music was keeping me going in one sense although It was also distracting me from my schoolwork. I was still participating but my interests stretched as far as English, Art and History, and thankfully swimming and long-distance running, which I ended up competing in at quite a high level. Out of school hours, I wasn't interested in what most other lads were interested in but, being a lad that was pretty much a ball of energy, being involved with swimming and running competitions definitely allowed me to quell some of that energy. Overall though, my main interest was playing my music, discovering new bands and pretty much spending time on my own annoying my folks as the music become louder and louder, until threats of having the plug pulled were shouted by my Mum from the bottom of the stairs. And so at the same time as this early part of my journey was proceeding, the first inklings of an idea came into my head, and I decided to myself that I wanted to play an instrument. I didn't know what I was going to play or how I was going to learn, but I just knew that I wanted to be involved in music. Amazingly, fate stepped in, and from the most unlikely of quarters.

I had no aspirations of becoming a drummer up until that point, but the opportunity presented itself from the most unlikely of family members, my Grandad from my Mum's side. Let me explain. During the Second World War my Grandad enlisted with the Black Watch, the elite and highly respected Scottish regiment, at the age of 17. He didn't quite make the D-Day landings, by which time he was 18, but he was involved with some of the later waves of landings at Sword Beach and fought all the way back to Germany where he met my Grandmother, or Nanna as we called her. She was obviously a German lass who came from the Duisburg area. During this period, he acquired a set of bagpipes and years later learned how to play them. Fast forward the clock to around 1980/81 and he's involved with a gathering of like-minded souls who have formulated a full bagpipe band consisting of bagpipers, side drummers, a drum sergeant (big bass drummer) and tenor drummers. I was encouraged to go along and was introduced to a gent who offered to teach me how to play the snare drum. So I wasn't learning to play a drum kit as such, but I was being taught how to play military-style drumming on a drum with a wired grate about ¾ inches wide attached across the top and the bottom skin (giving it its distinctive sound) known as the 'snare'. The snare was able to be switched on and off when not in use. My interest was piqued when I heard these chaps doing their thing, as I definitely felt I wanted to do this and learn how to play. Before I was allowed to go near a drum, I was going to have to learn from scratch and so, on a weekly basis early on, I went to this chap's house. His name was Terry and he had originally been in another Army regiment. Terry gave me some sticks and a wooden practice pad. We would sit opposite each other and he started to show me the rudiments. The first thing I ever learned was the 'Mumma Daddas' – two hits with the right hand followed by two hits with the left hand, repeated over and over again until a momentum and rhythm is achieved. The left hand stick is held like a chop stick and the right hand stick placed in the palm of the hand facing forward. The aim of this first exercise was to get to a point where the technique is practised and perfected, sounding like a large piece of paper being ripped slowly from one end to another. In short, a military roll. Terry had a lot of patience, bless him. After a number of our weekly meetings and with myself practising enthusiastically in between, I started to get the hang of it. To give you an idea how this sounds in its slow form, have a listen to the song *Radar Love* by the group GOLDEN EARRING. After the song's intro, the drummer comes in with exactly the rudiment that I first learnt. 'Mamma Dadda, Mamma Dadda, Mamma Dadda' repeated rhythmically in accordance with the other players. Along with this, Terry also taught me what is known as a 'Paradiddle'. Using the right and left hand technique, one half of the Parradiddle was LRLL, and the other half was RLRR. Learning Mamma Daddas was hard enough, but perfecting the Parradiddle was very difficult indeed. I can only describe it as being similar to getting one's words mixed up or getting tongue-tied, as the saying goes, only in this instance with your hands. The idea is to be able to play the exercise over and over again until it flows naturally. What would happen is that I would begin and after only a few paradiddles I would lose my coordination and I would be lost and have to start again. Slowly but surely, and through repeated practising, I started to progress and it wasn't too long before I started playing them as good as my teacher. This was my introduction to drums – I was off the starting blocks so to speak. If I were a drum teacher and if a kid wanted me to show him something with regard to drumming, for as much as these military rudiments have nothing to do with playing a drum kit, for me they represent the essential starting point in regard to getting your hands working in harmony with each other. I swear by them and still practise them today. This would be a healthy distraction for me as I wasn't the easiest kid. I can't say that I didn't like my parents, but looking back everything was still a bit raw for me, whether I was conscious of it or not. I was starting to show the first signs of rebellion towards my elders. I would push the boundaries and would seldom take much notice of my stepfather.

At school I would notice the older lads and they would have names of bands on their bags or badges fastened on their blazers. The SKIDS, SHAM 69, GENERATION X, ADAM AND THE ANTS. As 1979 slipped into 1980, music was finding its way into my head and I was soaking it all up. And as always, there were the PISTOLS. By this time they'd obviously split up, but records were still being released in their name and I was an obsessive fan. And so, what with these rebellious bands being played in our house, the dissatisfaction with the world I was seeing around me deepened. I was doing ok at school but I wasn't giving it the attention I should have. I couldn't concentrate for long periods though, and would easily get bored and lose interest. To add to this, I was always in a rush. One thing remained unchanged, though. If and when something did attract my attention, I was entirely engaged and focused. So after initially being taught how to play the military rudiments by Terry, it was time for me to start learning the actual drum patterns that would accompany the actual bagpipe tunes. No doubt you have heard a bagpipe band before. For some I respect that it is an acquired taste, but if you have been in the presence of such a thing, you can't fail to be impressed by the power of it. All the drums that you hear, the precision rolls and machine gun-type beats, that's what I was being taught to do. I really enjoyed learning this stuff, which in turn made me eager to do it to the best of my ability. With each passing week I was getting better and better. The aim was to be able to start and play the songs all the way through. In a marching band as this was, there is always a Drum Sergeant, with us at the back, who is more often than not a big geezer, with a huge bass drum strapped in front of him, as he would provide the beat. Boom, boom, boom, and we march in time and play to his beat. I loved it and was progressing to the point that the prospect of actually going out and performing with the band was on the cards. It was also around this time that another amazing band with an amazing double live album found its way into my hands. That band was the RAMONES and the album is called IT'S ALIVE. I can also remember arming myself with singles by other bands, too. THE ANGELIC UPSTARTS, the STIFF LITTLE FINGERS and THE RUTS. No doubt this aural assault emanating from my bedroom must have started to annoy my folks, but I didn't care. Regular shouts from my Mum at the bottom of the stairs stating that tea was ready and to 'turn that bloody racket down' became more frequent. The regular weekly practice sessions with the bagpipe band that I frequented with my Grandad continued and I was improving quickly. I wasn't playing brilliantly but I was starting to master playing the songs from start to finish. I would practise intently at home, honing my playing until that, too, was starting to show real promise.

To give you a fuller picture, after becoming sufficiently acquainted with the rudiments I had learnt, I then started to become involved with the rest of the bagpipe band, whose place of practice was at the local Army barracks. Regular weekly get-togethers that required the pipers being in one room practising and the drummers in another, or us drummers using our practice pads whilst the pipers used their chanters (this being the part upon which the player creates the melody and it basically looks like a recorder). I was the youngest addition to this set-up by a long way. I was barely 13 and at the time I joined there was a mixture of ages, with gents even in their fifties. I took to it like a duck to water, and with a big engagement coming up (not a gig as you lot know it), I was deemed ready to participate and was eager to do just that. I don't know how it came about but the band had some association with a local stately home-type place called Belton House, and so the band was called the Belton House Bagpipe Band. Eventually the band would perform there on numerous occasions and we also ended up rehearsing there beneath the main building. The engagement, as they called it, was a request to lead the local town carnival. Now, back then, the carnival was a rather grand affair with a large assortment of floats advertising local businesses, etc. and often lots of other marching bands all doing their thing, starting off at one point and all in a procession ending up where everybody and the general public came together and had an enjoyable time. Well, we were requested to lead the carnival and this for me would be my first public performance playing a drum. The day of the carnival was approaching and we were to lead from one end of the town to the other. A fair distance that was to be marched rather than walked. Now, these snare drums weigh quite a bit and there was absolutely no way, at that age and limited height, I could carry the thing for nigh on two miles. So, as I wasn't going to be playing on all of the songs as I was still learning, somebody (I can't remember who) would pass me the drum and I would join in from a certain point on our route. As my memory serves me, all this went ahead and I have a vague memory of marching down the middle of the streets that were lined with people cheering and waving. The day was a particularly jolly one, looking back. I'd like to think that my folks were pleased with what I'd done, but the one person I really wanted to please was the person who'd initiated me into this position, my Grandad. I'm sure he was pleased as I am sure Terry was, because from there on in, I was a permanent fixture in the band and would progress more and more as time went by. I was in the fortunate position of possessing a natural ability and over the next five years, as well as having Terry teach me, I had another guy take me a step further and tutor me on more complex drum patterns. With my inbuilt desire to be the best, I overtook them both as a player. Not in the teaching way, I add, but as we performed more and more engagements, the standard of my playing started to surpass theirs. As well as appearing at various other carnival-type events, we continued to play regularly at Belton House. We played every year on Remembrance Day or Armistice Day, as it is known, either in my home town or in Leicester. The high point for me from that time was playing on New

Year's Eve or Hogmanay, as it's also called, at De Montfort Hall in Leicester. I really enjoyed that one as I also knew it was the venue where a lot of my punk influences had also played. By the time I got to this period it was right at the end of that phase of my life and I would have been just 17 or so. Going back to those early days of me playing in the bagpipe band, there was a lot of fun and it was challenging because I'd found something that I truly excelled at and, aside from my sporting activities, I'd found something that I liked doing more than anything I'd ever done before.

So, I'm this 13/14-year-old kid who's got quite a lot going on. I'm still at school and a keen swimmer at the town club. I'm drumming during the week and, in between all of that, I am managing to explore all of the different bands that I've seen coming out of the 1977 punk scene. The list was endless. If you mentioned a band, I'd have more than likely heard of them. It's 1980/81 and my life was progressing in a somewhat interesting trajectory, depending on how you saw it. Looking back now, I can see that my out-of-school activities were becoming detrimental to my educational expectations as I was becoming more focused on the things I enjoyed rather than what I was actually supposed to be doing. I was losing interest in school work right at the time I needed to be buckling down and starting to prepare myself for exams and qualifications, etc. On top of this, over the next six months and so on, things were moving very quickly and I was enjoying myself. Unfortunately for my parents, they weren't.

Every year at Christmas for as long as I could remember, I would get Beano and Dandy albums as part of my present selection. I'd read them and then put them aside to go with the previous year's editions. I did like the books, but once I'd read them once that was pretty much it. However, one day I found a way of getting something extra from those books. I destroyed them in the name of creativity and here's what happened. Earlier on, I mentioned getting my hands on a copy of the IT'S ALIVE double live album by the RAMONES. I absolutely loved this record and it still gets played now after nearly 40 years from when I first heard it. Before any of the British 1976/77-style bands, you had these American bands like the DICTATORS, IGGY AND THE STOOGES and the NEW YORK DOLLS, but for me it was the RAMONES who were the first band that sounded like a punk band. Short songs, no lead breaks, just downstroke power chords and played really fast. They looked weird and cool at the same time. So I'm playing this live album and it's just one song straight into another, non-stop, with DEE DEE hollering 1,2,3,4 at the end of each song – I was captivated and I must have started air drumming along with the music. Now, I was a fair way from getting a drum kit as I was only 14 or so and hadn't even entertained the idea of even playing a full drum kit. Yes, I was playing in a military band, playing these admittedly complicated patterns and songs, but the thought of playing a kit hadn't even entered my mind. Now this is where these DANDY and BEANO annuals come in, and this was a pivotal moment. I grabbed a number of these books and set them down on my bed. I situated one down where I thought the hi-hats should go, one for the snare and the other in place of the tom toms. I got my sticks and, while the record was playing, I started to make an attempt at playing along to the song. I didn't have to worry about stopping and starting because no sooner had one song finished, another one had started with the famous count in that brought me in at the same time as the band. And there we have it. The seed was sown. No doubt my improvisations would have been a bit 'all over the place', but again I had some flair instilled in me due to the military stuff. A head start, so to speak. There I was, now actually attempting to play a make- believe drum kit made from the books I had received as Christmas presents. It was the RAMONES that gave me the idea of attempting to drum along to that album. I thought, 'Maybe I can do that, I'm going to have a go.' And from there, there was no stopping me. I knew that I was going to have to practise and practise to master this new-found outlet, but I was already used to that anyway. So as I was playing along to the record, I starting practising along to the other records that informed me. Obviously the PISTOLS were at the top of my priorities. I learnt to play along to all of the classic songs of that period and it wasn't too long before these poor books started to bear the brunt of my incessant banging. Also, my folks must have thought 'What the hell is he doing up there?' as there is no way I could have done this exercise quietly.

I was also becoming an avid record collector as I wanted to own and treasure as many of the punk bands' music as I could. The great thing about the advent of punk was that it signified a new direction with regards how bands released their records. Different coloured vinyls, picture discs, 12-inch editions and of course some of the artwork was so striking that it has become quite iconic over time. As always, the SEX PISTOLS were at the top of my list for collecting. They were the kings, and any release that I didn't have would be sought for my collection. There was a huge array of bands to collect with fantastically designed sleeves, album and single-wise. And not just predominantly punk records were on my 'wants' list. I also liked so-called 'new-wave' bands: those deemed a little more pop-sounding than the overtly labelled punk bands. I loved the BLONDIE singles, I liked SPARKS and THIN LIZZY. I ended up owning as many records as I could. Singles were about 99 pence in the early 80s if I bought them from a record shop, and back in those days there were always decent record stalls on the town market. So some records that were already a couple of years old I could get for less than the price of a new release. I was getting a decent collection together and a lot of the records that I accumulated all those years ago, I still have now. I would continue to collect until I was well into my forties, and every now and then some new additions will be added to my collection that is preserved in my music room at home.

I started getting the impression that my folks were getting a little irritated and annoyed with what was now becoming an obsession. You see, I come from a working-class family. My Grandad, through his good business acumen and eye for money-making opportunities, had amassed a fair-sized property portfolio and had become quite wealthy. My German Grandmother had become a head nurse at the local hospital and, in the eyes of a lot of people they knew in our small town, they were seen as being well off. My Mum and stepdad were market traders and again they were both hard-working. At weekends I would work with them too, and more often than not, most of the money I earnt would go on my next single or album. The thing is, I started to get the impression that they were all bothered with what other people thought about them. My grandparents were 'old school', and with that fairly opinionated, and I suppose it started to rub off on my parents.

What happened was, as well as collecting all this punk music, there were posters and magazines coming out all of the time and I was also starting to display some of the bands' artwork around my bedroom. Again top of the list, and by far the most popular, were the PISTOLS. My folks must have caught glimpses of these great unwashed individuals and thought, 'My God, this is what he's getting into.' From here on in, a battle of wills began whereby if there was any chance that they could get to suppress my interest in punk, they would. I'm sure that I speak for thousands of kids up and down the country who went through exactly the same thing, including some of you reading this. Looking back it wasn't the right approach because, as we all know, if you ask a kid not to do something, as soon as your back is turned, that same kid will go off and do exactly what you told them not to do.

To add weight to the slow deterioration of my relationship with my elders, it was around this time in about 1981 that I started recognising punks in the town. Donkey jackets with 999 imprinted on the back, bleached blonde hair, Dr. Martens and monkey boots and T-shirts with band names on them. I was immediately drawn to these individuals as they were obviously into the same type of music that I was discovering, but they were a bit older than me. I was just 14 and these people were probably 16/17 or even older. At that time that seemed a huge age gap to me!

I was quite steadily getting on with what I needed to do. I did as much schoolwork as was necessary to keep everyone off my back. I was still swimming a lot and competing at the same time. I was out with the bagpipe band and, no doubt about it, I was still wrecking the annuals that were meant for a different purpose rather than being battered to death. As I stipulated earlier, though, my mind was often away with the fairies as my sole intention was to take in as much music as possible. I suppose that this could have been the first inklings of possessing an addictive personality. It was also at this point in time that I found out that Grantham had its own newly formed punk band. In 1978 some lads got together and formed a first wave band known as THE BRICK WALL BAND. As far as I'm aware they only ever recorded one song (*Distant Drums*) for a compilation album, and pretty much dissolved not long after. Well, the bass player (JOHN MURRAY) was only just getting started and immediately set about putting another band together, and so with three other lads, namely Wakey, Wattie and Pinch, they formed the band known as ENGLISH DOGS. So it's sometime in mid-81 and, looking back, punk had shifted quite dramatically from its early beginnings in 76/77. The kids who were the original fans of the first wave bands were all a little older and were now taking it upon themselves and starting their own bands. Thousands of kids up and down the country were picking up instruments and forming bands, and ENGLISH DOGS were a perfect example of this. I'd start to see lads and lasses that I recognised as punks and it wasn't long before I started to see the ENGLISH DOGS logo on the backs of leather jackets. Well, I lived on the outskirts of Grantham in Barrowby, then a small village, and I couldn't believe it when I heard that they were going to play at the Memorial Hall in the village. It was the most unlikely venue, looking back, but that's what new bands did then! I thought, 'Sod this, if this is gonna happen I want to be there,' so I found out the date and waited to see if the gig would go actually go ahead. I was amazed this gig was occurring literally a few hundred yards from my home. I can't remember if I told my folks about myself attending this gig, but I can't imagine that I did. I arranged to attend with a couple of acquaintances, but once again I can't remember who that was. Well, the night of the gig was here and so myself and my companions made the short walk up to the Memorial Hall. As we approached we were greeted with an unbelievable sight. As part of the Memorial Hall activities, it must have been used in conjunction with a children's group, or something like that, because various punks were riding round on kiddy-sized tractors and cars, etc. They obviously found them under the stage area but they were having a whale of a time riding round on the road. There was a fair few outside the hall and I was taken aback with how hardcore they looked. Punk was now a lot more hardcore in a lot of ways to the first wave punk look. Leather jackets were in, with artwork all over them. This I liked. The coloured spikey hair was more extreme and defined, and I also liked this. To top it off, though, the Mohican had been introduced and a high percentage of punks back then had one. I wasn't overly keen on the look, and I know I'm going to piss some of you off here, but for me, the Mohican defined the dumbing down of punk as it became a rather more uniformed look. But hey, I know loads of people on the scene with Mohicans and they're perfectly nice people, it's just that I preferred, and still do prefer, a mixture of the different 70s and 80s styles. Let's be honest here, Sid Vicious had the look down perfectly.

3. THIS LOOKS A BIT SCARY, BUT I LIKE IT

Back to the gig, and after our initial surprise and, I suppose, shock, we decided to venture into the gig. I can actually remember feeling a little nervous and even scared as we went in. There was a feeling of tension in the air. I was only 14 and most in there were, like I say, a good few years older than me. I had nothing to fear though, as nobody bothered me at all. We kind of stayed on the outside of the crowd that was in there and waited for the music to begin. Looking back I can't remember much about the music. It wasn't that the music was bad, but I was too busy taking in the people and the overall atmosphere. Everybody looked different. Three bands played that night, and I can vaguely recall them all, but only in snippets. THE HERBERTS, who were rubbish, THE DESTRUCTORS from Peterborough, who I really liked, and lastly the ENGLISH DOGS, who again I liked immediately. They weren't professional as they would later become, but I can remember that they had proper songs and an excellent geezer on vocals known as Wakey who was very good at interacting with the audience. The bands and the atmosphere of that first gig definitely left an impression on me, and a lot of the people that were there, including members of THE DESTRUCTORS and the ENGLISH DOGS, would become lifelong associates and some, even friends. For me, what was so great about the gig was that it represented something that I could be a part of. I was too young for the 76/77 bands when they started, so to go and be able to start seeing bands at this stage was great. And to have a band in my own town was the focal point for me to start getting involved.

There was a shift from the style of first wave bands to the sound of the bands that appeared in the early 80s. The dress style had got a little more extreme and brash, and the music became for the most part a lot faster and, if anything, not as melodic. There were exceptions to the rule and another noticeable addition was the mixture of styles. So, moving on from the 76/77 mob, we had bands like the UK SUBS and the amazing RUTS just as an example, but then I started to hear of faster and more extreme bands like THE EXPLOITED, DISCHARGE and GBH. Then there were the more melodic bands, for instance CHRON GEN, PETER AND THE TEST TUBE BABIES, and the ADDICTS. There were the so-called Oi! bands, a label I've never really warmed to, because for me it was all punk. I didn't like and still don't like those labels. Anyway, the bands I mention were just a select few in what was becoming a massive underground scene that was sweeping across Britain in the early 80s. To top it all off, there came along another flurry of bands that brought with them a totally different but vibrant and positive although somewhat naïve outlook and attitude. The main band was CRASS and they inspired what become known as ANARCO PUNK. I loved CRASS as they completely did things their own way and incorporated other bands who were of a similar mindset to them. THE SUBHUMANS were amazing, RUDIMENTARY PENI had a classic first album and then there was CONFLICT. These were the bands that really told me about the way the world really was, and it became almost like an education when I read the lyrics and absorbed the information on the record sleeves. I can definitely state that some of the ideas and views that I hold today stem right back to those CRASS-related records and bands. The sheer volume of music on offer at this time was huge, and with that in mind I was collecting as much of it as I could. It would also have been at this point I reached 15. I was enjoying playing for the bagpipe band but playing along to music in my bedroom was wearing a little bit thin. I mentioned to my folks that I wanted a proper drumkit so that I could learn properly. To them, the fact I was already involved with playing for the bagpipers was good, so they probably thought that it was a natural thing for me to move on to playing a full kit. They had their reservations but I was a pushy little sod and hoped that I would get my own way. For now, though, my main intention was to go and watch the local ENGLISH DOGS and the similar bands they were involved with as often as I could.

4. A JACK OF ALL TRADES, MASTER OF ONE

Come 1982 and I was having a good old time. I'd been playing with the military band for three years or more and I was excelling in that department quite nicely. What saddens me a little is that there wasn't the technology around then like there is these days and there isn't any film footage or audio of me playing stuff. A real shame, considering the complicated nature of what I was playing. Today, one can record anything you want on a phone, but back then nobody had the foresight to do such a thing. Not long after I'd finished with the military band to concentrate on playing a full kit, I started to forget a lot of what I had learned. I can still play a couple of the basic patterns but the large majority has been forgotten. At that point, though, I was getting better and better and was out regularly with my Grandad, doing our thing. I had all the get-up that went with playing in a military band. The kilt, the feathered bonnet, all the classical attire. I also had a fantastic PREMIER snare drum that wasn't actually mine but that was provided to me by the band. I was still heavily involved with my competitive swimming on a weekly basis, training twice a week on Thursdays and Sundays but also competing at weekends. I had some great times being involved with the club aspect and made some good friends. We did a lot of travelling to galas and for a club of its size and with the trainers that were involved I took that side of my life to its logical conclusion. I would have been deemed an excellent swimmer but, to be honest, I didn't have the training facilities available to me, what with being involved in a small town club. I also didn't have the natural physique associated with professional swimmers – those boys were usually six foot-plus and with feet like flippers but, like I say, I took it to its logical conclusion and would bow out in the next couple of years. 1982 was a watershed year with a multitude of record releases on the punk rock scene. Most of the bands that had started in the wake of the 77-style bands were now releasing their debut albums and I collected pretty much all of them. As well as the usual suspects, I loved the album DEFECTIVE BREAKDOWN by the Irish band, THE DEFECTS. I played that one to death at the time and, lo and behold, years later Buck the vocalist and his good lady would put us up when 999 went over there to do some gigs. Compilation albums were being released left, right and centre with titles such as PUNK AND DISORDERLY, RIOTOUS ASSEMBLY and HAVE A ROTTEN CHRISTMAS. There were actually some half decent Oi compilations and loads more I can't remember off the top of my head. Add all of the singles that were being released by the RIOT CITY, NO FUTURE, WXYZ, SECRET, SMALL WONDER, CRASS and various other independent record labels of the time, and this kid's appetite for music is well and truly being taken care of. I was also getting to a few of the town gigs that were taking place, and I would gravitate towards any gig that the ENGLISH DOGS were involved with. By now, they were gigging all of the time with other bands out of town and so every time I saw them they just got better and better. On top of that, visually they looked great as they all had their own look going on. It hadn't passed me by that their drummer was also getting better too, and obviously because I had an interest, albeit a different involvement with drums, I was drawn to what he was doing. This and watching the other bands I witnessed at the time only enforced my desire to get a drum kit and to become a full-on drummer and get in a group like these lads were. The downside to all of this activity that was going on was that I was in my final two years of school. My work wasn't conducive with achieving the final exam results that were expected of me. I had started to skive off school and I really wasn't giving my work the attention that was required, and with exams appearing not too far on the horizon it didn't look good. I wasn't mature enough to be thinking about any long-term prospects and I really didn't have a clue what I wanted to do with myself after leaving school.

Along came Christmas time and, lo and behold, my folks had treated me to my first ever drum kit. Looking back, it was an old, mottled silver one with what can only be described as a wallpaper-type finish on the actual drums. I never knew how much it had cost but, like I say, it wasn't one of the main brands that were available such as Premier or Ludwig. I suppose they thought I'd have a play around for a short while and then just leave it in a corner for it to gather dust. Not a chance, because it wasn't long before I had it set up in the large double garage that was situated at the end of the house. I was fortunate enough to be living in a house that had a long driveway and with a large garage included. I could pretty much lock myself away and start to get to grips with learning how to play. And so for the duration of the time that we lived at that place that is exactly what I did. My family could just hear what I was getting up to in the garage and it was just what I needed in that this allowed me the space to start getting a beat together. Stopping and starting, getting a momentum together. The coordination it takes with four limbs doing something at different times to make the pattern sound proper and fluent. Getting the bass drum beats down in between the hi-hats and then the snare. Attempting to perform rolls around the kit then hitting the cymbals at the same time as hitting the bass drum. And what with the inherent drive to master something that is enjoyable yet challenging, I started to practise more and more. I never had any formal tuition from anybody. I taught myself to play through hours and hours of repetition and my sole ambition was to be able to play as good as all the drummers who played on the punk records I owned. When I first set up that first kit, I had a bass drum, a snare, two toms that would go on top of the bass drum and a floor tom, hi-hats, a ride cymbal and two crash cymbals, one on the left and one on the right. This would become the perfect setup for me and is one that I still use to this day. I don't remember having all of the cymbals in place at that time, but everything else was as I wanted it. Years later I would mess about with having extra toms and bigger kits and China cymbals etc., but I always ended up returning back to this 5-piece setup. Most rock and punk drummers these days usually just use a 4-piece, missing out one of the toms on top of the bass drum, and I've learnt to adapt to that set-up, especially after years of gigging all over and venues or support bands providing just the 4-piece on the night. It's no big deal but I do have a preference. The way I play the drums is also completely different to most other drummers. And this is where the influence of those years of playing military drumming comes in. If any of you watch any of your favourite bands, be it live or on video, you'll see that the drummer is playing with his arms crossed. Watch carefully as they use the right hand to hit the hi-hats and the left hand to hit the snare drum. PAUL COOK, TOPPER HEADON and RAT SCABIES all played in this orthodox manner.

There are exceptions to the rule, but more often than not rock drummers play in this way, including the likes of slightly more advanced players such as DAVE GROHL, STEPHEN PERKINS from JANE'S ADDICTION and NEIL PEART from RUSH. Now myself broaching the idea of learning to play a kit had a slightly different approach. As a fledging snare drummer learning to play the military stuff, I was taught to hold the sticks in a certain manner. The left-handed stick is held like a chop stick and the right-handed stick held just as if you were holding something in your hand but facing forwards, like holding a knife for instance. That way the sticks are perfectly angled so that the rolls and techniques can be played properly. Like most drummers, I'm right-handed so felt it was imperative that I hit the snare with my right hand. The problem was that, the way I held my left stick didn't allow me to have as much power and dexterity as my right hand due to the awkward angle I was holding it. You have to imagine that I'm not just playing one drum here, so to make both arms and hands equal I turned the way I held the left stick into the same way as I did the right. Both held exactly the same. And to top it off, rather than teaching myself to play cross-handed or orthodox, as the saying goes, I just started playing open-handed. Basically just an extension of the way I had been taught to play military style, but now I had started to develop my own style of playing an acoustic drum kit. In short, I learnt to play in an unorthodox style. Over the coming years and as I progressed as a player, I would seek out players who were beyond the punk rock style. One of those was a guy called STEWART COPELAND who played for THE POLICE. He's one of my all-time favourites and I still like listening to those early singles and albums that he played on. Ironically if you happen to watch him, he plays his own way too. He holds his sticks as if he were military playing but with his hands crossed. A mixture of orthodox and unorthodox style. Fantastic!

My final year at school was a bit of a disaster really. I hadn't been paying a lot of attention to my chosen subjects and, with the prospect of exams coming, I just buried my head in the sand, not really caring what would happen. A couple of incidents at school also took place in that final year that kind of showed where I was going. The first I wouldn't have deemed too serious although the outcome did come to the attention of the Headmaster. Funny how this incident came about actually, because believe it or not, it was music that ignited the spark. I can remember that forms or classes were allowed to use an allocated association room one day of the week, where all pupils from my class could congregate and socialise. We were allocated a tape recorder and I distinctly remember playing one of my favourite bands on this deck. It was the DEAD KENNEDYS. I wouldn't have been allowed to have it blasting out or whatever but I'd just taken the opportunity, as that was what I was able to do. All of a sudden, this other boy came over and proceeded to yank my tape out of the player and put his own in. I think it was AC/DC but I can't remember a hundred per cent. He basically muttered something about 'turning that shit off' and I was quite taken aback. Well, I wasn't having none of it because he'd actually done a pretty good job of showing me up, or at least that is how I saw it at the time. So without hesitation I responded by yanking his tape out, but with that, things soon began to get physical. We squared up to each other and, if one of the teachers hadn't walked in then, no doubt we would have gone for it there and then. This had obviously raised the attention of everyone in the room but the intervention of the teacher, who made it quite clear that this was not to be taken up outside of that room, quickly killed the tension that we'd both created. After this heated exchange had died down we all headed to our next classes, and for me that would have been the end of the matter. I did observe, though, that during the dinner break he'd got his mates on side and I got the distinct impression that what had happened earlier was going to once again escalate. Scraps, as we called them, always happened. I had witnessed a few, often egged on by a group that would shout SCRAP, SCRAP, SCRAP, gaining the attention of anyone in earshot. Before you knew it, a fight was happening with an audience consisting of other lads or lasses cheering for one or the other of the two fighting. Now I didn't want to fight this lad, but as the day progressed it came to my attention that he was going to be waiting for me at the shop where we had to pass after school. I'd resigned myself to the fact that this was probably going to happen and, for as much as I didn't want it to, I was not going to back down. Come home time, myself and a couple of mates left school and, lo and behold, there was a sizeable crowd waiting at the shop and that's when it became apparent that this was really it now. Although I didn't want to get into any fisticuffs, I thought if this was going to happen I was going to give it my all, as there was some sense of pride at stake. I walked towards the throng that had gathered and matey boy came towards me, and as soon as we met on the grassy part where the shop is we started fighting. Now I wasn't a better fighter than him or anything like that, but I was a fit old boy and had the edge strength-wise, and so after God only knows how long, I ended up on top of him and just started pummelling him. A couple of lads stepped in to split us up and then we would start again. After another short round of exhausting blows, once again I got him down and went for it again. After this happening repeatedly, I can remember one of his mates pulled me off my opponent and headbutted me straight in the face. I can remember reeling from that but within a flash I knew that that was my cue to get out of there. Myself and my mates who had bothered to hang about, and I was grateful that they had, scarpered and I remember getting home and feeling absolutely fucked. I was battered and bruised but to me, and in my mind, I'd proved a point. I was surrounded by this lad's mates yet I'd not backed down and they'd seen that. As it turned out, I'd broken a finger but I still went to school the next day, although there was no sign of matey for a week. I was questioned by one of the head teachers and that's when my parents were informed and called in to discuss the matter. Nothing really came of it as it was just a case of two lads fighting.

But it had been noted by my school that I courted trouble. Looking back I'd do the same again. As I say, I'm not into violence and I would shy away from it if I can, but if I'm pushed into a certain situation, and this had happened thankfully only a few times in adulthood, then it's almost as if it's like 'do or die time', and then I act accordingly.

5. MEADOWS, I WANT TO SEE YOU IN MY OFFICE

The second incident that took place would have more serious repercussions for me, although again looking back I don't think that I was that bothered. I'd been on a school trip down to London and in total there were two coaches with about 120 pupils included. Females on one coach and male pupils on the other. We'd been in London all day and were on our way back when the coach drivers started humouring everybody by overtaking each other, giving all of us pupils the opportunity to wave and pull faces as one coach overtook the other. This must have happened a couple of times when a few of us who were situated at the back of our coach decided it would be hilarious that if this happened again, then we would pull down our trousers and as the buses were adjacent to each other, would moon the other coach, giving the girls one hell of a shock. So, that's what we did. Myself and three others were waiting to see if the drivers would once again line up alongside each other, giving us all the opportunity to wave and cheer at each other as one coach overtook the other. Only this time the female coach got a little bit more than just flailing arms and jeering. As they passed by our coach, they were greeted with plenty of what was going on before, only this time also the sight of 3 or 4 puny arses pressed against the side windows greeted them, along with a lot of hilarity from the back end of our coach as the expressions on the girls' faces turned to shock and disbelief. It seems that this had been one joke too far, because very shortly after this our coach was stopped and one of the teachers came to the back with a look of thunder on his face, wanting to know who was responsible for such a dastardly deed. I can't remember if any of my fellow 'mooners' held their hand up to it at the time, but I know I didn't, and that no way was I going to admit I was one of the guilty party. I was already getting some shit at home, and knew I'd be in some right bother if I got found out for this, so I kept schtum and never gave myself in. The incident had been deemed that serious that the whole coachload of lads who had been on the trip were threatened with being banned from all future trips if the culprits weren't exposed. With that, the other lads involved handed themselves in, but I never did. All I can remember is being in one of my English lessons and the year head teacher entered the room, came over to me, bent down and whispered in my ear, 'Meadows, I want a word with you in my office at lunchtime.' And with that I knew I had been dobbed in and that I was now in deep shit. I went to the head teacher's office at lunchtime and was basically told that this sort of behaviour was just not acceptable, and that there were going to be consequences, one of those being that a letter was going to be given to my mother and that she would be asked to come into the school to discuss my deplorable behaviour. And so for the next day or two I had to wait and wait until the letter arrived. There was no way that I could intercept this letter and not let it get to my Mum, as the school would be waiting for her to act on their request for her to go and discuss the matter. I hadn't said anything to my Mum about me being involved in the prank, although I had joked about some lads doing it the night after we got back. I remember the morning the letter came, my Mum shouted at me to go and get the post as I was getting ready for school. I went and got the mail, gave it to her and waited for her reaction. Let's just say that she wasn't happy. Once again she was being called to one of the head honcho's office to discuss my attitude and behaviour. To them, doing the deed was bad enough as it was deemed almost criminal that I had exposed my arse to a busload of girls. The fact that I hadn't owned up, and it had dragged on until I was informed on, made my behaviour worse to them. And so after my Mum had been to my school, I was informed that I was banned from attending any more school trips EVER.

It wasn't to be all doom and gloom for my parents, though. There were some moments for them to think that all wasn't lost. As I turned 16, I achieved a minor victory at school, although saying that, it had nothing to do with my educational abilities, so to speak. By now I was hitting a peak with regard to playing in the bagpipe band, and it became quite well known throughout school that I was doing this. And so, over the space of the last year or so, I had also got a couple of my schoolmates involved. In a bagpipe marching band formation, for the drum section to be complete there are three parts. Snare drummers like myself, a big bass drum player and tenor drums. Tenor drums are basically the same as the snare drum and played at the same vantage point. By that I mean a strap is located all the way over the shoulder that hangs over the body and then the drum is attached at waist height. Now, tenor drums don't have snares on them, and beaters are used rather than sticks. These beaters are twizzled in between hitting the drum at the same time as the bass drummer hits his drum. Basically, these two combine to hit the beat as we march from left to right, left to right. The two mates of mine had learned to play their drums on our meet-ups with the full band, as was always the case. Learning to play a tenor drum was nowhere near as difficult or time-consuming as learning to play the snare, although an element of skill and timekeeping is always required. A school show had been arranged and I can't remember how it came about but we were approached and asked if we wanted to be involved. Well, we must have jumped at the chance because before we knew it we were on the programme to take part. As part of any marching band that is worth their salt, a decent drum section will have a drum salute or solo to add to the entertainment. Well, we had one, and so we decided that we would go with that. If it's good enough for the grown-ups that we usually played to when out with the full outfit, then it should be good enough to play in front of the school. So, to set the scene, this is how we went about it. I would be in the middle playing the snare drum solo on my own and I would have my two mates either side of me providing the marching beat on their drums and twizzling their sticks. Well, the day came and the show started and we were set to go on some way towards the end. We were resplendent in our uniforms and white drums at the ready. I have to say that we were all rather nervous as this was completely different to anything we'd done before. Also, this was no small gathering, as we were playing to the whole school. We needn't have worried, though, as we had made sure we were ready. On cue we started, marched out in front of the whole school and for the next 5 to 7 minutes marched up and down between the two sides of the gathering in front of us. I can remember us sounding huge as we kicked in. In a big assembly school hall the sound reverberated around the hall, and as far as I can remember we played really well and went down a storm. My Grandad even attended and stood at the back watching us, and I know for a fact that for that short time I had, along with my mates, made him proud. So yeah, that was a good moment - a small victory, so to speak. The only other positive thing that was coming out of this phase of my final school year was that I was excelling in my sporting endeavours. Due to being an avid swimmer and being involved at club level, there was nobody who could touch me at the different strokes. I was particularly good at backstroke and butterfly, both of which I did well at in competitions. I was also making a name for myself as a long-distance runner and I was entered into competitions and tournaments for the school, which took me around the county. But again, like my swimming, for as much as I would be classed as an excellent runner, I would only be as good as the backing I received and my physical attributes would allow me to be.

Let's be honest here. The overall reason for us going to school was to further our personal development and to educate us to be ready for getting on with life as adults. After the age of 14 I'd shown a normal interest in my schooling, but at 15 and 16 I'd lost a lot of interest and, with my final exams coming up, I hadn't prepared or taken them seriously. I hadn't done the groundwork needed to gain what would be classed as good results. When it came to sitting my exams, for the most part I really struggled, and would be sat there not understanding some of the questions put to me. As well as feeling a little thick, I also felt a bit ashamed, as deep down I knew that I hadn't prepared for this important part of my life. And so with that I came out of school with my exam results being well below what they could and should have been. Leaving school in 1983 with hardly any decent qualifications, I didn't have a clue what I wanted to do now that I was a school leaver. My parents would have been trying to no doubt steer me in the right direction, but what with my lack of positive outlook and direction they must have been rather concerned as to what they were going to do with this 16-year-old directionless kid.

I'd now been practising for some time at home on the drums and had got to grips with almost being able to play songs all the way through. I can just remember right towards the tail end of school, getting together with a couple of lads who were the same age as me. DARREN CHANTRY and ANDY EDWARDS. Darren went to school with me and he knew this lad from another school. They were both into punk and I had got this kit and Darren had a guitar and an amp of sorts. Well, Andy's folks were landlords of one of the town's social clubs and we were allowed to use the stage there, and that's where I first realised that I wanted to play in a band format kind of thing. Let's just say that we were terrible, but that didn't matter because we were enjoying ourselves. We called ourselves THE FALLEN. Andy made an attempt to be a vocalist. The thing was that he was such a laid-back character that his delivery was just so very monotone. But, like I say, it didn't matter as we were just enjoying it. Darren was a bit of a lunatic and he liked THE DEAD KENNEDYS, and he wasn't a bad rhythm guitarist for a beginner. The sum total of the little repertoire that we got together consisted of UK82 punk songs of the time. Thinking back I do remember a bassist trying to keep up with us, but I can't remember his name and he didn't last long at all. I can remember us trying to do *Blown To Bits* by THE EXPLOITED and *So What* by the ANTI NOWHERE LEAGUE, and there were others but I honestly can't remember them. We must have got a few tracks together because we managed to secure a gig at one of the United Reform Churches in town. My memory of that night is sketchy, but I do remember us playing fairly amateurishly, which was to be expected, but for me the main thing was that some of the town's local punks were in attendance and so at least I had made myself known in some form, even if it was just by playing in this shitty covers band that didn't have a bass player. And that was that, THE FALLEN never progressed beyond that one gig. I think that was partly something to do with my folks observing what they thought was not the right company. This would be a bone of contention from now on until I left home. I was into the punk rock thing big time, and as much as I loved them all, there was a bit of a small-town mentality thing going on. This, 'Oh, what would the neighbours think?' kind of attitude. As you read this you will notice that I go to extremes regards my behaviour, and to them at that time, I was getting into this thing on an extreme level. So, looking back with regards to playing music with the lads, I can't say for sure whether my elders intervened or not, but they were definitely keeping an eye on me, and would in future try and coax me in a direction that was much more in keeping with what they thought I should be doing. Those lads that I was first involved with were rough round the edges but that didn't mean anything to me. Ironically, over time they both went off and got on with their lives unhindered, and it was muggins here who went off and got himself into all sorts of skulduggery.

Grantham in 1982/83 had a great little punk scene, made all the better because of local heroes ENGLISH DOGS. Throughout the last year I'd attended a couple of their gigs played at the local army barracks. Also, sometime during 1983 they managed to get the local nightclub owner to agree to put punk bands on every couple of months. I remember attending most of them and they got better and better. Grantham had the ENGLISH DOGS, but things were happening elsewhere too, and not too far down the road. We had THE DESTRUCTORS from Peterborough and another band called AVOID, who were from Derby. Now, I was barely 16 and as much as I would have loved to have travelled to those places to see the bands in their home town, I wasn't well acquainted enough with the in-crowd to be invited on board. Also I was still of an age where I was still slightly shackled to my parents. To have this new venue to go and see these bands was great, because all of a sudden I've got this thing I'm really into right on my own doorstep. I suppose you could call it networking because back then I found myself being drawn to these events, and I started to see the same faces over and over again whilst observing a scene developing between these bands from the three different places.

I started to acquire band T-shirts, which was the start of my blending in. My folks definitely knew what I was getting into, and I'm sure they weren't best pleased with the direction I was taking, but unless they tied me to the house there wasn't much that they could do. They did try to block me from wearing what I wanted to but I always had a strategy up my sleeve. If I was off to a gig I would have a carrier bag with my fucked up jeans, T-shirt and Dr. Martens in and proceed to a mate's house to get changed and then go to that night's gig. I acquired a bullet belt and that was me, ready to roll. I acquired leather jackets and adorned them with badges and even painted a couple up with some good artwork, as was the thing back then. I used to love seeing all the jackets with the backs painted with a different variety of bands that were around at the time. Jackets festooned with band names from the late 70s as well as the more current bands of the early 80s. And the girls were something else, too. Now the ENGLISH DOGS were making a lot of progress as they had secured a record deal with this Stoke label called CLAY records. The label showed interest due to the band's association with Birmingham band GBH, who were also signed for the label alongside DISCHARGE, ABRASIVE WHEELS and a few others. Now that ENGLISH DOGS were associated with these like-minded bands their reputation grew as they started gigging all over the country, with their name growing all the time. So as the first gigs featuring THE DESTRUCTORS, AVOID and the DOGS passed I started to see gigs coming up with other bands from around the country, too. So in the space of what seemed like a few months I got to see THE VARUKERS, who were OK but just a bit samey for me, and ONE WAY SYSTEM, who I remember looking real cool but being able to back it up musically, too. The best gig of that era for me, though, was when GBH came to play at that venue that the DOGS had secured. It was great, as punks came from all over and I can remember being outside the gig, and it being the largest-attended gig that was put on down there. I remember the night quite well and I loved it. It felt like I was part of something and I was eager to get more and more involved. For me, though, I was still on the side-lines and waiting in the wings for the opportunity to do just that. It was OK going to these early gigs but eventually I would hope to get involved in a more musical role and go from being a punter at the gigs to actually being on stage playing to a crowd.

6. HELLO MATE, DO YOU WANNA PLAY IN OUR GROUP?

At the same time that this was all going on, and after my very brief time playing with THE FALLEN, I got a phone call from a lad called KEITH DAVISON. Now, I didn't know this old boy and all I can remember him asking were words to the effect of, 'Do you wanna play drums in our band?' Well, I wasn't doing anything and from what I could gather the lads that were in the band weren't really that much more advanced than me as individual players. So I thought, 'Fuck it, let's do it.' I'd been practising as regularly as I could and I must have been confident enough as it wasn't long before a meeting was arranged for me to go and introduce myself and see what they were up to. Well, these lads had known each other as kids as they came from the estate on the other side of town. They'd been knocking about with each other and a couple of them got guitars and started playing about. Now Keith, who had originally contacted me, was already a fairly competent bass player due to having an older brother who was very competent indeed. There were three other lads. LEE FARDELL on rhythm guitar, STEVE BROWN on lead guitar and MARK HODGKINSON on vocals. They were 18/19 at the time so I was definitely the baby of the bunch at 16. But I was pleasantly surprised when they appeared to have everything in place to get this new band up and running. Everything was there, guitars, amps and a small PA. Even a really decent practice place at the youth centre that was right on the edge of their estate. Now these lads weren't punks at all, but I was thinking at the time that didn't matter. I'd got to a level of competency with my drumming that I was eager to take it to the next step and actually be involved with some lads who were intent on playing songs in their entirety. From start to finish. Like myself, these boys had been brought up on music from the 60s and so it was their intention to pay tribute to that and play music from that era. So yeah, we were going to be a covers band. So with that in mind I moved my drum kit from home into the practice place and it was from there that I at last started to learn how to play properly. One of the first songs I learned to play, and which was a predominantly drum-based track, was *Wipe Out* by THE SURFARIS. This is where my military drumming experience came in. The song has periods of just drum rolls going through it. I got to work on it and before too long I'd pretty much mastered it. We also did stuff by THE BEATLES, *Back In The USSR* and *I Saw Her Standing There*; THE ROLLING STONES, *Jumping Jack Flash*; THE KINKS, *All Day And All Of The Night* and *Tired Of Waiting*; THE WHO, *Can't Explain*, as well as a few that I can't remember. I can remember us doing more current stuff too, like U2, *New Year's Day* and also THE CARS, *Best Friend's Girl*, which we actually ended up recording. We weren't bad for a new band who had never done anything before, and as much as I wasn't overly keen on playing this stuff it was a good introduction to learning how songs are played and structured. Most rock'n'roll has a basic and similar structure, and I soon learned how this worked. From the outset I immediately started to improve as a player. As a unit we got quite close and decided to call ourselves THE SYSTEM. We were keen to play a gig and so after a few months practising regularly, we played a debut gig for all the kids who frequented the youth club where we rehearsed. After that it was sporadic gigs in the town, in local pubs, culminating with a gig at a social club at a 60s revival night. Aside from a couple of gigs we did out of town, this would be the largest audience we ever played to. There were about 300 to 350 people who were all fans of the 60s era, and as a young band playing that stuff we went down really well. We weren't too bad, but personally I was itching to play something with a bit more power to it. Now these boys knew that I liked punk music because I had made it quite clear, so I mentioned bringing PRETTY VACANT into the set. Well, I can't remember much disapproval from the rest of the band but Steve, the lead guitarist, got really shirty to the point of being quite threatening, basically saying, 'We're not playing any of that punk shit.' And so, with that, I pretty much lost interest with what we were doing and decided to leave in pursuit of something that was more interesting to me. One good thing came out of the experience, and that was that all of the lads never held it against me for clearing off, as there was a mutual respect due to us all being part of something right from its humble beginnings. And throughout the years since that mutual respect has never waned, because whenever we see each other, it's always good to see them and I get that the feeling is mutual. THE SYSTEM carried on, albeit without Steve Brown, and are still together today. In 2015 I played a few gigs with them for old time's sake, playing a selection of covers from all genres including this time a cover of THE CLASH'S, *I Fought The Law* and other songs by bands such as THE KILLERS and the like.

Having finished school there was a bit of a break, but to be honest I hadn't a clue what I wanted to do with myself career-wise. Does anyone at that age? I suppose some kids do, but what with all the things that were going on in my life, I'd become somewhat anti-everything. I hadn't anticipated further education as I'd had enough of that by the time I was 15. My end of school exam results reflected that, and to have it pushed on me that I should go to college to redeem myself didn't fill me with a lot of joy. But I reluctantly agreed and was enrolled at my local college to attend and get myself a diploma in Business Studies. This would prove to be disastrous, and looking back, I can't blame my parents as they were just trying to make the best of a bad situation. From the outset I had no interest or inclination to better myself and again, from my elders' point of view, this must have been most irritating and very concerning. From this time a familiar pattern would start to emerge. And I suppose from a personal point of view, this would be labelled as a character defect. I was 16 nearly and I started to lose interest in the things I had been doing since I was a real youngster. First there was school, of which the last two years I had pretty much wasted, resulting in shit grades. Then there was my involvement with the swimming club. By the time I was 17 I'd pretty much stopped attending training nights and galas. And lastly it was around this time that after playing at De Montfort Hall with my Grandad's bagpipe band, I removed myself from that. I felt that I had achieved my personal goals with these phases in my life. In retrospect I hadn't. I could have gone on to do more but my attitude was shifting and with that attitude I developed a line of thinking that meant that if something didn't interest me, or the chance of something I thought was better came along, then I would just drop whatever I was doing and move on to the next thing that did interest me. And so with that, the same applied to my introduction to attending college. I displayed a modicum of interest in a couple of the subjects, as I became quite adept at typing, would you believe, and I displayed an initial interest in computing. But everything else I found tedious and boring. One, because I struggled with the particular subjects. Book keeping, for instance; I was useless at maths and to be any good at this subject, at least a little understanding of mathematics was required. Two, if I wasn't interested in a subject then I was easily distracted and my concentration would be off somewhere else. And talking of distractions, I'd only been at college for a short time and I only had interest in a few things, and none of them were in any way connected with concentration on furthering my education or preparing for life in the adult world. One was punk rock, and as much as I didn't look like one, I was now a punk rocker whose sole intention was to immerse myself into that scene as much as I could. And then there was sex. I'd been aware of sex and all its loveliness from a very young age. At 16 I lost my virginity, and not long after starting college I embarked on an insatiable conquest of sexual activity with as many girls as I could. Most lads at that age are feeling those impulses, I'm sure, but let's just say that I was very highly strung in that department. And lastly, I came into contact with something that ironically came from my interest in music and punk rock. Only this time this would end up having more far-reaching consequences than anything I'd been involved in up to this point.

Throughout 1984 there was a flurry of gigs that were occurring in my area, and with being a regular on the fringes of these gigs I started to acknowledge some of the regulars that I saw there. One such guy was this tall fella a few years older than me and I recognised him as being one of the crowd that gravitated towards the people that hung around with the ENGLISH DOGS. Turns out he was the band's driver taking them down to London for gigs at the 100 Club and all over the rest of England. Well, I don't exactly remember how it came about, but at some point at one of these gigs he must have said, 'How do' to me. From then on we acknowledged each other whenever we saw each other. I liked him straight away as a lot of the others were a bit aloof, you know, but he was always alright. He wasn't one of the Mohican brigade with the studs and all that, but more of a standard 70s-looking punk with short, spiky hair. Anyway, his name was DUNK and over time we must have got chatting and we kind of hit it off. Now, back in the day most punks were on the dole and Dunk was one of these lads who did fuck all during the day, pretty much slept until midday or whenever, and was driver for the DOGS by night. He said to me 'If you're stuck for something to do come round my gaff and we can play music and stuff.' Well, I was at college during the day and, as I've said, I wasn't that interested in that side of things and his place was just up the road from the college. So when I soon got bored at college I started bunking off and going to see Dunk. We'd usually just hang around and listen to music and talk about what he'd been up to. He was also a big TOY DOLLS fan and had ended up driving for them too. Well, I was only 17 and still very much wide-eyed and a tad impressionable. I looked up to a lot of these lads who didn't seem to give a fuck and were out there doing what I wanted to do. Well, one day I was up there and he asked me if I wanted to get stoned. Being of an age where I was wanting to find out about this kind of stuff I thought, 'Yeah, why not?' I relayed to him any fears I had about being completely out of it and he assured me it would be cool and there was no need to worry. And so with that he gave me a dope cake, which I proceeded to chomp down on and finish. Well, I didn't know what to expect and, after being informed that I wouldn't feel anything immediately, just relaxed with him and listened to some music. Now I distinctly remember drumming along to THE CRACK album by THE RUTS on a table and then, whoosh, it hit me. Now, consuming a hash cake is somewhat different to taking a few puffs on a joint, and as a rule, consuming cannabis in the manner that I had was far more potent than, say smoking a little. It really knocked me back and I came to, stood rigid against a wall feeling very disorientated, scared and unsure of what was going on. It's a long time ago that I first took that cake but as soon as it hit me I can't say that I enjoyed the feeling. I told Dunk this and he just said, 'Don't worry, you'll feel fine, just let it happen,' or words to that effect. And so that's what I did. I can remember us getting in his Mini and heading off round to the ENGLISH DOGS bass player's house. This was WATTIE, who I'd obviously seen on occasion, what with attending various gigs etc., but I can't recall us ever having spoken to each other. Anyway, as I remember it, he was still in bed in his loft room of his Mum and Dad's house, and as I was with Dunk, we exchanged pleasantries and I sat down and just tried to chill out. I was still feeling really weird and as I was observing what was going on I was hallucinating mildly, as everything seemed a little bit trippy. And then something happened. Wattie, like a lot of punks by this time, was starting to listen to a lot of heavy rock and metal, IRON MAIDEN and BLACK SABBATH with the heavier hardcore punk stuff like DISCHARGE and GBH. Anyway, OZZY's BLIZZARD OF OZ album was playing and the space cake must have started to wear off, because all of a sudden the combination of the dope and the music made me feel really euphoric. For the first time ever the music sounded brighter, more colourful, so much deeper than I'd ever heard before. It was quite overwhelming and I loved it from that moment until the cake started to wear off. I felt fine and really enjoyed the experience. That was the first time I'd taken a mood-altering substance, and though it would be some time before I partook again, that first experience would place me on a trajectory of wild times - most of them enjoyable, but ultimately it would also lead me into a whole lot of trouble and a long, dark descent into full-blown drug addiction.

7. AN INTRODUCTION TO AN ENGLISH DOG

I got over that getting stoned episode and proceeded to get on with whatever was going on at the time. Amidst all this activity another chance meeting came my way with someone who I would end up having some involvement with in the future. I don't recall why I ended up at this house but I do remember being somewhat surprised to find hardly anybody there. I think that I had some records with me to play while I was there, so it must have been sort of a house party-type thing. Anyway, I just recall myself only being in the presence of a certain gent called Peter Wakefield, otherwise known as WAKEY 'O' WALRUS TUSKS. Now, Wakey's six years older than me and I have to be honest in saying at that time being 17, as much as I was a bit of an outgoing person myself, I was rather impressed to be engaging with the singer of the best punk band in the area. Being the pushy little sod I am, and was, I engaged with him and probably made a bit of a nuisance of myself, talking about bands and the scene, etc. I also happened to notice that he had a record on his person. And this record was a test pressing for the ENGLISH DOGS' debut album, INVASION OF THE PORKY MEN. Well, I was like Wow! as the album hadn't even been released yet, and here was the singer talking to me about it and showing it off to me. Well, while we were in conversation I was trying to impress him with my knowledge about punk rock and stuff when he asked me how I knew so much about it all. I just told him that I'd been interested since I was a nipper. No doubt he'd spotted me at one of the number of gigs he played and probably thought I was just some nondescript spotty-faced kid who was having a good time. I was really impressed that he'd got his album on him, and then being the forward little brat that I was, I asked him if he would trade it with me. I was being cheeky I suppose, but I didn't care. I wanted that album. Of course I didn't think he would go for it, and at first he declined. I can be rather persistent when the need arises and so I started to press him on it. I know that we'd been discussing the ENGLISH DOGS playing one of the big all-day punk fests that had happened recently. CHRISTMAS

ON EARTH, or one of those similar type dos, I think it was. He'd told me how impressed he'd been with THE DAMNED, who had headlined, and explained to me how much he loved one of their new songs called *Generals*. Well, it just so happened that I had a DAMNED live album with me at the time. It's a pic disc called LIVE IN NEWCASTLE and I'd been playing it loads due to it being a really good recording, unlike most live punk recordings of the time. Well, he was most impressed as the song *Generals* was on the album, and so after some more brief discussions we actually came to a deal. I gave him my live DAMNED album and he gave me his debut album on a test pressing. I was fucking buzzing about this as nobody else except the band would have had one of those. With that we struck up a friendship which would ultimately lead to us getting a band together a year or so after he'd left the DOGS for the first time. I took the album home and played it consistently and memorised all of the songs, some of which I would play myself a good few years down the line. I still have that test pressing in my collection after all these years. You collectors out there would pay handsomely to own that now, wouldn't you?

Well, my year at college soon passed by and my end of year report and attendance report, or lack of it, pretty much reflected my efforts there. I came away with pretty much nothing and totted up 30 days of absenteeism. I was too busy pursuing my own interests rather than being concerned about any long-term prospects. The fact that I'd performed so poorly at college obviously hadn't gone unnoticed by my folks. I can't recall any big sit-down to discuss my lack of enthusiasm or direction, but it was pretty much decided for me I would be enrolled on a Youth Training Scheme, otherwise known as the YTS. So as an extension of the work that I was supposed to have done at college I was sent to become an apprentice at the local Electricity Board where I would work in the offices of the Accounts Department. Basically, I would be dealing with people's electricity bills and accounts, etc. I tried to show some commitment to this new avenue that had been put to me. At first I was doing a lot of filing but then slowly progressed into working on a VDU (visual display unit) as it was called, a computer I suppose, to view people's accounts. The department I was working in dealt with customers who were struggling to pay their bills and so I saw a lot of disconnection orders been sent out, and lots of phone calls with pay plans put in place to help them keep up to date and ultimately stop them having their electricity disconnected. Once again I soon found myself tiring of the monotony of it all. I found every day was the same and, as much as the people there were OK, it was just so fucking boring. I couldn't see myself doing this year in, year out and, what with having to attend the local college for one day a week again as part of the course, I soon started to lose interest. So on the days I was supposed to go to college I didn't bother, and my first initial little bit of enthusiasm I'd had at the beginning of this YTS scheme soon waned. It wasn't too long before I was summoned into the office of one of the bigwigs there to discuss my position. He was one of those toffee-nosed cunts who looked down on me as if I were just a waste of time, and looking back, I suppose to him I was. I didn't want to be there and my dull response to his questioning probably said it all. I couldn't account for not attending college and I couldn't really tell him that I found the place really depressing, and the job mundane and boring. My demeanour probably spoke volumes, and with that he dismissed me from the place. I was relieved in a roundabout way, but I knew one thing. This wasn't going to go down well at the YTS organisation and it definitely wasn't going to go down well with my Mum and stepdad.

8. SEX AND ROCK'N'ROLL , WHAT CAN GO WRONG?

Well, as you can imagine, to my parents and my grandparents my life seemed to be taking a somewhat downward trajectory and this didn't bode well with life at home. I wasn't the easiest teenager on the block and, what with my lacklustre attitude towards them and my failed attempts at being a responsible young man approaching adulthood, it would only be a matter of time before things came to a head and drastic measures would have to be taken. I started seeing this girl called NICOLA who, in effect, was my first girlfriend. For both of us it was akin to a sexual awakening and we fucked at every given opportunity. We began what would be a tempestuous relationship for the next 3 to 4 years and, to be honest, I was very fond of her. But it wouldn't be long before my self-seeking behaviour in all areas would start to cause problems. We ended up having a love-hate relationship and, what with both of us still being in the care of our parents, neither sets of them were in favour of our relationship continuing, being as hot-wired as it was. It was around this time that I also went to my first gigs out of town. Through my attending the gigs in town I was getting to know some of the older lads who were fans of the same scene. Well, two gigs came up on consecutive nights and myself and these lads attended both. The first was at THE PALAIS in Nottingham and we went to see JOHNNY THUNDERS AND THE HEARTBREAKERS, LIGOTAGE (BEKI BONDAGE'S BAND) and another band who I don't remember the name of. I think they had TEXAS in their name. Anyway, this was a giant leap for me as the Palais was what you would call a proper venue. There was a big crowd in as well and I was overjoyed to be there as I really liked the HEARTBREAKERS, and the fact that they'd reformed with the original line-up was great. I'd never got the chance to see the early VICE SQUAD so this was a treat as MISS BONDAGE had one of my new-found favourite drummers on board. His name is STEVE ROBERTS and I knew his style and delivery from albums he'd played on by THE EXPLOITED and the UK SUBS. I got right up front to watch these bands do their thing on a proper stage. The first band, whose name I can't recall, were OK but my enduring memory of them was that their drummer had arms that were not fully developed but he could still play, a thalidomide. Anyway, LIGOTAGE were on next and I must admit that Beki did look great and her band backed it up musically too. The only thing was they were a new band and nobody really knew the songs, but they were still good. And yes, most impressive to me was their drummer. He was shit hot and I watched and learnt a little after watching him. Lastly the HEARTBREAKERS came on to a rapturous response from us in the audience. Thankfully Thunders and all of the band were on form that night and really knew how to work a stage. A truly great rock'n'roll band, and they went down really well. I can't recall if I went home that night or stayed at one of my mate's houses. I wasn't too fussed because I was having a bit of an adventure. On the next day, which was a Saturday, we then made our way to the RETFORD PORTERHOUSE to see THE FITS and PETER AND THE TEST TUBE BABIES. This was a smaller and quite a different kind of gig, but still no less exciting for me. We got to Retford via train and got to the venue, and again it was packed. There was a bit of tension in the air. I can't describe it but I started associating this with punk gigs. You can feel it, sense it. I wasn't scared as such. It was a combination of the music, the energy and the average age of audiences back then lent an air of menace to the atmosphere. I hadn't heard a lot by THE FITS but they were good and looked sharp as well. They got themselves associated with the TEST TUBES through a double-sided 12-inch EP they'd both released recently. They went down okay but most people were there for the TEST TUBE BABIES. Now, this lot had released their debut studio album recently, THE MATING SOUNDS OF SOUTH AMERICAN FROGS, and it's an absolute belter. I can remember purchasing it the day I left college. Anyway, they came on and the place exploded. Having a sense of humour but taking their music seriously really impressed me. I got stuck in there with the countless other freaks who were enjoying what they saw and heard. And just to top it off, WATTIE BUCHAN was at the gig too, in his leather jacket that he's wearing on The TROOPS OF TOMORROW album. Me, being the cheeky little cunt I was, I asked him if I could have my picture taken with him. He duly obliged and I was buzzing. It was only at the end of the gig that I came to realise that he was at the gig because of Peter from the TEST TUBE BABIES. As everyone was being asked to leave the venue by the security staff, I spotted them both deep in conversation and I actually witnessed the doorman giving them a bit of grief, telling them that they needed to leave. That rounded off two great nights for me and I've never forgotten them. I'd seen four completely different types of band that all flew under the punk rock banner, and most of all I'd witnessed two great drummers, OGS from the TEST TUBE BABIES and Steve Roberts. I was gonna really get practising now because I wanted to do what these boys were doing and I wanted to do it as good as them.

I'd been practising my drumming constantly and so naturally wanted to get back involved in some sort of band or other. Well, I ended up getting to know this lad who was the same age as me and he'd attended the local grammar school and he could play a bit of guitar. His name was NEIL TRISTRAM and we hit it off immediately. He had another old school mate and his name was MARK THOMAS, who was also a guitarist. Now these lads gravitated towards the more rock-sounding type influences. At that time the likes of STATUS QUO, AC/DC and bands of that ilk were huge and appealed to the likes of my new acquaintances. Well, I can't fully remember how it came to be, but as well as myself and these two cohorts, I drafted in two of my old mates from THE SYSTEM, Hodgy and Keith. This would only end up being a short-term project as I remember it not lasting very long. As a five-piece we were quite good, definitely a step up from the stuff I'd done with THE SYSTEM. We decided on a name, and called ourselves CRIME AND PASSION, and once again we tackled a selection of covers, but this time they had a little bit more punch to them. With the two quite nifty guitarists on board we were able to do songs like BILLY IDOL's, *White Wedding*, THE DAMNED, *Disco Man* and THE RAMONES, *Daytime Dilemma* some justice. I distinctly remember us going to a studio in Leicester that was owned by the famous rock'n'roll revivalists SHOWADDYWADDY. As I say, it didn't last very long and after only a few gigs, it fizzled out. There were no arguments or anything. I think Mark the guitarist had to go to university and the lads from THE SYSTEM went back to doing what they were doing. I'd made an ally out of Neil, the other guitarist, though, and we would definitely be involved with something else very soon. I do remember one of the little gigs that we did in the town and a gent I instantly recognised as Wakey being there with his lady. I know he watched us play as I can recall seeing him in the audience. This would prove to be quite a pivotal moment, because now he'd seen me play. It would put us on course in the not too distant future whereby we would end up being involved in our next band together.

Life at home was becoming a real strain and to be honest most of the problems, I suppose, were down to me. I wouldn't and couldn't remain consistent with any form of progression towards full-time employment. And so I was, in my parents' eyes, a lazy little bastard. On top of that I really didn't get on with my stepdad. I hated him telling me what to do, and it just caused more conflict in the household. I had not long been dismissed by the YTS scheme and it really was a case of 'What do we do with him now?' Well, my folks had a friend in the town who had another associate who had his own business. He needed somebody to work in his office and basically cover all aspects of the admin side of things. Well, I wasn't completely clueless after what little I'd learnt at college and the Electricity Board, and also I was really in a position whereby I needed to try and get my shit together. And so with that I went to see this guy and within a short time I started working for him. His name was John, and this would turn out to be a real eye-opener. This wasn't an organisation like the Electricity Board or an up and running company. This basically was a one-man band who had his fingers, so to speak, in all sorts of pies. Some of them I suspected were probably not within the realms of legality. He was a bit of a dodgy bastard to be fair, but he was alright with me. I think one of his main sources of income was through a pallet-repairing service he provided. He had this huge yard and the office that I worked in was a portacabin situated to one side of the yard. Well, the yard was packed with pallets and he had these two Herberts working for him who used a forklift to move them into position. They would then strip them down and make them whole again. I bet there was good money in that. My duties, as I say, were to run the admin side. That entailed a lot of filing, answering the phone and basically keeping things up to scratch and whatever he requested I do. He was a real wide boy and quite a character. He was very open, which I found was a complete contrast to anybody I'd witnessed before in authority above me. By that I mean he swore a lot and didn't hold back. I quite liked him. I know he was married, with kids to boot, but I also learned that he had bits on the side, because phone calls would come through and women would ask to speak to John. It didn't take a rocket scientist to realise what he was up to and on occasion I know he was off out and up to no good. He knew I had a girlfriend and was open enough with me to the point of letting me use the office to bring her back to and have a good time, if you know what I mean. We were still in the midst of the lustful period of our relationship and I took him up on his offer, and we ended up going back there a few times when we had nowhere to fuck. Yeah, we got on quite well, me and John, but once again my behaviour in this term of employment ended up being a somewhat brief one. On this particular day he was off out somewhere, in fact he was away for a few days on business, or up to no good, and his team that he had in the yard overseeing the pallets were off too. I was merely there to make sure everything was running smoothly. There wasn't much going on at all and I was rather bored. Well, the devil makes work for idle hands, and that's exactly what happened. I eyed the forklift in the yard and thought to myself, 'Well, I've seen them two driving it around. How hard can it be?' And with that I was off out into the yard, climbed into the forklift and started her up. No, it wasn't difficult at all, and before too long I was tazzing around the yard, relieving my boredom. Now, this wouldn't have been a problem, but as we all know these things have forks on them and I started to race around, lifting and lowering the forks as I did so, and this is when it happened. I'm in mid-flight and the forks are raised really high, and what does this little twat do? He slams it into the portacabin office and shifts it about 6 feet to one side. I'd caused some damage to it as well, but that wasn't my worry. How the fuck was I going to explain to the boss that his office had decided to move 6 foot? I was shitting myself but there was absolutely nothing I could do to rectify the situation. I suppose a professional forklift driver may have been able to manoeuvre the cabin back to its original position, but I didn't have a clue what to do and I didn't really want to be causing any more damage than I already had done. Let's just say that when he came back he went fucking apeshit at me and just said 'You'd better fuck off.' And that's how I came, once again, to be unemployed. Mummy wasn't happy, and in fact none of my elders were happy.

I did take some initiative after losing this source of employment as one of my mates was working for this Ugandan fella who had a pine furniture business. The business made and dealt pine furniture i.e. bureaus, tables and cupboards etc, but also took in second-hand furniture that was often painted or a little damaged, got it stripped, repaired and rewaxed, and then sold it on again. Now, my mate was getting in the region of £80.00 in his hand, and that was quite a tidy sum back in 1986. Some enquiries were made and I started working for the Ugandan chap straight away. Now this was going to be a complete departure from my other terms of employment I had already served. No sitting behind desks and doing office work. I didn't mind, as I hated that work anyway. This new source of income would involve getting quite dirty. I would be doing a lot of sanding down and then rewaxing, which was a strange one as the working environment wasn't totally adequate as we were working in an old school-cum-workshop. When waxing this furniture the wax gives off fumes that are intoxicating, and not necessarily in a pleasant way. I also had to strip painted pieces by immersing them in a huge bath-type vessel with a massive Bunsen burner-type device that heated up the acid in the big bath, which then stripped the paint off. Quite dangerous, so knee-high wellington boots and long-armed rubber gloves were required to do this without getting burned. After the furniture was stripped I would then power wash it and make it ready for repair, and then rewaxed to be sold on. Now, my boss was OK most of the time but he loved himself and could be a bit of a prick. He did push us hard, but like I say, the money was good. I hadn't long turned 18 and home life was not going too well. I'd started drinking by this point, but no more than any other young folk did. The relationship with my parents was getting worse and fall-outs were becoming more and more frequent. I was staying out till all hours, and as much as I had my girlfriend, which was an on-off thing, I was seeing other girls and bringing them back to our house for sex when my folks were out working on the markets. I got caught with my pants down, so to speak, on more than one occasion, and after a night out with my mates I ended up spending the night with this one particular female. I came home at 8 in the morning and things came to a head. My Mum had obviously been worried because I hadn't come home, and when I got in my stepdad got physical with me. It got a bit ugly and after that particular incident I never went back home for four days. The next time I saw my folks, it was at a late hour and I was trying to get in the house via a window. I was half hanging in and half hanging out when the kitchen light went on. Another confrontation ensued and it was there and then it was decided that it would be better for me to move out for good. I was a tad fearful of the prospect of having to fully take care of myself, but it hadn't passed me by that anything was now possible. In other words, I could pretty much do what I wanted. That was all well and good but this did raise the question of where I was going to live. I kicked myself into action and thankfully the question of where I would live wasn't far away, because my boss the Ugandan offered me a room at his place. I had an account with the Halifax and it had money in it that had been saved. Well, for starters I was going to need that. Only thing was my folks had it, and so when things were in place and I knew that this was definitely happening, I went to see them. I got all my records and any other essentials that I felt I needed, and my parting shot was the request to have my bank book, as I was going to need the money. Mum was reluctant to give me it, but I just stipulated that the money was mine and I had every right to have it. With that she handed it over and that was that. I'd now officially left home at the age of 18. I don't recall being that fearful about the future or even giving the future much thought. I just wanted to get out there and have fun. At least I had a job and a source of income, and although it wasn't a secure job I wasn't too worried. To me the most important thing is that I wanted to get involved in another band, only this time I wanted it to be a proper band inasmuch as I wanted to be involved with like-minded individuals who had an alternative outlook on things, and who wanted to do something completely fresh and original. As it happened, things fell right into place, because no sooner had I thought of the idea, everything seemed to fall into place just as I wanted it to.

I was working at the furniture place and for now I was living at my boss's house, which was fine. I had my own little room with hardly anything in it and I was just happy to get from one day to the next. I remember piercing my ears whilst I was living there. The only annoying thing about my short time living there was sometimes late at night, my Ugandan boss man would be entertaining this buxom lass in his bedroom, and so to drown out their bedroom activities, he would have the fucking BEE GEES blasting out at full volume. The music didn't so much annoy me. It was the thought as I lay there on my back, of the spindly Ugandan fella going for it with the big voluptuous sort to the sounds of *Stayin' Alive* that I found a little disturbing. As I said earlier, he wasn't the easiest bloke to work for, mainly due to him just having an over-inflated ego. He was the boss so he obviously had power over me, but it was just the way he used to interact with me. He almost relished treating me like an underling and that was okay for a time, but I wasn't going to be handling that for long. I was paying him rent, which was fine, but looking back he wasn't that much older than me. I'd say he was about 25 or 26 and I was 18 and I suppose, naively, we were mixing business with pleasure. It was not going to work long-term with me working and living with him. He would sub me money during the week and that's where the problems arose. It wasn't his fault as I wanted to be subbed, but I ended up in debt to him. It wasn't like I was actually work-shy at this point as I quite enjoyed the work, but he would be quite ruthless and passive- aggressive towards me, and I suppose I couldn't blame him. So it wasn't long before we pretty much had an altercation and I just fucked off out of it. I left the job and got out of his house. This would be a pattern that I would repeat for many years. They say that a rolling stone gathers no moss, and without realising it at the time, I would move from pillar to post on numerous occasions. But for now it was 1986 and I needed somewhere to live.

Now, as much as I had become the black sheep of the family, I always kept in touch with my Mum and to her credit she never once turned her back on me. A mother's love, I suppose. Well I wasn't really in favour with my grandparents but my Grandad did have a number of properties and he had a bottom floor flat that was empty, and I was allowed to rent this flat as long as the agreed rent was paid. Well, I'd just become unemployed once again, so for the first time, I went on the dole and got the rent paid through the DHSS. The flat was situated near the local train station, and to be perfectly honest, it was a place that needed bringing into the late 20th century. It needed some attention but I was just pleased to have my own roof over my head. I was grateful to my Mum for helping to secure his place for me but I wouldn't see much of her at all. And aside from my brother, who was just leaving school to go straight into a barber's apprenticeship, I never saw any others from the family because, as I say, I had by this time become the black sheep. I now pretty much began living life as a full-on 80s punk rocker, and my flat would eventually pretty much have that written all over it, and it was also from this point that my new network of friends would grow. For me the shackles were off and I could pretty much do as I pleased. I didn't want for much, and as long as I had my music I didn't care, so living on the dole at the time was no major hardship for me.

Thousands of us up and down the country were living that way already. Hundreds of people squatted in the cities back in the 70s and 80s, and for that generation of people it was pretty normal. I was just lucky to get a hold of this place through my family. Can you believe that my toilet was still outside, even back then in 1986? I settled into my new pad quite quickly and got myself a cat called Splodge. I was still seeing my first girlfriend and we enjoyed having our little haven to do whatever we wanted. A lot of the faces I'd started to see at the gigs I'd been frequenting, I now knew by their first names. I gravitated towards a select few who I wanted to befriend. I made it clear that they could come round and doss about round my place and, through that, new associations and friendships were formed. I was still a tad naïve and a little impressionable but I was having a good time. I even had my drums with me and I had them set up in the front room down the hall. But the drums would start to cause problems a little later due to the obvious fact that they were too fucking loud. At weekends I'd meet up with a few of my mates and we would go down the pub and get pissed. I could never drink beer or lager as I didn't like the taste, so I drank sweet cider and cheap white wine. I did get into some states as any youngster does as I didn't drink for the enjoyment of drinking, but to feel the effects of the alcohol. One night I got a visitation from 3 lads a few years older than myself. One of them was Wakey from the ENGLISH DOGS. I was buzzing having these new guests around, and basically just went into DJ mode, playing loads of different punk singles. They had all been drinking and I hit it off with all of them, especially Wakey. I don't remember whether it was on this particular night, but it was definitely around this time that I was introduced to a ritual that I would repeat over and over again for the next few years. He asked me if I had a milk bottle and a couple of normal knives.

Well, milk was still delivered and bought in bottles then, so I produced a bottle and the knives. He broke the bottom off the bottle and then stuck the knives into the gas fire that was in my room. I wondered what the fuck was going on here. One of the lads then produced a lump of cannabis and started tearing tiny pieces off and placing them on top of the fireplace in a row. One lad took the bottle and placed it up to his mouth. Wakey took the knives out the fire, that were now literally red hot, placed one knife onto the little piece of cannabis, then placed it under the now exposed bottom of the bottle and then placed the other knife so that both knives came together with the cannabis lump in between, which now billowed smoke. The lad with the bottle to his mouth then sucked in the smoke that now filled the bottle until he'd inhaled it all. All of them took turns to do this and then it was my turn. Maybe I shouldn't have done it, but I did. I wanted to try new things out. I was told it would feel good and not to worry, and with the experience that I'd had only 18 months earlier in my head, I went ahead and had my first hot knives. This time though, the effects were a lot more subtle. Not just a whoosh feeling, but a lot more pleasant as my brain took in the drug. To be honest I felt great, and once again the music sounded fantastic and it also made me laugh. I'd found something new that made me feel really good, even better than the effects of alcohol. And so this would be a ritual I would repeat thousands of times over the coming years. Wakey informed me that he only lived just round the corner from me with his wife and two daughters, and he said I was welcome to go around his whenever I wanted. Within a few days after that he informed me that he was going to form a new group and that he hoped that I would be the drummer.

Come 1986/1987 most of the classic punk records that we all know and love had been released, but there was still some little gems being on offer. *Too Tough To Die* by the RAMONES was one. I discovered the BAD BRAINS, who were absolutely phenomenal. *From The Cradle To The Grave* by THE SUBHUMANS, and one of my favourite all-time bands was a band from Vancouver called DOA who had one of the best punk drummers ever, CHUCK BISCUITS, an absolute powerhouse with a dynamite- like flair. The DEAD KENNEDYS were still giving it some, just. And then came a blinder of an album that influenced me no end. Not just for the power of the music on offer, but also its lyrical content that just reinforced how I was viewing the world at that age, and that band was CONFLICT, with their album THE UNGOVERNABLE FORCE. So aside from these bands that were keeping me interested, there was music from other genres that I started to take on board, especially as I myself was progressing as a drummer. A lot of us were listening to more rock-based stuff like early IRON MAIDEN, and with that the thrash metal scene was also taking off big time. And so, out of the myriad of 80s-style punks, new bands like GAY BYKERS ON ACID, ZODIAC MINDWARP and CRAZYHEAD, who all had their own styles, started to appear. There was goth too, which was to become very well-known indeed, and at the same time that I took all these new bands and new sounds in, there was still a huge array of bands and music from the past that I'd yet to discover. More often than not it was via other musically minded people that I would be exposed to something new and unheard. And so, it was in this atmosphere with everything going on, that the next band I came to be in formed. I started going round Wakey's place quite a lot. We would invariably get stoned and just listen to music and just waste our time. Now his involvement with the original ENGLISH DOGS had dissolved due to him leaving midway through a German tour. Punk gigs back then were frenetic affairs anyway but throw a load of right wing skinheads into the mix, and things could get very unpleasant indeed. So it was in this climate that Wakey said, 'I've had enough,' and came back home, and with that, he was an ENGLISH DOG no more.

9. WALTZING WITH WAKEY AND THE COSMIC SPACE TOADS

Well, that was a good while ago and he was ready to do something else. We got our heads together and started to ask people if they'd be interested. I got hold of Neil, my rock guitarist mate, who I'd been in CRIME AND PASSION with. We got hold of one of the original ENGLISH DOGS fans on board, a lad named TROY, who was now playing a bit of rhythm guitar, but we still needed a bass player. In the meantime we started to congregate round at Wakey's and practise in his cellar. Just to get things moving I'd just use a floor tom and snare to provide the beat and the two guitarists would have their amps just at a sufficient level so that we could get to grips with coming up with tunes, etc. We'd get stoned first by ingesting a few hot knives, and then heading down into the cellar we got on with things. It was a lot of fun and Neil and Troy really complemented each other, with myself plodding away and keeping things in time. Now as much as Wakey had his punk thing going on, in the last couple of years he'd been broadening his horizons with what he was listening to musically. I'd go round his place and he'd be listening to really diverse stuff like PLANET GONG, IAN DURY, THE SENSATIONAL ALEX HARVEY BAND and THE STRANGLERS. Throw into the mix a steady diet of hot knives and booze and the lyrical vocabulary he was coming up with was starting to get really interesting, thus when he showed us his new style of lyrics we'd be rolling around with laughter. They were brilliant. The word was out that we were getting this new band together and while we were round at Wakey's there was a knock at the door and a guy with a bald head, biker jacket and jeans said, 'I hear you're looking for a bass player.' I can't recall us trying anybody else out but that wasn't a problem because this guy was perfect. He went under the moniker of FELIX, and he looked pretty weird, which was pretty much how we all looked back then. He was a very adequate player too, and so with that it seemed that the line-up was now complete. Wakey's lyrics were a mixture of styles, mixed up and then thrown back out again. Imagine JIM MORRISON, IAN DURY and adding his own punk rock style, intermingled with subject matter that verged on the most amazing hash, mushroom and alcohol-fuelled Alice in Wonderland trip imaginable, and that gives you an idea of where he was going. The music was also a mixture of styles that in short can only be described as acid punk. No fast hardcore music or just basic three chords. There was mixtures of good solid rock riffs and melodic interludes all played at a relatively mid-paced speed, and unexpected changes that flowed into each other and back again, making everything interesting but still catchy. With all of this in mind we called ourselves THE COSMIC SPACE TOADS. It was time to take it to the next level and find ourselves a proper room to rehearse in and start harnessing the songs into a full and cohesive set. There was a buzz around the town about what we were doing way before we even did a gig, and with that in mind we found ourselves a room at the back of one of our local pubs. We were practising regularly and I would never practice straight, although as a drummer I never made a habit of playing drunk. It just can't be done, but rest assured I was always stoned.

Up to that point I'd never smoked cigarettes, but now I wouldn't turn down the offer of a spliff if it came my way, but I did prefer smoking cannabis raw as in hot knives, or in a pipe etc. I was smoking regularly now, and by that I mean every day if I could. I just found that it enhanced my music listening experience to another level. Food tasted great on it, hence I used to experience the munchies, and sex was also a more deep and sensual experience when under the influence, and with that in mind, myself and my girlfriend would have some wild nights at that point in our relationship. Like I say, a buzz was flying round and so it was decided that we needed to start gigging. We immediately went down well and we had no problem finding little venues in our area. We had a different mix of people who came to see us, a fair few who were from the original punk crowd, but a lot of people came out of curiosity just to check this different thing out. The fact that Wakey was the front man definitely gave us a head start and he never failed to deliver as he had learned his craft with the DOGS, only now he took it up a gear and, as front men go, he was very good. Musically, though, the band were also on top form. We gelled perfectly, and for me personally I was loving it. My playing went up a notch here, and from here I'd realised that I had become a half-decent drummer. Life for me at this time looking back seemed to be one big party, and a lot of it was focused around the band. My social circle was growing with a large mixture of people. I was still seeing people I knew from school, I'd bump into people I'd been involved with in the swimming club days, but we were all moving on. A lot of the new people I was socialising with were more often than not a little older than me, and due to the band and the people we attracted who were the more alternative or bohemian type, with the passing of time, I'd pretty much become one of those myself. The relationship with my girl was becoming a little strained, for as much as I did feel that I loved her, I was away having a good time when I wasn't with her, and I suppose there began to be some distance between us. For my part I was no angel. If I wasn't busy getting wasted during the day, then I would be in our local pub/club type place that catered for us alternatives, getting off with various young women behind her back. I was also now dressing differently and experimenting with things that would also begin to drive a wedge between us. The problem with me was that I wanted to try out different things and she was more strait-laced, not boring but just a little bit more normal. We should really have split up at this point because her parents were not overly enamoured with this reprobate who wasn't working and who looked like something out of Mad Max. If the truth be known we were infatuated with each other, but rest assured, with me being a bastard, it would come back and bite me on the arse. A lot of the older people gravitated towards Wakey, and so what with myself and him being neighbours and being in the band, I also became acquainted with most of them too. I remember a coloured guy called COCO who gave me a black capsule, otherwise known as a black bomber, or speed, and I loved the way it made me feel. I was already flying round like a wild dervish anyway without anything to help me but taking speed for the first time again just intensified how things were going on at the time. Punk rock and speed were designed for each other, and now I found out why. THE COSMIC SPACE TOADS proceeded to rehearse regularly and we were getting better and better. And the regularity of gigs was reinforcing that. Meanwhile the party lifestyle that was happening round at my gaff was starting to take its toll on my neighbours. One was the noise factor, never mind the constant barrage of music blasting from my record player, but I was now living a 24-hour party people kind of existence. Up most of the night and then sleeping till midday or whenever, I'd get up and get stoned with a few hotties and then go from there. Then I'd probably go round Wakey's and there would be one or two of our circle there. Then we would proceed to get more stoned and then go get some booze, get rowdy by playing card games for drink and basically end up having a right laugh. Even band rehearsals could turn into mini gigs as our hangers-on would all come along, usually pissed and stoned. Not ideal really, but we didn't care and it was usually fun. Like I say, complaints were being made about myself and the motley crew that were congregating round my place and the level of noise being emitted at ungodly hours. It was causing some friction as this place was in the family and no doubt my Mum was getting some grief from my Grandad about my supposed unruly behaviour. I received written warnings from the local council and I would make a bit of an effort to curb the noise and other shenanigans. Meanwhile, the TOADS were now making headway out of town with gigs in Nottingham and Telford, and these gigs turned into mini events as our local following would be in tow, ready to boogie on down to our space rock tunes with Wakey as the Pied Piper pulling them in. I can remember when we played in Nottingham, myself and somebody else who I can't remember went to the sex shop just down the road and bought up all the bottles of amyl nitrate we could, and these we dished out to all and sundry at the gig.

I'd played one gig a few years earlier with THE SYSTEM, where we were miked up properly with monitors and the like, but this was even better. A proper venue with proper sound and with an audience that loved what we were doing, which obviously made us better. The band was going well and it was decided that we needed to get some promo photos done. It was a Sunday and we all met, and at this point in time we now had the inclusion of a young lass on board who would dance on stage as we played. GEORGIE was her name, and she was great fun and didn't mind letting her hair down, so to speak. These pics were taken just on the outskirts of town out in the countryside. Well, we started to find magic mushrooms scattered around the ground. We all got picking and when we'd picked enough we all headed back to Wakey's to boil them up and ingest. Let me tell you that mushroom tea tastes fucking vile but the flipside of that being that I've never laughed so much in all my life. Another first, and this time the effects were even more pronounced and more intense than hashish. Colours, sound and the senses are all heightened tenfold. A bit strange coming down off them, but It wouldn't be the last time I partook of hallucinogens. I was still attending other band's gigs too, and two that stick in the memory were fantastic. The first was when my band mate Troy and I went in his little green mini to see the RAMONES at the Birmingham Odeon. I'd never been to a big venue before, although saying that, I myself had played at De Montfort Hall a few years back, but never to see a band. And to get to see one of my favourites was great. It was on the back of the TOO TOUGH TO DIE album, and as expected they were on fire, playing at breakneck speed. I can distinctly remember wanting to get right down the front for when they came on, but security were only letting certain people down there. I had no need to worry though, because when the intro music kicked in, signalling that they were about to hit the stage, loads of us charged forward and lucky old me got past the security, and I pretty much watched the whole gig right in front of DEE DEE RAMONE.

The second gig was better but for a different reason. CONFLICT were putting on a gig that would become known as The Gathering of the 5000 down in London at the Brixton Academy. On the day of the gig I travelled to Derby, where a fair contingent were going down too. There was a band from Derby called THE CITY INDIANS who were actually involved with the gig itself. This was a big gig as CONFLICT had in a roundabout way picked up where CRASS had left off. And to show that this was part fact, STEVE IGNORANT from CRASS was now a member of CONFLICT, dual vocalling with COLIN CONFLICT. To be the premier anarchist band in the country and to secure the Brixton Academy was a major thing in itself, and the powers that be surely can't have realised who they had truly booked. I have since found out that this was in fact exactly what had happened. Unbeknownst to the venue the gig had pretty much sold out, and whether they liked it or not 4,000-plus hardcore punks were going to be converging on the Academy. I suppose that it was inevitable that problems would arise with such an event taking place. I can't actually remember getting down to the gig, but as always once I was inside I headed straight towards the front of the stage. I can remember the Rasta poet BENJAMIN ZEPHANIAH doing his thing, but the crowd were getting whipped up and ready for CONFLICT, who at this time were hugely popular. The atmosphere was fucking electric and I was thinking, 'Fuck me, this is gonna be great.' I loved the band's direct approach and Colin's lyrics were inspirational. And although I haven't adhered to everything the band informed me about, a lot of the views that they espoused, and opened my mind to, I still carry with me to this day. There was the regular feature of TV screens showing riots and stuff relative to their subject matter, until finally the lights went down and PACO, the CONFLICT drummer, kicked in with the intro to the CRASS song, *Banned From The Roxy*, and with that the place erupted. From then on in we were bombarded with a whole selection of CRASS classics and CONFLICT standards. It has to be said that the sound wasn't brilliant but I didn't care because I was lost in the sense of occasion. Tonight, for one night, we the punk scene were all together and I was loving the fact that I was there. Amid the sound problems other factors started to take over as the Academy security was starting to get heavy with sections of the audience. Midway through one of the songs Paco had seen some shit going on and he just jumped off his kit and waded into the security, who were being overly brutal to some of the young punks. With that the gig was stopped and then started again. This went on and on until eventually the gig was finally ended for good. With that there seemed to be a bit of a stand-off, and then finally 4,000 angry punks started to leave the venue. The constabulary were waiting outside and inevitably there were some substantial clashes outside. We came out of it unscathed but I know for a fact that what with public transport and tube stations closing down earlier than usual, there was chaos and running battles with the cops. As much as the whole event turned into a bit of a shambles, it was still great to be down there and seeing the coming together of all those like-minded souls.

Back at home, momentum was gaining pace with the COSMIC SPACE TOADS. Our gigs were well attended and we came to the attention of a couple of businessmen who thought they could play a hand in managing the group. I don't think they realised how out of their depth they were going to be, dealing with an admittedly great band, but also the individual characters and especially Wakey. These fellas had never come across anything like us. They paid for us to go into a studio and record our set, but unfortunately the recordings came out crap and really didn't give a true representation of how the band really sounded. They even invited us over to their place to discuss some sort of strategy, but being the way we were, we turned up a bit worse for wear and when one of the clan made provocative remarks to one of these guys' wives, who I have to add was rather dishy, that pretty much brought that avenue of progression to a halt. We just carried on as if nothing had happened and forgot about them and got on with the gigging when we could. For me though, by now I had just about burnt all my bridges with staying in my flat. The noise and disorderly conduct continued and so with threats of intervention from the courts I moved out and into a house I shared with a new acquaintance. I was now using drugs quite frequently and this guy I moved in with was too. Again, he was a bit older than me and it was good of him to put me up, but I didn't stay there long. He was a bit of a dark character and I didn't always feel comfortable around him, but we remained sociable after I'd left and he did eventually sort himself out, but sadly he passed away only a few years back with some underlying health issues. I got quite ill while I was staying at that place. I'd been taking quite a lot of speed at this point and was scoring from this dealer who was cutting it with something that he shouldn't have been doing. I started feeling rough and my mouth and lips started to blister up really bad, and so, like a twat, I scored some more of this dodgy cunt's speed, thinking, 'Oh, I'll feel better if I have some more,' and all it did was make my symptoms worse. I ended up being bed-bound for a few days and word got to my mother, who ended up taking me to the doctors. I can't recall what the diagnosis was, but in short I'd been mildly poisoned. Poor old Mum, she must have been worried sick. I moved out of matey's house and ended up getting a bedsit in a large house that was rather swanky, to be honest. The only thing was the landlord and landlady also lived there and, as much as I know how to conduct myself in an appropriate manner when the need arises, I don't think that they were particularly enamoured with having to share their communal living space with a punk. Well, they had other properties too, and suggested it may be best if I could move into one of those. Well, this place was nowhere near as salubrious as their main place and I was given a room upstairs that was very small indeed. I wasn't very impressed but it was a roof over my head. As luck would have it a chance meeting with someone I met down the pub came in very handy, whereby within a very short time I would have a whole house to myself, and where more merry crazy goings-on would take place. This guy was known as MONTY, he was your typical biker stoner, beard, jeans, cap and cut-off top type fellow, but we hit it off straight away. I mentioned to him that I hated where I was living. With that he told me where he lived and stated that I was welcome to rent a room off of him as long as his rent got paid. The house was quite big and I took the large bedroom upstairs. This suited me down to the ground as Monty was a very down-to-earth type of character, probably too down-to-earth, and that was probably down to the amount of dope he was smoking. I could come and go as I pleased and his rent was paid into the bank via the DHSS. As much as he lived in the place too, it was basically bare, with hardly any creature comforts in it, but just the basics to live quite humbly. Well, I moved in all of my records and my stereo and made my room as comfortable as could be, and while he would be blasting out JIMI HENDRIX, DEEP PURPLE and that kind of stuff, I was discovering bands like SNFU, NOMEANSNO and loads of other American bands. One day, Monty came to me and said that he was fucking off somewhere. I can't remember where exactly but I think it was something to do with a bird. Anyway, he basically left me with the responsibility of looking after the place and simply fucked off. I never saw him again, and so here I was with this large house all to myself. Well, first my pal Neil, the guitarist from THE TOADS, took on a real small room next to mine. I can recall a skinhead I met in town who was a Londoner. I befriended him and he moved into one of the rooms downstairs. He came across as being a bit thick, but I do remember him being really good at art. He could do those caricatures of people really well and I can remember us giving him his new name, TREVOR, after the skinhead TIM ROTH played in the film *Made In Britain*. What with the place being so big, I came up with the bright idea that the band could practise in one of the other rooms. And so that's what we did. I was having a good old time, but at this stage, the cracks were definitely starting to appear between myself and my girlfriend.

I was smoking a lot of dope by now and she didn't agree with it, as I could be quite nasty if I didn't have any. By this time we were pretty much having an on-and-off kind of relationship. I still always had my eye on other females if the chance arose and I know for sure that she copped off with other fellas too. I couldn't blame her as I was a loose cannon who was out for what I could get. It really hurt me when I realised that she'd been out fucking someone else, but like I say, I couldn't blame her. She decided to leave town and we kept in touch as there was still a bond between us, but she just felt that she needed to move on. She had never really been into what I was doing anyway, but there is one of the memories that sticks out for me where we did something together. We went to see STIFF LITTLE FINGERS on their first comeback tour in late 1987. We went to Rock City in Nottingham and we both had a great time and the place was absolutely packed, but alas, that was one of the last times we'd do anything together. We were both starting to go in different directions, and within a few months we'd both go our separate ways.

10. ELLO ELLO ELLO, WHAT WE GOT HERE, THEN?

My main objective was to carry on the way I was. My mind was purely set on making something of the band. We really did have something and it was all of us as a collective that made it that way. At this time Wakey was a phenomenal front man and on a personal level me and him were the best of mates. A very funny guy who was great fun to be around. Not everybody got his sense of humour and some people found him to be too much, but not I. We had plans, plans that included eventually taking the band to the next level, on tour and hopefully on to a record deal. But you can only do that one day at a time. We were definitely going in the right direction though, and that was because we really were a tight unit and the fact that the songs that we had and our growing reputation as a live band seemed to suggest that it could definitely happen. Yeah, we were definitely on a roll, and then what happens? Old muggins here goes and gets busted for drug possession.

I'd been on one of my many nights out and I had ended round at a mate's place that was just round the corner from a local haunt. I'd gotten stoned with a couple of mutual acquaintances and after some time one of them bade us farewell and left. Well, I hung around for a short while and then left myself. As I came to the top of the road I noticed a cop wagon parked outside a club. I just proceeded with caution and carried on towards home. I crossed a couple of roads and was not far from my house when the cop van I'd seen a little earlier screeched to a halt and a couple of cops jumped out. I was startled, to be fair, and with that they instructed me that they wished to search me for drugs, as they had information I was in possession. Well, I had a small quantity of hash on me, nothing that would warrant a major crime, but back then in 1988 any possession could still be dealt with by heavy fines being imposed. Well the game was up and it didn't take them long to find my stash. With that they informed me that they also wanted to search my house. I was escorted back to my place. Unbeknown to me one of my associates had left dope in my room in a matchbox. Again, not a considerable amount but I was going to get charged for being in possession of that, too. I'd already had a couple of brushes with the law. Petty stuff, shop lifting etc., but this was deemed considerably more serious. And so with that I was taken to the local station, charged, and given a court date. I'd just turned 19 and this incident threw a spanner in the works. Quite obviously I had to inform my mother and, to be expected, she was really upset. And worse, she was going to have to inform my grandfolks. Not good. For now, though, I just pretty much carried on as I had done and thought it was just a case of bad luck and that I'd been in the wrong place at the wrong time. I did find out that I had been grassed up by one of the lads who I'd got stoned with after my night out. He'd left the joint and told the police that I was carrying. Bastard. The court date came and the system was trying to do me on an 'intent to supply' charge, which is deemed a lot more serious than just possession. I got found guilty of possession and received a rather hefty fine.

It was rather a big deal for my family and my Mum immediately started badgering me about going to South Africa and staying with my Dad for a while. If I remember correctly, she started on with this idea before I went to court, thereby if I agreed to it then it would look like I was working to change my ways, and was willing to go to certain lengths to achieve just that. Well, I really didn't want to go at all, but to be honest my Mum was feeling rather desperate and so I just relented and in the end I agreed to go for a short while. For me that meant getting on a plane and getting to South Africa and living with my Dad who I hadn't seen for years, and his wife who I'd never met at all. Ultimately it meant the end of the band and that was the thing that hurt the most. The lads all knew the story and were fine about it, and Wakey just said we'd just crack on when I got back. And so not long after being dealt with in court, I flew off out to Johannesburg.

For my elders, the hope was that after a stint away from England I'd either stay out there and build a life for myself in some form or other, or I'd come back and put my past behind me and get on with a life that would be, in their eyes, a tad more normal. Sadly for them, and ultimately for me, this was not to be.

I arrived in South Africa and in truth I didn't particularly want to be there, and no doubt my father and his wife had their reservations too. Dad came to meet me and although I knew this wasn't going to be easy for any of us, I was actually pleased to see him, although it was quite strange being halfway round the other side of the world. It wasn't as if I was there on holiday or anything. I'd been gotten rid of to keep me out of trouble, or that's a little bit how it felt to me at the time. My South African parents lived in a little town about an hour or so from Johannesburg, and they lived in a large open-plan bungalow with a swimming pool. It felt a little bit strained, but they did make me feel welcome, and for the first few weeks I was there I just chilled out while they went out to work. I'd taken a lot of cassettes with me and so that brought some light relief to any boredom that I started to feel. I met a few of my parents' friends and they were nice enough. But it wasn't long before I was asking myself the question, 'What the fuck am I doing here?' I couldn't just sit around for months on end and my parents certainly didn't want that either. So I decided to get a job. Steakhouses were, and still are, all the rage in South Africa, and so I applied for a job as a waiter in a place called The Porterhouse. And this was where another whole new adventure started. I was drug free for the first time in a couple of years, but I suppose I still looked alternative as I had long, bleached blond hair and didn't look too dissimilar to a young Kurt Cobain. I slicked back my hair and wore some relatively appropriate clothing to the interview and voila, they asked me when I could start. I was quite chuffed as now I was going to be doing something productive, and hopefully also meet some new people who were of a similar age to myself. I had to wear black trousers and white shirt and a dicky bow, and I had an order book that would go in a waiter's apron around my waist. I'd take the orders for drinks and then food, and this would all have to be documented. One copy to the relevant station that prepared food or drinks, and the other to the reception who would then tot up the customer's bill for them to pay at the end. I was quickly shown the ropes and would be working two shifts. One in the afternoon, the other in the evening. The wage was quite meagre but one could make up the money via tips. On starting the job I soon realised that most of the waiters and waitresses were all young like myself. Being new in the place, and being English, I soon blended in really well, my accent instantly being a source of interest to those who I worked with, but also the customers that I would be waiting on. This would serve me well as I was quite good at laying on the English accent. Add to that I took to the job relatively easy and, more often than not, my tips were generally very good. I liked the job because it was quite fast-paced and I liked a good few of the people I was working with. It's 1988, right, and at that time apartheid was still in place with restrictions with regards blacks and whites mixing in the workplace and socially, or whatever. It was bullshit, but that's how it was, and just to put you in the picture, this place I worked at was quite big, catering for about 200 people if the demand required. So all staff who worked in the main part of the restaurant, in the front, where the customers were, were either white Afrikaans or Portuguese and mostly English-speaking.

All kitchen staff, of which there about 30 to 40, were coloured. Like I had my uniform they had theirs too. They dealt with the preparation of all the food that the waiters, people like me, would go and serve to the punters. I soon got to grips with how the system worked and I really did actually enjoy the job. Before too long I was making some new acquaintances amongst the other staff, male and female. And it wasn't long before I caught the eye of a gorgeous dark-haired lass called CLARA. She was Afrikaans but spoke near-perfect English. She was doing the same job as me and so we were always in close proximity to each other. After initially getting to know one another, she claimed that she had noticed how I looked at the other girls. I didn't know I'd made it that obvious. We started flirting with each other, and after telling her that I'd had some experience with regard to sex, she turned around and told me that she wanted me to teach her. And with that we started a brief relationship that would last for the duration of my stay in South Africa. She had her own flat and not long after we started sleeping with each other, I pretty much stayed at her place by night and we would go to work together during the day. And so, as well as Clara there were a few other people I got to know too, and we all used to go out and socialise when we weren't working. Now it must have been in my mind as it wasn't long before I was making inquiries about the availability of cannabis. In Africa cannabis has always been widely available and over there they call it 'dagga'. After some more probing I found out that the guys in the kitchen could get me some. Well, I was now earning a tidy little wage and I wasn't paying any rent. So I could at least afford some, as well as doing a little drinking and socialising with my new-found friends. Now from the moment that I started this job I'd immediately set about sussing out the coloured guys and gals that worked in the kitchen. Not at all to suss them out for my own ends, but because I was genuinely interested in them as people. I've never been a racist person at all and coming from where I come from – meaning little, small-town England – to be in the company of these people who were literally a whole world away from mine, what with the political situation and the restrictions imposed on them, I went out of my way to bond with the few who didn't eye me with a slight air of suspicion. I viewed and treated them just as I would anyone else, and as much as there could be a language barrier sometimes, I struck up a good working relationship with a few of them. That being said I also knew that they had access to getting hold of some dagga and, after a few failed attempts at securing some, I finally got my hands on some. In England in the late 80s cannabis still came predominantly in resin form, but in South Africa it came in a weed form, pretty much as it does all over Europe now. Well, this stuff stinks when smoked and I hadn't smoked any blow for a good few months now in any form.

11. JO'BURGS A HOOT, BUT ENGLAND IS CALLING

Well, I'd just scored this amount that was wrapped in a cigar-shaped package in newspaper not long after starting one of my afternoon shifts. Well, I slipped off to the toilets and locked myself away for a moment, just to see what I'd just bought. I opened the package carefully and there it was, weed with quite a lot of pips in as I remember. Living in the moment I thought to myself, 'Well, I'm not going to get the chance to smoke any of this soon.' One, I wasn't smoking cigarettes at that time, and two, if I did get the chance of smoking some I would smell of it afterwards. So without further ado, I got a fair amount and just crammed it into my mouth and washed it down with some water. It wasn't very pleasant at all as it was very coarse and bitty, but after washing it down thoroughly I brushed myself down and went out and got on with my shift. A little part of me was needing to know that it was actually proper weed I had bought, and this in a roundabout way was my way of testing it to see if it was real. Ingesting cannabis takes a lot longer for the effects to take hold rather than smoking it, which only takes a few minutes. I was about 2 hours into my shift and the stuff I'd swallowed hit me. It was real alright. From feeling very straight one minute to having this all-encompassing feeling wash over me was quite stark and I can remember feeling very paranoid, as I was in the middle of serving people food and drinks. I retained my composure and just got on with what I needed to do and amazingly, with the way I was feeling, my customers didn't seem to notice at all. Well, I suppose they wouldn't do, would they? In fact I just kept very calm and if anything, with the euphoria I was feeling, I think that I added a touch more panache to my waitering skills. I repeated this ritual a few more times but it wasn't long before I would resort to smoking it like most people did. If only some of these people knew that the strange-looking Englishman serving them was quite zonked out on South African bush. I was good at my job and I took a certain amount of pride in doing it to the best of my ability. And as a reflection of that, at the end of each working week, the management would get all of us waiters and waitresses together and inform us all who were the top tip earners, and lo and behold, for the number of months that I was there I was top scorer! The management even offered to send me on a course to become a restaurant floor manager. Looking back it would have been a great opportunity for me to get involved in a line of work that I seemed to own a certain aptitude for. Who knows, if I'd decided to take that on and stay over there, my life may have taken a completely different route.

The truth of the matter was that as much as I was enjoying myself over there, from the moment I landed there I was already thinking about getting back to England and cracking on with what I really wanted to do. So yes, I did have an adventure, I did renew my relationship with my Dad and I got a job that I really enjoyed. And this beautiful lass I spent my time with and some of the wild nights I had over there were fantastic, but England was pulling me back all of the time. It wouldn't be the first time I experienced that feeling because in the coming years I would return to South Africa again on numerous occasions. And yet every time the allure of England would always bring me back. There's one final tale about that time I spent over there. Before I went out there, and my mother had literally begged me to go, I'd originally said I'd go for three months. My Mum had said repeatedly that I should go for at least six months and we argued over and over again until she finally gave in and said okay, my ticket would allow me to stay in South Africa for three months. It was only when I made plans whilst out there to come home after three months that I found out that my ticket was actually for six months. She understandably conned me into going for six months. I was fucking livid and set about getting the ticket changed. There was some slight conflict between my father and myself as I stipulated to him what I wanted to do. He wasn't happy about it and pretty much said, 'You're not going back,' and I said that I was. There was a bit of a standoff between us but underneath he could not really stop me, but to be fair I was a stubborn little sod and I'd made up my mind. I didn't even know if I could get my ticket changed but after visiting the airlines in Johannesburg, and paying over some cash, my ticket was changed. And so after a return date was set I was given a really nice farewell from all the people I'd got to know at The Porterhouse and a bit of an emotional goodbye from the girl I'd been with. The next day my Dad and his wife drove me to JAN SMUTS airport in Johannesburg, whereby I said, 'Thank you very much for having me,' and with that, after a four months stay, I flew back to England.

And so I landed back in England. My Mum wasn't pleased as I'd changed my ticket and I was back a few months before she reckoned I should have come back. My family this side of the pond were hoping that I'd end up staying out there, but to be fair I had no intention of doing that whatsoever. I love England and I love being English, so it wasn't even viable. I was just turning 21 and I wanted to be where the action was. And that for me meant getting straight back and involved in a rock'n'roll band. Amazingly within a day or two of arriving back in Blighty I bumped into Wakey, who seemed overwhelmed at my return, and almost immediately we set about putting THE TOADS back in a rehearsal room and getting straight back out there to do some gigs. There was just one problem. In the four months that I'd been away Felix the bass player had cleared off somewhere, and Neil the guitarist had gone to live in Nottingham and joined another band over there. This was a blow as both of those fellas were really good players and they were also part of the dynamic that made the band what it was. Not being in the habit of showing defeatism, we just set about recruiting other people to replace them. As much as it was a priority in my eyes, there was the question of where I was going to live now that I was back in England, because living back at my parents' house wasn't an option.

So for a brief period some friends of the family put me up whilst I tried to gain some form of employment. Well, I got a job at a food manufacturers which was basically a factory that churns out quick meals. My job was to probe the food after it had been cooled with this device that gauged the temperature. Once it reached the appropriate temperature then it is taken over to another section and packed, ready to be sent off to the relevant outlets, etc. I managed to stick this out for three weeks before I thought to myself, 'I can't be arsed getting up every day and doing this for 8 or 9 hours.' Once again I decided to go back on the dole, which didn't go down well with the elders, and also I didn't want to be a burden on the friends of the family. So I ended up staying with some of my own friends. For now the band was the only thing that I was motivated towards. We ended up finding a half-decent bass player, although God knows what he thought of us. We were a loud and brash bunch, and he was your typical bass player-type character, quite laid-back. For now we got to grips with practising as the four piece, and the fact that our main guitar had gone was felt. But Troy, our rhythm guitarist, did a really good job of tackling the songs on his own. Before I got busted and had gone off to South Africa, the aim was to get into a studio and get some decent recordings done, so as to promote the band further down the line. Well, within a short space of time of me being back and us getting things rolling again we were now ready to get some of our best tracks down on tape. As well as having this in the pipeline when we were ready, we also got back to doing a couple of decent gigs. We played Telford and Derby and both were riotous affairs. And we ended up finding a guitarist to beef up the sound so that we came across heavier as a live unit. It was none other than my old mate Dunk, whose place I used to go to when I was skiving off college. My overall feeling was that with this new line-up we were good but there was just that little bit of something missing. Yeah, we were still really good, but the line-up we had before was phenomenal. Well, we cracked on from day to day and once again I was usually getting stoned, pissed, high on speed or on all three if I had the opportunity. We got a studio booked and so we got our heads down in preparation for that. It was always fun to be involved with Wakey back then as he was always up to something that would usually end up with us all rolling around with laughter. And the studio was no different. In saying that, when it came to laying down his vocals the man was totally serious, as we all were. And as it happened, what with the high spirits that we always found ourselves in, things used to come together spontaneously. That ended up making our time in the studio more creative and thus coming out with a better finished product, because of that willingness to explore things to the max. To give you an example, we decided that there wouldn't be breaks of silence between tracks, instead we would record sketches that were relevant to the songs and place them at the end of one song, and have the sketch that would then lead into the next song. So with subject matter that ranged from riding round Mars on a rocket ship, smoking hash and songs to do with fucking, you can imagine what we got up to. It was great because those snippets just added to the whole character of the band and also added that extra little twist to what I thought was great music. We came away from that studio with an amazing document of that time, but this was just before the age of CDs really kicked in, and so we decided to release it on a cassette only.

We decided to call the tape LETS EAT, which had its meaning tied into the munchies, which went with smoking dope. We had a certain amount recorded and they all flew out really quickly. These recordings became almost legendary around my way, and sadly I don't own a copy. Although I know someone who does own one. I really should try and get hold of it as it would be a nice memento of that time. At the same time that all of this was going on I bumped into Neil, the original lead guitarist from the TOADS. Now myself and Neil went back even further, if you remember, as we'd done a little bit together in CRIME AND PASSION before the TOADS. We were good friends and it was good to see him. Well, what with me fucking off to South Africa he didn't hang about. He moved to Nottingham and immediately got himself involved with some goth rock band that was pretty much on its last legs when he joined. When we got chatting, though, he couldn't stop telling me how good the scene was in Nottingham and that he was in with this other guitarist who had some good contacts. And some of these contacts were all involved with the venue over there known as ROCK CITY. Well, I'd been going to Rock City for a couple of years now, to go to gigs or to go to their great alternative nights that they used to put on on Saturday nights. Well, because of Neil's new affiliation with this guitarist fella, he was now well acquainted with all the people at the venue and basically had free entry whenever he wished to go there. Neil also impressed on me that he and his buddy wanted to get a new band together and that I should seriously consider joining them. Immediately my impulsive nature triggered off all these different thoughts. It seemed to me that here was an opportunity to get right into the thick of things in the city. I kept the offer to myself and arranged to meet him again in Nottingham. Firstly, it was good to see him and to catch up, and well, he did seem to be doing all right and was full of confidence with regards to whatever else he was going to do. For now I just carried on doing what I was doing with Wakey and the TOADS. If Saturday nights weren't spent getting wasted and looking for sex in town then I would usually, along with a couple of my bandmates and a few others, end up going to Rock City to do exactly the same. I always loved that place because of the anonymity and there was always loads of birds and other like-minded souls there having a fucking good time. Well, not long after I'd first met Neil again I ended up meeting him in Rock City and he said, 'Come with me,' and proceeded to take me underneath the club where it was usually off-limits to punters like me. As we progressed through the place he was greeted and exchanged mild pleasantries with the door staff and security guys. Turns out that all of the team that took care of that side of things were all members of arguably the most renowned and infamous biker gang ever formulated. Use your imagination and you'll know exactly who I'm on about. We ended up in some dressing room and Neil started telling me that this new band would have a good few rungs up the ladder before they'd even started, due to the involvement of his new-found guitar buddy. Since I had last seen Neil he'd actually made an album with this guy and the band he joined. But due to internal differences or whatever, things had come to a head and now they wanted to do their own thing. Neil pretty much sugar-coated what the prospects were before us if we got it together. And with his very optimistic predictions I was pretty much sold on the idea. Neil's guitarist mate's name was ROGER, and Neil said I should meet him and see what he had to say. It was Roger who was well in with the people at Rock City and it seems that they all knew him on first-name terms, and him them. I said, 'Yes, why not?' and so a meeting was set up and then we went back into the club and cracked on with our evening. At the back of my mind I had this nagging feeling in my head I was already in a shit-hot band back in Grantham, but for me things weren't happening quick enough. I'm still quite highly strung now, but back then at 21 I was a livewire always looking for action. I had a low boredom threshold and I think that's why I loved getting stoned, drunk or out of it on whatever I could get my hands on, just to relieve any feelings of normality or tedium. Music was another avenue out of that headspace and, as much as I loved playing with the COSMIC SPACE TOADS, with what my mate Neil was telling me I was already finding excuses and justifying why I should pack it in and get involved with something else that seemed have a lot more to offer. With the TOADS at that time, yes we had built up a reputation as a great band in our area, but out of town we were hardly known at all. We had no offers coming in as of yet and I didn't want to just peter out and dissolve into nothing, whereby I'd be back at square one and having to start something all over again. As I write this now, it makes me realise when looking back at how impatient I was back then. I think the phrase 'instant gratification' is the right terminology for what I was always seeking. I want it all and I wanted it now. I was being rather hasty here because it was still relatively early days with the TOADS and a career in music doesn't happen overnight.

Back then I didn't see it like that. I was young, naïve and wide-eyed. When the prospect of something I felt was better came along I pretty much made up my mind what I was going to do. With that in mind I had to tell Wakey and the others that I was leaving. My memory is a bit sketchy here as I can't actually remember telling Wakey of my intentions, although I have a recollection of being somewhere and telling the others that I was going to hook up with Neil and do something new with him in Nottingham. I imagine now that they weren't happy about the situation, but there was no major drama as I can remember. When Wakey found out, it was different. I was sat in the public waiting place in the supermarket and I saw Wakey's wife and said, 'Hello', and she carried on out. A few minutes later Wakey came in, saw me, and came over and went into a tirade about me leaving his band, etc. I didn't really get a chance to say anything back, and that was when he bent down to my ear and said something very strange. He said, 'Just remember who your master is,' and with that backhanded me in the face. And off he went. Ouch, that fucker hurt. With that I'd now just left the COSMIC SPACE TOADS officially and I wouldn't see Wakey again for about a year after that. The TOADS never stayed together, which looking back was a bit strange. Although I didn't expect them to regroup, which was selfish of me to think that they couldn't have found another drummer and carried on, but no, nothing more was heard of them, and one of the last times I saw Wakey back then was when he came to score some blow off me and he informed me that he and his wife were leaving town and that they were going to become new age travellers. He made up with me and as a final gesture and as a parting gift he gave me his prized and fucked up GOD SAVE THE QUEEN T-shirt. One of the last things he said to me was that I was wrong to quit the TOADS and that I should have stuck it out. Looking back he was probably right. With that, within a day or two he'd left town and did exactly what he said he was going to do. It wouldn't be the last time I'd see Wakey, and it wouldn't be the last time I'd hear from him either. As for all the other TOADS, well they just got on with their lives, and thankfully there was no long-term animosity from them towards me. I was excited because now I would be doing something new that would open up a whole new world for me. The next two years would be a wild time for me and I absolutely loved every minute of it. Unfortunately, it would get me into a whole load of trouble, too.

12. LETS GO TO ROCK CITY, FAITH NO MORE ARE PLAYING

I'd been flouncing about staying on mates' couches and basically being a fucking burden on certain people who had extended me enough charity, when a good bit of fortune came my way. Through my bandmate Troy I'd gotten to know this thrash metal dude called PETER, through working at the same steel factory as him. Well, Peter had his own house and car, which wasn't bad for a 22-year-old at that time. He had a sense of fun about him and, not having anywhere permanent to live, he said if I got the rent sorted through the DHSS then I could go and have a room at his place and share the use of the house. This was great news for me as I at last had a new permanent address. This coincided nicely with me getting involved with the boys from Nottingham. Peter would go to work early in the morning and I would leave later on in the morning and catch a train to Nottingham. Neil was now living with Roger, and they were living in the top two rooms of Roger's parents' house. Well, after an initial briefing between the three of us, it was decided that we'd practise as often as we could, and with regard to music we'd be going down the thrash metal route. Roger was your typical hair rock guitar player, with a style that was reminiscent of GUNS N' ROSES meets METALLICA kind of type-thing, and he was very good at it. Neil was just as good, but with a bit more of an alternative feel to his playing, but still heavy rock influenced. And myself, well I was a mixture of punk and rock. I could play fast D-beats or I could play more ploddy-type beats if required. By this time I'd had my long hair put into dreadlocks, partly due to my love for the BAD BRAINS. And with the other two, with their own sense of style, we were an interesting trio. They'd pick me up from the station and then we'd head off to Roger's place. We were really lucky as we had a soundproof room in his cellar and it was really good as Roger's parents were totally supportive to Roger and what we were doing. My kit had been moved in and we immediately set about getting some music together. Well, these boys had already got some pretty nifty riffs together and it was easy for me to slip straight in and start providing the beat that gave their tunes some substance. We managed to get the basics together for a few tracks and then the subject of a player came up. Well, I suggested getting hold of FELIX, the original bassist who had played for the COSMIC SPACE TOADS. He reared his head again when the TOADS MARK 2 had reformed after my stint in Africa.

Well, his place had been taken but he still hung about and we kept in touch, and so with this new project up and running I gave him a call and without hesitation he came on board. We really did have some musical muscle behind us now. Aside from Felix, who was four or five years older than us, we were in our early twenties, but we all knew how to play. Now all four of us got together and things really started to shape up. And it wouldn't be long until the final addition of a decent vocalist would need to be taken care of. It turned out this would prove to be more difficult than anticipated. Now that I was spending more and more time in Nottingham practising with the new band, and using the band as a focal point, I was now starting to frequent Rock City at weekends too, meeting up with Roger and Neil Friday night, which was rock night, and Saturdays for the alternative night. Good music was one of the attractions that drew us to the place, and yes the place always played a great selection of music depending somewhat on which night you went. Rock nights were OK, they catered for your very commercial and, dare I say, more clichéd form of rock. If you remember the late 80s it was all MOTLEY CREW, POISON, GUNS N' ROSES and the kind of stuff that catered for big hair and the glam side of things. And I have to say that some of the females who frequented there on Fridays were gorgeous. Saturday's in-crowd were markedly different. For one, there was more of a difference with regards the music that was on offer. You'd get a mixture of styles from new romantic, indie, goth and punk. And Saturdays were my preferred nights. One, for the music and two, for the females. I always stood a better chance of pulling on a Saturday because the rock chicks on Fridays were looking for the latest SEBASTIAN BACH look-alike, or some twat who looked like he played for DOGS D'AMOUR. Well, me being the way I looked I didn't stand a chance in that atmosphere. That's not to say I didn't get involved on the odd occasion or two, but I always felt a little more comfortable when there was a bit more of a mixture of people who didn't pose as much as the Friday night fraternity. Rock City happened to be, and still is, one of the best mid-sized venues in the country. Over the years I've seen some great bands there. Since I'd joined Neil and co. my social life improved tremendously, and as I became a little more known by the door staff there, this being because of my new association with Roger etc., I didn't have to pay to get in and it became my new regular hang-out. It also has to be said that at this time, and with even more increased regularity, I was smoking dope every day. After arriving back from South Africa I just pretty much picked up where I'd left off. I loved playing whilst stoned and I loved socialising stoned. Back then you could still smoke in pubs and clubs, and it's mad to think that I used to skin up in these places and, unless you were too open about it, nobody gave a shit. More often than not I'd usually take some speed when out on these weekenders, and usually we'd carry on partying somewhere for a good few hours after we'd left the club. All in all I was having a good time. The music side was coming together nicely, and my playing was still improving, what with the amount of practising. And I had a great social life. Now the Rock City connection, and the fact that I was becoming a regular face in and out of the place, was through the connection with Roger and then Neil. But it was Roger who was really in with the biker gang that I've mentioned. Well this crew, as well as being the main source of security for the club, were partly the organisation behind a massive biker festival known as the BULLDOG BASH.

Their annual get-together was coming up at Stratford-upon-Avon and Roger, myself and Neil were offered the chance of working there. It was a three-day event and there would be thousands of bikers turning up on their bikes. Our job was to act as marshals, signalling them where to go as they entered the festival. It was easy money and we'd be able to enjoy the festival when we weren't working. We were all up for it, and the intention was that we all camp down together and just enjoy ourselves. On arrival at the festival site we were issued with marshal bibs and instructed where we'd each be working. With that the gates were opened and, slowly but surely, people started to arrive on their bikes and all I had to do was stay at my post and direct them towards the relevant campsite. It was unbelievable how many bikes that must have arrived over the three days. It was constant throughout. And then from where I was working

I could also hear the rumble of the music that was emanating from the area the large stage was situated. The work was a bit tedious, stood there for hours herding the two-wheeled traffic to their designated spot, and I hadn't been doing my first shift for long when, probably because I looked like a man who was in the know, someone came up to me and asked rather sheepishly, 'Hello mate, do you know where I can score some hash?' Well, I'd seen this rather burly and tall fella milling about. He looked like a typical biker-stroke-grebo type who I'd say was in his late thirties to early forties. For the benefit of myself, and to protect certain people's anonymity, I'm going to call this fella BIG GEORGE. Anyway, I went up to Big George and told him that this geezer was looking for some dope. Well, he told me he was carrying and how much did the geezer want? Back in those days, blow usually came in sixteenths, eighths, quarter ounces, half ounces and ounces.

Well, this old boy wanted, say, an eighth or a quarter ounce. I went back and told him that I could get it for him, and what the price was. With that he handed over the relevant cash and I told him to wait there. I went back to Big George and, bosh! the deal was done. For my part I took a little bit of the hash for myself and the geezer fucked off. Happy with that done, Big George said to me, 'Anybody wants anything else come and see me and I'll sort you out, OK?' Well, that was fine by me, because not long after this I started getting a steady flow of people coming up to me and asking for speed, and acid as well as hash. Big George was carrying all three and so, with the regular toing and froing, back and forth, through sorting people with their medicine for the weekend, as well as getting all of my drugs for free, I had struck up a weird attachment to this dealer that lasted for the whole weekend we were there. It just so happened that he was from Nottingham, and he also frequented Rock City. Our working weekend turned into a great weekend all round, and that was partly due to this happening. It made it a little more exciting doing a bit of wheeling and dealing, and because I got my drugs for free, I had a blast, and was out of my skull for the duration. And due to the acid I took I actually really enjoyed some of the live bands. I remember a band called the HAMSTERS who played stoner rock covers like STEPPENWOLF and HENDRIX, etc., and with the shit that was in my bloodstream, the sound was spectacular. So for me the weekend working out there was a success, and to top it off, it wouldn't be my last dealings with Big George. I can't specifically remember how the topic was raised, but more than likely I had said to him that I could get rid of gear for him in my home town of Grantham.

I'm figuring that that is what happened as he, I'm sure, would have had most avenues covered in his own area. I informed him that there was a gap that could be filled in town, and that I could get rid of quantities of hash and speed (amphetamines). Well, through his contacts he could get the amounts and so with that we came up with a strategy that entailed me meeting him at Rock City, usually on a Friday night. We would spot each other and we would then proceed to a spot underneath the club out of the way of prying eyes. He would hand over an amount of hash, usually a matter of ounces, an amount of amphetamine sulphate, usually an ounce or two. These were given to me on credit, and then I would get rid during the week. We would do exactly the same thing the next week, after I'd paid him for what I'd had the week before. I was of an age where the consequences of my actions played second fiddle to my reckless and impulsive behaviour. A large part of it was down to the fact that as well as earning money out of this new little venture, it would also give me a steady supply of my own two favourite drugs of choice. And so after just turning 22 I had the band going on, I had a great although hectic social life that had brought me into contact with a lot of females, and to top it all off I was out financing my lifestyle through the dispensing and sale of Class B drugs in my hometown. Peter, the guy I was living with in Grantham, didn't seem to mind the fact that there would be knocks at his door at all times of the day. He was out all day anyway, and at first most of the punters were part of the crowd we knew anyway. I would be out until four or five, as I would be over in Nottingham rehearsing with the band and would always have a flurry of activity from about then until 8 or 9 at night.

I had a room upstairs when I first lived at this place, and as soon as I moved in it became a party house, and I have to say that Peter was most accommodating. As things progressed, though, and when I started dealing, I moved down into the front room, and that gave me the opportunity to be nearest the front door to deal with customers and the like. People would want hashish all through the week but speed was a weekend thing, and come Friday afternoon onwards that's when that stuff would literally fly out the door. It all seemed rather hectic looking back, but I have to say that I revelled in it all. What with being that young I was living in the moment, although underneath all of this nefarious activity my goal was to make good with my musical endeavours and hopefully make what would be classed as a career out of it. And so at that point the band took precedence. We needed to call ourselves something because through the Rock City connection and the people that my new band mates were involved with, a buzz had started due to the fact that these boys had got something new together. We decided to call ourselves SONIC ASYLUM. We'd been holed up for a few months now, getting our shit together. The addition of a vocalist was now paramount and, with that, Roger happened by chance on some bloke completely randomly who was from up north somewhere. I can't even remember the bloke's name, but he definitely stood out, he'd been playing in a band called BASTARD, and we found him through this bird that Roger knew. What happened was that Roger's folks were away for a long weekend and it just so happened that that's when we started rehearsing with matey from BASTARD. He was about the same age as us but remembering back, and just being around him, I could tell that he'd had more experience in life than us, and from what I could gather, a lot of it was not necessarily good. With us having Roger's place to ourselves the whole weekend turned into a drug-fuelled 48 hours. That didn't necessarily interfere with what we needed to do, but that was because we were all cranked up on loads of speed. So we headed down to the cellar and started work on the songs. He immediately showed some promise. He knew what he was doing and he displayed a mixture of styles with the way he looked up and the way he sang. Goth meets punk meets metal, is how I would have described him. Like I say, he came recommended from this goth lady who was another of Roger's acquaintances. I can remember her being at least 10 years older than us, and like us she had a liking for amphetamines. We'd been offered a gig at an all-dayer that was to take place at Rock City, so it was with this in mind that we knew we needed to really crack on and make sure that we were ready. Things seemed to be coming together nicely and the line-up of the new SONIC

ASYLUM seemed like it had been completed. Now this goth bird had seemed OK, but I did notice that after a while of getting to know her that she was prone to periods of instability. She came across as a very confident personality and our new vocalist seemed to be just the same. They'd obviously known each other for some time, and I started find it a bit overbearing. She was, in a roundabout way, probably seeing herself playing a management role with regards to the band. I didn't mind as she did seem to have some clout with the people she knew. She was also doing a little bit of dealing on the side, and on this mad weekend we all had at Roger's, I took her to bed and shagged her. It was on that weekend that I also saw the darker side of our new vocalist's nature. Most people who took speed back then and who were of a similar age to us would snort it or bomb it, but this boy injected it. I'd not witnessed anything like this before and I did find it a little unnerving. But I just thought, 'If that's your thing, then crack on.' It certainly wasn't for me. He was a talented guy actually, as I can remember just me and him being down in the practice room and he turned on the bass rig, strapped on the guitar and started playing, shirt off and speeding like fuck. He was a great bass player, sounding not too dissimilar to CLIFF BURTON or LEMMY even, and he had a good personality with a certain charisma. Underneath the confidence and bravado, though, I could sense a feeling of tragedy in him. It was a big deal for us to be doing our first gig at Rock City, and by the time the gig came I wouldn't say that we were completely ready, but we went for it anyway. I remember the gig now and it turned out to be a bit of an anti-climax. We played only about seven or eight songs as we were on with loads of other bands. The headlining band were called LAWNMOWER DEATH, who were like local heroes in Nottingham. Well, it was our first gig and we were a bit ropey, and we were all very nervous too, but we'd done the gig and we hadn't completely bombed. It certainly didn't put us off as we all knew that we had to start somewhere. So it was back to work with the intention of honing our songs. We hit a stumbling block at this point, though, because our vocalist just cleared off back to where he lived up north and we never saw him again. To us it just hit home that for all that he had to offer as a musician the guy was quite troubled and couldn't commit to what was really required of him. I knew that I was a bit of a loose cannon, but I still had my shit together to the point that I could still function in the world. So it was no major loss, and so we just decided to find a singer who was a bit more stable.

And so for the next few months we carried on with our usual routine of me going over to Nottingham and rehearsing with a view to finding a new vocalist. By now I'd been dealing for a good few months and business was good, and I noticed an upsurge in customers. I never ripped anybody off, and to a select few I would give credit, which was another headache altogether. Most of the time people paid me back when they said they would, as they would want to score some more. You always had the arseholes that would come and have some credit then I wouldn't see them for God knows how long. I only sold in small amounts so as to maximise my profits. So it would be sixteenths, eighths or at the most quarter ounces I would sell. Any larger amounts than that and then you are expected to sell them for a little less. There was one little problem in that I was smoking a hell of a lot as well, and for as much as I saw it that I was getting my dope for free, I was actually smoking my profits. This was also the case with the speed I was dealing. I only sold £10 wraps individually, and I could turn an ounce bag of speed that cost me £120 into 28 £10 wraps. As time went by and as I got busier and busier my profits were obviously increasing, but at the same time my own usage started to increase. A typical case of one getting high on one's own supply. To be honest, it was just like one long party. I did notice one thing back then, though. There were different kinds of personality for the drugs that I dealt. Cannabis users were stoners, laid-back and usually quite amiable. With speed users it was completely different. Shifty, paranoid, unnerving, on edge and unpredictable is how I would describe the odd few that I had dealings with. On a good few occasions I had to deal with a few people I wouldn't have entertained at all had it not been for the fact that they were paying customers. So yeah, things were gathering pace in that department. My regular jaunts to see Big George continued and as each month passed onto the next I was handing him over a fair-sized wedge, to which he would hand over another consignment of blow and speed. I got to the point where I was selling a quarter of a kilo of hash a week along with two ounces of speed. I can remember after one weekend I counted up over £800 in takings. That was a lot of dough back then. But as I've said, I was also using a lot myself and my speed intake jumped too. I was never straight and I was living life very fast indeed. I had plenty of girlfriends but, because of my usage of the drugs, I started to get a little bit sloppy and let things slip. I should have been stashing money away because the longer I was doing this for, the more chance there was that I was going to get caught and end up in some right bother. One night I very nearly did get caught. I was getting regular lifts to and from Nottingham now. I hadn't passed my driving test but I always knew a geezer with a motor who was willing to help me for a free bit of blow, or whatever. This particular night it was my landlord, Peter, who was driving us back from Nottingham when we got pulled over by the cops. Well, I'd picked up a hefty amount of gear a few hours earlier and it was laid out at my feet as I was sat in the back of the motor behind Peter. There were four of us in the car and we were shitting bricks as the copper approached our vehicle. As he did so I just told everyone to keep fucking calm as Peter wasn't over the limit and it would more than likely just be a stop check. Peter wound down his window and so did I. The policeman bent down and started to ask Peter the usual questions, along the lines of, 'Where have you come from?' and 'Where are you going?' I recognised the chap and, lo and behold, he recognised me. At my first flat a few years back I'd had a bit of an incident round there and the cops were called. I hadn't done anything wrong at the time and the copper who was now questioning Peter was the same copper that had come round to my gaff back then. As soon as he recognised me we exchanged pleasantries, and with that he told us that we could be on our way. Let's just say that he wouldn't have been quite so amicable had he realised that I had nigh on a thousand quid's worth of Class Bs at my feet. You could say that that was a close shave.

After we set back off on our way we were all amazed at how close we had come to getting rumbled. With that I just got back on with the everyday job of being a drug dealer. I'd been doing this now for over a year, and to be honest it was getting a little bit out of hand. My services were in demand more than I really needed them to be, but because I was in the thick of it all, I really wasn't observing the signs. Anyway, I was still having a ball during this period. I was frequenting Rock City, and not just for the business side of things. What with it being a fantastic venue I went to see a lot of bands there as well. FAITH NO MORE in 1989 were fantastic and the most memorable. It was during this time that myself and the crowd that I was associating with in town all descended down to Reading for the annual rock festival. This was a real eye-opener and I absolutely loved it. I got to see THE CRAMPS, FAITH NO MORE, MUDHONEY, THE BUZZCOCKS, JESUS JONES and LIVING COLOUR. I loved the experience and the festival vibe. One massive party and thousands of us all in one place. I dropped some acid at Reading, and after experiencing the drug a couple of times in the past, I found that it was in a festival setting that I enjoyed that drug the most. I was also still connected with a good few of the punks from Derby. And so what with me being in possession of plenty of dope and speed I soon sold out of everything whilst down there. Back on home ground and the band was progressing. We tried out another vocalist who was a long-haired blonde chap but, as it turned out, he wasn't really right for the group. He was a good vocalist, but a bit too namby-pamby for us. We were a thrash band and needed somebody who could step up to the mark and deliver a vocal as powerful as the music we were playing. I was working on my playing by this time and that was partly due to playing with three others who could really play. I had a couple of serious incidents also occur around this time, too. There had been a bit of a drought on the dope front and I'd not been able to secure my usual batch from Big George. So Felix, my SONIC ASYLUM band mate, used to borrow his Dad's flash motor and drive me about to do my dealings and whatever else needed doing. Not having any dope to smoke we thought we'd go over to Nottingham to the Hyson Green area and go and see if we could score some to tide us over until I scored from my usual source. The area was well known and frequented by Rastas and the like. You'd be able to spot them on the street and, with the right body language, a deal could be secured. Well we didn't want a lot, so we drove around for a brief period and it wasn't long before we spotted a potential seller. We drove by him and then passed by once again and he got the message that we were seeking some stuff. Obviously a bit of discretion is required, and scoring in full view on a main road is not the done thing. Anyway, after being as discreet as we felt we needed to be, the guy gesticulated for us to go down the next road, which was slightly more out of the way. With it also being dark we didn't think there would be a problem. We stopped and he came over to us, we told him what we wanted, and sure enough he produced the goods. I handed the money over and we left pronto, happy that we'd got ourselves a little bit of personal to tide us over. We'd not long set off on our journey back to Grantham when all of a sudden the rozzers pulled us over. It all happened very quickly, and after stopping us and coming over to the car they informed us that they wanted to search the car. We were busted. The three lumps of hash that we'd scored were hidden underneath my car seat and the cops found two of them. With that we were informed that we would be arrested and charged with possession. We had to go to Radford Road police station where we were charged and told to appear at Nottingham magistrates at such and such a date. As it happened Felix, my driver friend and bandmate, got away with just a caution, whereas old muggins here got a fine of £120 for possession. This was due to the fact that I was a repeat offender. That aside, I can remember us being let out of the police station and we couldn't wait to get in the car and make our way back to town. On the way I was happy to find that beautiful bit of dope that the coppers had missed, and we proceeded to get royally stoned.

The second incident took on for me an even more serious undertone. Ever since I'd been physically able I'd been a fucker for chasing girls in pursuit of sex and everything else that goes with it. I always had my eye on young women. It wasn't like I saw myself as being better looking than anybody else or anything like that, but I was quite fortunate in being quite successful when it came to pulling the odd bird or two. If the truth be known I was a slag, and now my dastardly behaviour was about to bite me right on the nose. Through my dealing activities I was coming into contact with a lot of different people. I'd also come to the attention of some of the recreational drug-taking fraternity from the nearby town of Sleaford, and they would come across and buy whatever they needed off me. Most of these people were a year or two older than me and it seemed that there was a shortage of speed over in their neck of the woods. Well, I didn't mind them coming to me as I was of the opinion that the more the merrier. Well, I'd started having sexual liaisons with a Grantham lass called Debbie who I'd known before I started dealing in the town. What with her being a bit partial to a bit of speed, our paths had crossed once again, and one thing led to another. Now I knew that she had been having a relationship with this lunatic in Sleaford, but I'd been assured that they had finished and that they were both going their separate ways. Well, he didn't quite see it like that when he heard that we were fucking each other. I knew him well enough as he was one of the Sleaford mob that would come and buy a few wraps of whizz every now and then. Well, this lunatic was also pals with another speed freak from Grantham, a chap I knew quite well. These two had bonded through the use of amphetamines. I just need to reiterate what I've said before about speed users being completely different than pot smokers. The Sleaford geezer wasn't a happy bunny and so himself and his mate thought they'd come and show me their displeasure and teach me a lesson. There was a knock at the door and so, thinking it was another sale in order, I opened the door. And there he was, and he immediately set about telling me what a cunt I was and that he was going to kick the fuck out of me. I can't remember responding verbally, but I do recall backing off as he came inside the house in his threatening manner. That was bad enough as I contemplated him setting about me, but then the unbelievable happened, because right behind him was his mate brandishing what looked like a shotgun. Well, this really shit me up big time, and as I kept backing up, matey with the shotgun started saying shit like, 'Don't fuck with us, Stoo.' Well, I had no intention of fucking with them, but I do remember calling out, 'Don't shoot me, man.' I didn't know whether I was going to get beat up or shot at, but let's just say that I was really scared. Who wouldn't be? The thing is that Peter the landlord was there and another friend of ours, who had both witnessed what was happening. Strangely though, as soon as the lad who came in to do me harm for shagging his girl saw my distressed reaction at the appearance of the gun, he just backed right off. And in a shot (excuse the pun), they both skedaddled off. We couldn't believe what had just happened and we were all just gathering our breath when there was a knock on the door once more. Only this time I didn't open it straight away. I wanted to know who it was, and unbelievably it was the twat who'd been brandishing the gun. Only on this occasion he was apologising for what he'd done. Now as I've explained, I knew this geezer a lot better than his thug mate and was trying to get to the bottom of why he was doing this kind of shit. I then said something stupid along the lines of that I knew people in Nottingham who would happily come and sort him out, etc. Well that was it, he started ranting and raving about starting a war, or something ridiculous like that. This was obviously a clear case of speed psychosis in action. Things calmed down and thankfully he fucked off and I never saw him again for a matter of years. With what had just happened and my mate and landlord bearing witness to it all, understandably on his part, he stated that things were getting far too heavy for his liking and that it would be a good idea if I moved out. I didn't argue in any way as I knew that he was right. I understood completely, and so with that myself and another of my friends found a small house to rent and I went on from there. It was the end of an amazing time for me, living in that place. I'll never forget the laughter, the different people and also the not so colourful episodes that took place there. I still remained friends with Peter, but it was time to move on. And so, after acquiring this new gaff with my mate GINGE, I carried on making money, but at the same time trying to keep a somewhat lower profile than I had been doing.

After moving into the new place that was very close to the train station, I was now once again using that mode of transport to get myself to and from Nottingham. The lifestyle I was leading wasn't impeding the pace at which I was working with regards making progress with the band, as we'd now found a good possible replacement vocalist and we'd been rehearsing with him on a regular basis. At the end of the day all of us in the band were living our lives as we were so that overtures within the band could be met. Again we were at a point where some studio time was required so that we had something to show for ourselves. A product of some sort would also go some way to having something to pass on to prospective venues, management companies and even record labels so as to take us to the next level. So a studio was secured in Redditch and we booked ourselves in for two whole days. As I remember it, we worked all through the night, and as was often the case when doing something like this, the process was aided by quite extensive use of amphetamine sulphate. We got three tracks down and we were all pleased with the results. And so we now had something to provide a reference point for people who hadn't heard the band before. Having that as a document would definitely help us, and so naturally we were looking forward to the next phase of the band's development. It was business as usual back in Grantham. Another weekend was approaching, and I needed to make the customary trek over to Nottingham to pay off Big George and obtain more gear. Earlier in the week I had been approached by an acquaintance who had a friend who wanted to purchase a quarter kilo of hash and he had the money to buy it up front. Now this wasn't just a little bit of personal. It was a huge block that looked like a slab. Not something you want to be getting caught with. I had been scoring quite large amounts like this for myself to sell on after it had been cut down into the smaller weights that enabled me to keep my profits up. I was falling into a bit of debt with my dealer and so I thought I could diminish that debt a little by purchasing a large amount for a set price from my dealer and thus charge my customer a certain amount extra on top. This would then go some way to alleviating my financial situation. A price was set and the customer handed me over the cash, which amounted to around £800. I already had my own money which would provide for my own gear, so that night, which was a Friday, I travelled to Nottingham with the intention of scoring about six to seven ounces of hash, two ounces of speed and a few acid tabs for myself and a couple of friends. I headed over to Rock City with a considerable amount of cash on me, and after being in the club for however long, myself and Big George made the usual exchange. I can remember him being in a particularly grumpy mood with me, as he often would be, and it was often due to the fact that I wasn't producing enough money, or whatever. I kept my cards close to my chest and broached that I needed a quarter kilo amount and that I could produce the cash immediately if it could be got at short notice. He came up with a price that didn't work in my favour so I just brushed it off and informed him that I'd probably get back to him shortly. With that I just kept the money on my person and left him. I now had the six ounces of hash, two ounces of whizz and the acid tabs, plus the £800 on me.

13. MEADOWS, THIS IS YOUR NUMBER JH1660. DON'T FORGET IT

That night I ended up staying in Nottingham at Neil's new place just outside of Nottingham near West Bridgeford. I'd recently changed my routine with regards to getting to and from Nottingham as my usual lift wasn't always available, so now I was using the train more often to get to Nottingham and back. On the Saturday morning as I planned to take the train back to Grantham, I decided to leave the two ounces of speed at Neil's, hidden in an old piano just for safekeeping, and then I planned to come back later that day and get it after I'd done some business in Grantham. I was practising caution here as I knew that I had a lift secured for when I left Rock City later that Saturday night. Well, I never made it back to Nottingham that night because, unbeknownst to me, the drug squad and the police were waiting for me in Grantham. I caught my train at Nottingham train station in the late morning. I was feeling a bit rough due to the late night before and was looking forward to getting back home, which was only a small walk from Grantham station. I arrived back in Grantham with the hash, the acid tabs and this geezer's 800 quid on me. The money I was going to give back as I'd not been able to get the gear for the right price, and that would be the end of it. I got off the train and walked towards the station exit. As I walked through the reception area I got jumped by about four or five blokes who grabbed my arms and informed me I was under arrest for suspicion of being in possession of narcotics. There was no escape. I was asked if I had drugs on me, to which I replied that I did. I was then bundled into a car and taken to the local police station. After being booked in I was informed that I was to be strip-searched to ascertain what I had on me. A big white sheet was laid out on the floor and I had to stand on it and remove my clothes, and as this was done they would find what was on me. Well, it didn't take them long to find the hash or the money but I had concealed the wrapped acid tabs up my arse. Acid is a class A drug and I didn't want to get caught with it, but these fuckers weren't having any of it, and after a little more probing, so to speak, it fell out and they could now charge me for that as well. So that was that.

I was to be detained at the police station for further questioning that would take place over the next day or two. I was now in serious trouble as it had only been a couple of weeks or so earlier that the drug squad had raided my mate Peter's house where I'd been dealing from for nigh on a year or so. They weren't best pleased when realising that I'd moved out just a few days before they raided the place. Now that they had me it looked like some serious charges were going to be put before me. My sex, drugs and rock'n'roll lifestyle had just been brought to a sudden halt, and the seriousness of the position I found myself in started to sink in. I was placed in a cell and this is where I would be staying for the next 72 hours. Later that night after getting initially busted the first of a number of lengthy interviews began. It was obvious to me now that I'd been on their radar for some time. They'd collected enough evidence to prove that I had been supplying class B drugs for some time and the fact that I'd been caught with an amount of hash plus the significant quantity of cash seemed to point to just that. Well for one, the cash wasn't mine, but they weren't going to believe me. The fact that I hadn't got any amphetamine on my person must have come as a disappointment to them because they informed me that they had evidence that I'd been supplying that too. I obviously kept schtum about the two ounces that were stashed away in Nottingham. I was questioned at length about my source of supply but there was no way they were going to get that out of me. It would be more than my life was worth further down the line if I told them that my contacts were one of the world-renowned biker gangs and it got back to them. It wasn't like I was going to be banged up forever, and besides, why the fuck would I tell them that anyway? I tried to be shifty with them but these people had done their homework, and it seemed that there was no way out of this one. They also asked me about my use of drugs and that's when I can recall for the first time saying out loud that I had a problem. I sounded really rough to them as my voice was very gruff, and this was partly due to the amounts of hash and speed I'd been taking. A couple more visits to the interview room and it was then that they came up with the charges of intent to supply cannabis and amphetamines. The acid was just the lesser charge of possession. The cash was classed as proceeds of crime and I would never see that again. Next, I would be attending court in Grantham where the charges would be read out with the probability of being remanded in custody to Lincoln prison looking very likely. Oh, fuck.

After attending Grantham court I was immediately remanded in custody. This was serious, and to be honest, I was scared. By now all of my family and everybody I'd had dealings with were finding out that I'd been busted. The fact that I owed people money i.e. my dealer and the punter who had fronted me £800 was of no consequence to me at this point because, let's be honest, there was nothing I could do about it now that I was on my way to the clink. There was also nothing I could do about the fact that I was owed money too from various sources. I was completely on my own and, as I say, it really was quite scary and at the same time daunting. This was going to be a whole new experience and it sure wasn't going to be a pleasant one. I was taken to Lincoln in a police van and from now and for the next few weeks, my life was to take on a whole new meaning. It was as if I were a deer facing oncoming headlights. On arriving at the prison gates my heart sank and I thought to myself, 'Here we go.' I was herded into a reception area where I had to wait until being called. I can just remember having to stand in front of these screws who were sat at a long desk, and them asking me questions about my clothes sizes. I had to take off all my clothes in front of these uniformed strangers and it sank in about the situation I was in. There was no telling this lot to fuck off and, like I say, I was scared shitless. I was a criminal and I was being treated like one. I'm stood there bollock naked and they hand me my prison clothing. Brown trousers, a blue T-shirt, a blue and white striped shirt and a pair of slightly ill-fitting shoes. There was a very long, narrow corridor with cubicles that fit one individual in. I was escorted to one of these and told to get dressed and wait. They closed the cubicle door behind me and there I waited for what seemed like ages. Eventually a screw came to collect me to take me onto one of the prison wings. New sounds were entering my ears. Lincoln nick really was a prison like you'd imagine one to be. The 70s programme *Porridge* springs to mind, and back in 1990 that's very similar to how it actually was. The clanking of keys, a very echoey place with long wings that had three to four landings. By the time I'd been taken through what seemed like a labyrinth of different sections I'd arrived at my cell. This was about eight or nine at night and so everyone was banged up and the wing looked huge and daunting. It was quite dark and I ended up in a cell on the third landing. The cell door was opened and in I went. I was sharing a cell with another con whose name I can't recall. The cell door was closed behind me and locked. I made my introductions to my cell mate and sat myself down on my new bed. This cell would be my new home for the next five months, and to the screws my name meant nothing. I was now a number and I certainly wasn't a free man. That number I've never forgotten even to this day. I was now prisoner JH1660. The next morning I got up and a huge dark cloud was hanging over me. All of the cons coming out of their cells were slopping out. There wasn't a toilet in the cell, there was a bucket, and from whatever hour it was that one got banged up in the evening until the morning, the bucket was to cater for one's natural bodily functions until slop out at about 7.45am. If one needed a number two during those lock up hours, we always had a supply of newspaper at hand and so the deed was done on the paper, wrapped up and then lobbed out of the cell window and onto the courtyard below. This was known as a shit parcel and some poor soul would be designated to pick these up as part of their cleaning up duties.

It was all very intimidating at first, and not necessarily because of the screws, but because of some of the other cons. I was a 23-year-old white Rasta punk who'd been thrust into this overtly male and very macho-dominated atmosphere. One of the first things I did notice was that the wing population pretty much consisted of half white and half coloured chaps. Being on a remand wing, this meant that all on the wing, having been charged, were waiting for the judicial process to take its course until sentencing. After sentencing, individuals are then moved to start their sentence on another wing with the rest of the prison population. My brown trousers I was given at reception signalled that I was on remand. I would be eventually sentenced and from then on and until my sentence was spent, I'd be wearing the traditional blue trousers. Those first few days were horrible. But my cell mate, who wasn't new to this game, filled me in on how things worked. I didn't say boo to a goose and proceeded to keep myself to myself, and thankfully had matey to guide me through the coming weeks. It really did seem like time slowed down as every day seemed to last forever. The legal process with regards to my case kicked in and every two weeks I'd be taken from the wing, placed in a prison van and taken back to court in my hometown, only to be remanded once again and taken back to Lincoln. I wasn't allowed to work whilst on remand and so I was banged up all day except at breakfast, dinner and evening meal times. I was allocated exercise every day, an hour before dinner time. All the cons on remand were allowed out onto a huge courtyard to walk around and get some fresh air. Pretty much as soon as I was shipped to prison I was allowed to start contacting people on the outside on special designated prison handwriting paper and envelopes. I was allowed to be sent a small amount of cash to buy myself a few little essentials, i.e. tobacco, batteries, biscuits, crisps, etc. I'd managed to get a tape Walkman sent in and this was a bit of a welcome relief from the boredom that I experienced whilst on remand. I can particularly remember playing over and over again METALLICA's AND JUSTICE FOR ALL album and THE ACE OF SPADES album by MOTORHEAD. At weekends, which were really hard as I was always imagining what people were getting up to in the outside world, we were allowed out of our cells on what was called 'association'. Saturday afternoons and Sunday afternoons a section of the wing was set up so that we could watch a film laid on by the prison. Also at this time visits from friends and family were permitted, which again went part of the way to relieving the tediousness of the time in there. When I used to be banged up on a Friday night, I'd look out of the prison cell window feeling a little sorry for myself, and one night I remember thinking to myself, 'Don't worry about it Stu, you've got loads of weekends to look forward to once you get out of here.' Those little thoughts just gave me that little bit of hope when I needed it. After a few weeks I had a nice bit of fortune, as some lads I knew from my home town had arrived and one of them, who I knew quite well, ended up being put in my cell. This immediately made life a little bit more bearable. These lads were of a similar age to me, but they were all in for burglaries and TWOCKING (taking without owner's consent), in other words nicking cars. My original cell mate had been moved on and so I was quite chuffed to have somebody familiar in with me. One thing that became a little unnerving, after not being in there for long, was the high number of true Rastas who I noticed started viewing me with looks of suspicion. I was the only white Rasta in the place, and for as much as I'd taken up the smoking of the dreaded herb, I wasn't at all interested in their preaching and worship of HAILE SELASSIE and Rastafari. For me my prized dreadlocks were there because I absolutely loved and was influenced by the amazing all-black American punk band known as the BAD BRAINS. Strange thing was that for half of the Rastas that checked me out they would click their tongues to mock me or show their disapproval. The other half were totally sound with me and would exchange mild pleasantries. From what I could gather, a lot of this clan were mostly in for poncing, which on the streets means pimping or dealing like myself. The most unsettling aspect of this new-found atmosphere that I found myself in was the fact that blokes with all manner of offences were all banged up together. There was no difference between dealers, murderers, burglars, pimps and violent offenders in here. We were all under one roof. The only people who were not welcome in this environment where the nonces (sex offenders). Their presence was not tolerated and let's just say I did witness a couple of incidents that would make your blood run cold if you had seen and heard what I did. There were efforts by a couple of blokes who did try and bully me with intimidation tactics. But I stood my ground and thankfully no violence was needed to prove myself.

Now at this time in 1990, cons were only permitted to have a bath once a week, which was no good to me, so I ended up killing two birds with one stone by immediately signing up to go to the gym. One, to get my physical fitness back, for which I used to take part in circuit training-type activities rather than the weightlifting facilities. That didn't appeal to me at all, and through my gym membership I also got to take a shower every day, thus keeping myself adequately clean. I was also fortunate enough to be getting regular visits off some of my friends, and letters from girlfriends and plenty of other folk, that bolstered my morale whilst I was in there. Now the old adage that there are just as many drugs in prison as there are on the outside is very true, and I would find that out a bit later. Early on, though, I never witnessed much going on, partly due to being banged up for most of the day. However, myself and my cell mate from town had the chance to procure an acid tab which at the time seemed a great idea. Anything to relieve the sameness for a few hours. Well, I swapped this tab for some of my goodies. The goodies being treats that came from my private cash allowance i.e. crisps, Jaffa cakes and dilutable juice. You have to remember back then that everything was up for grabs. Dodgy deals were still going on all the time. The main form of currency was tobacco, followed by cannabis. Anything could be traded and so after securing the acid we got banged up for that night and we took half each. My god, all I can remember was us conspiring to commit all these dodgy things we were going to do once we got out, and laughing our heads off until the early hours. There were a few disgruntled faces in the morning once our cell was opened, and this being due to us keeping a few of the others awake with our fits of laughter. So for the next three months I managed to get through this period of my incarceration without getting into any trouble. I'd overcome any problems that I'd initially had, especially with the Rastas who now didn't have a problem with me. And I'd soon learned to suss the cunts from the decent lads on the wing. As time had gone by my case had been moving forward and I'd had some counsel from a couple of people who would speak on my behalf when it came to my trial. The charges had been classed as being quite serious and I knew that a custodial sentence was inevitable. It was just the length of the sentence that was causing me some anxiety. I'd been on remand for a bit of time and so no matter what the length of my sentence turned out to be, the time already served would come automatically off the end of my eventual time dished out to me. My mother, bless her, supported me throughout and came to visit me as often as she could. We did, however, have one bone of contention, and that was my hair. She insisted that I have it cut but I didn't want to. It wasn't a problem for me but for her, and with the trial coming up, she chipped and chipped away at me, but I still didn't get it cut. The date of the trial was set for just before Christmas 1990, so I had some decent clothes shipped in so at least I looked like I had made the effort. Come the morning of my trial I was taken back down to the reception where I was allowed to change into my normal clothing. I looked well smart and had my dreads tied back. I was taken with a number of others to Lincoln Crown Court, which was a castle- type building. From there I had to wait in a large cell with all the others who were also up before the beak. It was a long old wait but I distinctly remember the guy who went up before me. He'd been gone about an hour, but when he came back down his face was grey. He'd been handed down a ten-year sentence for armed robbery.

A short while later, I was called for and taken from the cell by a screw, who then told me to go up these steps when called. I got called and proceeded up about seven stairs, and as I reached the top this large Victorian, dark and predominately wooden-type courtroom came into view. I was told where to stand and before me, but quite a lot higher up in the vestibules, was the judge in his wig looking down at me with what looked like pure disdain on his face. My mother was there and a gent who had come to speak on my behalf. I can recall only having to answer my full name, the rest was done by the prosecution and by the kind gent representing me. The charges and a description of my activities were read out, and to be perfectly honest they didn't present me in a positive light at all, and the prosecution stated that my flagrant disregard for the law should be dealt with as harshly as possible. Next the guy acting for me proceeded to explain that I'd gotten in with the wrong crowd, or words to that effect, and basically said that I'd showed some remorse for what I'd done, as well as accepting that I knew it was wrong, and made a plea that a bit of leniency be granted. Well, the judge was having none of it and, in short, for the possession and intent to supply charges I was given ten and a half years. The judge then said that the sentences were to run concurrently. I didn't have a clue what that meant but I was informed that I would be serving a total of three years. I was a little stunned, to be honest, and was told to be taken down. With that I went back down those stairs and back to the large cell. I was allowed to go and see my mother very briefly. We spoke to each other through a thick iron gated door and she was visibly upset, as was I. We said goodbye to each other and I was returned back to Lincoln prison later that afternoon. It was dark when I got back into the prison and I can remember looking out of the windows of the prison van as I was returned to jail. All the Christmas lights were on everywhere and here I was going back to jail. Doom and gloom was pouring out of me, and that night I was sent to the long-term wing, out of my civvy clothes and into my new blue trousers and other prison attire to start my three years. Oh shit. Having been moved on to the new wing, for the first two weeks or so I walked around in a bit of a daze. I wasn't expecting to get such a lengthy sentence at all. I got a bit of support from a few of the other cons and just resigned myself to the fact that moping about wasn't going to help at all. Now that I had been sentenced I was allocated a job in what was known as 'the ropes' department. Here I would be taught how to build children's climbing frames made from thick blue rope. My wages were £3.75 a week and I worked in the morning and again in the afternoon. I shared my cell with a few different lads and became quite well acquainted with a Rasta known as STEPPA. He was a pimp and came from Nottingham, and it seems that we had something in common. We'd both been seeing the same girl but at different times before we had been apprehended for our different offences. I was still going down the gym regularly and for my remaining time in Lincoln I just got my head down and counted off the days. Lincoln is a category B nick which, as I've said, caters for almost all offender types, but it's also an allocation nick. Basically the purpose of the place is to remand, sentence and then move prisoners on to other relevant prisons for them to serve their sentences. After just over five months in Lincoln I found out that I would be allocated to STOCKEN PRISON near the town of Oakham, which is a category C nick. I couldn't wait to get out of the place as it was a sure sign that my time was moving on somewhat. A couple of things I do remember about being in there. One, I hadn't seen my father for a number of years and he obtained a special pass to come and see me for a couple of hours. He was visiting the UK from South Africa and so with that in mind he was granted a privileged visitation because of the situation. It was good to see him, although it was a little strange. I was grateful that he had made the effort. And two, come New Year's Eve the whole of the nick is banged up and from about a minute to 12 every cell door started to rattle as we all started banging away to bring the New Year in. It was a good feeling and an experience that I won't ever forget.

I forgot to add also that during this last brief phase at Lincoln I found a kindred spirit in a guy who made my time in there a lot easier. I was working away in the ropes department and this fella asked me what I was listening to on my Walkman. I told him and we immediately hit it off around our love of music. Turns out he had been given a life sentence for manslaughter. That aside, he'd moved round everywhere and was finishing off his time. He'd learnt to play acoustic guitar since being banged up, and he wasn't bad at all. On our association times we'd meet up and he'd play some of his tunes and I'd drum along to them. We also had a similar sense of humour, so when my cell had become vacant with just me in it he got moved into mine and we had a right laugh most of the time. It wasn't long, though, before he got shipped off to Sudbury prison and then I got moved out to Stocken. I landed in Stocken and as much as I was overtly pleased about having to go there, I appreciated the change and I welcomed leaving the hell hole that was Lincoln behind. This place was a far more modern nick than where I had just spent the last five or so months. In all honesty it was like a holiday camp in comparison to Lincoln. I was placed on a brand new wing which had a centre reception area and the wings went off to both sides. I had my own cell on the first floor and I would remain there for the duration of my stay. The place definitely had a lot more of a laid-back atmosphere about it, and it didn't take me long to settle in. I was allowed the usual visitation rights and I would be allocated a job within days of getting there. At the end of the day we were still criminals serving our time, and we still viewed the screws with suspicion as much as they did us, but this really was a lot easier than being in a category B nick. The wings were more personal and so I soon got to know most of the faces there. This was a place for people with life sentences who were finishing off their time, non-violent inmates, although that didn't mean that it didn't kick off every now and then between people who were pretty much of the same temperament. I applied for the job as a wing cleaner, which had its perks, the main one being that I would be out of my cell longer than most of the other cons. I did manage to do the odd bit of wheeling and dealing from cell to cell. I still had a few loyal friends that would come and visit me at weekends, and through them I used to smuggle lumps of hash concealed in my mouth back onto my wing, and this would keep me going at night later on when I was banged up. I did notice while in Stocken that cannabis was quite a major thing. You could always tell after we'd been banged up after work and then let out an hour or so later for association, a lot of lads were walking around with really bloodshot eyes due to having a smoke, especially for association. Also hooch (prison alcohol) was another thing, but this was a risky business as it had to be made whilst also being hidden for the duration while it brewed. If one got caught with drugs or hooch then one could find oneself being taken down the block, as it was called, and put into isolation for however long the governor deemed necessary. Of course the authorities knew that this shit was going on and, to be honest, I think they turned a little bit of a blind eye to it. Although saying that, if cons were getting large amounts in, and by that I mean say an ounce concealed up their arse or other parts of their anatomy, again there could be serious consequences, but it did happen as I witnessed it. I tried my best to keep it very cool as I certainly didn't want extra time adding on to my sentence, and thankfully I never got into trouble in that department.

I very nearly came unstuck due to another incident that took place and that came about because of my work duties. For a brief time I actually worked on the servery dishing out the food to all the cons. Again this was a cushty job as it meant I was out of my cell early and always out more than the others, preparing and doing the stuff that goes on in a kitchen. Last thing at night I used to have to go to one of the main kitchens and collect a massive urn for the wing and a massive vat of milk. Now, I'd got some little scam going whereby I'd smuggle some eggs in the milk to trade with the lads who liked their weightlifting and took it rather more seriously than most. These eggs I'd trade for hash or other stuff and also skim some of the milk for myself, as it was also a precious commodity. Well, I had to go through various security doors to get to the main kitchen and back. Well, screws are everywhere and I'd got from my wing to the main kitchen to collect the tea and milk. I found myself in the presence of this screw, who was okay as it happened, but he decided to check the milk. He plunged a ladle into the milk and scooped up these eggs that had been put there for me to move on. I'd been rumbled and he said, 'Right, what have we got here, then?' Not exactly the crime of the century, but it was against the rules all the same. I thought, 'Here we go, I'm in trouble now,' but no, he smirked and just told me not to take the piss, and he let me take the eggs. His parting comment to me was, 'Stay lucky,' and with that I swiftly went on my way. Working on the servery was OK and I'd like to have kept the job. I was working with a few gay blokes in there and they were always taking the piss, what with their sexual innuendos and stuff, and I just used to take the piss back. Yes, it was a good job that, but eventually I got caught for pilfering food for myself and so I was relieved of my duties and was soon back with my mop and bucket cleaning up the wing. The most surprising part of being in Stocken was the large array of educational facilities that were on offer. Loads of the lads were taking degrees and doing computer courses, none of which interested me at all. What did interest me, though, was the fact that they had a music department and this facility ran when we were on association or free time. I signed up for it just to see what was going on and, lo and behold, there was a shitload of equipment on hand, i.e. guitars, amps, drums and even a PA. Now this stuff wasn't all top notch gear but it was better than nothing. So I got involved and got the kit together and with a couple of the other cons we started to do something. Anyway, we got some music off the ground really quickly. It was all covers but at the time I didn't mind. It was my way of escaping the fact that I was still serving a sentence. It was enjoyable and for the most part prison isn't meant to be enjoyed. What with us getting a little bit of a band going, our progress hadn't gone unnoticed and there was mention of us doing something under the guise of a gig. One for the cons and another playing to invited guests. Who they would have been I don't know, but with this news we were obviously enthused and were making ourselves as ready as we could.

For me though, events and fate were about to intervene, meaning that none of this would transpire, and I shall explain to you why. Right from the outset of me being sentenced I was advised to appeal against what was deemed quite a hefty sentence. This process can take ages and nothing is ever done quickly, so I just sat quietly and got on with my time whilst still monitoring this process as it took place. I had to have a viable excuse for thinking that I'd been over-zealously treated. All appeals against sentences at the time were being dealt with down in London at the Old Bailey. Well, after a lot of waiting and loads of mitigation from people acting on my behalf, I at last received the news that my appeal had come through and I was to travel down to London to see my case come through. There was no guarantee that the appeal would even be successful but in my eyes I had nothing to lose. This would be like another court case. Once again I prepared myself for what lay ahead. I was to be taken down to London the day before my case was heard and so I would be spending the night in Brixton Prison. And so the day before the appeal I was driven down to Brixton whilst all the time being cuffed to a screw, booked into the nick, and all I can remember is having a terrible night's sleep. The next morning I was taken to the Appeal Court and again dressed very smartly with my dreadlocks tied back. I can remember being in some open cell at first, and then being taken up into the building somewhere, and I was told to sit on this wooden armchair. A prison officer sat opposite me at one point told me that RUTH ELLIS, the last woman to be hanged in England, had sat in the exact same chair. Moments later the door opened and my name was called. I walked through the door and was startled to find myself on a balcony alcove. I looked to my left and there were three judges all dressed in their attire, wigs and all. I looked down and to my right a collection of people who could have been anybody off the street were sat in the gallery. In front of them was the duty barrister who would speak for me and a couple of other barristers. It was all a bit surreal. I hardly had to say anything at all, the details of my case were read out and that was the part that took the longest. There was a bit of toing and froing with exchanges from the bigwigs, and before too long I was informed that my sentence had been deemed a tad excessive, and so with that in mind it was to be reduced to two years. I was very pleased, and said, 'Thank you' when asked to leave. This was good news for me, as on a three-year sentence the likelihood of getting parole comes after about fifteen months. On a two-year sentence one is eligible for parole after only eight months. Well, I'd served nearly eleven months, and with that in mind I knew that my release had just been brought forward to within weeks, if not days. I was taken back to Stocken and I wouldn't say that I was buzzing about my successful appeal but I was certainly glad that my sentence was coming to an end. There was a bit of back slapping from my mates back on the wing and even a few of the screws congratulated me on my result. I'd informed my mother of my appeal and this all of a sudden posed the question of where I was going to stay when I was released. My Mum came to visit me twice more before I was released and, after agreeing that I could go back home to stay, she laid down one stipulation, and that was I had to get my hair cut. She pleaded and pleaded with me until she got really emotional about it. With that I agreed to have my beloved dreadlocks shorn. We said we'd see each other on the day of my release. I went back to the wing whereby I had to formally get permission to cut my dreads off. Changing one's appearance in prison is not allowed unless you're given the go-ahead. I got hold of some clippers and shaved my hair down to a couple of millimetres. Afterwards I looked like a suede-head, not bald but definitely short. A few days later at the grand age of 24 I left prison after eleven months. What an experience that was. One I'm glad I did in retrospect, but not an experience I wished to go through again. I'd served my penance and at 8 o 'clock on a sunny morning I was picked up from outside the nick and at last I was a free man. There was no big homecoming celebration and I don't recall any overwhelming feeling of joy at being released. I was out on parole and with that there were certain stipulations. I'd be staying with my parents and I would have to attend the probation office once a week as that was part of the conditions of being on parole. I was very fortunate as it was soon agreed that I'd get involved with the family business. I was well up for this and didn't have a problem with getting on board. Back then my folks were market traders. Stepdad ran a hot dog wagon and Mum sold cards on four different markets five days a week. I'd double up with my Mum and we'd go from there. Although I didn't show it to them at the time, I was eager to meet up with a few of my close pals, have a shindig and more than anything else have sex with the first willing female who was up for a bit of heavy petting. Eleven months without some sort of intimacy with a female is a bloody long time, and so it was only natural that that avenue of pleasure be satisfied. No sooner was it the weekend and we all had a get-together, got pretty smashed and fortunately for me I got my rocks off with some pleasant little chubby lass.

14. SOME CHARMING QUALITIES, BUT THERE'S A FLIPSIDE

It is at this point that I feel that I need to change tack slightly. The reason I'm adding this is because It's for the benefit of the ongoing story, and not wishing to keep repeating myself over and over again. At the same time it is important for me to explain what happened as it happened. In short, a pattern was starting to emerge with regards my character which was ultimately impeding a lot of the progress I was hoping to make in my life. Let me explain. After doing time in prison and with hindsight now in plain view, being a 23-year-old that had just been banged up, I would like to have thought that whilst and during my incarceration I could have had the opportunity to attend some sort of help group or educational course with regards to drug abuse and where my involvement with drugs had landed me. Probably more so after I'd been released and on parole and involved with the probation services. Being really honest about it, if the help, or some sort of compulsory group that I had to attend, had been put in place, it is questionable whether it would have made any difference to me at all, for although I'd been an active criminal leading up to my time in jail, that now wasn't the case as I had no desire to return to that nefarious way of life. In short, what I'm saying is that I was dealt with by the courts and while this was happening it had become quite obvious that I had developed a drug problem that ultimately led me into criminal activity. Well, now that crime element had been discarded I was still stuck with the problem over my use of substances. I didn't know any better at that time and I was still young enough to think that I could use recreationally as most people did; it was only years later on down the line that it was quite apparent that I couldn't. At 25-years old I was the last person to think I may have had a long-term problem. With a new start in life in front of me I got on with my life one day at a time. I now had the opportunity to go straight, as they say, and earn my money the normal way. Add to that also the burning desire to reacquaint myself back into activities that were of the musical persuasion. From the age of 25 to 26 things were very steady for me. I was working four to five days a week on the market and my time on probation went rather well. It was no major hardship to attend and keep up with appointments and, to be truthful, something came from that period that proved, one to be very beneficial and two, it came for free. As unbelievable as it may sound the probation service paid for me to take driving lessons, which ultimately led to me passing my test. I remember getting my first car, which was an orange Ford Fiesta, which now allowed me to spread my wings a little further. As I was earning some honest money I restarted my record collecting again too and I can distinctly remember getting myself over to Nottingham to SELECTADISC, which was the main record shop in Nottingham back then and purchased two great albums. METALLICA's BLACK ALBUM, and POISON IDEA's FEEL THE DARKNESS album. As I was staying at my parents' house, my weekends would entail me not going too mad on a Friday night as I needed to be up and ready to stand on the market early on a Saturday morning. On Saturday nights, though, I'd score some whizz and blow and take a load of CDs or albums over to a mate's house where he'd let me take over the stereo, blasting out JANE'S ADDICTION, MINISTRY, RAGE AGAINST THE MACHINE and various other alternative rock bands, as well as my beloved punk rock stuff. We'd all head down to the pub and then return back later for much of the same. I also got my drums back together and started practising regularly. I'd had a little stint practising on the inside, but now it was time to get back to a level I knew I was capable of. I always loved the presence of females too, and after coming out of prison most of my weekend activities would in one way or another always entail the pursuit of some fun with a woman.

It was around about this time though, I hoped to find someone to probably have a relationship with. Well, I'd fancied this one lass called VICKY way before I got banged up and I happened to see her down at our local haunt. After some effort from myself it didn't take long before we engaged with each other and from then on began a relationship that was to last for about three years. She would also become the mother of our daughter. The chance of a new musical project came through as well. A couple of my old associates had got something new together. They were living in this huge house and were fortunate enough to have the cellar as a practice room. I was asked to come on board and I immediately jumped at the chance to do something new. They were calling themselves AHAB, and musically it was quite a bit different to anything I'd done before. Think KILLING JOKE and FAITH NO MORE, and that gives you an idea of where it was heading. The inclusion of keyboards also gave the sound an edge. I'd been working on the markets for some time now and I'd been given the responsibility of running them on my own, driving the van to whatever town I was standing that day, setting up and then hopefully take some decent money and then pack up and head back home ready for the next day. It was a good crack, to be fair, as I'm better at dealing with people on a one-to-one basis. Also the card game was still in demand and profits were good. The downside of that occupation is that it's not so pleasant to work out in all weathers during the winter and as an enduring prospect this was my primary reservation and I started thinking about the long term. My brother James from the time he'd left school immediately gained an apprenticeship at a barber's shop and had become fully qualified and was earning good money. So I did some research with a view to doing exactly the same. On my mind though, was a way of skipping the three-year apprenticeship and finding a quicker way in. I found out about crash courses and within the space of a couple of months I had one. I left my folks' place and moved in with my bandmates at the large shared house. With the money I'd made from my market days I embarked on the six-week crash course in barbering. This proved to be a very productive time for me, what with moving out of my folks' place, changing my long-term job prospects, being in a relationship, albeit quite a rocky one, and I was out doing gigs again and stretching myself musically. With music always at the forefront of things, I made sure that my quest for live music was satisfied. I got to witness one of the all-time greats in the shape of CHUCK BERRY in Nottingham. He was getting on a bit back in 91/92, but he was still really good and still very nifty on the old guitar. I resumed my yearly pilgrimage to go down to the annual Reading rock festival in 92, which also took in the usual acquiring of illicit substances to keep us going for the whole weekend. Reading 92 was fantastic because I got my first chance to see JOHN LYDON play with the then rejuvenated PUBLIC IMAGE LIMITED. I think it was at that festival I got to see a band called JESUS LIZARD who I'd recently discovered. The highlight for me, though, was witnessing NIRVANA, who were fantastic. So yeah, I was packing quite a lot in.

It wasn't long after that my barbering course court had finished and with that done I immediately went into the working environment with my brother, who had his own shop. I'd picked up some of the skills that barbering required, but there was still some way to go with obtaining the skills needed to get to a level of proficiency that meant that I was doing the job confidently. My brother nurtured me along in that department and before long I was really pleased that I'd decided to go down that route. It would prove to be possibly one of the best decisions I ever made for myself as I now had a skill that would allow me to earn a few quid and keep my head above water without having to return to my old wheeler dealer days. My band AHAB was going along fine but there were some issues going on with the odd member or two. Gigs had been arranged but we'd end up having to pull out due to over-indulgence. For once it wasn't me that was not pulling my weight, and so after only doing a handful of gigs and recording a couple of great demos the band petered out. There was no long-term animosity and I remained well acquainted with these lads. There's no point in having long-term resentment, is there? It's only a fucking band and, let's be honest, life is too short. I just picked myself up and got on with something else. One thing remained a constant throughout this period, and beyond, and that was my appetite for using mainly cannabis, but amphetamines too. My use of drugs had a detrimental effect on the relationship that I was in, especially when it came to the end of a weekend of speed, booze and pot indulgence. Come-downs from speed are pretty horrendous for anybody, but I think they can be even more severe for females, and my lady was no exception to the rule. I would still be flying around like a wild dervish on Sundays and she would be feeling like shit. It wasn't a good mix and we would fall out, only to make up again, only for the same to happen again a couple of weeks later or whenever. I did possess some charming qualities but there is always a flip side, and that meant that I possessed the ability to wear people out very quickly. Finding myself without a band to play in I decided to recruit one from scratch. I wasn't going to be the leader or anything but just wanted to get something going with some like-minded chaps. My brother was an avid music fanatic and I suppose, what with having a big brother around who'd done nothing but inflict it on him from a young age, it was only natural that he followed in my footsteps with regards similar tastes and the like. Whereas I was always into music first and the vocals or lyrics second, my brother was the other way round. I'd introduced him to BILLY IDOL, ADAM ANT, JOHN LYDON and JELLO BIAFRA when he was about 10 or 11 years old and he very much took notice of what they were singing or how they sang, a little more than I did. Anyway, my brother didn't have a bad voice and he could write lyrics too, and so with myself and him up for doing something we found an average bass player and two amazing guitarists who had been bouncing off each other for a while and needed the right people to get involved with. Once again I was up and running with something new musically. We wrote all of our own stuff and it really was quite good. I can only describe what we were doing as like a crossover of metal and punk but with a twist. There was some talent here and an awful lot of energy. My brother came up with some fantastic lyrics and sang in such a way that you could tell he had been influenced by the vocalists I mentioned. My brother and I were working together in two instances. One in the shop and two in the band, not always an ideal situation as we could end up being at each other's throats, but at the time we just went with it. I remember discovering a fantastic new Irish band around this time called THERAPY. I loved them and made sure I went to see them on the occasions that they came to Nottingham. Another band that fused punk with tinges of metal. A crew of us headed down to Reading once again for another drug fuelled weekend where we witnessed RAGE AGAINST THE MACHINE, PORNO FOR PYROS, STONE TEMPLE PILOTS, SIOUXSIE AND THE BANSHEES, THERAPY and, amazingly, my beloved BAD BRAINS. Back at home the new band I'd got together was making really good progress. We had gigs on our minds, and so using the practice room that I had at my disposal where I lived we got ourselves ready. We came up with the name UK 95 which in hindsight was a tad short-sighted. 1995 wasn't that far off but we didn't care. We were fucking good, to be fair, and having created a bit of a buzz round our way, we set up our first gig in a neighbouring town, and for this I'd formulated quite a novel way of recording gigs, etc. I'd got one of those old separate tape players that one would use as part of a separates sound system i.e. record player, amplifier, CD player and the like. Well, a lot of the tape players had microphone inputs in them, so you would just plug two microphones into the player. Where you situated them was key as equal amounts of sound needed to go into the mics otherwise when playing back whatever had been recorded, if the sound wasn't balanced, it could come out louder from one speaker compared to the other. So, I taped the microphones high above and situated them at equal distances. Come the night of the gig and the place was packed. Full of our friends and other like-minded creatures. There was a lot of speed about and I remember being particularly cranked right up, as was everybody else. The gig was amazing and I still have a cassette recording of the night in question that's slowly deteriorating with each passing year, and for me it's a document from that time. We were on fire and the night was most memorable. Sadly again, it was not to be a long-term thing. We played a few more local gigs and got to support the reformed ENGLISH DOGS in Birmingham who then had GIZZ from the DESTRUCTORS on board, at a club called SINATRA'S that was apparently owned by GBH back then. We also went into the same studio that I'd recorded stuff with Ahab and recorded two three-track demos. One was really good and the other not so good due to it being a little rushed. A combination of personality differences and again too much over-indulgence put paid to any longevity, and once again the band burnt out too quickly. By now my partying was starting to have a detrimental effect in other areas of my life. I was using at work whilst just being able to keep myself functioning sufficiently and retaining a work ethic that enabled me to live.

What was not going so well was my on-off relationship with my girlfriend. I was always up to no good, which would result in us having a mighty row and her fucking off. This would usually mean that we wouldn't see each other for a week or two and it would end up with myself going more off the rails with drugs and sex. I did care for her and in my own twisted way I did love her, but I was still immature and too much of a good time Charlie for her to take. We'd always get back together though, and then one night she called me at my place and I can still distinctly remember her telling me that I was going to be a dad. That came as a bit of a shock and I didn't really know what to say to her. To my surprise she also sounded a tad indifferent with the news that she was pregnant, but I do know that we decided that now was probably the best time to move in with each other and face up to what was coming. In the meantime I would try and curb my outlandish ways, crack on with my day job and at least show that I was showing some commitment towards becoming a father. We ended up moving into a nice little house that was owned by her parents. For a short while there would be a bit of calm and we made the place quite homely. Looking back, and what with us both being so fiery and with her being 21 and myself being 26, there seemed to be more differences than similarities in the way we viewed life. Don't get me wrong, she was very intelligent and fun-going but she was also quite responsible with things and I was not, and that's where we always seemed to hit a brick wall which would pave the way for some fairly raucous arguments between us. For my part I wasn't the easiest as I had a very blasé attitude towards everything. I remember us having the mother of all rows at which she cleared off for the longest time yet. As per usual I just went out, got wasted and pulled another bird. The dust was settling after what seemed like ages and I realised I needed to sort my shit out. I knew that my cavalier attitude was part of the problem, but part of me really wanted to be there for her and our child, so once again I set about trying to put things right. My banding activities had once again come to a halt and it seemed to me that a lot of my problems derived from my activities and influences in my hometown. After us making up I suggested that we move out of town to make a fresh start. Vicky agreed and from then on we made plans to do just that. I suggested Derby, as I knew some folks there from bands and stuff and that would mean that at least we wouldn't be totally isolated, not knowing anybody. It was also only an hour's drive from Grantham which meant that she wouldn't be too far away from her family. We got all our stuff together and found a nice little house on the outskirts of Derby and in early 1994 we moved out of town. 1994 was an important year for me. I can remember one of my associates informing me that this famous geezer had died. I asked him, 'What geezer?' and he said, 'You know, that geezer from the band that you like.' I said, 'Who do you mean?', and he said, 'That Kurt geezer.' He was referring to KURT COBAIN. I was gutted,

I really liked NIRVANA and Kurt Cobain was just a couple of months older than myself and so it hit home quite hard. A member of my own generation killing himself. I felt confused about it and initially thought he was a selfish cunt for doing what he did. Now that I've had more life experience one can assume that all was not well with the guy's mental health. NEVERMIND is one of my favourite albums alongside the likes of NEVER MIND THE BOLLOCKS. I can stick it on any time and it still sounds as good as the first day I heard it. Within a short while of settling ourselves into our new home I found a job at a barbershop in the centre of the city. The money wasn't brilliant but it was a start. We knew it wasn't going to be easy, but having kids never is. I was kind of prepared for being a dad and really wanted for us to make it work. My main point of contact was a good friend of mine called JIM, who I'd known from the COSMIC SPACE TOADS days. We bonded through our love of music and he was a good guitar player. He wasn't doing anything and so we set about getting something together. At home, thankfully we had some neighbours who had a young family with another on the way and so they warmed to us when they saw that we were expecting too. This was most welcome as we needed a little bit of support, which made things a little bit easier for Vicky. Now the idea of us moving here, like I say, was to create a new start for ourselves, and for me that new start meant curtailing my drug-taking ways. I couldn't see myself totally stopping so I made a decision to only smoke dope and quit doing everything else. Vicky was quite long into her pregnancy and everything was going quite smoothly. My job was going OK and myself and Jim had started getting together at a local practice room setup that allowed us to get some tunes together.

Jim had a mate who was good on the bass and could sing too. His name was MAZZ and with him on board we pretty much had a full band together. A few years earlier I had read a book about DENNIS NILSEN, the serial killer from the 70s and 80s. The book was called KILLING FOR COMPANY and as a suggestion that's what we decided to call ourselves. On 2 June 1994 Vicky gave birth to our daughter, who we named JADE RAMONA. She was born in Derby City hospital at about 11.00 in the morning and I was there at the birth. A wonderful moment, as any parent who has witnessed the birth of a child will definitely understand.

I remember going out with Jim to wet the baby's head, as the saying goes. My favourite new haunt was a club called the ROCKHOUSE. I'd played there years earlier with the COSMIC SPACE TOADS and now it was where I would spend quite a lot of my time. Within a couple of days, both Jade and Vicky were at home and we were all very happy. Her family came to visit, as did mine, which meant that I would have to hide my bucket bong, which had pretty much become one of the staple ornaments tucked away in the corner of the main front room. We got on with our daily lives with the added addition being Jade. I'd go to work and at the end of the day I'd quite happily sit with her in my arms for an hour or two. Within weeks of Jade being born we started to extend our social circle. Jim's mum, a lovely lady, offered to babysit for us just so that we could have a bit of time to ourselves. With regards to the band we'd decided to get another guitarist on board, and with all involved having girlfriends or wives we had little get-togethers. We were very much newcomers to the area and so it was good to have that little group to bond with. Good for me as I had the band lads, and good for my other half as she could talk lady stuff with the other girls. The band was coming together and there were all sorts of little venues in the city for us to cut our teeth in. In 1994 SOUNDGARDEN released a brilliant album called SUPERUNKNOWN. Now Jim and Mazz were into this kind of stuff and so what we were playing didn't sound too dissimilar. We were all of a similar age and the other three all had long hair and I had my peroxide blonde look even way back then. It wasn't long after I'd had my dreads shorn off. We looked quite a handsome bunch, to be honest. Now Jim and I were kindred spirits and we both shared a love of getting pretty hammered, although some of his habits turned out to be a little different to mine. Like I say, we'd known each other for a few years now and I started to realise that Vicky was starting to become a little irritated at how close we were. She definitely thought that he was a bad influence on me and started to view him with an air of suspicion. Jim was like me I'm afraid. We were our own worst enemies whilst at the same time we were really good mates. I can't blame her for feeling this way as we had a child, whereas none of the others did. She needed my full attention and I had a habit of always getting side-tracked. For the time being though, we were still doing OK. She was handling early motherhood really well, and I was still bringing in the dough so that we could keep ourselves. In September, when Jade was just a few months old, Vicky and I went to Rock City to see THE RAMONES. We had a good night and that also coincided with my new band starting to play gigs around the Derby area. As soon as things started to happen, my circle of similar like-minded people started to grow and it wouldn't be long before an old friend came knocking. That old friend was amphetamine sulphate and I hadn't touched any of the stuff for some time. I had a day off work and I met a new acquaintance and through him I scored some bass speed, as it was called back then. It wasn't like sulphate or in powder form. It was like putty and very, very strong. I loved the stuff and on this particular day I was as high as a kite and had to go home. This didn't please her indoors at all but I did manage to convince her that it was just a one-off.

A few weeks would go by and every now and then my mates from Grantham would come over for a night out and the same would apply with regards to Vicky's friends. The band was starting to become more active too, and as much as Vicky wouldn't come to all of the gigs, we made sure that she attended the ones that she really wanted to. KILLING FOR COMPANY were using a place to rehearse that catered for the majority of bands in the area. Well, one day we bumped into BRIAN ROBERTSON. He'd played for THIN LIZZY and MOTORHEAD. Now, this guy was a shit-hot guitarist, and we struck a bit of a conversation with him and he seemed alright, if just a tad aloof. He was there with his own band doing some stuff, as were we. We were preparing for a two-night slot that was booked for the coming weekend at one of Derby's small venues known as the OLD VIC. He showed some interest in what we were doing and said he'd pop down to one of the gigs to come and check us out. I never gave it any more thought as I wasn't overly struck by the bloke. He looked a bit rough, as I remember. Not surprising I suppose, what with the lifestyle he'd probably had up till then. Anyway we went off and played our first gig on the Friday night, which went as well as could be expected. We were leaving our gear set up on stage for the next night's proceedings. We got to the venue on late Saturday afternoon only to discover that the gear had been moved round somewhat, and more disturbingly that Jim's guitar was broken. Well, naturally he flipped. Who the fuck had done this? We had a gig to do in a matter of hours and at this stage everything was up in the air. Thankfully, Jim got a replacement guitar and we sorted ourselves out and did our second gig. Also we managed to find out who the cunts were that had taken advantage of our gear. After being told that our gear was secure after our Friday night slot, later on that night after we'd left, Mr. Robertson and his crew had turned up and proceeded to have a jam session on our gear, which I may add at the time was all tip top stuff. Downright fucking cheeky, if you ask me. Jim's guitar would've been one of the high-end spec types and not cheap. One of the bastards had damaged his guitar and didn't have the bollocks to own up to it. As it happens we never saw those fuckers again. A bit of a dark episode that one, but hey, you live and learn. A lack of respect on their part, but I'm sure karma will have evened things out somewhere down the line. All that aside, the band was gathering some momentum. We had some professional promo pics taken and, along with the gigs that were coming our way, we booked ourselves into the same studio where I'd done stuff with AHAB and UK 95. We went in and put down three tracks. The results were really good, showcasing what we were capable of. It was definitely a nod towards the grunge sound along with a bit of punk and ballsy heavy rock thrown in. We were capable of writing singles. By that I mean songs that had commercial value, along with other songs that would sit nicely on an album. At this point, it needs to be noted that what with us doing a geographical or moving to a new place was all well and good, but the idea was to put the past behind us and make a fresh start so that I could step up to the mark, so to speak. I had this vague and naïve notion that, what with moving to a new location with new people, I could possibly make changes in my life that would enable me to focus my attentions on being there for Vicky and my daughter. All that happened was I'd moved myself and my problems from one place to the next, and whilst at that time it wasn't plain for me to see that I had some issues, with them going unchecked, no matter how hard I tried it was only a question of time before they would return. By this I'm talking about my hedonistic habits and where they took me. For Vicky it was different, she didn't have an issue. She'd partied hard for a few years but it had never been a problem for her inasmuch as it hadn't affected her ability to function. In short, her days of living that way had come to an end now that she was a mother, whereas for me I pretty much wanted to have my cake and eat it. Cracks started to appear again in our relationship and we had been in Derby for barely six months. My use of amphetamines was slowly starting to creep in again and people who use speed don't keep normal hours. I was still working normal hours and I was still living a relatively normal life, albeit I was still pursuing the hope of an eventful breakthrough with KILLING FOR COMPANY. That was going to take time and commitment, which meant focusing a lot of my efforts towards that. In the end she just couldn't handle me and the way I wanted to live my life and, looking back, I couldn't blame her. One day I returned home and another member of her family was with her, and she informed me that she was leaving and going back to Grantham. One of our friends had hired a van and they loaded all of her stuff into it. After the many times that we'd split and then got back together she left me for one final time, taking Jade our daughter with her. I was devastated. Deep down I kind of knew that the chances of us making a successful life together were slim, but all the same the fact that she and Jade had gone hit me really hard. I slowly resigned myself to the fact that I was now on my own again. Wanting to keep myself afloat and the house going I immediately took in a lodger, who I hardly ever saw, and I cracked on the best I could. KILLING FOR COMPANY were getting a steady flow of gigs so for me all wasn't lost. We'd ended up getting our studio recording printed on CD and they were circulated around the musical hotspots of Derby. There was definitely something on offer here and we found ourselves coming to the attention of a lot of people, notably the iconic rock mag *Kerrang* who favourably reviewed the disc, along with the likes of releases by FAITH NO MORE and EXTREME. Always liking the company of the opposite sex, the idea of having a new girlfriend didn't appeal to me at all, but that didn't stop me from getting involved with a few lasses just for some fun and frolics. The most notable change at this time, though, was my increasing appetite for speed. As much as I was putting on a brave face, underneath I was grieving over the loss of my daughter and Vicky. Losing Vicky was bad enough, but to have my daughter taken away was what hurt the most. I know now that I'd partly brought this on by my own actions but there was no denying the hurt I was feeling inside. So to fill that emptiness I started using more speed, that would for a short time make me feel better. It was creeping in though, with ever more frequency and I knew that it was becoming a problem as I was using the stuff to play on. I can remember not being able to get some whizz at one time and because of that I didn't want to do the gig. That was very unlike me. I was starting to struggle playing and the others knew it too, and this started to cause some resentment. I could just tell that my predicament was pissing them off. One thing that did cause some amusement before all of this I must share with you. Not long before Vicky upped and left, and when everything seemed to be going along quite nicely, I had an accident and it was all because of my daughter. Well, not because of her directly, but due to something of hers. When Jade was born we obtained a fold-up style pram, and we stored this pram in its folded-up state at the bottom of the stairs near the front door. Well, as always I was bounding around the house and I came down the stairs and hadn't calculated my footing right. I swung and slammed my right foot right into the folded-up pram. Oh my God, I was in so much pain. I immediately realised I'd done myself some mischief, being the clumsy oaf that I am. I was in agony and had broken the little toes on my foot. The thing was that we'd got a gig coming up in a couple of days and I use that foot to play the bass drum on my kit. Well, I wasn't going to cancel the gig for something as trivial as a broken toe or two. Come the day of the gig I strapped my foot up, bearing in mind that it was still throbbing like fuck. Jim produced some elephant tranquiliser-type pain relief tablets. I bunged a couple of these down and, hey presto, I did the gig and hardly felt a thing. I felt a bit raw when the pain relief had subsided and the gig had been done, but the band thought it was hilarious.

With Vicky and Jade gone I was feeling a little isolated in Derby, so I started to go to Grantham at weekends via train to catch up with all my old mates. I'd go over on a Saturday afternoon and return on the Sunday. As time went by I was starting to spend nearly all of my social time back in my home town. I was still grieving inside about the split from my ex but I knew that that was final. I'd stopped enjoying myself in Derby though, and I'd started to lose interest even in the band. Whatever happened I still wanted to be a part of my daughter's life, and with myself being in Derby this would prove to be a difficult thing to do. I didn't have a motor and my ex wasn't going to bring her to me. So sometime in mid-1995 I made the radical decision to pack everything up in Derby and move back to Grantham. Leaving the band behind was neglectful and I'm sure the lads weren't happy about it, but I'd made up my mind. Jim, however, was fine with my decision and we remained friends to the point that we got involved with something else a couple of years down the line.

15. ONE'S TOO MANY AND A THOUSAND'S NEVER ENOUGH

I managed to secure myself a flat through my family. One of my Grandad's places that really needed a bit of attention, but for now I was grateful just to have a roof over my head now that I was back on home turf. I arrived back in town with hardly anything except for my hefty record collection that had moved with me on God knows how many occasions over the years. Now I had his first-floor flat in a large old building. There was a massive living room, a small kitchen and bathroom adjacent to each other and a small bedroom upstairs. I had no job, no band and no woman so I signed on so that I could keep my head above water and immediately settled back into my hometown. I had a lot of acquaintances, some older from the days back when I was involved with the COSMIC SPACE TOADS, and some younger that I'd known for just a couple of years. Well, I'd been away from town for a year or so but I noticed that certain things had changed . Becoming sociable again and reacquainting myself with a lot of the people that I hadn't seen for a while, I developed this kind of distorted respect from a lot of them for being this bohemian type who liked partying hard and living every day as if it were my last. Now whether this was a good or bad thing is irrelevant as my family and significant others certainly didn't see it that way. I seemed to have this knack of attracting people of a similar ilk, and through them I was able to use them, as they did me, to survive. I was known for my music and I was known for my propensity to party hard. My new pad where I was living was fantastic because I had this massive room that became ideal for having little get-togethers, especially after pub hours, or at any hour to think of it. I'd obtained a decent sound system with sizeable speakers and with all the music I had in my collection, I would act as DJ and people would congregate at mine and bring with them booze and blow and we'd have a bit of a knees-up. I was still smoking a lot of hash but it's at this time that my appetite for speed started to take over. I loved speeding because the effect lasts for a long time, meaning I could stay awake longer, but the downside being that there would be an eventual comedown, and that's when I would smoke hashish to cushion the horrible feeling that went with the speed crash. Before I'd moved to Derby some new faces had appeared in town a year or so before. These individuals were a couple of years older than me and, like myself, I would call them 'free spirits'. I liked them and they had fallen in with our crowd. They had moved from Scunthorpe, and their motivation for getting away from there was one thing. Heroin. I've since learned that Scunthorpe in the mid-to late nineties had a huge problem with heroin. These lads had upped sticks and landed in Grantham. Now I liked these lads but at that time, and unbeknown to most of us, they had a dark past. Earlier I mentioned that when I arrived back in town certain things had changed. One of them was that before I left to live in Derby there was no heroin at all in Grantham and it had never been mentioned. After being back in town for a month or two I can remember it being mentioned, and that a small selection of people were using it. I thought nothing of this as I was too busy speeding; however, there was one particular threshold I did cross and it would do me no favours at all. I'd known some of the more hardcore older lads who lived and breathed getting shit-faced twenty-four-seven. When I say older I'm talking about six or seven years older, and when I first met them it was predominantly booze that most of these people abused. A few years on though, and now a load of these lads had moved on to getting anything inside them just to get a buzz. I wasn't in the best headspace at the time and I was almost pretty much open to trying anything too. My barriers were completely down and the intrigue of what I was about to do overtook me. I requested that one of my acquaintances help me, and so sometime in early 1996 I got one of them to inject me with speed. Of course I was nervous at the prospect of what I was about to do, but with all my reservations gone, I went ahead with it and waited for the effects. The rush from the drug running through my bloodstream was almost instantaneous. To ingest speed the way most people did, either by snorting or orally, the effect takes time to come on. I should have left that little experiment there and then, but to be honest I enjoyed the instant hit, and although I didn't repeat the ritual for some time, it was only a matter of time before I was wanting to experience it again, only now I intended on performing the ritual myself.

I started dealing again, albeit nothing on the scale that I used to do a few years back, but just a little to pay for my own. I knew a wide array of people of all ages and I'd known one particular youth through music since before the UK 95 days. When coming back to town from Derby I met up with him on a regular basis and instantly fell in with a load of his mates who were all different, but who all shared the same kind of free-spirited attitude towards life. Whilst I was heading towards 30 these folks were all in their early twenties, but that didn't matter. I knew I'd dropped out and so did they. Like I say, they were a mixed bunch of personalities and a select few were definitely alternative, and so when I realised that a couple were very musically minded I made overtures with regards to getting a band together with them. I found that one was a very adequate bassist, and another looney-type character was keen on becoming a vocalist. Luckily we found a guitarist who wasn't directly involved with the other two but was of a similar age. There was no intention of playing covers and, after finding a practice place in a local pub cellar, we started meeting twice a week and making some new music. I was just happy to be playing again. Our first names were STOO, KOLIN, ALAN and MARK. So, using the first letters of our names we called ourselves SKAM. Being back in town was turning out to be in some ways the right move, but as I mentioned earlier on, my main motivation for returning was to be involved in one form or another in my daughter's life. It was never my intention to not be around, so to speak. Thankfully my mother and co had retained good contact with her mother who, it has to be said, didn't like me much at this time, and so wasn't at first prepared to let me see Jade on my own. Slowly but surely though, I started to get her a few hours one day a week, or I could see her whenever she was in the care of my folks. This pleased me no end and it was important to me that she at least knew who her Dad was. Also, aside from everything else that was going on I became involved with another woman. Her name was EMMA, and I met her through one of the older geezers I knew. They'd been together for some time but I did notice that the relationship wasn't exactly harmonious. So, when given the opportunity after they split up, I seized the opportunity and gained her trust. It wasn't long before she moved in with me, bringing with her two huge dogs. We would end up being together for four years, in what I can only describe as a most tempestuous relationship.

I'd been enjoying the new circle of people I'd met that gravitated around the lads in the band. Weekends were always good fun, and more often than not small gatherings would end up round my gaff until the early hours. The intention of the new band "SKAM" was obviously to get out there and do some gigs, and so that's what we worked towards. We got some half-decent songs together and I would loosely describe what we were doing as punk rock. I was certainly enthused by the lads' enthusiasm and the slowly gathering little fan base that was growing as we progressed towards being ready to play a gig. At the time this was happening I remember hearing the wonderful news that the SEX PISTOLS were to reform, starting what would be a world tour, and the first gig would be at Finsbury Park in London. This was like sweet music to my ears. My favourite band, who I had been too young to see in their heyday, were playing just down the road. Jesus Christ, there was absolutely no way that I was going to miss this. So through a friend and her credit card, I got myself a ticket to the gig. For me 1996 was turning into one hell of a party. I don't know how I managed to afford to live through those times, but I did. I lived very cheaply really and never wanted for much. I didn't drive and so all I wanted and needed was food, drugs and enough money to pay my bills. I was claiming rent and dole money, or Income Support, as it was called then. Emma, my girlfriend, was working part-time and so one day just drifted into the next. The PISTOLS' reformation was all over the news and with about 30,000 others, we'd all waited for the day to arrive to witness the kings of punk making a triumphant return after splitting eighteen years previously. It was going be a hot day, and I travelled down to London with a couple of friends. Trainers, ripped jeans and my leather plus a day's supply of speed was all I needed. It turned out to be a long day as we got there at about noon. I just parked myself up on the field somewhere and waited. I remember seeing a little bit of IGGY POP and a little of THE WILDHEARTS, but none of the other bands. When I knew that the PISTOLS were going to be coming up next I made my move for the front of the stage, which wasn't going to be easy as a few thousand other bastards had the same thing on their minds. The atmosphere was building up big time. The stage now displayed the hugest backdrop ever that covered the front of the stage so that nothing could be seen behind. One of the 76/77 newspaper headlines commenting on the *Filth and the Fury* was emblazoned across the backdrop. DOLLY PARTON'S *Jolene*, and other late seventies' pop ditties came through the sound system and then the music stopped. On the front right-hand side stage, England legends STUART PEARCE and GARETH SOUTHGATE appeared. They were there to introduce the band. With that one went 'Ladies and gentlemen,' and the other, 'The Sex Pistols.' With that, the whole crowd cheered. There was a brief moment and then amazingly the band themselves burst through the backdrop, which we now knew was paper or something similar. It was a dramatic entrance and thousands of us roared our appreciation. They got themselves ready and then ROTTEN shouted 'Are you ready?' Fucking right, we were ready. And then the opening notes of the song *Bodies* started. Fuck, it makes the hairs on the back of my neck stick up just writing about it. With that, the place literally exploded as the song kicked in. I was lifted off my feet and then thrown back down. This went on for about a minute or so and I have to be honest, it was too rough even for me. This wasn't a small crowd with a handful of people cascading to and fro and bashing into each other. It was like the battle of Agincourt, and so with all of my strength I started to push back until it felt that I was safe. Honestly, it was that bad. From then on, though, the gig was fantastic. The band looked and sounded great. This was special. One may have thought that they could have fallen flat on their faces as they had not played together for so long, but they had made themselves ready for this, and I could see that they were relishing putting the record straight and having the last word. For me the PISTOLS were and always will be the kings of punk. A very special day indeed.

Getting back home and daily life carried on and I wasn't doing myself any favours. I was now fixing myself with speed more and more often and, for the first time since I'd started using drugs, I now had a woman who'd developed a taste for speed that matched mine. This meant that if I scored some she would want her share too. I'd never been in this situation before where a girlfriend could match me with her intake, and I can't say I was happy about it. It meant I was having to share my gear with her. At the same time another move was in order as the raucous nights at my gaff had raised some complaints, and once again I thought it best to get out from under my family's feet and find a place independent from them. Just before we moved though, my 30th birthday was approaching and SKAM were ready to do a gig. We did the usual thing of putting up posters and handing out flyers and we secured a large room at the back of this pub. Come the day of the gig and all the gear was taken to the venue. We set up and looked forward to the night's proceedings. Absolutely loads of people turned up, which we were half expecting anyway. We had another young punk band playing with us and they were called DAGOBAH, and over the next year or so we did numerous gigs on the same bill. Well, they'd brought a fair few of their own crowd along too. It was a fantastic gig, a perfect punk rock night with people crashing into the gear, us having to stop and start again. I employed my technique of using a tape recorder and microphones from the ceiling to record our set, and after the gig I listened back and the night was absolute chaos, but at the same time most enjoyable. I was in a quite unique position at this point as my social circle ranged from the older people that I'd known from the punk scene in the 80s, guys in their mid-thirties or thereabouts, and then this new group of people around myself and the band that were predominantly in their early twenties. There I was at 30-odd, now mixing with both circles. Myself, my lady and her two dogs moved into a third-floor flat near to the main street in town. It had three metal stairways leading up to it, and it very much reminded me of those kind of backstreet stairwells that you would see in American films. Well, after settling in there we pretty much just carried on as we did before. The added advantage of being in this new place was that we didn't have any immediate neighbours. Below was an Indian restaurant on the ground floor, and on the second a storage room of some sort. Once again my place became a magnet for any one of a number of people. Most of them were recreational drug users and, for as much as my using was starting to take on more of a habitual role, my gaff was always available to them as long as they didn't mind sharing a little bit of what they had with me. Once again I'd got my sound system set up and music would always be playing. Always music. It was always the one constant if people came round. It was one of the things that attracted people. It wasn't the fact that they liked my music, or whatever. It was the fact that if you came round mine you could relax as I was so easy-going, too easy-going really. An atmosphere where you could skin up and get stoned and just enjoy yourself. Now I was up for anything really but my thing was still hash and speed. I'd use speed and then use dope to come down on. Emma, my lass, was getting prescribed dihydrocodeine, a mild opiate pain relief for a knee complaint. To me these were known as DF118s. Well, through one of the circle I was involved with I was informed that if you took a couple of these pills, they gave you a nice buzz. They weren't wrong and I soon found them to be an almost ideal remedy when coming down on speed. It wasn't long before I was abusing these too.

One shining ray of light was that I was seeing my daughter quite regularly. By my own admission I was the typical absent father, but when I could be there for her I made the effort. On knowing that I would be picking her up I wouldn't use beforehand and so, when she came to my place, my gaff would be off- limits to everyone. My intention was to cement the bond a parent makes with their offspring and I believe for as much as I wasn't there as much as I should have been, I was there to let her know who her father was. It meant a lot to me when she called me 'Daddy'. My girlfriend also made the effort with her and for those few hours that we had her a little bit of normality shone through. I've spoken to Jade and asked her if she can remember that time. Taking into consideration that she would have only been four to five years old, she tells me she can remember very little and almost nothing of Emma who, like I say, did make a bit of a fuss of her. No sooner had I taken her back to her Mum's, or her coming to pick her up, I immediately went back to doing what was normal for me back then. Creatively my get-togethers with the lads from SKAM were also bringing in results. We started to get regular gigs in and around the area, and even started getting the odd one or two in Nottingham. We now had a full set of songs that were our own, but I do remember us doing a cover of the song PRIVATE AFFAIR by the Australian band THE SAINTS as well. We even played a gig in someone's house. It was in his front room but it was a fair-size. This guy being a fan and a friend of various band members wanted a party for his birthday. This was to take place after we'd all been down the pub. There must have been 40 to 50 people turn up at his place after pub hours and we were all set up and ready to go. Another riotous evening was had by all. God only knows what the neighbourhood, never mind the next-door neighbours, thought. Reckless abandon knew no bounds back then and thankfully my circumstances have changed as I wouldn't wish to, or dare to, inflict that sort of mêlée on people who aren't used to it these days. One great thing that did transpire from this period was that I encouraged the chaps that we need to get some of this stuff recorded properly. So, using the exact same studio I'd used with previous projects, we went to Mansfield and laid down four of our songs. The results were brilliant. I can't remember the engineer's name but he did a great job of mixing the tracks. They still sound great now. It was also at this time that I crossed one final threshold, one final taboo. The cardinal sin of the punks and the one thing that would end up taking me to a very dark place indeed.

I'd been out speeding all weekend, as I'd done on many occasions, and it must have been late on a Saturday night, but more than likely the early hours of Sunday morning as I was slowly starting to come down from that weekend's revelry. For years I'd combat a speed come-down by smoking lots of hash. It always helped to take the edge off that feeling of still speeding a little whilst starting to feel absolutely fucked. I ended up round a friend's house where there were other folks ending their weekend just as I was. Now, I've mentioned that I knew a wide array of people of all ages. I was for the most part at this point socialising more with the younger contingent and that in part was to do with the people who were following the band. One of the individuals was smoking heroin, 'chasing the dragon', so to speak. This is done by placing the brown powder onto a small sheet of tinfoil. Using a lighter, the powder is burned so that it liquefies. The brown liquid runs and as it does so, it gives off a vapour or smoke. This is sucked up through another tin foil flute. I was offered the flute while my associate burned the tinfoil underneath the brown dot. As it started to run I inhaled, sucking up the smoke, and held it in my lungs for as long as possible and then exhaled out. I'd just ingested heroin for the first time. After repeating the process to or three times, a wonderful feeling overcame me. Any nastiness from my speed come- down evaporated almost immediately and I felt calm and relaxed, whilst at the same time euphoric in a way I had not felt before.

My girlfriend wasn't there, as she had made it quite clear that she vehemently disliked heroin and people who took it. I'd heard and read about smack from an early age. JOHNNY THUNDERS, MALCOLM OWEN and one of my early anti-heroes, SID VICIOUS, had all succumbed to the drug. There was all the evidence I needed to tell me that I shouldn't be messing around with such a thing. The strange thing is, no one ever thinks anything's going to happen to them; well I didn't, anyway.

And the truth of the matter is that a little part of me didn't care, and because of that I had no fear of where it may take me. Living in that moment as I inhaled the heroin I wasn't thinking about the long-term consequences. I just wanted to change the way I was feeling right there and then and I suppose that's the difference between someone like me and someone else who would read the danger signs and say 'No, I'm not doing that, it's too dangerous'. Deep in my heart I knew I would try it again. As I write this I'm wondering to myself why I chose to do such a thing, to go down that route that was pretty much everything I was against. OK, I enjoyed getting wasted and being a bit reckless, but what with the stigma attached to that drug in society and especially in the punk scene, with the knowledge I have since gained through being educated, it was a case of my drug using progressing from one thing to the next. Add on top of that the amazing high the drug gave me and I now appreciate the fact that everything I'd ever taken before was going to lead me to this. From that first dope cake I had at seventeen, to taking heroin at 30, it's so obvious now, but back then and whilst in the thick of it, I was blind to the fact I was, and still am, an addict. It wasn't that long before I tried smack again. Only this time I wasn't on a come-down and I can remember the feeling being a lot more intense, and I must have taken too much as I threw up after using it. It's from here on in that my downward spiral accelerated. The cunning thing about heroin is that one only needs a small amount at first to feel the effects or the rush that I've mentioned. As the user starts to use the drug more frequently though, the little amount used at first is not sufficient to achieve the same high, and thus a larger dose of the drug is required. This compulsion and a desire to achieve a high leads to habitual use, which subsequently leads to higher tolerance and full-blown addiction. I started using the drug just at weekends at first, with speed still being my drug of choice. I would start speeding and partying on a Friday night and then use a little bit of smack to come down on the Sunday. I was still smoking hash as well, but it was the smack that brought me down really nicely. It didn't stay like that, though, and eventually I started using more heroin and it wasn't long before I completed the circle and became the epitome of the word 'junkie' and started injecting the stuff. Speed to go up and smack to come down. I was still involved with my band mates and we were still doing the odd gig or two, but personally I was starting to lose interest and I'm sure my mates could see the change in me too. It wasn't a case of me losing interest in music, not at all. It's just that my erratic behaviour and unreliability was starting to show. After only using heroin for a few months I got to a point whereby if I didn't have the drug then I would start to feel the effects of withdrawal. 'Clucking', or 'rattling', as the terms go. These symptoms are unpleasant, to say the least. Mild at first, I used to feel like I'd got a cold or mild flu-like symptoms, and the only way to alleviate these symptoms was to use more gear. As I got more addicted the withdrawals got worse. Lack of sleep, the sweats, and then the shivers, retching, involuntary bodily movements, especially in the legs, and an overall feeling of powerlessness and misery that can only be quelled with a fix.

This wreaked havoc on my already fractious relationship too. My girlfriend had always despised heroin and the people who took it and she made this perfectly clear as my alliances with other smackheads started to develop. To her credit she tried her hardest to keep me away from these people and the drug itself, but my addiction grew in strength. I would just use at another junkie's house, which brings me to the people I was now associating with. Junkies stick with their own, and now that I'd sunk that low and become one of them, I was leading a double life. My lass wasn't stupid though, and she had me sussed and it was only going to be a matter of time before things came to a head. I got to the point where I was now having to search out a fix every day, and to do that I needed money. To pay for my drugs I was now resorting to crime. Theft, rent book fraud, all manner of crisis loans, and dealing, albeit on a small scale. I'd rip people off if I could, anything to get a tenner together just to stave off withdrawals, anything to just feel normal. One thing is certain, as an addict and as much as it's a sordid and horrible existence, I became very resourceful, but truthfully it was a nightmare. I would get high some of the time, but using became a quest to just function as normally as possible and to make sure that I had a hit later on in the day just so that I could get through the night. The next day the same routine would start all over again. By now the band had fizzled out and a lot of the younger people I had been associated with were moving on, getting jobs or settling down in new relationships. I was still hanging out with a few of them, but they were the ones who were using gear. Most of the other people I hung out with were old punks, traveller types, dropouts like myself, and normal everyday Joes who'd ended up with a habit, too. I was playing a risky game here and it was only a matter of time until my lifestyle decided to bite me on my arse. The heroin was taking over and on this particular day, for a change, I hadn't used any speed beforehand, but I had money to score some smack. I went to a dealer's house and scored two bags for the price of one. I asked the dealer if I could shoot up there and he offered no objections, so I prepared a hit using both of the bags I'd scored. I shot up and within a very short time passed out. I'd OD'd and I didn't even know it. All I can remember is that the guy I had scored from had realised what was happening and had gone into action to revive me. I came to with him leaning over me and shouting at me in a panicked voice, telling me that I'd 'gone over', street talk for OD'ing. He had been slapping me about the face to help me regain consciousness. To me it was just like waking up but he really was freaking out. Without his intervention there was a good chance I would have slipped deeper into a coma and my heart may have stopped. I was quite out of it once I'd come to, but what could I do? I just brushed myself off, thanked him, bid him farewell and went off on my way. Things were getting heavy and this was a sure sign that I needed to do something about it. For the time being I just carried on as normal. Most logical-thinking people would have heeded the danger, but when you're a junkie that's not an option. For me to have been able to stop, it meant literally locking me in a room and not opening the door again until I'd gone through the withdrawals. If you've ever seen the film *Trainspotting*, then that gives you an idea of the kind of life I was living. I'm lucky that I never caught Hepatitis

C, because if I were round somebody's place to have a fix and I didn't have my own works, I'd be happy to use somebody else's. I'd flush them out with boiling water and do what I needed to do. One of the worst side effects of withdrawals is the lack of sleep. To be fair, my experience of drug using or even drinking is that always my sleep pattern is affected first. I registered with my doctors and started getting weekly prescriptions of sleeping tablets and DF118s to help with the withdrawals. I could have got myself a methadone script, but to be honest I never wanted to get onto that stuff as I just felt it was another ball and chain that I could be doing without. I know people now that are still on a methadone script that they were first prescribed twenty-odd years ago.

Late in 1998 I had a terrible accident and there was nobody else to blame except myself. I'd been hanging about with this right dodgy little bastard, and I was getting up to all sorts of skulduggery. Anything to procure cash quickly and I'd be up for it. This old boy said he knew of some offices where there was cash waiting if we could get inside. Well, in turns out that the only way of entering was through the roof, and to do that we had to scale a drainpipe to get there. I was desperate so like a twat I went along with the plan. It was a Sunday night and that's when we made our way to this place. It was pretty cold so I was pretty well wrapped up. Matey boy scales the drainpipe, which is about 20 to 25 feet high, and as he was a little fella he was up there in a shot. I thought to myself, 'Well, if he can do it then so can I.' With that I started my way up. It wasn't easy but using all my strength in my arms and legs I got to the top. As I was about to reach my arm over to pull myself onto the roof, the drainpipe gave way. I fell like a stone and hit the floor with an almighty thud. I can remember letting out a blood-curdling scream as the pain hit me. Amazingly I didn't pass out, but as I lay there I knew I had done myself some serious harm. I tried to move my left arm but as I did so the pain was unbearable and I let out another yelp. My arm didn't move. My partner in crime, realising what had happened, shouted down to me that he was coming down to help me. I managed to sit myself up and began sweating profusely. Out the blue a couple of lads came towards me as if just walking by, and I pleaded with them that I'd just fallen, and if they could help me get to my feet. I put out my right arm, which was also injured, and one of them pulled me up. They cleared off pronto and I didn't blame them. Fuck knows what they must have thought. God knows where my mate had gone, but I assume he must have called an ambulance because within a short space of time one arrived and I was taken to hospital. On arriving at the A&E I was immediately whisked through and taken to a room where I was assessed for the damage I'd caused to myself. With it being October, as I mentioned, I was well wrapped up. Well, the nurses managed to get my Crombie-like jacket off me. But the rest of my clothes on my top half had to be cut off because I couldn't move my arms at all. It was whilst doing this that the main lady who was removing my clothes noticed my arms. Not the damage I'd caused that night, but the track marks on the inside of my arms. She didn't judge me though, and just carried on with the job in hand. I had rings on my fingers and strangely a couple of those had to be cut off as well. This actually took some time. After being stripped of everything I was immediately taken for X-rays. I was sedated and put on a ward. I do remember getting to sleep, although I think it was more a morphine-induced haze than anything. The following morning the doctor came to see me with quite disturbing news. I was told that the injuries to my left arm were very serious. I'd broken my arm in five places and the elbow had been shattered. My left elbow was also snapped and I'd also cracked a bone in a very awkward place on my left foot. As I'd fallen, my left side had borne the brunt of the fall, hence most of the damage was on that side. My girlfriend was obviously upset and came and visited me. She knew what I'd been up to, but it was too late now as the damage was done. The hospital didn't hang about and within a day or two I underwent the first of two operations, the first being the most extensive, with the intention of fixing the damage to my arms. My left arm was going to need a lot of attention. I was in a lot of pain and I knew that there was going to be a long road ahead. The operation itself took over six hours and thankfully I knew nothing about it, but I can remember coming to as if being brought back from the dead. Once I'd awoken I wanted to know what they'd done to me and I couldn't believe it when I saw my arms. They both looked like they had zips on them where the surgeons had obviously cut me open, done their work and stapled me back up again. A couple of days later I had a second operation performed on my left foot. They fixed it but I had three pins inserted which were protruding out of the top of the foot. Then a cast was placed around the bottom half of my leg covering the foot. I was in a right state. I could barely wipe my arse, never mind do anything else. I was placed in a private ward and put on a morphine drip which gave me regulated doses when I pushed a button. Being the fuckwit that I was I repeatedly pressed the button to hopefully get a nice increased dose, but was promptly informed by a nurse that it didn't work like that, and only an appropriate amount of pain relief would be administered at one time. I do believe that while I was left to start recuperating I went through a forced detox. I know hospital wards are known to be quite hot and stuffy, but for about a week-plus I sweated profusely. I felt like absolute shit for a while, but slowly I started to come round. My girlfriend would visit me in the early evenings, and through the use of a wheelchair she'd wheel me to the A&E entrance and we'd have a crafty spliff. I had a few visitors whilst I was in hospital, and my Mum was beside herself, bless her, and it was brilliant when she brought Jade in to see me. I ended up staying in hospital for nineteen days, after which I was told to stay at home and rest.

The next six months were really hard work. Within a few weeks the injury to my foot wasn't healing properly and it got infected. By the end I was screaming my head off as the pain came and went. My foot was encased in a cast and it felt to me like it was expanding. Like a bloody fool, when it initially gave me problems I scored some smack to ease the pain. It worked for a short time but an infection needs professional treatment. My girlfriend was disgusted that I'd used gear and from here on our relationship would deteriorate as I once again slipped back into my old ways. My mother came to see me, and when she was informed about the infection in my foot she took me to the hospital where my cast was removed, my foot given the once over to make sure that the pins hadn't moved, and a new cast fitted. I was prescribed antibiotics and then sent back home to recover. What made it so much more difficult during this time was the fact that we lived three storeys up, so getting up and down stairs was quite problematic with one leg out of action. A wheelchair was provided and every now and then a friend or two would take me out and wheel me to wherever we needed to go. Slowly but surely I started to heal and, as much as my arm injuries were serious enough, the injury to my foot was more uncomfortable and was taking a lot longer to deal with. The surgeons had done an amazing job of fixing my arms, and the fact that I can still drum and do my job today is testament to that. I was told that the crack in the plate of my foot was a very awkward fracture and so would take some time to recover. As a lot of you will know, if you have had broken bones, the bone never completely recovers. I was very lucky as my arms don't give me a lot of grief and I have some awesome scars to show you if we ever meet. My foot, however, took longer to come right as the cast was on for over two months and there was a lot of muscle wastage. I also walked with a limp for nearly two years. Saying that, I'm very grateful to the amazing fellow and the nameless people who put me back together again. I've never been able to thank them though, as I soon returned to my old ways. As long as I was just using speed, then relations between me and my girl were fine as she loved the stuff too, but as soon as I ventured back towards smack she would turn really nasty, so I just used to do it behind her back. I'd use at other smackheads' houses and then go back home when I was done. I was returning back to where I was before my mishap, and she didn't want to know. I don't blame her, looking back on it, and as I have already stated, she tried her best to stop me. I was having none of that though, and soon we were still living under the same roof whilst becoming totally distant from each other, and it was only a matter of time before she felt she needed to leave. So that's what she did. One day, with what little belongings she had, she and the two dogs left. We'd been together for four years. In reality that was about two years too long, as our relationship had become almost what I have since learnt to be a co-dependent one. I had mixed emotions about her leaving. On the one hand I was upset and on the other I was relieved. We'd been no good for each other and after getting over the initial idea of now being on my own, I soon came round to the idea. As chaotic as my life was, there was always one thing that had never left me and didn't do me any harm, and that was music. I'd got to a point again when nothing else interested me except the acquiring of and the using of drugs. My main drug of choice was heroin, followed by speed and then cannabis. I was also back on a steady diet of sleepers and mild opiate substitutes acquired through my doctor.

Music was still there every day though, as it always had been. I even found another couple of younger chaps who expressed a desire to get involved and put together something new. After coming out of hospital a year or so back, I'd slipped back into full-blown heroin addiction, but I still had the desire to play. OK, I was never going to be able to give it my full attention, but this was the thing. I was leading this double life whereby I knew and associated with other junkies in my own time, but also tried to function properly when other areas of my life came into play. I was still seeing my daughter, I was still seeing my mother, and I still wanted to play music with people who had no true idea of the severity of my addictions. I used to hide it well a lot of the time, although I'm sure that most could see that I wasn't firing on all cylinders. The time that I spent with my daughter meant a lot to me as it was those brief moments of reality that I needed. Now that I was on my own again I even got quite close to Vicky, Jade's mum. We got on well but there was no way I could let her know how bad things were. I didn't expect for her or anybody out of that using circle to understand how heroin addiction works. I felt guilt and shame because of it and I didn't want to unnerve her to the point where we fell out and I had access to my daughter denied. For as much as I was in full-blown addiction, when she saw Jade and me interact, there evidently was no need for her to be concerned. We started to arrange day trips out which for me was great in one respect, but also posed problems in another. For me to function I'd need a fix in the morning. That would tide me over, thus allowing me to do whatever I wanted to do. I would need another one within eight to twelve hours though, otherwise I would start to feel rough, anxiety would set in and then the withdrawals would get worse until I'd sorted myself out. Town and the using network had become like a ball and chain. I couldn't spend too long away from my source of supply otherwise the inevitable feelings of withdrawal would begin. On the few occasions that we ventured out, one camping, and one on a bus trip down to London, I was caught short and I started to experience the onset of withdrawal. At the same time I didn't want to show Jade and her mother what was going on. This was horrible and it just showed me that my double life was a real problem. Add to that I was running more and more risks to get smack. I was getting into problems with dealers, I was ripping people off, I was thieving off people, I was thieving out of shops, and it was getting to the point where no amount of smack could satisfy me. Also, my body was starting to bear the scars of repeated intravenous abuse. I was coming to the end of my tether and for the first time I was getting scared at the prospect of where this would all end. Jade's mum and I did a couple of car boot sales together to get a few quid and my mother came out to one of them. The time was now to tell her, so I got her on her own for a chat. Just short of breaking down completely, I let her know what was going on and that I needed help. She knew that I was in a mess, but now she knew how severe it really was. She mentioned getting out of the country and going to South Africa. I didn't quibble or resist. I was ready to do anything. I'd hit rock bottom. My father was notified and now, at last, I let Jade's mother know the full extent of my problem. A plan was put in place, but these things take a bit of time and with a plane flight out of England planned for just under two weeks away, I carried on using. My habit was costing me at least £25 a day, and to finance my habit I'd taken to nicking stuff out of electrical stores, taking more risks and just generally becoming more brazen in my antics. Dealers would swap this stuff for gear and, if they were happy, so was I. On this particular day a copper had noticed me entering Currys and thought he'd wait to see what I was up to. No sooner had I picked up this radio and was heading out the store when he pounced on me as I got outside. This was really bad luck as I'd gotten away with so much shit over the last couple of years that to get busted now I didn't fucking need. I was taken to the local cop shop and charged with theft. I was given a court date to appear to answer the charges. Having been informed of the date to appear, I immediately realised I was due in court a couple of days after my proposed flight to South Africa. I said nothing to the police and just thought to myself, 'I'll deal with that when I eventually come back.' Nothing was going to stop me from getting out of England. It was 'do or die', and I had no intention of dying. Over the next few days I emptied my flat and put all my stuff in storage. I got a letter and a supply of DF118s and sleeping tablets from my doctor. I said my goodbyes to Jade and her mum, promising to stay in touch, and the night before my flight I stayed at my brother's place. On the day of my flight, in the morning I had one final fix to get me through the next twelve hours and the flight. My mother came and picked me up and with that my mother drove me down to Heathrow. I bid her an emotional farewell and with that I caught a plane to Cape Town. I didn't have a clue what was going to happen when I got to Africa.

16. HITTING ROCK BOTTOM/RECOVERY

It took eleven hours to get to Cape Town and when I landed I wasn't in good shape. After about eight or nine hours in the air, withdrawals came on. There was no turning back now though, and I just had to grin and bear it. To add insult to injury one of my suitcases had been waylaid, and that was the one that had my prescription drugs in. Aargh, I really was fucked. I went to meet my Dad and immediately informed him of my condition and how I was feeling. It was horrendous. I told him that I needed to get to a doctor asap. Fuck knows what he must have thought. This wasn't what he was expecting, I'm sure, but he didn't fuck about. We ended up at his doctor's and, after explaining the situation, they prescribed something. I can't remember exactly what it was, but in short, whatever it was had an adverse effect on me. We got to his house and I was all over the place. It was a terrible situation to put my Dad and his wife in, but bless them, they handled it the best they could. I stopped taking what I had been prescribed immediately and had to just get on with it. The next week was the longest week of my life. I went into full-blown cold turkey. No sleep at all, the sweats and then the shivers. Pains all over my body, agitated, anxious and feeling really depressed. I wouldn't wish heroin withdrawal on anyone, but here, 6,000 miles away from home and cut off from a supply, I knew that this was the only way of giving myself a chance. Some phone calls were made as my parents knew I was going to need professional help. This was way out of their hands and thankfully they got hold of someone who was willing to come and see me. A woman came over and she immediately knew that I was withdrawing from heroin. She was an English woman and a former user herself, but she had straightened herself out many years previously. She was now a counsellor, and after a consultation she suggested that I should go into a rehab facility that was doing amazing work for people such as myself. I had nothing to lose and I just wanted to get well. Going into rehab was going to cost and, as I had no money, my Dad was willing to pay for my treatment. I'd been in Cape Town for just over a week and I felt really ill, but after some quick arrangements I was driven the 1½-hour journey to a rehab centre right on the coast called STEPPING STONES. I bid farewell to my Dad and step mum and said I'd ring them as soon as I was allowed to. I was now entering a primary care rehabilitation facility for people with addiction problems, and this would be my home for the next 28 days. The first week of being in rehab and I was still going through intense withdrawals. I was helped with this through being given a heroin substitute not unlike methadone to help me with the withdrawal. I was given this daily, with it being reduced slowly just so that I could cope. After five days I had to finish off the rest of the cold turkey raw. I still wasn't sleeping and that was one of the hardest things to deal with. Insomnia and involuntary leg movements made the nights go very slowly. It almost sent me insane. I was initiated straight into the community in there and at first it was quite daunting and I felt a little disorientated, but everybody was very kind to me. I was a bit of an oddity, due to the fact I was from England. I was given the lowdown of how things worked and basically as soon as I was fit and able, as I was slowly coming to be, I would join the programme, as it was called. This being a structure to every day, and strict rules and guidelines that one had to adhere to. Group sessions would start every day after breakfast and would go on all day until just before teatime, whereby the rest of the evening was spent as free time. I started smoking cigarettes, as everything can be quite intense and raw. There's a lot of people dealing with their own shit and so fag breaks were always a welcome relief after an intensive group session. I slowly started to come round, whereby the withdrawals started to subside, and I started to get little bits of sleep. After nearly two weeks, and aside from a brief spell of sobriety when I was in prison, my body was free of drugs for the first time in seventeen years. My faculties were returning whereby I could start to concentrate for periods of time and take in what was going on around me. As a junkie I can't recall having an outlook, so to speak. I very much just remember possessing a tunnel vision-type way of viewing the world around me. Now that I was drug free the world I saw around me started to open up. For instance, as much as it sounds slightly barmy, hearing birds sing sounded new to me. The truth of the matter is that I'd been numbing everything with drugs for years and now that the drugs were gone everything became magnified and my emotions were raw. I was in the right place though, a safe place for me to get to grips with what was going on. I was introduced to what is known as the *12-STEP PROGRAMME* and the NARCOTICS ANONYMOUS programme of recovery. When I was deemed to be ready and able, I started to attend NA meetings, whereby along with everyone else we were picked up from the faculty and taken in vans to meetings that were quite local in and around the area. It was at these meetings that I would introduce myself as an addict. Along with written work that I was given and this new daily program, I knew that it required 100 per cent commitment from myself if I were going to succeed in what was being put to me as a new way of life. I started to see a little bit of light at the end of the tunnel.

For as long as I could remember I had tried to be self-reliant about a lot of the things that happened in my life. In rehab one is encouraged to speak or share, and now that I felt free to do so I took every opportunity to do just that. I was getting a whole new education with regards to the kind of person I was and am, and although a lot of it was unpleasant, to be told I was an addict and that it is a disease was a revelation to me. I just thought for years that I was a bad person who was incapable of being a good person. Now, for those of you who see this as a cop-out, please let me explain. The DISEASE concept comes about from the fact that, in my case and many others, I have an allergic reaction to using mood-altering substances. I can't use alcohol or cannabis or anything successfully like you can. I have an addictive personality and drugs are a symptom of that personality. In short, addiction is incurable, it's progressive and can even be fatal. The only way for a person such as myself to live is to put down drink and drugs altogether. In other words, totally abstinent, and to do this one day at a time. As much as having this information put to me came as a relief it didn't, however, excuse me from the behaviour and the things I had done in order to obtain drugs. Counsellors offered words of wisdom and came out with some great one-liners. 'I am not responsible for my disease, but I am accountable for my actions' was just one. By the time of my third week in rehab my body was clean of all toxins and my head was clearing. I was working the program that was being put to me. I was instructed to work the twelve-step programme, a programme that would, if I worked it, help me stay clean and sober and enable me to have a new way of life without the use of drugs. I met some great people in Stepping Stones, and as my time progressed I came to realise what a golden opportunity I'd been gifted. A chance to do something I'd never been able to do before, to actually live a life free from active addiction. Whilst in there I was constantly being assessed by counsellors who were all recovering addicts themselves. The core of my problems ran really deep and it was put to me and my father that 28 days just wasn't going to be a long enough period of time with which to send me back out into the everyday world. An extended course of treatment whereby I could carry on doing recovery-based stuff under the guidance of other counsellors was put to me. I agreed, and so when my 28 days was up at Stepping Stones, I left there and went straight to another facility in the heart of Cape Town.

This is called 'secondary care' and I would stay here for two months. I would carry on where I left off at Stepping Stones. There was a somewhat different aspect to this new place. This was a large house whereby up to fifteen to twenty recovering addicts lived together, cooked together, maintained together, attended meetings together and learned how to live back in society drug-free. Having picked up the tools that I'd been given whilst in treatment, I did everything that was expected of me, reluctantly at times, but with professional people overseeing and monitoring everything, cutting corners wasn't an option. More written work, especially regarding the twelve steps and daily group meetings, were the norm, albeit sometimes with a somewhat different approach than in primary care. I would have one-to-one sessions with the counsellors who really helped me. Living in such close proximity of each other under one roof, I soon got to know all of the other residents and also their own unique personalities, male and female. Fraternising was a big no-no in there as this was considered as a huge obstacle towards a person's recovery and could lead to a relapse. Totally understandable of course, but that doesn't mean it didn't happen. Natural urges return after years of abuse, and in there it was no different. The counsellors were constantly watching for this and if anything started to happen, or there was evidence to suggest that something was happening, it would be stamped on straightaway. If two people were found to have had sexual relations then they could be asked to leave the house with immediate effect. I got into trouble a couple of times but, to be perfectly honest, I wasn't going to jeopardise my place in the house over what I saw was a bit of harmless flirting. The counsellors didn't quite see it that way and when it was put to me that people's recovery was at stake, I complied straight away with the 'no fraternising' rule. This facility also acted as a halfway house whereby, when it was deemed appropriate for me to do so, I could actually apply for a job. It would act as a final step towards re-entering society and becoming an active member of the community. Well, I had a trade as a barber, and so after being in secondary care for just over a month I applied for a job in a huge American-style shopping mall. I couldn't believe my luck and I got the job working in a plush new salon. Now my days were fuller than ever. I went to work during the day and then returned back to the house in the late afternoon, and then attended meetings every night of the week. At work I wasn't overly busy, but it was a slow initiation back into a workplace existence whilst still working on my early recovery. I was starting to get my strength back and I started to look the healthiest I'd looked in years. I was also making new friends, all of which were in recovery like myself. My life was turning right round and I was enjoying myself. I wasn't making loads of money but it didn't matter. I was clean and sober. I completed my two-month stay in secondary care, and with the 28 days in primary care included I'd now had three months of rehab treatment, paid for by my South African parents. I was very grateful for a couple of reasons. My old man had been there for me right when I really needed it and it went a long way to cementing our relationship after years of bitterness on my part for him leaving us all those years back. After I came out of rehab I went back and lived with my Dad and his wife and we did a lot of talking and bonding, and I got to hear his side of things. Secondly, if it wasn't for the fact that I'd had the opportunity to go to South Africa and get myself right out of the chaotic life I was living, I doubt at all whether I could have got myself clean and back on track. I developed some good friendships in Cape Town and in between working and attending meetings I had some great times. Going to beach parties, swimming in the sea, going for coffee with other recovering addicts and enjoying a little bit of the South African way of life. Relationships were still a no-go area, but I have to admit that I was a naughty boy, and to quell my overpowering urges, on three separate occasions I visited a brothel in Cape Town. In my eyes, women of colour are just as appealing as white women and besides, I didn't feel guilty, it was sex. I was feeling healthy again and it had been some time since I'd been intimate with anyone. Throughout my time in Africa I maintained a steady line of communication with my daughter through her mother and also my mum and brother, and after nine months I decided that it was time to come back to England. I had a few primary objectives on returning to England. To get involved with Narcotics Anonymous and to carry on working on my recovery. To seek full-time employment so that I could be there for Jade and have a proper father-daughter relationship. And finally, I was eager to start playing again, only this time doing it clean and sober. In May 2000 I returned to England. My future was unknown but I had every intention of keeping my life on track.

Mum, Stoo and James 1971.

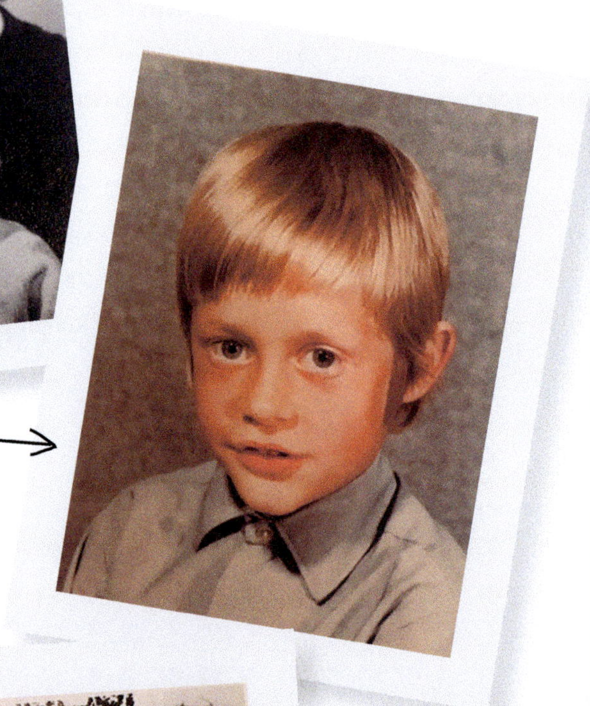

Five years old and a look as if butter wouldn't melt in my mouth.

Little drummer boy. Can you recognise which one's me?

With my Grandad. Doing it properly and realising that I was actually quite good.

I wanted to be part of a gang. I found punk rock.

At an early English Dogs gig in Grantham with drummer Pinch.

THE COSMIC SPACE TOADS. Notice Wakey, ex-English Dogs on the far right.

Playing with THE TOADS at the local Guildhall in 1987. Check out my T-shirt.

My Dad, who without knowing it would have made a good drummer. Taking the piss with a pair of sticks and a Resistance 77 shirt on.

Reading rock festival 1990, a drug-dealing white Rasta. King for a day, fool for a lifetime.

With my daughter JADE RAMONA. A brief ray of sunshine amid the chaotic existence I was living at the time.

PART 2.

1. CAN ANARCHISM AND CAPITALISM MAKE GOOD BEDFELLOWS?

I returned back to England and I was pleased to be back. My Mum and stepdad offered to put me up whilst I got myself on my feet. Within a week I'd found two NA meetings a week to attend. This would keep me in touch with my sobriety and help me build my associations with other addicts who were actively staying clean. Seeing my daughter for the first time in nearly a year was a great reward. My brother James had his own barbershop and he kindly let me work there for a short period, enabling me to earn a few quid. Before I'd gone out to Cape Town, just under a year before, I'd been meeting up with a couple of lads with a view to playing some music. I got straight back in touch with them and within a short space of time we got back together. Nothing was changing with regard to what direction to take musically. It was going to be loud, heavy and probably quite fast. With a renewed sense of purpose I got stuck in with my new way of life back in England. Working with my brother was never going to be a long-term prospect and so, after borrowing some money from my folks, I'd come up with the idea of opening my own barbershop. I found a shop to rent, and with a budget that I had I got everything in place with a view to opening up as soon as I could. Throwing myself back into anything musical, I attended for the first time what was originally known as the HOLIDAYS IN THE SUN punk festival, only now in 2000 it went under the banner of the WASTED festival. I went to Morecambe with a mate and we had a really good time. It was good to see some of the bands I'd never got the chance to see back in the day. I also remember on 31 July going to see a band called THE VANDALS in Nottingham at an all-dayer. I remember that date because the next day, on 1 August, I opened my new shop for the very first time. Everything was falling into place and, to top it all off, the music that I was writing with my two mates was taking shape. We were definitely a hardcore punk band and with that we decided to call ourselves SKWERM. These two lads, ANDY and DAN, were very laid-back chaps indeed and they were considerably younger than me, but they were both avid music lovers and we were certainly kicking up a stink with this heavy music we were practising. We started to do a few gigs in and around the town and ventured into Nottingham on a couple of occasions. Since being back from Africa I'd had a couple of dalliances with a couple of females. Nothing serious, but it was around this time that I met a woman who I would end up having a six-year relationship with. REBECCA was her name and for me she would be the first woman I'd ever been in a relationship with clean and sober. I was still officially living with my parents but was spending more and more time at her place. She had two kids but that didn't bother me. Being of a certain age, 34 at the time, most women of a similar age had littluns anyway. Within a few months she asked me to move in and a short while later I did. When I'd decided to start my own business I was financially limited with regard to how the place looked. I'd used the loan money to get myself up and running and slowly, through focused commitment, the business started to take off and for the first time ever, I was in a position to start paying off my loan, make the shop look that little bit more professional whilst also putting away some savings every week.

It was around this time that a slightly different aspect of my addictive nature showed itself and It had nothing to do with my former destructive patterns of behaviour. I'd always been an avid record collector and thankfully that collection is still nestled away in a room in my house today. I'd read an article in a record collector magazine about my favourite band, THE SEX PISTOLS, and the interest was not only in their records but the memorabilia surrounding them. Posters, tickets, banners, flyers. Anything to do with them was now becoming highly collectable. I found a contact for a guy in the back of the magazine who happened to live not far from me. He had stuff for sale so I got in touch with him with a view to meeting up, and probably procuring an item or two. Now, I've always loved posters and as I started to delve deeper, I knew that the PISTOLS had had a full-on graphic designer man behind them in the shape of JAMIE REID, but I didn't realise how much different stuff of theirs was out there. I went and met this guy and after spending some time at his and parting with a few hundred quid, I'd just entered into a new chapter of collecting. I came away with a couple of rare posters, both from the late seventies, and a few records. I definitely got a buzz purchasing this stuff but knew that it wasn't going to mess with my personal health. In fact, if my predictions were correct, I'd just made myself an investment. With the PISTOLS being such an iconic band, I could only see this stuff going up in value as long as I got it for a good price first.

I got to one year clean and sober and then I got to eighteen months. My recovery was going well and I was attending meetings regularly, and because my recovery was running smoothly, that meant for the most part everything else ran smoothly too. The lads and I from SKWERM went and recorded some of our songs, which came out rather well. We got them printed onto CDs and soon sold or distributed them to people who'd appreciate them. I did, however, end up clashing with one of them over their laid-back attitude. I was being a bit full-on, to be fair, as I just wanted to get things done. In short, I was being pushy as I felt that I'd wasted enough time fucking about in the past. There was no major fall out or anything, but I lost my rag and basically said that I couldn't be arsed if he couldn't be arsed, so that was the end of that. Help was at hand for me though, because no sooner had I jacked SKWERM in than I got a call from an old mate who'd moved to Nottingham, telling me of a band that needed a drummer. The name of that band was POUNDAFLESH and they were a five-piece hardcore band from that area. This sounded good to me as I'd now grown tired of playing in small-town bands. This was a refreshing change. To be part of something in the city was just what I wanted. I knew that I'd got something to offer to the right people and so with that I arranged to meet up with them in the hope that I could get out there and play to a bit more of a wider audience. I met them at Nottingham train station. SEAN the vocalist and MARK the guitarist, who looked a quite imposing couple of brutes, picked me up and we went off to their practice room. I'd been sent some songs beforehand and worked them out, and after we'd had a good couple of hours working on them, they seemed most pleased with what I had brought to the table. I was in. The music was very fast and very heavy and I liked it. Like myself, these lads had all played in bands before and they'd got some gigging experience under their belts. They knew what they wanted to do and had loads in the pipeline with regards gigging, touring and recording. On the home front, my business was growing in stature with each passing week, and I was working hard to keep the momentum going! I'd set the place up for it to be able to cater for another two workers as well as myself, and before too long I was going to need somebody to come on board to help the business fulfil its potential. I was putting cash aside each week and eventually I was able to give the shop a decent makeover that pretty much had my stamp all over it. For a start, I changed the colour scheme on the outside to red and black, my favourite colours. And on the inside punk rock posters adorned the walls. It gave the place a retro and unique feel, and for the first time ever, at the grand old age of 35, I was really happy being a self-employed person. This place was mine, and if I gave it the care and attention it required I could have myself a decent living without having to go back to some of my old ways of getting cash. To be honest, I was never going to be able to work for somebody else, I just didn't have it in me. I could never be told what to do and I tried factory work a couple of times when I was younger and walked out after only a couple of hours. I have to thank my brother JAMES here because if it wasn't for him I definitely wouldn't have taken this route of employment as an option. Earning some decent dosh allowed me to delve deeper into the collecting of PISTOLS memorabilia too. I started making sporadic visits to my mate up the road and every time I came back I had some more booty with me. Amazing artefacts from the band's heyday. Promo posters for *God Save The Queen, Anarchy In The UK, Pretty Vacant* and *Holidays In The Sun.* I was a right SID buff, so getting the promo posters for his singles was a delight. A lot of this stuff would end up on the walls of my shop. Mum reckoned that that kind of stuff would scare off my customers, but that wasn't the case at all. In fact, the customers seem to love that kind of thing. Mainly because it's a bit different from the usual shit you see in a barber's shop.

In 2002 I got myself to two years clean. Quite an achievement when one considers that my former life entailed using every day. I put my success here down to the regular meeting attendance and constant contact with other recovering addicts, that kept me topped up with positive input and healthy feedback from others who were in pursuit of the same thing as myself. The shop was going well and I was now able to afford a motor for the first time in years. On the home front, I was happy in my relationship and had also gone a long way to having restored some faith back from my family. I was going over to Nottingham on Sundays rehearsing with POUNDAFLESH and as a band we were making great progress, a real powerful unit. In wasn't long before we started gigging and for a start that was mainly in the Nottingham and Derby area. I immediately felt in my element as I was meeting and playing to people I'd never seen or met before.

The band and its followers were well and truly embroiled in the punk rock scene and that's just what we wanted. A lot of people would say that going back into such an environment, with all its temptations and the like, I was putting myself at risk, and yes there is some truth to that, but to be perfectly honest at the time I was too busy enjoying myself and had my eyes firmly on staying clean and sober. Booze was everywhere but I built up a mindset whereby it was almost invisible to me. One of the band was using speed, but again, it didn't bother me. For me, playing a good gig and people commending me on my drumming or expressing how good we were was all I needed. That was my new buzz. Through my returning to Derby to do gigs, which often took place at the Vic Inn, which has sadly now turned into a posh restaurant, I met up with my old mate Jim who I'd played with a few years earlier in KILLING FOR COMPANY. It was good to hook up with him again and he expressed his desire of getting a new band together.

On further discussion we decided to give it a go. Jim knew a vocalist and a bass player and so with that we started practising at the same rehearsal rooms as POUNDAFLESH. We'd be playing punk rock but this would be a completely different style to what I was playing in my other band, POUNDAFLESH, who, as I've mentioned, were a hardcore band. This new project would be somewhat slower and some would say a lot more tuneful, and lyrically completely different. Whereas the hardcore band dealt with serious issues, this new outfit was all about getting pissed and taking the piss out of anyone and everything. So there was quite a lot of humour involved. I was all up for that, and besides, I liked the idea of playing something different to what I was already doing. The name CHIMP BISCUIT was decided upon and so another night of the week was taken up with rehearsing and getting a set of songs together. I was setting a new standard for myself here that has pretty much remained ever since.

From here on in I would always be involved with more than one band at a time. It might be something to do with there being a lack of drummers, but for me it's about not getting bored with just doing one thing. I'm adept at remembering the songs and I've found that I can step from one style into another, although I don't think that it's too difficult anyway. It's all just a slight variation on a different theme. POUNDAFLESH were out and about and soon started to get noticed in the area. Some gigs were arranged abroad, which was great. I'd been wanting to do this years ago and now here was a golden opportunity. Thankfully I'd got somebody working in the shop with me by then and so that freed me up to go on tour. Before that though, we managed to find a recording studio run by a guy called KARL and he called his place ZOO STUDIOS. We went in there and recorded five of the first songs we got together and immediately put them on CD. We called the EP OBSCENE DISPLAY after one of the song titles, and sold them to followers of the band ourselves.

2. HEADS DOWN, NO NONSENSE, MINDLESS BOOGIE

For our first tour and In keeping with the DIY spirit of things we'd be taking all of our own gear in the van. It would be hard work but I didn't mind. I was up for it, no matter what. As I remember it we played in Hengelo, Groningen, Amsterdam in Holland; Berlin, Hanover, Hamburg in West Germany; Chemnitz and Leipzig in the East, and Liège in Belgium. Amsterdam was a bastard as I'd always wanted to go there when I had been using, so it was a real test for me now that I was straight. We couldn't go there and not look around the place, and it was definitely an eye-opener. I got offered hashish and cocaine as we ventured around the red light district. Thankfully I didn't succumb, but as I say it was a test and I was quite glad to get out of there. The festival that we played in Leipzig was by far the best gig. A lot of venues in Europe, especially in Germany and Holland, are former squats so believe me when I say that they aren't the cleanest of places. And they certainly look different by day than they do by night. In Groningen we played at an old hospital and people were actually living in the place. In Berlin we played at a famous squat called THE KOPI and as much as the gig was bang on, where we had to sleep that night, just above the venue, will probably go down as the filthiest place I have ever had to rest my head. As I say, the Leipzig festival was brilliant, and not just for the music but the different array of people there. On entering the venue I remember greeting these two blokes who to me looked like typical thrash metallers. They had the distinctive long black hair and they were worse the wear for drink and a tad dishevelled. It turns out these two gents were from Chile and, as much as we couldn't understand each other, they were really friendly. Well, all the bands were allocated bunk beds that had been made in dormitory-like rooms. My enduring memory of these two Chileans was on the morning after the gig we'd got ourselves up and ready to leave for our next port of call when there was a bit of a kerfuffle in the adjacent room. We all went to see what the commotion was, to be confronted with the two Chilean lads spit-roasting a very young lady on one of the top bunks. All three of them knew we were there but they didn't give a fuck and just got on with what they were doing. Very funny indeed.

I was hitting a peak with my playing and I prided myself on being as tight and on the ball as possible. As a hardcore band, POUNDAFLESH were very good. There was one weak link though, and that was FLIPPER, the lead guitarist. He was a great player but he had a speed problem which made him become somewhat unpredictable. He snapped at me one night towards the end of our time over there and I put it down to him coming down and a lack of sleep. I let it lie as he was a bandmate and these things happen. I was angry about it but I forgave and forgot about it. With regards completing the tour and not succumbing to any temptations on the road, I felt that I'd scored a major victory. I came back from the tour absolutely knackered, but I hadn't dropped my guard once. I hadn't used anything and I'd proved to myself that I could do it. I was still clean and sober. As soon as we got back to England we hit the ground running and within a short space of time we entered Zoo studios once again to record another five-track EP. We were going from strength to strength and the quality of the songs and the recordings were getting better and better. As well as the five tracks of our own, and as an added bonus on the CD version, we recorded a cover of the song *Decontrol* by DISCHARGE, which came out really good. The EP went out under the title CRY FROM THE PEOPLE, another song title, and we even went as far as getting four of the tracks printed on limited edition vinyl via a French independent label. A collector's item for hardcore record collectors here. Also the gigs we were getting were on the up. First we played gigs in the UK supporting one of our favourite bands from Portland in Oregon, POISON IDEA, in Sheffield, and a fantastic gig in Derby which brought me back in touch for the first time in years with my old mate Wakey. We supported THE WERN'T, who for you people not in the know, consisted of Pinch and Wakey from the ENGLISH DOGS and JOCK and ROSS from GBH. POUNDAFLESH were absolutely blistering on this night, as were THE WERN'T. I happened to spot another familiar face in the audience that night too. No other than JOHN MURRAY, the ex-guitarist from the ENGLISH DOGS. We spoke to each other briefly and through seeing the two ex-ENGLISH DOGS members that night a seed was sown that would flower a couple of years down the line. We'll get to that later. We also supported The SUBS and GBH on separate occasions. Also, during this period we went back into the studio to record another five-track CD which ended up being an absolute corker. The crafting of the songs was gaining momentum all of the time and that showed on the new recordings. Sadly we had a major setback when Mark, the guitarist who had founded the band, went down with a major health issue. Thankfully, and mainly for his own benefit, Mark made a recovery and we got back to business as usual. Another trip across the pond was in the making. Now I did have reservations as my business was still in its early days and I didn't want to jeopardise or neglect it in any way. But I managed to get myself covered for the tour. We went for a week once again taking in Holland, Germany and Belgium but also including a gig in Zurich, Switzerland. The tour went well and once again I really enjoyed it. Aside from Mark's unavoidable health problems the band really were on a roll again and I was looking forward to what might lie ahead. The main highlights of that year for me were playing at the WASTED festival in Morecambe for the first time ever. I'd also been rehearsing hard and had started gigging with the side project with my mate Jim from Derby. Going out as CHIMP BISCUIT, we played a few of the same venues that I had been treading the boards at that time. This outfit was a completely different entity and our sole aim was to just have a laugh. Not that being in POUNDAFLESH wasn't without its fun, but in all honesty the dynamics and the different personalities were totally different. That aside, we still took playing our music very seriously. We were doing quite a few pub gigs and they were always good fun. We supported THE VIBRATORS in Mansfield and we also played there again with GARY BUSHELL'S band THE GONADS. I can just remember them being absolutely terrible. We got ourselves into a recording studio on three occasions, as I remember. Fantastic comedy punk, ripping the shit out of everyone and everything. Songs about reruns on telly, songs about dead rock stars, songs about drinking Stella Artois and songs about one's gran being in the Taliban. You get the picture. One night in the week, it would most probably have been a Wednesday evening, as I was on my way to an NA meeting, out of the blue I got a text message from Jason, the singer of CHIMP BISCUIT, telling me that I'd been kicked out of POUNDAFLESH. All of a sudden I'm feeling very confused so I ring him up and, lo and behold, it's gone out on social media. Bearing in mind that Facebook hadn't even been started by then, and people used Myspace, I wasn't savvy with regard to these communication platforms. No fucker had rung me or contacted me. And to find out this way I thought was pretty fucking low. At that time the band meant everything to me and I was very upset about it. The fact that no one had communicated with me made it worse. Now, I am rather a sensitive person and unfortunately for me, as sad as it sounds, it brought up feelings that I thought I'd dealt with. Feelings of abandonment and rejection, and to be perfectly honest I didn't handle it well at all.

I did get hold of Mark, the poorly guitarist, and it transpired that the band felt that I was holding them back from doing all of the things that they needed to do. I had stated that I was partially limited with regard to all commitments due to my ongoing business responsibilities, and so with that in mind they decided to get this other guy in on drums. Also Mark's health issues were a lot more serious than any of us had realised and he was wanting to do as much as he could, whilst he could. For me, it would have been nice to have been spoken to first. Like I say, it did hurt. Not a word from one of the others until a few years later. In my book that's called 'cowardice'. Anyway, I had to just brush myself down and crack on. So that's what I did.

We've all heard the saying 'You never know what's round the corner'. Well, that was definitely true for me at this point. I was really pleased with myself as I'd just got to three years clean. My business was doing well and I was very happy with my homelife. An associate from town got in touch telling me that this certain band were looking for a drummer. Well, I was all ears, especially taking into consideration that I'd just been dropped. That band was called RESISTANCE 77 and I was immediately stoked as I can remember discovering them when I was about eighteen or nineteen and I liked what I had heard. They still sounded like a seventies punk band but in the eighties, and I was immediately drawn to them. I love the eighties stuff, but if it wasn't for the late seventies punk style there wouldn't have been an eighties style. I emailed the address that I had been given and it turned out that it was KIERON EGAN I was speaking to. After exchanging details, and being given a list of songs to learn, arrangements were made for me to go over to their neck of the woods for a rehearsal. I knew what I was capable of and relished the idea of playing for them as their style was right up my street. I just had to go along and hopefully they'd be impressed enough to take me on board. The band were based in the Derbyshire area and they had their rehearsal space in Alfreton, about a good hour's drive from my place. So, I met ODDY/vocals, Kieron/bass guitar and ELLIS/guitar, and after getting set up we ran through some of the songs I had been asked to learn, and it went brilliantly. These lads took their music seriously. Kieron and Oddy were founder members and Ellis was the new boy on the block, and he was an absolute whizz kid on guitar and they were lucky to have him. We all got on great and arrangements were made to meet the next week and the week after that. I was in. But first there was the topic of the drummer I was replacing. He was still in the band but had given them notice that he was quitting, hence the drafting in of me. They had got a gig at the Rock City venue in Nottingham and this was to be his last gig, and after that I would be taking over. I was invited to the gig just to get the idea of how they did things live, and besides, I was eager also to see how this guy did things. I got to Rock City an hour or so before they came on and got to meeting the soon-to-be-ex-drummer outside with Ellis the guitarist. They were sharing a pint and at first this old boy didn't seem to be too bad, but then out of the blue the conversation changed and he made some comments and expressed some views that I was completely opposed to. His comments completely surprised me and in a second I had made up my mind that this geezer wasn't the type of person I would associate with for long. We moved on and went into the venue and I needed to just get something straight with the others. I told them all what I'd heard and I was glad when they all expressed the same opinion as myself with regards the radical views he had. And, in so many words I was told that they were glad he was leaving as it didn't fit in with their agenda either. I was relieved to hear it and with that he played his last gig and from then on I was the new and permanent drummer for RESISTANCE 77. And so for the next month or so, and after a lot of rehearsing, I played my debut gig with the band at THE BOARDWALK venue in Sheffield. I was quite chuffed as this place back in the seventies was called THE BLACK SWAN and it was where the SEX PISTOLS played, supported by THE CLASH. At last I was playing in a decent punk band who had their own audience and the fact that they were damn fine people made it all the better. The prospects looked good with plenty of gigs to look forward to and there was talk of recording an album in the future, which enthused me even more. Just for the record, in 1980 the band formed and called themselves the ANTI-HEROES but what with the influx of new punk bands back then, a lot of which had Anti in them (e.g. ANTI PASTI, ANTI NOWHERE LEAGUE), they decided to call themselves RESISTANCE 77 instead. They were resisting the urge to sound like the heavier eighties bands that were coming through and were tying their allegiance firmly to the mast of the 77-style bands. The name was firmly acquainted still with wanting to sound like a first wave punk band and nothing else. At the same time as doing this I was still involved with my mate Jim and CHIMP BISCUIT, albeit on not such quite a busy level. But I was enjoying the two.

3. A SLIP IS NOT A SLIP. IT'S A RELAPSE

Something out of the blue occurred about this time which gives credence to my comments about 'not knowing what's around the corner'. Everything was going really well in all areas of my life: work was good, music was good and I was very happy in my relationship, but something must have been amiss because I didn't even see what happened coming. It was Christmas Eve 2004 and I'd had a really busy run up to Christmas in the shop. Gigging had been quiet as it often is round that time of year, which enabled me to be at the shop when I needed to be most. Being in the barbering trade one gets to meet people from all walks of life. And for as much as I knew a lot of respectable, and without sounding clichéd, normal people, I still knew a few reprobates, so to speak. By that I mean people that were drug users and by the same token, I don't mean casual users. Out of my hometown, coming into contact with those kind of people was almost non-existent in the punk scene. In Grantham though, I've got a past, and sometimes mud sticks. Now I'd been clean, and I mean totally clean, for three and a quarter years and was intent on keeping that going. One of my last customers of the day came in and I knew him as a likeable rogue, and I just treated him like any other customer. Well, he was under the influence of speed, wasn't he? The longer he was in the shop the more unnerved I was becoming as he was talking about it. He applied some product to his hair and asked if he could wash his hands in the back of the shop. He did that and as he came through to the front he informed me that he had left something in the back for me. I took his money for his haircut and he cleared off. I went off into the back and he'd left an open Rizla paper with an amount of speed on it. Well, this took me back. I was on my own, I'd had a good day and I had a wallet full of cash and was feeling good about myself. With no hesitation whatsoever I wrapped the gear up in the Rizla and bombed it down my neck. I'd just relapsed. Fuck. I actually really enjoyed my evening after taking speed again. But for as much as I had enjoyed the short-term buzz, I knew that I had let myself down big time. What had happened? What had shifted? Looking back I can now see what happened. I'd become complacent and I'd taken my eyes off the ball. I'd become a little too comfortable and forgotten that my primary purpose was not to take that first drug. What was done was done and I'd just blown three years and three months of sobriety time, to end up back on day one. I felt guilty, and with that came feelings of shame, too. But I had no time to mope about. I had a lot going on. I had a woman and two kids to think about as well as my own daughter, the shop and the bands. So I just got on with doing what I needed to do and carried on as if nothing had happened. What I should have done, but didn't do, was go straight back to Narcotics Anonymous and admit to my slip and get the help and support that I'd received in the past. I needed to get back on track, and I did attend some meetings with all of the above in mind, but the disease was on me, and this again is not a cop-out and it happened really quickly. In a short space of time the wheels of my recovery completely derailed and I was using again just as frenetically as I had in the past. I was in a very strange position as now I had money, I had a decent car and I wore clean and decent clothes. But here I was back again in scuzzy places with their scuzzy smells, visiting dodgy people to score drugs. At first I was smoking a little bit of hash but I was soon returning to some of my old acquaintances that I'd known when I was using heroin, and I started scoring that shit again. Smoking it at first but eventually returning to the needle. As if that wasn't bad enough, I got involved with a drug that I thought I never would and that had never crossed my path. That was crack cocaine. I remember smoking it for the first time and oh my God, the rush was unbelievable. Only thing is, the rush subsides very quickly after only two to three minutes and I felt the need for more. The first hit is always the best and so subsequently one can never quite get the same high after repeated hits, and that's why it is so moreish. And it's not cheap either. This all happened within the space of a two to six-week period and I needed to get on top of this before it got any more out of hand, as if it wasn't out of hand already. Everything I've been working for was in jeopardy because I now had the unhealthiest distraction to contend with whilst trying to keep all the good things in my life going smoothly. Firstly my relationship started to suffer as my lady had no experience at all when it came to drug abuse and it hadn't gone unnoticed to her that my behaviour was changing.

I'd started smoking crack on the way to band rehearsals, which entailed me stopping on the way, parking out of sight and doing the business. It all became a nightmare once again. Having to score and then use. Lying about where I was and then going home to my family set-up and trying to act as if nothing was wrong. It was horrible. I'd got myself a heroin habit again and the cracks were starting to appear. I had lost control and once again I was in active addiction. I'd saved up quite a bit of cash, so knowing there was no other alternative I decided to go back to the rehab I'd been to in South Africa to detox myself. Rehabs in England were mega expensive, thus the option to go to South Africa, which was a lot cheaper but with the treatment being just as good, if not better. Being a junkie is a full-time occupation and I'd had enough. So I shut my shop for three weeks, got in touch with the rehab who knew me from the past, informed my Dad about what was going on and flew back to South Africa. My lady was most upset but this had to be done. I didn't tell any of my bandmates. I pretty much just went AWOL. I emailed them once I'd got there and had a few days detoxing, and informed them that I'd be back soon. I spent seventeen days in rehab and came out pretty much fully detoxed. I was still feeling a bit raw though, and after spending a few days with my South African parents I thanked them and returned back to England. It was good to get back and home back to work, and back to playing with my bands. The lads all took it on the chin, especially the RESISTANCE 77 boys who were, and have always been, a strong source of support to me. I also got straight back to my regular NA meetings in Nottingham and back into the swing of things. Opportunities with RESISTANCE 77 started to come in. My days with CHIMP BISCUIT had come to an end after we'd recorded a not so good demo just before I left for rehab. I felt like I'd done my bit and was for the time being wanting to focus on RESISTANCE 77 as there was talk of writing and recording the new album. This would take up a lot of my time and so I packed that in but I still kept in touch with my old mate Jim.

For now I had plenty of gigs to do in the UK and then we were handed a golden nugget. We were invited to go out to the former Czech Republic to play at a large three-day punk festival called ANTI FEST. This promised to be good, with bands such as PETER AND THE TEST TUBE BABIES, ONE WAY SYSTEM, VIBRATORS, 999, GOLDBLADE plus a slew of bands I'd never heard of before on the bill. This was the kind of gig I'd been wanting to do for years. We flew out there and the organisers picked us up, and it just so happened that we were to be travelling to the gig with THE LURKERS on board. That was where I was first introduced to a great bloke who would become an important part of my story, although at that time neither of us were any the wiser. Original LURKER, ARTURO BASSICK and his mates DAVE and NELLY travelled with us in the punk mobile and Arturo, being the full-on raconteur that he is, regaled us with tales of being involved with punk rock right back in its salad days. Fascinating stuff, and a pleasure to hear from someone who was there in London when punk kicked off. We got to the festival site and it was huge. It was then that I realised for the first time that punk rock was still a big deal in the Eastern Bloc countries. I'd played at the dome venue with POUNDAFLESH at the Wasted festival in Morecambe but this was a totally different ball game. A massive stage with a big drum riser and just open space with a large crowd to play to. This I liked and come showtime I was really stoked. To be honest the anticipation and nerves were almost like a drug high without the drugs. It was August so it was hot as hell out there, and when we went out onto the stage we had a few thousand people waiting to greet us. We kicked off and for the next 45 minutes I was in heaven. I loved it. To finally play to a large, frenzied audience definitely makes for a better experience as a player, especially when you've got them dancing to your beat. I was buzzing for hours after the gig and, while all the others went off and got a bit pissed, I hung about backstage. That was when I met a fellow drummer and someone whose records and drumming I loved - PABLO LA BRITAIN from 999. Another lovely and humble chap who was milling about, but the silly sausage hadn't got his cymbals with him. As a rule I wouldn't lend anybody my cymbals, but at the time I didn't care, and happily lent them to him so that he could do his set. It wouldn't be the last time we shared a stage, as when we got back to England we supported 999 on various occasions and Pablo returned the favour by letting me use his kit when we did. We got back after the Czech Republic gig and began immediately writing new songs for a new record that would be released in the New Year. Writing an album's worth of songs is no easy task and it takes a lot of time and commitment. For me it wasn't a problem to throw myself into it as I'd never done that before. And so, for the next six months, as well as playing a few gigs here and there, every week's rehearsals were donated towards getting the new songs together.

On the home front I had nothing to complain about either. My shop was doing great and I had taken on an apprentice. I'd ended up saving a nice tidy sum of money and it was then that I thought about buying a house. My relationship was in good shape and I'd got some more clean time under my belt. Unfortunately I relapsed again and once more put everything into jeopardy. There was so much at stake but I let the bastard get under my skin once again. I was using smack again as well as crack. I don't mess about, do I? Not just a few drinks or a couple of joints here and there, straight back out there and involving myself with two of the most addictive substances known to man. This just shows the power of the addictive force within me. The amazing thing is that I was managing to function in my day job, and I was still playing to a decent standard. There was something coming up on the horizon though, that gave me a great cause for concern. RESISTANCE 77 had a gig booked in Italy and myself and my lady decided to tie it in with a holiday to South Africa. So, we'd all travel together to Milan and from there Rebecca and I would fly down to Cape Town for a holiday. Now, I'd developed what I thought was a mild habit and we had this trip coming. I needed to make a plan. I managed to procure a heroin substitute in tablet form called SUBUTEX. My lady was in a right state about it but really had no option but to go along with my plan. I bought an amount of this stuff I thought would enable me to do both trips and, thinking that I'd only been using smack again a short period, I imagined there would be no problems. I was wrong. The trip to Italy and the gig went really well. Being cut off from my supply I just downed a couple of Subutex tablets and that seemed to do the job. No withdrawals whatsoever. There is no high with this prescription drug although I didn't get it for that anyway. I knew people who had their own habits and so there's a network of people who mix in those circles that are prescribed this stuff to try and come off. But more often than not, these people sell it to fuck-ups like me just so that they can buy some street smack and get high. Anyway, we flew to Africa and checked into our hotel. We were booked to stay with my South African parents a few days after we arrived. After three or four days I'd finished the last of the pills thinking that I'd be okay now. Again I was wrong. I started to go into withdrawals. I was supposed to be on holiday and here I was 6,000 miles from home with my girlfriend who, bless her, didn't have a clue what was going on inside me. It was baking hot and I felt fucking awful. I cannot put it into words, but I started to really panic. As it got worse and worse I made a decision. I needed to get to a doctor, tell them the truth and see if they could help me out. This was going to cost me but I didn't care. I needed help. I managed to get hold of a doctor's surgery who were willing to see me. On getting the appointment I told the doctor everything, and that I was in South Africa on holiday and that I needed something to tide me over till I got back to England. Thankfully he agreed and gave me a prescription for something that was similar to the pills I'd been taking. It cost me in the region of £120 for the consultation and the prescription. Thankfully, within twenty minutes of taking the dose of medication I started to feel human again. The anxiety, panic and all that goes with opiate withdrawal left me. I was so relieved and so was my woman. We got on with the rest of our holiday with no hiccups whatsoever. We had a really good time under the circumstances and I ended up showing my lady all of the places I'd been to in the past. Beaches, the sights and she got to meet my parents. We flew back to England after two weeks away and I remember getting back into town and I made my excuses and went out and scored as soon as I could. I went back to work in the day and returned to rehearsals with the band. But it was no good. My addiction was progressing once more and within a month or so of being back from holiday I decided to once again book myself, for what would be the last time, into rehab. Once again I told the RESISTANCE 77 boys and things were put on hold. My Mum knew, my Dad knew, my daughter knew and my workmate knew. I flew over to Africa once again and was taken straight to a different rehab than I'd been in twice before. I would stay there for the customary 28 days and hopefully relearn everything I'd forgotten in the past. I went through the usual withdrawal programme whilst under observation. Once I'd started to straighten out I went through the usual group sessions and then going to Narcotics Anonymous meetings every night. Again I made new friends, if only for a short time. I was happy to be there in one way as I was getting help. Although I was concerned at what cost. Never mind the financial cost of flying to South Africa and the cost of the treatment. But the personal cost. I was repeatedly fucking up big-time and it was pissing a lot of people off. I completed my treatment once again and couldn't wait to get back home. I was supposed to be buying a house. I had a business to run and I also had my bandmates to consider. And then there were the people that really relied on me. My folks, my daughter and my partner and her kids. I got back to England safe and sound and, as always, threw myself back into keeping busy.

Early in 2006 I bought a house, which for me was a first. I put down a hefty deposit and thought that investing my money into a property was a good move forward. It was quite a spacious gaff and plenty big enough for my little family setup. As soon as I'd got back from rehab the band immediately reconvened and we worked on the new RESISTANCE 77 album. We composed and rehearsed twelve new songs, a couple that had been done before, and then booked ourselves into Zoo studios in Nuneaton. I recommended the studio after the numerous occasions that I'd been there with POUNDAFLESH. RESISTANCE 77 would cement a bond with the guy from Zoo, and we would use his facilities again and again over the next few years. We were also back to gigging regularly, which meant also appearing at what was now known as the Rebellion Festival. A little-known fact about RESISTANCE 77 and their affiliation with the festival is that, aside from 999, who have appeared at every one of the yearly get-togethers, RESISTANCE 77 have played more than any other band. We went into the studio to record the new album and I was fully prepared. We'd rehearsed extensively and with that I was looking forward to getting to work on it. Now, for you people out there who don't know how the recording process works, let me explain. It's not just a case of going in and the group playing the songs, and an engineer pressing the record and that's it. No, there's a method and as a rule it's always the drums that are recorded first. I'm set up in the main recording room ready to play the song. I have headphones on and the rest of the band are set up in another room. I can hear them through the headphones and they can hear me through theirs. I count the song in as I would always do and from then on we play the track. Now to get the best results I have to play the song perfectly, and while we are doing so it will be recorded. But it is only the drums that will be laid down on their own. If I've done a good enough job, and I'm happy with it, then we move on to the next song, and so forth. This can take hours as drummers very rarely play the same song exactly the same twice. We make mistakes or we speed up or slow down. This is not good enough. It has to be just right, otherwise later on when everything is done, the listener will know that something is not right and that ruins everything. A recorded song has to be treated as if it is a masterpiece. Perfection is key. I know to some people it's only punk rock, but that's not the issue. I always want the song to be the best representation of that song ever. Once all of the drums have been recorded, of which we did twelve, the foundation has then been laid down for the next layers to be included.

Usually that would be the bass, then rhythm guitar, then the lead guitar and finally the main vocals and backing vocals. I was under quite a lot of pressure, what with being the first up to get the drums down. But once I got going I was in my element, and after two days the drums were completed. After that everybody else got on and did their individual parts. The album took weeks and weeks to complete but eventually it was done. We decided to call the album SONGS FOR A NANNY STATE, which pretty much tells the government what we were thinking of them at that time. The album was released on CD only through a label known as CAPTAIN OI! We also sold copies ourselves. As the album was released we started to air some of the new songs at gigs and it soon became apparent that we had written a song that would resonate in certain parts of the punk rock scene all around the world. That song is called *True Punk And Oi Will Never Die*. The song would become an anthem and we would always pretty much end the set with it. The fact that I had written an album with the lads was a proud moment for me, as I'm sure it is for all musically-minded people who get the opportunity to do so. Some great gigs abroad came our way too. We played in Finland, France, Belgium, as well as more gigs in the UK.

It was not long after the album was released that I relapsed again. I just couldn't seem to get a sufficient amount of time under my belt in those days. Deep down, I yearned for the day where I could get a year onwards clean. Funny, isn't it, that I was always surrounded by booze at all the gigs I was doing, but it was never that that drew me back? I had a taste for the hard stuff, and knowing where it always took me, I just couldn't and wouldn't resist the temptation. I was also having problems at home. Let's just say that taking on another woman's children is not an easy thing to do, but I was open-minded enough to know that if you love the woman enough you take on the baggage. I had my baggage too, but in all honesty I was struggling with it and it started to cause friction between myself and my lady. The fact that I'd started using again only made things worse as I was again resorting to the devious tactics that I'd employ when I want to use and don't wish for anyone else to know about it. For a brief period I was injecting heroin again and subsequently soon developed another habit. I was also flirting once more with crack cocaine, but in a vain attempt to curb myself I quit using needles and just smoked heroin and gave up using crack altogether, only to replace it with a drug I'd not used for nearly seven years: speed. 2007 arrived and things could have been worse, but for me things could have also been better. A lot of people can function quite well with a drug problem, and for a time that's what I was doing. Only thing is, with me having such a ravenous addictive streak in me, it was only going to go one way. And that was down. I really needed to get on top of this and I came up with a solution, a solution to put down smack once and for all.

The desire and need to stop fixing heroin came about through another near-death experience. On this particular day I'd been at work with my young apprentice. He'd been making progress and had been doing the job long enough for me to leave him while I nipped out. Unbeknown to him I wanted to score, so I made an excuse and made my way to someone I knew was in possession of some gear. I parked my car in a secluded area and made my way to this guy's place. He let me in and I told him I wanted a tenner's worth. He offered me 20 pounds' worth for 15 pounds. I agreed and asked him if I could have a fix at his place. He agreed and, like a twat, I did it all in one go. I can remember leaving his place, but the next thing I remember is waking up and I was lying on my back with two panic-stricken women bent over me, trying to revive me. I'd made it to my car but had collapsed just as I did so. In short, I had overdosed again. This happened years before and the fact that it had happened again just showed that

I was once again playing a dangerous game. An ambulance was called, and I can remember being put in it. And whilst I came to I was being asked all sorts of questions. I evaded any questioning regarding drugs, although it must have been so obvious. The eyes say it all when someone is under the influence of smack. For one, pupils reduce to a pin-like size. Also the voice drops slightly, and also nodding out can be a symptom that shows that someone is under the influence. I didn't like to get to the nodding out stage, but no doubt it happened to me on plenty of occasions. Sat in that ambulance, and after regaining my composure, I certainly felt really out of it, but amazingly after convincing the medic that I was OK I was allowed to go. I shouldn't have even contemplated going back to work because I was really high but that's what I did, and it didn't go unnoticed to my young apprentice as I was struggling to remain coherent. Let's just say that this was just one close shave too many. If those two women hadn't found me then I could have died there and then on the pavement.

Hence my decision to stop fixing. With a plan in my head to finally come off the gear altogether I had one final dilemma to contend with before I put that into effect. I had a big gig coming up with RESISTANCE 77 at the punk festival known as PUNK AND DISORDERLY in Berlin. For this gig we were required to bring our own guitars and I needed to take my own cymbals. Now, the dilemma I faced was that I was going to be out of the country, which meant I was going to be cut off from gear, and that meant disaster for me. I wasn't prepared to go into Europe to do a gig only to go into withdrawal as soon as I got there. So I hatched a plan. On getting to the Airport at Stansted, Gatwick or Luton, I can't remember which, I'd have to put my cymbals through checkout and they would then go through in the hold and I'd pick them up in Germany when we got through customs. I decided to conceal enough smack and speed to get me through the trip. I had a perfect hiding place for it. My hi-hat clutch had a deep space going right through the middle. If you don't know what one of those is, look it up and you'll see what I mean. I packed the gear in there and applied a lock to my cymbal case. Job done. Looking back I can't believe I was willing to take those risks, but I did. I was putting myself plus the other members of the band in harm's way. But at that time that's what I was willing to do. We got to Berlin, proceeded through customs check and went to collect our instruments without a hitch. Once we got to the hostel where all the bands were staying, thankfully I had my own room, which meant I could sort myself out. Firstly I needed to find some tin foil. I made my way to the nearest corner shop-type place and purchased some. Went back to my hotel, chased the dragon, got a little bit high and then got on with the weekend. We weren't due to play 'til the next day, but after having a spruce-up and getting ourselves ready, we were taken to the venue to suss out the festival. On getting into the venue, which was an old school if I remember correctly, we were handed a load of free drink tokens. The leash was off for me, and so, doing something completely different for me, I decided to get really drunk. I managed to piss away all of my tokens on vodka and orange. My everlasting memory of that night was being able to sit right at the back of the stage and watch THE RUTS up-close and personal. I can't remember the geezer's name who was singing that night, but he did a really good job of singing and sounding like MALCOLM OWEN. To watch PAUL FOX (rip) up-close was an honour. The next night we played our slot and I really enjoyed it. Another big stage with decent monitors and everything done with quality in mind. It was quite apparent in the band that I wasn't firing on all cylinders and a few words were said. Not in a sarcastic or derogatory way, but in a caring manner. I told them that I was struggling but that I would sort it out. We got back to the hostel after the gig and all the gang decided to carry on with the night's festivities. We were all in high spirits when I noticed a young woman buzzing around. She made a beeline for me and she had a friend in tow. We happened to engage in some idle chit chat and before long we were all having a bit of a knees-up. There was quite a lot of flirting going on, and when it came to them leaving one of them gave me her room number. To be honest, with my home life starting to suffer, I was just happy living in that moment and was also quite enjoying the flattery. I never took the woman up on what seemed like quite a pleasant offer.

Having got back to England I put my plan into effect. I went to see my local doctor and admitted that I had a heroin problem and that I needed help. From a personal point of view I wasn't interested in a methadone programme because I don't think it works and, as I have already mentioned, one can still end up being on that stuff for years. I mentioned the option of a Subutex programme. This form of medication is taken in tablet form and the way it works is to stop the user from going into heroin withdrawal, but at the same time if the person uses heroin, it is pointless as it acts as an inhibitor and thus the user does not get high. This could actually work for me as long as I took the medication when I was supposed to take it. I really had had enough of the vicious circle that heroin put me on, and so, after a couple of false starts, I started to really take it seriously. At first I was on a high dose, but as the weeks passed by I would visit my doctor and get repeat prescriptions, but with my dosage being reduced on a weekly basis. It was working. Now Subutex is still an opiate, but the truth of the matter is that I wasn't using street smack anymore, and that is what I wanted.

The subutex wasn't giving me a high and although I would end up having to use the drug to treat my addiction for some time, I'm happy to say that after using Subutex properly and responsibly I did eventually finish the course of treatment and I've never used heroin or opiates since. This was a major victory for me, but my war wasn't over yet. Knowing what I do now, I am the type of addict who has the propensity to get addicted to almost anything that comes my way. Well, I'd started using speed again, and as much as I knew that it wasn't physically addictive like, say, heroin, it definitely started to get a grip on me mentally. For the time being I just got back to business as usual and everything was going along quite steady.

4. IF YOU'RE GOING TO ACT LIKE A DOG, BECOME AN ENGLISH ONE

I was at the shop one day and it was early afternoon when I received an unexpected guest. A guy called John Murray popped in with a proposition. Now the last time I can recall seeing John was at a POUNDAFLESH gig a few years back. It was the night that we supported THE WERN'T. Anyway, he mentioned that he had been speaking to Wakey and that they were wanting to put the ENGLISH DOGS back together. Using Pinch, the original drummer, was out of the question as he was off playing drums with THE DAMNED. To them I was the obvious choice to do the job, and if I said 'Yes' they wanted to crack on straight away. I was quite taken aback and at the same time overjoyed. It seems that my playing hadn't been going unnoticed, and here was another opportunity to do something that I could have only dreamed of a few years back. All we had to do now was find WATTIE the bass player, and if that could be done and he was up for it then the band would be up and running with three out of four of the original line-up. I knew how to get hold of him and so, after a quick telephone call explaining the proposed plan, he was delighted with the prospect and counted himself in.

With everything finalised we found ourselves a practice room on the outskirts of town. The intention was to come back with all of the band's classic songs, i.e. *Max The Millionaire, The Fall Of Max, Psycho Killer* etc. Basically, nearly all of the band's early tracks but with some new ones written and included. Wakey hadn't lived in town for some years and was now still living in a bus with his wife Sally. So with that in mind John, myself and Wattie started rehearsing on a weekly basis. We were all really keen and we soon started to whip some of the old songs into shape. Wakey came and joined us when we gave him the nod that we were ready for him. I remember the first rehearsals and, to be honest, it was a bit chaotic.

Wakey and Sally would turn up in their bus and more often than not Wakey would be nursing a hangover from the night before. Or, if that wasn't the case, he would usually be in one of his outlandish moods, which wasn't a problem as there was always a laugh to be had with that mad cunt around. I was using speed quite regularly again and especially at band practice. So that made me a bit scatty and twitchy. Jon and Wattie were fine, as I remember. It was just a case of us all connecting together as a band, and before long that started to happen. I was loving this as I hadn't seen myself doing this a couple of months before. I had the utmost respect for them all as musical individuals and the fact that we were all together, working on the most popular of their songs, for me was a dream come true. We practised week in, week out with the exception of Wakey who made it up a couple of times a month. When we did know that this was definitely going to happen, word got out and there was a tremendous buzz that went round the town. Word spread to Nottingham, Derby and beyond that the ENGLISH DOGS were going to be doing some gigs very soon. We relearnt all the songs off the band's first EP, MAD PUNX AND ENGLISH DOGS, and a number of the best tracks from the band's debut album, INVASION OF THE PORKY MEN. Funny how things turn out, eh? All those years ago I'd managed to get hold of Wakey's test pressing of the album and now here I was practising the same songs in preparation for some up and coming gigs. Anyway, it was decided that it would be best to come back with the first gig being in Nottingham. THE OLD ANGEL pub had its own venue upstairs and was known for its alignment with the punk scene in Nottingham. Regular gigs were held there and bands from all over the world had passed through its doors. Now, it's not a huge venue but it was deemed just the right place for the band to make themselves known once again.

With the prospect of gigs on the horizon we really knuckled down and worked hard on the set as good as we could. It wasn't a question of half measures here, we wanted to come back and show that the band were just as good and energetic as they used to be. Also, this wasn't going to sound anything like the metal-sounding outfit that appeared in the late eighties. This was punk rock, loud and in your face. We secured a date at The Old Angel and with that, posters and promotion via social media went out. Jon the guitarist was a wizard on a computer and immediately set up an ENGLISH DOGS website, which also created a lot of interest, especially among the diehard fans of the band. The gig itself was absolute chaos, but at the same time most enjoyable.

There were another three or four bands on the bill but the only ones I can recall were F.U.K. (GABBA from CHAOS UK) and SICK ON THE BUS, who were fantastic. The place was absolutely rammed and, in hindsight, a bigger venue would have been more appropriate. Half of the people that turned up couldn't get in, which just added to the chaos. I was speeding, as was Wakey, along with God knows how many others. I distinctly remember it being very hot in there. When we finally came on the place exploded, and thankfully I have some great footage of that night on DVD. The lads loved it and so did I. The ENGLISH DOGS were back. And so after that first gig, more were hastily arranged and the idea that new material should be written was soon put in motion. The band started to gig regularly, taking in Nottingham, Derby, Leicester, Peterborough, Wakefield, Leeds, Bristol and Stoke. And in between all of the gigs myself, John and Wattie were meeting up regularly, getting some new music down. Wakey would be sent the new ideas and he would put his lyrical ideas down over the top. The momentum was growing and the band got the opportunity to go to Berlin and play the PUNK AND DISORDERLY festival. As much as the ENGLISH DOGS and my time with RESISTANCE 77 was all going along nicely, things on the home front weren't going so well. My lady knew I was using speed with increasing regularity and, along with a few problems we were having at home with the kids, our relationship was getting a bit rocky. I decided to take her with me to Berlin, which in the end didn't necessarily turn out to be a good idea. She really wasn't used to the seedier side of rock'n'roll. Drugs and booze has always been synonymous with music from every genre. Now I'd made the decision not to use on this trip because I had my girlfriend with me. And to be honest I didn't have a problem abstaining as I was just happy to have her with me. Well, let's just say the others didn't compromise their liberal attitudes at all and as soon as we got to the venue, just hours before we played, the rest of the band met up with SICK ON THE BUS and various potions were traded and imbibed, all within eye shot of my lady.

She wasn't impressed and I immediately got the impression that she'd sussed out that if she hadn't been with me, then I would most definitely have been doing the same. She was also struggling with Wakey as a person. If you know

Wakey then you know that he's one of life's more colourful characters. To some, he's a bit of a kind of Marmite character. You either like him or you don't, and my lady's attitude and opinion of him was definitely leaning towards the latter rather than the former. I could tell that she was forming the opinion that a band like the ENGLISH DOGS were definitely not good for my health. Whereas RESISTANCE 77 she warmed to, as they were nice clean-living boys in comparison. We played the gig and it went really well. The next day, my girlfriend and I headed into Berlin to spend some time on our own. When we got back to our hotel that night all the rest of the band were there, and everyone was feeling a little worse for wear. What ensued was the first of many occasions where myself and Wakey had major differences of opinion. I didn't always like his attitude with regard to certain things, and he didn't like the fact that I would question or challenge him with regards to what I considered his outspoken outbursts. I didn't respect the guy any less, it's just a well-known fact that he can be quite outspoken sometimes. Don't get me wrong, over the years I've definitely been guilty of not engaging my brain before I act or speak, and sometimes I've had to admit I was wrong, but Wakey really didn't like the fact that I had a go back at him, and thankfully, Jon took me aside to calm things down. I'm glad he did, as coming to blows was the last thing I wanted. I was just not willing to back down when I thought I was justified in saying something and standing by it. With the situation calmed down we all retreated for the night. The next morning when it came to for us all to leave, we both agreed with each other that spirits were high and we made up. I was pleased.

Back in Blighty I was still doing a lot of stuff with RESISTANCE 77, and once again we got invited to play at Anti Fest in the former Czech Republic. The set of songs with the RESISTANCE boys was very strong and we were always very well-rehearsed. Oddy is an amazing front man, and he really knows how to whip up an audience, and the band were hoping to capitalise on this trip as we were going over there nearly every year by this point. Once again we've got to this festival and I'm walking about catching some of the other bands, preferably someone I've never heard of. On one of the smaller stages I checked the line-up and noticed a band from the UK are playing. They call themselves DOGSFLESH.

This piqued my interest is I'd never heard of them before. So as they were about to go on I watched their set from the backstage and was quite impressed. After they had finished, and they had had a chance to chill out, I went over and introduced myself and told them about my ENGLISH DOGS connection. I credited them on their performance and came up with the suggestion that with the two bands having similar names it would be a good idea that the two bands go out together and do some gigs. They thought that this was a great idea. After exchanging contact details I told them that I'd put things into action on my return to England and get back in touch. In the meantime, RESISTANCE 77 played another great gig in front of a full, packed field. The next day we flew home. Come the Summer of 2007 and the Rebellion festival was on the horizon in only a matter of months or so. ENGLISH DOGS had whipped up enough of a stink to be asked to play at the biggest and most popular punk fest in the world. Being one of the classic bands from the early eighties and reforming, we were in the position of being able to command quite a nice fee. Well, a fee that's good by punk rock standards anyway. This meant for me that I would be up in Blackpool playing for both RESISTANCE 77 and ENGLISH DOGS. Things were looking up. As is often the case with a lot of bands, RESISTANCE 77 have always had the fortune of having who I would consider to be the unsung hero of the band. Someone who would design and sell the band's T- shirts and other merchandise. Someone who is doing band stuff behind the scenes. RESISTANCE 77's unsung hero goes by the name of GREN, and with his efforts thousands of shirts with the band's name emblazoned on them are owned by people up and down the country and abroad. As well as it being a source of income, it's also a great promotional tool to keep the band's name out there. Gren would also film every gig the band played. These people are a valuable addition to any band, as they primarily get involved as non-musicians but are still lovers of the music. With this knowledge in mind I suggested that ENGLISH DOGS should do the same. Being back on the scene, and the band generating a buzz, as it was, we had nothing to lose. And so, with that, a load of merch was printed up via a friend of the band called HENDY. With the Rebellion festival looming I was preparing for it with both bands with a couple of weeks' extensive rehearsals.

With two sets to play, I felt like I was being spoiled, I just took it in my stride. I'd practised intensively as a young kid, and now the hard work was paying off all these years later. The weekend of the festival was upon us, and so I made my way up to Blackpool. I was as excited as ever to be playing with RESISTANCE 77 as they have a massive fan base who always turn out in droves when it comes to playing Rebellion. But in 2007 the fact I was playing for ENGLISH DOGS too only filled me with hope that this festival for me was going to be rather special. It was. RESISTANCE 77 played in the pavilion venue in 2007, and I have to say that it wasn't the best gig that we'd done there. We didn't actually warm to the venue settings but we still put on a good show. The nice touch came after we had just finished playing. As I was coming off the stage a certain gentleman offered me his hand and said, 'Well done'. That gentleman was no other than STUART PEARCE, or PSYCHO, as he became known in his footballing heyday. It was a nice gesture from someone who was as passionate in their own field as I was in mine. Kieron, our bass player, is an ardent Nottingham Forest fan and got to know Mr Pearce through that connection. What with Mr Pearce being a fan of all things punk rock, they had struck up a friendship and would go to gigs together. Mr Pearce is a fan of RESISTANCE 77 and has come to see us on loads of occasions. He stays in the same humble hotel as us when we are at the Rebellion weekend. No egos involved there, and just a nice down to earth bloke who likes his punk rock. With that set done I could now relish the thought of playing with the ENGLISH DOGS. My lady came up on the train on the morning of the gig. We got back to our hotel room and I had left some drug paraphernalia about. A bag of speed, as I remember it. She wasn't best pleased, so we didn't get off to a good start. But hey ho, we are at a festival and these things happen. I was very pleased that she was there, and to show some solidarity, what with all of the girlfriends and wives in attendance too, all of the ENGLISH DOGS, band and followers met up in the afternoon for a sit-down meal. We all knew that this was a big gig and I suppose there must have been a lot of expectation. This was a good way to prepare for the gig. Everybody together, with a fine sense of camaraderie in the air. The DOGS were the last band on the Sunday evening, and by the time we were able to go on, the arena in the Winter Gardens was absolutely packed to the rafters. We came on, started, and from my vantage point the sound was brilliant. As soon as we hit the first note the place erupted. This just propels you on as a player and so for me, the audience is just as important as the band. Wattie and John were ice cool although like me they were probably very nervous. Once you start though, those nerves disappear and you've just got to get on with it. As for Wakey, well he was in his element and was loving the reaction the band were getting. Wakey, being the front man that he is, had brought some props with him, and these turned out to be bin liners full of varying hats that came in all shapes and sizes. He must have dished out about 30 or 40 of these monstrosities to members of the audience and he insisted that they wear them and dance around proudly in their new head gear. We played all of the classic early ENGLISH DOGS songs which included *Pig Dog Killer* and *Mental Breakdown* that Wakey had recorded with his side project, THE WERN'T. It was an awesome experience and after finishing the set we came back on and finished the festival with the classic song, *Psycho Killer*. It was one of those moments where the hair stands up on the back of your neck. We ended the gig and afterwards backstage there was a fair amount of back-slapping. Everyone was buzzing, and rightfully so. The next day we all went home knowing that we'd proved that the ENGLISH DOGS could still be a fucking great live band. I was very happy to be a part of it. Within weeks of having done the Rebellion festival it was back to business as usual and playing sporadic gigs in and around England with both bands. ENGLISH DOGS were hoping to capitalise on their new-found interest and to keep the momentum going. Myself, John and Wattie had started to come up with some concrete new ideas for songs and Wakey was adding the finishing touches. Having an open mind they were happy with my choice of studio to use, that being once again Zoo Studios and my mate Karl. And so with a completely different band, once again I went into the studio to record five new tracks. This would become the TALES FROM THE ASYLUM EP. As per usual we financed everything ourselves, and that came from the decent money we were making from the gigs like Rebellion and also the merchandising money. John was brilliant and pretty much treated the band as if it were a business, which was good as he kept everything in order.

5. PUNK AND DISORDER IN EUROPA

As I headed into 2008 it would prove to be a pivotal year. There would be lots of highs, but there was also the lows in equal measure. I mentioned to the lads from the DOGS about meeting the boys from DOGSFLESH in the Czech Republic, and my thoughts about going out as double headliners. All agreed that it was a good idea, and soon connections were made. Again, John was incredibly good at arranging things. He became the manager in a roundabout way, and before too long he was in constant contact with ROB, the singer/guitarist from DOGSFLESH. ENGLISH DOGS were now getting offers here, there and everywhere. And so, when an offer came in for us to do a couple of gigs in the Czech Republic, one in PRAGUE and another in the city of Brno, DOGSFLESH were invited to come along as well. For me, the trip back to the Czech Republic would be eventful for a number of reasons. I'd been taking speed continuously throughout this period and, to be perfectly honest, my habit was gaining in strength. Taking into consideration that I was still taking prescribed medication to help me with heroin withdrawal, I wasn't the healthiest kid on the block. Just before we left for Prague I went down with something and started to feel quite rough. It wasn't a question of pulling out of the trip or anything like that, but I really did not feel well at all. I don't recall taking any speed with me on this trip, but I definitely took my medication with me and that was in my cymbal case, which as per usual was flown across in the hold with the band's guitars. So we get to Prague airport and it transpires that all of the instruments have been left at Stansted Airport and won't be arriving until the next day. This wasn't good news for me. What with feeling very rough anyway, and the symptoms that pretty much told me that I had gastroenteritis, I now had the prospect of going into withdrawal until our instruments turned up, whenever they turned up. For the time I just had to wait it out, and for the next 24 hours I had to continuously keep rushing to the toilet. After being in Prague for 24 hours I started to feel the onset of opiate withdrawal as well as feeling ill. I removed myself from everybody for a few hours and went out for a walk. Amazingly, and with a huge sense of relief, when I got back our instruments had arrived, and like a man possessed, I frantically got a hold of my medication and dosed myself up. Within minutes I started to feel better. Now it was just the shits and lethargy I had to contend with. To the band's credit they could tell I was not very well, and they rallied round and bolstered me up. The two gigs we did out there were really good and us and the DOGSFLESH boys got on really well. They were a good band although quite different to the ENGLISH DOGS, and that was no bad thing. If was at these gigs that Wakey took to wearing dark red face paint, which did go some way to giving him that devil-like appearance. Nobody could take it away from him that he was a great front man, ably backed up with us three by his side.

Back in England and RESISTANCE 77 had secured two gigs at Rock City in Nottingham. One was an all- dayer with loads of bands on. We were playing at the downstairs venue, and the likes of THE STRANGLERS were headlining upstairs. This was where I can remember having a bit of a flirtatious experience with PAULINE BLACK, the very charismatic lady from THE SELECTER. There is nothing else to say about that really, as a little bit of flirting is all it was. The second gig we played there happened to be a bit of a coup really. We managed to secure a slot opening for those yank horror punks, THE MISFITS. It was great to play on the main stage there, especially considering all the bands I'd seen there, and the wild nights I'd spent there in the past. I remember us playing to a completely different crowd than usual, and as always, we put on a fine show. As far as I'm concerned RESISTANCE 77 have a plethora of songs that can be pulled out of a hat. Songs that could suit listeners right across the board. If I have said it once I have said it a hundred times, RESISTANCE 77 are one of the most underrated and under- achieving punk rock bands out there. Hence the fact that I've played in the band longer than I have any other. In bands nothing ever runs smoothly all of the time, it's just not possible. The different personalities have to come together with a unifying goal to make the band and its music the best it can be. Throwing in egos, drugs, drink, mental health issues and sometimes too much time in each other's company, and it can often make for all sorts of problems. In 2008 I had a few problems of my own. As per usual my drug use could grate on my fellow band mates. The fact that I could play drums very well was all well and good, but it still didn't take away the fact that I could be difficult to work with. I became so erratic, and it was hardly surprising as I was ingesting speed far more than people realised, and a lot of the time I was bouncing off the walls. I started to turn up late for rehearsals with the RESISTANCE 77 boys, and it would be the same for gigs. Turning up at the last minute, leaving everyone on tenterhooks, not knowing whether I was going to turn up or not. For now I was getting away with it as I did always turn up, but I was slowly starting to slip with the amount of speed I was taking. I'd now resorted to buying sleeping pills off the junkies I knew in town. I was only taking them every now and then but it wasn't a good sign. Speed to stay awake, and pills to sleep. With the ENGLISH DOGS there could be some merriment too. Four completely different characters. Now, I'd seen this lot play when I was just a mere lad, and as the new boy on board I knew my place. But the thing is none of us were kids anymore, and we all have our own opinions and thoughts. I've never been backward at coming forward, and sometimes it's to my detriment, and there was already another member of the band who never held back from saying anything he wanted to, or doing anything he wanted to. For the most part myself and Wakey got on like a house on fire, but we could also have an uncanny ability to wind each other up. There had always been this mutual respect for each other, but working in close proximity to each other, and with us both having what some would say are strong personalities, we could either bring out the best in each other, or we could bring the worst out in each other. Wattie is the stereotypical bass player. Calm and seemingly laid-back. I found him to have strong opinions, but he always kept them close to his chest, until eventually he would give you an outburst of what he really thought when the situation demanded it. Then quickly he'd retreat back into himself. I liked Wattie a lot. A great bass player to boot. He liked to be known as the 'bassmeister general', and that was good. John's another character that I very much warmed to. He was the disciplinarian of the band. The one who used to make sure that everything ran as smoothly as it possibly could. This would prove to be very difficult, especially having to deal with his wayward bandmates, as well as all the stuff he was doing on the side. I liked the idea that he was totally focused on doing things right, and to add to that, the fact that the guy was very laid-back and calm evened things out, what with myself and

Wakey being quite full-on. A fantastic rhythm guitarist too, who definitely had his own way of doing things. A few years before the band had got back together Jon had had a mystery illness that had affected his brain. He'd made an almost full recovery, but after having told us about the illness, he warned us that every now and then he was prone to having momentary blackout-like symptoms. This was evident when we were playing. Sometimes we'd be midway through a song and all of a sudden, for John, it was as if somebody had turned off the lights for a couple of seconds. His playing for that couple of seconds became incoherent, but no sooner had it started, he would turn back on and kick straight back in. We all came to realise that it was part of John now and it wasn't a problem at all. For John it was great to see him playing and really enjoying being part of a band unit again. When I used to see the DOGS back in the early days, I always used to think that he was one cool-looking fucker. To be playing alongside him for me was an honour. Being back on the road for John wasn't so easy though. He obviously had to recover from quite a serious health issue, and doing some of the things he'd done years before weren't necessarily the right things to be doing now. John liked to have a smoke and no doubt every now and then he'd pep himself up with something for the gig. He was swimming in dangerous waters here. But we all were. When one's in the middle of a situation and it's exhilarating, exciting, and you are feeling totally free, it can be easy to forget about consequences while you're living in the moment.

I was playing for two great bands and I would be very naïve if I hadn't thought that absolutely none of them realised that I'd got problems of my own. Of course they knew, but when someone acts in such a way for long enough I suppose it becomes the norm. My life was starting to slowly unravel once again. For a start, my relationship was starting to crumble. It was becoming a struggle having to deal with another woman's children. I was just not prepared for it long-term at all. At that time one of the kids was being particularly disruptive and we were fighting a losing battle with keeping her under control. Let's put it this way: when you're invited into the school and then told that your child is being excluded permanently then you know there is a problem. There was always something going on, and any kind of short-term harmony would be undone with long-term in-house conflict and disharmony. Add to that my drug using, and the resentment it caused my partner, as you can imagine our home wasn't a happy one. I really did love my lady, and I knew the feeling was mutual, but looking back we were starting to buckle under the strains of our individual problems. Personally I was still managing to function. My business was still doing well and I was always there to oversee things, and besides, the bills still had to be paid. It wasn't as if I had any hardship in any way. I was in a good position, I'd got the business, I'd got the family unit and I'd got everything going for me with regards to the band work. I had nothing to moan about. It was just coming back to that same old thing though. I was carrying a monkey around on my shoulder and slowly but surely he was screaming louder and louder in my ear.

In April of 2008 DARREN RUSSELL, the manager who put on the Rebellion festival, decided to put on a similar event in Vienna, Austria. And both ENGLISH DOGS and RESISTANCE 77 were invited to play. It was another three-day festival and RESISTANCE 77 were to play on Saturday and the DOGS on the Sunday. I did my usual thing and smuggled a load of speed into the country. I was really looking forward to this, what with the added treat of playing for both bands. I flew out to Austria with the RESISTANCE 77 boys and after getting through customs we headed to our supposed digs. Well, we got the shock of our lives, because as a rule we were in a position where quite adequate accommodation was always made available to us, but when we got to this place we immediately thought that somebody must have made a mistake. This was a five-star hotel, and it wasn't the kind of place that usually catered for five punk rock types from England. Anyway, we weren't complaining and after finding our rooms the rest of the lads decided to venture out and take in some of the local scenery. I decided to stay in. I downed a load of whizz and took advantage of the huge selection of porn that could be downloaded via the internet. I also proceeded to drink the mini bar dry. Little did I know that this was all going to cost us at the end of the trip. I was just living out my dream of being abroad and playing in my rock'n'roll bands. We weren't U2 or the ROLLING fucking STONES. We were a poxy little band. But they were once weren't they? Anyway, the next day we headed to the festival site and it really was a bizarre location, although with it being situated the way it was, it worked. On arriving one couldn't fail to see a huge chimney a couple of hundred feet high protruding from the middle of the site. In short, the site was a former slaughterhouse, although you couldn't tell unless you were informed otherwise. There were three stages, a large outdoor one and two indoors. The festival had drawn a large crowd and from what I could gather there were punks and skinheads from all over Europe. RESISTANCE 77 played the smaller indoor venue and we put on a good gig. There were loads of our supporters in, and after the gig I just wandered around the site, speeding and socialising with loads of random people. Now I hadn't been drinking alcohol for some time now, in fact years, but I do remember going in search of booze, and as is always the case at these events, as an artist or performer one is pretty much given carte blanche when it comes to drinks. I was given a number of tokens and decided to use them. Having never been a beer drinker, I chanced upon a bar that was dishing out Jagermeister, and so I decided to whet my appetite with a load of that. I can't remember getting much sleep that night, which wasn't a good move on my part, as I still had another gig the next day with the ENGLISH DOGS. As I expected I felt as rough as fuck the next morning, but, as per usual I just got on with it. The RESISTANCE 77 crew were being picked up late in the afternoon to fly back to England, whereas I would stay over and come back on the Monday after doing my stint with the ENGLISH DOGS. Before they left we all went into Vienna and it was a gorgeous day, and we ended up all laid out in a park somewhere. We all had a great get-together and it was there that I opened up about some of my problems. As always, the lads listened to me with open minds and it was good for me to get a few things off my chest. When it came time to leave I was given the task of collecting the band's fee for the gig from the organisers and would sort the lads out when I got back. We got back to the hotel and the lads got their gear together and got into the van. I said my goodbyes and can remember waving to them as they left. Little did I realise at the time that it would be the last time I'd see or play with them for at least another two years.

I got my shit together and headed back to the festival. It was great to see the lads and lasses from the DOGS, and after us all getting together, we made our way backstage. We were one of the last bands on in the larger indoor venue that night. On getting to the dressing room we soon realised that we were in the presence of a band I loved at that time, THE DWARVES. They seemed like a friendly bunch and a bit of a party atmosphere ensued. A bit of coke and a bit of speed was imbibed and after setting our stall out it was just a case of taking in the atmosphere of the festival until showtime. Once again I went on walkabout. COCK SPARRER were playing on the outdoor stage. I never fully realised until then how popular they were in Europe, and they knew how to back it up as a band too.

Loads of catchy songs that appealed to punks and skins alike. They went down really well. We went on late in the day and had a good crowd in to see us. We put on a good show and went down well, although for me it was a bit of a struggle, partly due to feeling a bit knackered and frayed around the edges, what with the last couple of days up speeding. The next day we all returned back to the UK. After being back in England for a couple of days the ENGLISH DOGS were dealt a heavy blow. John had decided that it was best that he left the group as he had felt unwell and unsteady on his feet when we played in Vienna. This was obviously something to do with his health issues, and it was with a heavy heart that he had made that decision. The rest of us were all gutted as we all knew how much of an integral part of the band he was. Obviously his health came first, and all we could do was wish him the best. He decided to play one last gig, and that would be the upcoming Rebellion festival.

The weekend following the Vienna trip I was booked to go to Bruges with RESISTANCE 77. Well after getting back to my day job I came to the realisation that I had, for one reason or another, no staff to cover me whilst I was away. As I saw it, and as I always have done, my business is the nest egg. The thing that enabled me to go around Europe or wherever to fulfil my banding commitments. On this particular occasion though, I found myself stuck and closing the business on a Friday or Saturday wasn't going to be a good business move. I had to make a decision and I chose to stay in town and commit myself to shop open. This didn't go down well with the lads, which I completely understood. I was leaving them in the shit without a paddle and Oddy wasn't having any of it. They told me that I was out of the band. I wasn't happy about it but a little part of me felt resigned to the fact. I knew deep down that in recent times I had not been pulling my weight and my unpredictable behaviour was pissing them off. I soon shrugged it off because in my mind I was still on a high with the ENGLISH DOGS. They got their old drummer to fill in for me in Bruges and then got some other geezer to take over from me henceforth.

In the meantime, ENGLISH DOGS were getting on with business of their own. With John's days looking numbered, we cracked on and wrote a couple of extra new tracks. One was MUTINY and the other was called CAR CRASH PUNK. The latter was a real corker and would very soon become a live favourite. An offer came for us to have the songs included on a new vinyl album that was to be released. Along with the likes of DISCHARGE, ONE WAY SYSTEM, ABRASIVE WHEELS, BROKEN BONES and THE VARUKERS, all bands were asked to donate two new songs each and the two I've mentioned would be our contribution. I would record more stuff with the band in the future, but these songs were the final ones with this line-up that would be released on vinyl. The new songs were recorded once again at Zoo studios in Nuneaton and, as always, we were pleased with the results. The topic of a new guitarist was never far from our minds and I managed to draft in an old band mate of mine who had been in one of my old bands called UK 95. A Grantham lad like us all, he was a bit younger than myself, and quite a lot younger than the others, but that didn't matter. He was keen and quite capable of doing what was required. NICK was the new boy, and he was welcomed on board to the point that John met up with him to help him learn the songs. John was fully behind the band carrying on without him but there was still the Rebellion festival to do and, come early August 2008, we once again headed up to Blackpool. It was another packed venue and another great set with the added inclusion of some new songs. There was one slight difference to the set from the one we played the year before, and that was rather than handing out hats for the audience to wear, Wakey handed out 50 or so umbrellas for the punters to dance round with. It was great to look out from behind the kit to see a section of the audience all happily bopping away with their umbrellas. We also came away from the festival with another half-decent pay check and a small fortune in merch money. This was the last gig John would play for the band, and sadly as far as I'm aware, he has not done anything musical since. I was rather sad with him leaving, and for the record, I'll always have a lot of respect for John. It was him who approached me to join the band, and for that he will always have my gratitude. I did experience a somewhat sad and reflective moment whilst up at the Rebellion festival. I'd just finished my set with the DOGS and I was taking my gear off to the side of the stage area when I bumped into my friend, and now former bandmate, Kieron from RESISTANCE 77. He'd obviously come to check us out. It was really good to see him. We gave each other a hug, and after a brief chat his parting shot to me was that there were no hard feelings and that I was fucking nightmare to work with, but that I was the best drummer he'd ever worked with. With that we both wished each other all the best and we parted company. It was a bittersweet gesture but I was just pleased that I'd seen him and that he didn't resent me in any way. With that year's Rebellion out of the way it was time to break in Nick, the new DOGS guitar player. He'd been practising hard and we all got together and went through the set a few times, and within a short space of time an offer of a gig in Italy came up. We were to play in the city of Genoa, right on the coast. For that trip DOGSFLESH were once again onboard and also another one of my old bands, hardcore punks POUNDAFLESH would also be joining us. The Italians would be in for a treat if they liked this kind of thing. We flew to Italy and had to catch a train to Genoa. I can remember it being very warm and the journey there was a long and arduous one. It was whilst on this train ride that the personality clashes between myself and Wakey came to the fore once again. I don't particularly like it when people aren't there to defend themselves when they are being bad-mouthed, and especially when it's a person I'm rather fond of. I think the term 'two-faced' springs to mind. A former band member who'd got an illness was being spoken of in what I felt was a very unjust way, and the person being spoken of wasn't even present to respond. Well, it seemed that no other fucker was going to defend him, so I did. I didn't hold back either, and as soon as I'd said what I had, I immediately knew I'd hit a raw nerve. I felt really angry and felt that I had the right to defend a person who was not there to defend themselves. And like I say, it was someone I really liked and respected. The atmosphere became very frosty indeed but nothing else was really said until we got to our hotel. I had my own room and not long after we'd got settled in, Wakey came up to see me. Admittedly he was very calm and, in short, he asked me why myself and him couldn't just get along. I retorted that he didn't make it easy for us to just get along. I told him that I thought he was wrong for bad-mouthing this person, especially knowing the guy's circumstances. And again, I'll give Wakey his due, he tried to reason with me but ultimately we ended up agreeing to disagree. I can just remember him pretty much shrugging his shoulders in resignation that we couldn't and probably wouldn't always get along. He didn't like the fact that I'd stood my ground and, in hindsight, I'm glad I did. If push came to shove I'd do it again. The gig was okay as I remember it, and the new boy did a good job.

Another flight back to England and back home. And things were no more harmonious there. We had a problem child on our hands, and for my part I wasn't dealing with it in the best way. I was directing my frustrations at my partner as we couldn't seem to find a resolution to the problem. I was going to work and coming home and not knowing what kind of drama I what was going to come home to. Tensions were rising between us all, and it was only a matter of time before something would have to give. I wasn't this child's father and so my hands were tied. The only person who was really capable of doing anything was the mother and so, after repeated occasions of absolute dysfunction in the household, my girlfriend announced that she was moving out for the time being. I agreed that this was a good idea. And for my part I have to admit that my lifestyle hadn't helped the situation. I've never been abusive or anything like that but my drug using had definitely added to the situation between my lady and me, which obviously then puts strain on with regards to other problems. We'd tried to do the family thing, holidays abroad, school trips and days out, but it just wasn't working. The three of them moved out and I was left in the house. For the time being I had to just get on with what I needed to do. We were in constant contact with each other and from what I can gather her problems with the youngster were just beginning. The subject of my using came up once again as she desperately wanted me to stop using, or 'get well', as she put it. But I'd got myself in too deep again and for that I have to live with the fact that I played a part in putting the boot into what was an already fragile setup. Eventually a few months down the line she told me that we were just too different to each other. Our relationship was over, I was really upset about it, and it would take some time to get over it. One can't just brush six years under the carpet. I was on my own once again, in this massive house. I needed some company. So what did I do? I went and got a cat. All I wanted was something to come home to and for the time being he was great. He became my mate when I came home from work. I'd had enough of humans at the end of my working day and he was all I needed. I called him Tom and I loved him to bits.

Winter 2008 and ENGLISH DOGS decided to play a gig on home ground. The first time that had happened in many years. The fact that the band had made a comeback over the last two years had warranted enough interest to conclude that a gig in Grantham could only be a great success. Now Grantham had changed somewhat since the 80s and with the main venue that used to be in the town now long gone, we needed to find an alternative. We chanced upon a large bar up at the local leisure centre and asked three other bands to come along as well. As I remember it we had the DRUNKEN GRANNY BASHERS from Grantham, CERTIFIED from Nottingham, and our old mates DOGSFLESH on board. A PA was hired and publicity was put out well in advance of the gig. The gig sold out in no time and everyone involved was looking forward to a good night. Come the day of the gig and I got up to the venue and met up with Wakey and his lady, Sally. This was one of the occasions when Wakey showed what a kind and considerate fellow he could be. Now he knew that I was a fervent PISTOLS fan and he knew about my passion for collecting the band's memorabilia. Well, he was now living down in Bridgwater in Somerset and, lo and behold, he knew a gent who lived very close to him. That gentleman was no other than JULIAN TEMPLE. For those of you not in the know, this gent was one of the inner circle around the SEX PISTOLS back in their heyday. He was a film maker and had made a couple of widely acclaimed films all to do with the SEX PISTOLS. Well, Wakey had told me that he was on speaking terms with Mr Temple and that if I gave him a couple of my posters then he could get Julian to sign them for me. I got to the venue for that night's gig and, after greeting Wakey and his lady, he handed me the tube with my posters in. They were two posters with images of Sid Vicious on them and both had been signed to me from Julian Temple. A very nice gesture indeed. With that we proceeded to get ourselves ready for that night's gig. Everybody involved was turning up and everyone was in fine spirits. I was buzzing. At last I was playing in my home town and we had a ready-made audience who were well up for what we were doing. The fact that I was playing in one of the area's legendary bands just enhanced the experience. To be honest, I was really nervous about this gig and I like to think that was partially down to the fact that I knew a large selection of the audience. If not by face, then I did by name. It was definitely different to the gigs I'd been doing in the UK and Europe. The fact that I was speeding probably added to my nerves. A nice treat for me, although it probably wasn't for her, was that my daughter came to support her old man that night. After we'd got everything ready I had a few hours to kill and so I went and picked her up. It was good to have her by my side. She was aware about my new single status and just wanted to be there as support. Like I say, I was grateful. To be honest I can't remember seeing any of the other bands, and I kept myself out of the way. I was wanting to be focused on what I was doing and, as I say, I was as nervous as hell. It was showtime and so I got on stage to get my kit ready. There was a fantastic atmosphere in the place, and it was rammed full of people. Wakey by now had his familiar red face paint on, and after a delayed start, due to Wattie's bass playing up, we kicked off and into the set. From then on we had no problems and from where I was sat it looked like everyone out front was having a right good old time. It was like a typical punk rock gig. Fantastic. I do remember it being really fucking hot in there too, and by the end of our set, I was absolutely knackered. Loads of people came and said hello afterwards and credited us with putting on a great gig, the likes of which had not been seen for years. The night had been a total triumph for us, and so, after making sure that my daughter had got home safely, I spent the rest of the night celebrating.

The forward momentum I'd been enjoying with the ENGLISH DOGS was about to be brought to an abrupt end, and to be honest I hadn't seen it coming at all. Within a couple of days of the Grantham gig I received a message from Wakey saying that myself and Wattie had been sacked from the band. There had been no fall out, or anything like that. Just a message saying that he'd had enough of us and he didn't want to do it anymore. Fuck, this was not what I wanted to hear, but there was nothing I could do. It was his group and that was it. Looking back, yes I was gutted, but it was probably for the best. Wakey and I weren't getting on like we used to, and yes, I have to bear some of the responsibility for that. But it wasn't all my fault. In my mind, Wakey had changed a lot, and sometimes he was a very difficult person to be around. If you didn't agree with him, then in his eyes you were a cunt. It can be very difficult to be around someone like that. After a while it starts to wear thin. I'd known Wakey for many years now and yes, I stand by what I say when I say that he was changing. And that change wasn't necessarily for the better. When all is said and done though, it doesn't take away the fact that I was extremely grateful to him and the rest of the ENGLISH DOGS for letting me in. That also includes Pinch, because, let's be honest, I was replacing him and he was fully aware of the fact. They'd all had faith in me, giving me the job, and I absolutely loved playing all the songs, and I did the best I could. As it happened, this wouldn't be the last time myself and Wakey would be involved with each other in a musical capacity. Unfortunately it wouldn't be the last time that we would have major disagreements either. At that time though, this was definitely the end of quite a major chapter and I now had to consider my next move.

6. LET'S RIP IT UP AND START AGAIN

In late 2008 I believe I went through some form of breakdown. I woke up one day to the reality of my present position. In the space of a few months I'd lost the major things that made me tick. I was fully aware that my relationship was pretty much unsalvageable, but the fact that all of a sudden I was an unemployed musician, so to speak, really hit home. I also knew that I had not helped the situation with some of my behaviour, and because of that my feelings of guilt enabled me to just accept the fact that I had fucked up. I couldn't blame anybody else, but sitting with the realisation was still a bitter pill to swallow. Within a short space of time I started to feel quite isolated. Okay, I had the shop and that was still going very well, and I would converse daily with my customers and the two lads who worked for me. I still had my daughter, but in some way I didn't want to expose my vulnerabilities to her or the rest of my family. My problem was that I couldn't, and wouldn't, face life on life's terms. The way I had chosen how to deal with the difficult things in my life was to self-medicate. And here I was again, only now, what with the feeling of isolation and with my using going unchecked, I started on another downward spiral. It wasn't immediate but my use of amphetamines started to skyrocket. I developed a ravenous appetite for the stuff, that in turn required me to find sleeping tablets to get to sleep. Before long I was slowly becoming completely nocturnal. I'd finish work and drop some speed and spend the rest of the night bouncing round the house. I'd listen to music and watch pornography. I had no interest in sex with a real woman and so, with speed enhancing any sexual hang-ups that I may have had, I just got used to using that as a source of stimulation for me. Pornography has its place as long as it's used in moderation, but at this time and as my using progressed, using pornography became part of my using experience. Don't get me wrong, I used to enjoy staying up all night speeding and doing the things I did, but I also knew that it was unhealthy. I'd had a rehearsal room all kitted out above my shop. This had been done so that ENGLISH DOGS could practise up there. Well, my kit was still up there, and in these long nights when I'd be on my own speeding, I'd go down there at two or three in the morning and go apeshit on my drums. Good practice I know, but again not healthy, especially when one considers that I had to be at work in a few hours. And so the more knackered I got, the more speed I took. With no drumming with a band on the horizon I decided to get myself a guitar and amp, with the intention of teaching myself how to play. Over the years I'd picked up a guitar and learnt how to play a basic chord. And so with the free time that I now had, I would while away hours with the fucking thing cranked up really high at some God-awful hour until I'd eventually crash out. At the time I was having fun, but once I'd come down from the night before, reality would set in and I'd once again not want to face it. I was living in a house that I still had to pay the mortgage on. And with that the bills needed seeing to. Having a large house with just myself occupying it, I decided to take advantage of that and invited a mate to move in. I was starting to bury my head in the sand with regards to my responsibilities and if it wasn't for the fact that I had people working for me, I could have lost my business. I was starting later, finishing earlier, and basically everything was starting to slip. I honestly think that I was depressed, which was totally alien to me, and the using of drugs just compounded that. I'd got to the point whereby I was using speed every day of the week except on Sundays, as well as also developing a need for sleeping tablets. I'd now resorted to scoring all three strength tablets of the prescription drug Diazepam. I found these most pleasant, especially when wanting to come down from the amounts of whizz I was taking. I was playing a dangerous game here. Uppers and downers together were not going to be doing me any favours whatsoever. I ended up meeting a woman who would end up being a very good friend to me. She moved into another one of the spare bedrooms in the house. This was all my way of trying to keep my head above water with regards to my financial situation. I hadn't paid my mortgage for some time now and I'd started to receive letters of concern from the relevant mortgage people. I just chose to ignore them. The writing was on the wall regards to the house and it was only going to be a matter of time before the place got repossessed. I'd let things slip too much, and to be honest at the time I'd kind of got to the point of not caring about the house. My housemate saw this coming and promptly moved out. This was where my lady friend stepped in and helped me. She started scouting around and sussing out places for us to live, which I thought was really good of her. Others would have seen me as a liability and put some distance between myself and them, but no, she helped me get out of a bind of my own making. She knew I'd got problems and I hadn't actually been totally honest with her. When she moved into my place I was already up to my neck in debt and hadn't told her. No sooner had she moved into the house and within a short space of time she realised the situation I was in. To her credit though, she found us somewhere. Eventually the day finally came that my house got repossessed. I had that much stuff it was unreal. I'd been collecting all sorts of shit. I love antiques and anything quite old. I'd got old wooden furniture, pottery, old record players, and just loads and loads of stuff that I'd amassed since I'd become single. It was just another form of addiction really. This stuff, as well as all of my essentials, had to be packed and moved. Thankfully I had people who rallied round and helped me. As much as I was kind of gutted about losing the house, I was also glad to see the back of it. My main possessions, that I definitely made sure moved with me, were my extensive record collection and my now quite impressive collection of SEX PISTOLS memorabilia.

Myself and my lady friend moved into a house considerably smaller than the one we'd moved out of, and for a while, the new place resembled a junk shop. I started to get rid of the stuff that I didn't need and slowly the new place started to resemble a home. It was definitely a big weight off my shoulders not having to think about finding £700 a month for a mortgage. Sharing the rent and bills was so much easier, and I didn't have a problem finding the money for that. My main concern was making sure I did my best to keep the business going. I'd reached a plateau with regard to my using, as I couldn't really invest any more than I was doing. It was turning into a vicious circle and one that kept going round and round for a good two years. I had a couple of dealers that I could use to get speed, and I knew a few people who could get me the sleeping tablets and diazepam I needed to come down. My fixation with speed and pornography never abated and I knew I was in a rut because on numerous occasions that I'd go out to socialise, I'd pull a woman. Taking into consideration that I would have more than likely been under the influence, I just couldn't perform sexually as normal healthy people do. Now this had never been a problem for me in the past and I wasn't pleased about it. Truth of the matter is that I was a bit fucked up. I'd gotten myself into this weird routine by this point. I'd get up and go to work. I'd buy myself one of those massive bumper packs of mini cereal boxes and two litres of milk, and scoff the lot and bang some multi vitamins down my neck. This would set me up for the day. I'd do some work until about noon and then I'd go and score. Do my drugs at the dealer's place and then head back to work within an hour or two and as high as a kite, and then head back home. Now most people who use speed can't go near food for at least 24 hours. Well, I'd been taking the stuff that often I'd got to the point where I could still eat. Thankfully I still knew how important it was to eat regularly, and although I was definitely underweight, I tried my best to keep myself as physically healthy as I could. My nights would normally entail playing loads of music or playing the guitar and then using sleeping tablets to get to sleep. Weekends I would either spend at one of my dealers' places just socialising and burning up time and talking random shit until the early hours. On a Saturday night, at about 10 or 11 pm, I'd go with a couple of associates to a club in the centre of town. There I'd drink a couple of large shots of the drink called absinthe, which is a very strong spirit. Being under the influence of speed and drinking the absinthe gave me a very strange but pleasant feeling indeed. Any other form of drink wouldn't have touched me due to the amount of speed I'd ingested. Looking back, for the most part I wasn't a happy bunny at all, and I was just masking my feelings with drugs.

I can remember one little incident that did quite upset me. I'd seen online that my old bandmates RESISTANCE 77 had recorded and released a new studio album. I had a listen and immediately felt a sense of envy and loss at not being involved. I missed those chaps but they were out there doing their thing and here I was, stuck in a somewhat limbo-like situation. The flipside to a lot of the bad shit that was going down was that at around the same time, something really nice happened to me, something that at that point I really needed, and It was instigated by my housemate. She knew that I was a massive PISTOLS fan, and so one day she came home and told me that PUBLIC IMAGE LIMITED were doing a tour soon. We checked the dates and she suggested that we should go to one of the gigs. We decided upon the date in Oxford. She acquired tickets online and for once it was nice to have something to look forward to as I hadn't been to a decent gig for some time. The venue, the Oxford Academy, was only a relatively small place. I'd seen the PISTOLS four times and PIL once before at massive venues, and the thought of getting up quite so close cheered me up to the point where my friend and I joked about actually trying to meet MR LYDON.

Come the day of the gig, she drove us down to Oxford and on entering the venue I was pleasantly surprised to see that it wasn't massive and with a bit of patience I could probably get down to the front. And so that's what I did. The band came on and it was great to see the king of punk up close and personal. He looked healthy, although the fact that he was taking large glugs of brandy from a bottle did surprise me. I also noticed his long-term mate RAMBO stood to my left at the side of the stage. The gig was really good, and although it wasn't near as exciting as the PISTOLS would have been, I really enjoyed it. The gig ended and we made our way outside. We decided to hang about as I could see that the tour bus was parked within eyeshot of the venue. There may be just the chance that we could catch a glimpse of the man when he came out.

We weren't the only ones hanging about and I noticed some of the other folk milling about with records and stuff. I got into a conversation with a couple who had the same thing on their minds as us. I couldn't believe it because within about half an hour after the gig we saw him and his entourage coming down the lit passageway at the side of the venue. He duly came over to this little crowd of people and said that he just had go to the bus and that he'd happily comeback, sign stuff, and talk to us. A few moments later that's exactly what he did. I was hoping to secure a photo with him. Now we all know that he can be a frosty fucker, but on this particular night he was in a great mood, due partly to receiving a rapturous response after his band's gig. His mate Rambo was with him and so in an orderly kind of queue he signed people's records and chatted away while doing so. He came to me and I asked if I could have a photo with him and Rambo. I found myself somewhat a tad surprised as he was most accommodating and happily obliged. Rambo and John put their arms around me with myself in the middle, and my lady friend took the picture. I said thanks to both of them and wished them all the best. I couldn't believe what had happened and I was on cloud nine.

It was the nicest thing to happen to me in a long time. My friend knew I was really happy and I thanked her too. She was just as happy as I was that this had actually happened and said something to me that really hit home and I'll never forget it. She said that 'good things happen to good people' and the reason why it meant so much was because of late I hadn't felt like a good person for some time. This was a brief ray of light and positivity. Just the thing I needed. It cheered me up for the briefest of time, but within a couple of days I was still having to keep feeding my addiction. I couldn't stop and in my heart I knew once again that something drastic was needed to get me away from the cycle of using I was now living. I was getting to the end of my tether. My housemate never took drugs but she did like to smoke weed. I hadn't smoked it for a long time and around about winter 2010 I started to smoke it too. It was great and I really enjoyed it. It really mellowed me out, what with being pent up so much on the amphetamines. I'd forgotten how good music sounded on it too, and from then on I was smoking it regularly. We got Christmas that year out of the way, and with 2011 rolling in sight I needed to make a plan. This problem wasn't going away and I knew the only way of saving myself was to go away from it. That meant once again getting away completely from all my sources of supply. I got in touch with my Dad and asked him if I could go and stay at his place for a short time. I told him the severity of my problem, while stressing that heroin wasn't involved at all. This wasn't a physical addiction I was dealing with. It was a psychological one, and one that I felt I could repair if I could just have a bit of time and space to do so. He agreed, so I started to make a plan. First, I needed the flight money together.

After informing my English parents, my daughter and my workmates of my intentions, I spent the next couple of months getting ready. The final weeks leading up to me leaving I was using more than ever, and quite by accident I came across somebody who was selling really mild ecstasy tablets. On top of the speed I was taking they really enhanced the experience, but at the same time it totally reinforced in my mind the urgent need in me that this all had to stop. I was now 43 years old and had lived life in the mega fast lane for long enough. I was now using a combination of drugs that sent me up, down, sideways and asleep. In Narcotics Anonymous there is a saying for people such as myself. An active addict's prolonged life of using can only lead to three things. Jails, institutions and death. Well, I'd done the first two and I was getting pretty scared at the prospect of the third. I made plans with regards to the rent and the house with my friend. I made plans with my workmate to keep the business going whilst I was away. On Sunday 20 March 2011 my mother, stepdad and my daughter, took me down to Heathrow Airport. I think I slept nearly all the way down there. I said my goodbyes and it was a tad emotional, especially for my daughter. I was absolutely broken inside, I'd had enough of going round in circles trying to fill a hole that couldn't be filled. Most of all I was sick and tired of being sick and tired. After our goodbyes, I made my way into the airport. Before I caught my flight I drank a pint of cider and a shot of something, but I can't remember exactly what it was. I then got on the plane, and I'm happy to inform you that I've not used, or drunk anything mood-altering since that day. You see, miracles do happen.

English Dogs. A great punk rock band. This was a brief and final outing with them. But I was clean, sober and happy.

Post gig, hence the sweat. With Oddy and Kieron from Resistance 77.

Stuart Pearce. An ardent punk rock fan and champion of Resistance 77

Onstage. I took this picture from my vantage point at a gig with Resistance 77. What a buzz it is to play to a crowd such as this. Fantastic.

The reformed ENGLISH DOGS. Jon, Wattie, Wakey and myself. We could have taken this a long way, but strong personalities don't always make for good bedfellows.

THE LURKERS, Dave Kemp, Arturo Bassick/Arthur and myself. Backstage at the 100 Club. As much as it was a real treat to finally play the legendary venue, I found the overall experience a bit of an anti-climax due to terrible sound onstage. Set list and battered sticks from a batch of gigs we did in Switzerland, a beautiful country.

On walkabout in Luton.

I'd just come off stage and some lass came up to me, saying she'd just doodled this picture of me. I was quite flattered.

Meeting John Lydon and his mate. I was in a dark place at this point and quite unwell. This, however, cheered me up no end and not long after, I decided to get my shit together once and for all.

With my brother James at the Rebellion festival, manning the merch stall. In good spirits.

PART 3.

1. NOTHING CHANGES IF NOTHING CHANGES

After an eleven-hour flight I arrived in Cape Town. My Dad was there to meet me, and although it was good to see him, I was not in good shape. On long haul flights it's difficult to rest easy and on top of the fatigue I was already feeling, I looked like shit. On getting to his place and greeting my stepmother, and reacquainting myself with them both again, I explained what had been going on and the level of my problem. I explained to them that I didn't need rehab as such. My plan was to stop using, get myself into some form of help group, and pick up the tools that I'd put down years ago. NA meetings were a must, and getting a little bit of clean time under my belt to lay down the foundations for a long-term stretch of sobriety was the goal. Going all that way was drastic, but there was no way I could achieve or put my plan into effect anywhere in England. I'd been using multiple drugs and I needed to cut myself off from them all if this was going to work. Also this way was my last chance to get this right. A serial relapser is not conducive with being a success. In short, I needed to stop fucking about and start taking this thing seriously. I was now cut off from all the shit I'd been taking in England, and I knew the next few weeks were going to be really difficult.

For a start, I had not had proper sleep for as long as I can remember. I'd been inducing myself to sleep and now that I was cut off from all the pills that made me sleep, it was going to be a real struggle. I was going to have to learn how to sleep properly all over again. I'd been in a similar position before and, believe me, it's like torture. The brain is having to restart the natural process that allows a person to sleep, and it doesn't happen overnight. It was going to be a battle and it would be long and hard. But now I knew I was in the right place to get on with it. Thankfully the weather in South Africa was still good and it helped. The first week was hell. No sleep at all and I was really quite weak. My folks gave me some space, although we would all eat together at night. I could tell there was an air of disappointment coming from them, as they had seen me like this on numerous occasions and they must just have thought that I would never straighten my life out.

For me, something inside had changed. I'd had enough of the vicious circle. I was wasting my life away. Fortunately this wasn't a smack habit I was having to recover from. It was an addiction to amphetamines, and aside from the extreme tiredness and not sleeping symptoms, there were no other withdrawals. I wasn't craving any of the drugs I'd been taking at all, and I just had to slowly build myself back up again one day at a time. That's the attitude I adopted. One day at a time is an NA saying. It's a tool, and for me, it is one I have carried with me ever since. After a couple of weeks I slowly started to come round. My strength was up and mentally I was waking up. I'd been masking my feelings and now that I was clear-headed, I started to feel quite raw. I did some research and found a help group that dealt with people who'd had problems with stimulants, and so a couple of times a week, I'd go there and felt the benefits of the help the individual counsellors offered me. I also got in touch with one of my old associates who I'd initially been in rehab with in 2000. We'd stayed in touch with each other over the ensuing years and met up on my subsequent visits. He really was one of those people who I became friends with for life. It was great to connect with him once again, and he'd come and pick me up and we'd go out for coffee. Or I'd pop round his place to watch films. Within a month I was making good progress. I was having some good conversations with my parents and retaining the services of the help group. They gave me some serious insights into how the brain works normally and then what happens when the addictive brain kicks in. This was really beneficial as I could see how this had happened to me, especially on this last relapse. In short, my brain was having to rewire itself away from the addictive thinking to the normal thinking side of things. My sleep pattern started to correct itself, which in turn allowed me to think straight. Not once did I crave any drugs and I put this down to the fact I'd actually made up my mind to surrender to it all. I put in motion the mindset that to beat my addictive nature I had to surrender to it. Total abstinence was the only way forward and the way to live a life without drink or drugs was to do it one day at a time. I spent a total of seven weeks in Cape Town and it was to be the best break I'd ever given myself.

I'd gone back to a lot of the stuff I'd initially learnt on my first visit to rehab in 2000, and decided to put the main things that had worked for me into practise.

Special mention has to go out to my Dad and his wife for once again allowing me the opportunity to stay with them while I got my head together. My Dad was there just when I needed him most, and I owe him my gratitude. Today, years later, we have a great relationship and speak regularly. For a few years we went out there on holiday and it was great to go out there clean and healthy. For me, South Africa saved my life on more than one occasion, and I will always feel a connection to the place. A couple of nights before I was due to fly back to England I was with my good friend in a bar and it came over on the television that Osama Bin Laden's compound in Pakistan had been raided and he'd been shot dead. That certainly gave us all something to talk about. A few days later I was back on English soil. Now it was time to get real and finally fulfil my potential.

I landed back in England with a renewed sense of purpose. It was good to get back home and I was most pleased that my housemate had looked after the house and all of my stuff. It was time to get my head down and get cracking. I threw myself straight into work and I was pleased with my workmate, who had looked after the business while I was away. Having him on board made all the difference, and he was, and still is, a constant ally with regard to the shop. For him it must have been a revelation when I got back from abroad, as he hadn't known me clean and sober since he'd been working with me, so the difference must have been quite marked. I started attending NA again in Nottingham, and this was just to help keep the foundation of my new and early recovery in place. I reconnected with my family in England and I was really pleased to see my daughter.

It was good to be clean and sober. There were a couple of things on my mind that I wanted to sort out. Namely, getting involved with a woman, and the other, an increasing desire to get back involved with a band and drumming. Like I say, I was back and raring to go. I'd only been back a matter of weeks and I had some time to myself. I went for a trip into Nottingham and was walking through the centre when I heard a familiar voice shout 'I see it but can't believe it.' It was Ellis, the guitarist from RESISTANCE 77. With that, he bounded over to me and we gave each other a massive hug. We hadn't seen each other for a couple of years and it was great to see him. We got chatting and he told me that the band was going OK, but how much better it would be if I were back involved. I told him that I'd sorted myself out and I would love to be back in action with them, but that was going to be up to the others as to whether they wanted me back. We exchanged details and he said he would let me know after talking to them. He also told me he was about to get married, and that I was invited, and that would probably be a good time to meet up with them then.

I said I'd wait for his call and bid him farewell. A couple of days later I got a call from him expressing that they'd be pleased to see me and that would be the ideal opportunity to all have a chat. I was really pleased at this little piece of good fortune. On the specified date I made my way over to Ellis's wedding reception, parked up and made my way in. In short, we all met up, and it was all very jovial and just a good feeling that we were all together again. I knew I owed them some cash with regard to the fee from my last gig in Vienna, and I basically said that I would waive any money earned from my future gigs until my debt was paid. Their latest drummer was out and I was back in. This for me was another one of those 'you never know what's around the corner' moments, as I never thought for one minute that this would transpire. Within a week I was back over in Alfreton practising and preparing for gigs with RESISTANCE 77.

It was great to be back behind a kit again and back playing gigs. Another surprise was just around the corner too. And that surprise came under the guise of the ENGLISH DOGS. Wakey had reformed the band back in 2010 and recruited Nick, who I had originally found to replace the original guitarist in 2008. And with a new bassist and drummer they had started gigging again. Nick came to see me at my workplace with the offer of doing some recording for the band. Their drummer was not in favour, for whatever reason, and so, at the behest of Wakey, Nick came and asked me if I'd be interested. I was quite taken aback with this but was prepared to grab the bull by the horns, so to speak. For a start, being sober I was able to deal with stuff a lot better. And also I still respected Wakey and the ENGLISH DOGS' name. I told Nick that I was interested, along with my views being that we should see how things go, as myself and Wakey had the propensity to wind each other up. I was happy to start over and get on with doing something creatively new. The idea was to record four songs, two new tracks along with a couple of carefully considered covers. Nick gave me the rough ideas for the new songs along with my contact details to Wakey and TAT, the bass player. It wasn't long before Wakey got in touch and we buried the hatchet, so to speak. He informed me that he was really pleased that I was involved and looked forward to seeing me again. I returned the compliment and was happy that we had been reacquainted. Over the next couple of weeks Nick, Tat and I worked on the songs in the practice room above my shop, with rough recordings being sent to Wakey, so that he could arrange his vocals over the top. Wakey came up from Bridgewater with his wife Sally when he was ready. For the first time in a few years we were playing music together again. It was good to see him and Sally, and I was pleased that any animosity we'd felt towards each other was now in the past.

After getting a few rehearsals under our belts Wakey told me that he had hoped that I'd do some gigs with the band. I was a little sceptical, but with things going so well I didn't see it at the time being a problem, and so I agreed and just said, 'Let's see how it goes.' We once again went to our friend Karl's studio in Nuneaton and laid down the four songs. Now, the idea of this project was as a joint venture with Wakey's mates, SICK ON THE BUS. Along with the four tracks we were recording they were doing the same. All eight tracks were going to be released on one CD, and it was going to be called the DOG SICK EP. We laid down the two brand new compositions and we did a SICK ON THE BUS song, *I Don't Believe*, and *Shot By Both Sides*, by MAGAZINE. The results were really good and I really enjoyed the sessions. I was amazed at how well I'd bounced back into a fruitful early recovery. Staying clean was already paying dividends and I was getting myself back into a position where I was firing on all cylinders and doing it without the use of drugs. The shop was going great guns, and I was back gigging with two great bands. There started to be a little bit of backbiting and snide comments from members of both bands one towards the other, but I didn't let that bother me and I didn't take any particular side. I respected all of my bandmates, although I could definitely tell that there was a different vibe from one to the other.

With RESISTANCE 77 there had always been a more relaxed and even-scaled attitude with the way things got done. By that I mean that everybody pretty much had an equal say in things. They were also not into doing drugs, which was definitely good for me, although I would have handled it even if they were. With the DOGS it was somewhat different. The vibe was no better or worse, but you definitely knew that it was Wakey's band, and for the most part he would be, 'Let's crack on and be the best we can, and let's enjoy ourselves doing it.' The thing is that Wakey is a very complicated character, and he could be so unpredictable that anything could happen. He has to be one of the most outspoken people I've ever known, and as much as I respected that side of him, it could also lead to some very uncomfortable situations. All one could do was brush these situations off and realise that was just Wakey. One of his mottos was 'drugs and beer', and when under the influence this would only make his antics even more funny, or more cringe-worthy. To his credit he was a real taskmaster and always wanted to be the best he could, especially when we were in the studio. To my chagrin though, he did keep having a dig about RESISTANCE 77, which I did find annoying. At this point I was really on a high with the way things were going. I'd played the 2011 Rebellion festival and countless other gigs with the R77 boys, and I'd just had a new CD with the ENGLISH DOGS released as well as the few gigs I'd started doing with them.

To top things off quite nicely I'd just started a new relationship with a beautiful lass called MICHELE. I'd known her for years to look at, but had never engaged in much communication with her. Just before I fucked off to South Africa to get clean I'd bumped into her in one of the town's watering holes. We made some small talk and that was about it. A couple of weeks later I'd gone off abroad. Well, now I'd been back for a while and made some enquiries and got hold of her phone number. In short, I made a nuisance of myself until she relented and I went and met her. Within weeks we were seeing each other all the time. I would stay at her place most of the time, and at weekends she would come and stay at mine. Everything was falling into place quite nicely. Then there occurred an incident that knocked me back quite considerably. I suppose I was being quite naïve or foolish to think that it was ever going to last long at all. I gave it a try, but once again the clash of personalities between Wakey and myself came to the surface. A clash that would finally put paid to me ever wanting to work with him again. This was the badge incident, and this is how it unfolded as I saw it.

ENGLISH DOGS were headlining an all-dayer at some venue in Doncaster. It was on a Saturday. We didn't need to get there too early, but as I remember it we must have got there sometime in the late afternoon. I got into the venue and, as always, sussed the situation out. There seemed to be half a decent-sized crowd in. Knowing that we weren't going to be on for a good few hours I made my way up to the dressing room area that was directly above the venue. Just to chill out and stay out of the way of all the humdrum downstairs. I was going to be making enough of a racket of my own, never mind having to listen to it for hours beforehand. I'd nip down every now and again just to see what was happening, greeting the odd punter here and there that recognised me, or if I recognised them. Then I'd pop back up there and park myself up whilst everyone enjoyed the proceedings at the gig. One by one, the rest of the band turned up. We would all greet each with other a customary hug and relate how much we were looking forward to playing. I started to make a habit of using the dressing rooms at venues as a bit of a safe haven, due to the fact that I wasn't drinking. It wasn't that the alcohol side of things bothered me as such, just that at gigs everybody's drinking booze of some description, and having that little bit of space away from everybody at that time made me feel safe. Drinking wasn't an option for me, but at the same time I certainly didn't have a problem with those around me who drank. Anyway, Wakey and Sally turned up and they seemed in good spirits and as the afternoon turned into the night, more and more people were milling in and out of the dressing room.

I'd been up there for quite some time and was sat at a table. Wakey was one of the people that was in and out, basically soaking up the atmosphere of the gig. Everyone was in good spirits. I can remember Wakey talking to some bloke and we were the only three people in the room. Moments later this fella Wakey knew left the room and myself and him were stood opposite each other chatting. Well, I had my leather jacket on and as we were speaking he clocked something on one of the lapels of my leather. Now, I am collector of various things, records, flyers, posters etc. And also World war 2 ephemera. What he had clocked, was an original World War Two badge that was triangular in shape and about an inch or so in size. It was a badge honouring the unity between Germany and Japan.

What Wakey had seen was the swastika and completely went off on one. I was a little confused by his reaction at first as my view is, and always has been, that we're punks and use cultural items for another purpose. Think American Pop art. Dee Dee Ramone, Johnny Thunders, Siouxsie Sioux, Johnny Rotten, Sid Vicious, GAYE ADVERT and Lemmy from MOTORHEAD have all done the same. That didn't make them endorse the ideology, just repurpose the marketing. Wakey was having none of it. In short, in his mind I was well out of order and shouldn't be wearing it. I was trying to explain to him that it was part of the influence from the SEX PISTOLS, who'd also used similar imagery, and part down to the fact that I collected the stuff, as I know a lot of people do. A part of me felt like telling him to fuck off, but I really didn't want to fall out. So to reach a compromise I told him that I'd remove the badge, and duly took it off.

He thanked me and with that we agreed that there would be no mention of it again. I thought that that would be the end of the matter, but no, that wasn't the case at all. I admit some naivety on my part, but me being me, I hadn't even thought about it. My punk rock way of thinking was always more entrenched in the seventies scene rather than the eighties. Although that doesn't take away from the fact that I relished it all. I always leaned more towards the jeans, brothel creepers, leather jacket and spiky-haired look, rather than the more uniformed look of the Mohican brigade. Don't get me wrong, I see all sorts when out and about gigging, and I know some wonderful people and we all have our own way of doing things. And I'm afraid if we upset people then so fucking be it. It's punk. I'm not a Nazi and have never felt an affinity with those who lean toward that way of thinking - quite the opposite, in fact.

That night in Doncaster we went on and played a good gig. At the end of the night when we were all ready to leave I bid everyone a good night and a safe journey home. I got home in the early hours and got my head down. On the Sunday I got up and can remember having to go somewhere. I was in my motor and received a message on my phone. I glanced down to see who it was from and was suddenly shaken by what I saw. I had to pull over to read the message. It was a message from Wakey giving me a torrent of abuse with the threat of violence added on the end. This was all to do with the badge incident the night before. I couldn't believe what I was reading. I thought we'd sorted this out. I felt really angry and I needed to talk to someone. My lady wasn't about, so I went to a mate's house. I proceeded to tell him what had happened and the message that I'd received half an hour or so earlier, and after I'd finished relaying what had happened, my friend gave me the best advice that one could have given me at the time. I thought about it briefly and decided upon my response. I told Wakey he could stick the band up his arse. I felt vindicated. I felt that I'd compromised and bowed down to save any unnecessary conflict, and here I was still getting abuse. I'd had enough and didn't fucking need it. As that Sunday progressed I received more and more messages, and although they weren't as near as abusive, I chose to ignore them. I got the impression that he was on a come-down of some sort, but I didn't care. It wasn't any of my business. I remember receiving one last message in the early evening, basically saying that he still wanted me to be involved and hoped that we could sort things out. Yet again, I didn't respond, I'd said my piece and I'd made up my mind.

2. TIME TO TAKE STOCK AND RID ONESELF OF ALL NEGATIVITY

The next day I'm at work and Nick the guitarist came into the shop, wanting to know what the fuck was going on. I told him what I'd told Wakey and that I'd had enough of his belligerent manner and I wasn't prepared to work with someone like that anymore. Nick conveyed that Wakey wanted an answer with regard to me still wanting to play in the band, and I responded with a resounding 'No, I was done.' Nick seemed saddened by my response, and that was fair enough. This was nothing to do with him. With that he left and no doubt immediately got in touch with Wakey, giving him my answer. It was the following day that events started to take a real dark turn. Nick had obviously got word back to Wakey because later that same day a statement was drawn up and plastered all over the ENGLISH DOGS' website. In short, it read that the ENGLISH DOGS had kicked me out of the group because it had been found out that I was a Nazi and that the band couldn't tolerate anybody who had those kind of leanings. This to me was unbelievable, and it was downright fucking nasty. We'd been friends since I was sixteen, for fuck's sake, and we were now in our forties. I instantly lost respect for all of them as I would like to have credited them with a bit more intuition in thinking that this was as nasty a move as I thought it was. Then again it just exposed to me the difference between myself and them. They were prepared to go along with whatever Wakey either did or said, and fuck everybody else's feelings. In my mind they were just his yes-men, along for the ride as long as they got a little bit of glory. The basis of the statement wasn't true. My Grandad fought and killed Nazi sympathisers in the months following D-Day in 1944, and I'm grateful for the fact that he did. I don't possess any right- or left-wing views for that matter, for as far as I'm concerned they are both the same. If you don't believe in any of their views or kowtow to their way of thinking, then you have to be chastised or demonised to whatever degree they deem is necessary. I don't waste my time with that bullshit, and always try and maintain a safe distance from that kind of stuff. Secondly, I hadn't been kicked out of the group, I left of my own volition. I just wasn't willing to be treated like a cunt anymore, and for me that was it. What had started out as a storm in a teacup had now turned into a hateful and personal vendetta. I was fearful of a backlash, and within a short space of time that's exactly what happened. Don't get me wrong, I had a lot of people come out of the woodwork and defend me. People who'd known me for years, but the people who didn't know me and chose to believe that shit came out with daggers wielded. The PC brigade and the FB warriors claimed that I should have my head kicked in. There was even mention of me deserving to be stabbed. It was quite unreal, and for a few days I felt fucking awful about what had happened. It was upsetting, but thankfully the support I got helped. The lads from RESISTANCE 77 were right behind me and, to their credit, I owe them my gratitude. No sooner had the abuse started on me than certain factions took it upon themselves to start aiming abuse at my mates in RESISTANCE 77. This was totally uncalled for, as the incident in question had nothing to do with them. With that in mind, it's time for me to set the record straight. RESISTANCE 77 are a punk rock band. They are not a right-wing band at all. Everybody is entitled to their own views, but not in one song is there a mention of anything towards racism. In fact, Oddy's lyrics lean towards the exact opposite, and if anybody who's reading this feels that I'm talking shit here, just go away and listen to the song and lyrics of the band's main anthem song, 'True Punk and Oi!' and you'll get the truth there, in a nutshell. When all was said and done, I was really saddened by what had happened. I'd lost a friend, someone I'd shared bad, but mostly good times with. A person who was once a laugh a minute and great fun to be around. We've since seen and spoken to each other on a couple of occasions since the dust has settled, and to his credit, Wakey has apologised, and so for that I'm thankful.

It was time to move on and put all that negativity behind us. I had gigs abroad and in the UK with RESISTANCE 77, and there was now talk of recording a new album. Exciting times lay ahead. Also without realising it, I was about to embark on the most creative period in all my time as a player. With just having RESISTANCE 77 on my roster though, I was eager to do something else musically. Well, as luck would have it the opportunity wasn't far away. In fact it was right on my own doorstep. A couple of old associates got in touch with a view to putting together some music. Now these lads weren't punks and to me that was just fine. I was happy to do something a bit different, although in a lot of ways it wasn't exactly that much different at all, just a slightly different approach. For a start, keyboards were involved and the songs wouldn't be delivered in such a frenetic pace as how a lot of the usual punk stuff that I played was. Myself, the guitarist/vocalist, the keyboardist and the bass player started having regular practice sessions in the room above my shop and we decided to call ourselves THE MOONTHINGS. The sort of stuff we were playing I would loosely describe as soft psychedelic rock. We really were starting from scratch, but I was enjoying it. I had to change my style somewhat, with the emphasis being on holding back a little instead of my style of playing being in the full-on attack mode. Also, the songs were differently composed. They would start off quietly, and build up. In short, they had dynamics. Again, not something that is always a factor with a lot of punk or rock music. We rehearsed week in and week out and slowly started to get a repertoire together. At the same time as this it was business as usual with the RESISTANCE 77 boys, only now, we were writing new songs. Slowly but surely at our weekly rehearsals, a few new ideas started creeping in which eventually would flourish into fully fledged new songs, which in turn made the idea of recording a new album a real possibility. A gig for the band was arranged by myself in my home town of Grantham. We'd done the odd gig every now and then in town and it was always a good night. I somehow got to know of another long-standing punk band from Stamford, just up the road, called MARCH TO THE GRAVE. An agreement was made and they would play the gig too. The gig went ahead, and as I expected it to be, the night was a success, albeit with a few minor issues on the way. There was a little bit of a commotion with the MARCH TO THE GRAVE boys as they were supposed to go on at a designated time, the main reason for this being that a lot of folk who had come to the gig had to get transport home by a certain time. When it came to them going on, they were nowhere to be seen. So I went across the road to the pub adjacent to the venue and there they were, getting pissed. I expressed to them that they needed to get on stage pretty quick or RESISTANCE 77 would have to go on, and they'd have to go on after us. Well, they didn't bat an eyelid and said they were quite happy with that, and returned to their liquid beverages. RESISTANCE 77 went on promptly and played to a full little venue and went down as good as could be expected. MARCH TO THE GRAVE sauntered on in their happy-go-lucky fashion afterwards, and with their mix of original comedy-themed songs, mixed with some great covers, went down really well too. Things hadn't gone quite as planned but it didn't really matter as it had all gone well in the spirit of punk rock. A couple of weeks later I got a call from ANDY the vocalist, asking if I was available to do some filling in for their drummer who needed to take some time off. They rehearsed every Thursday in an old barn on Andy's farm just out of town. I agreed, and so within the space of a couple of months I was now in three bands playing three slightly different styles. This wasn't going to do me any harm as such, but I just needed to watch myself as the old behaviour patterns of taking too much on were never too far away. 'When is enough enough'? has to be the question, and this would be a theme over the next few years. All or nothing, and that kind of thing. The thing is that I was really enjoying my new-found sobriety, and although I'd only been clean for eighteen months or so, in my mind I was telling myself that I was making up for all the time I'd wasted getting wasted. Hence the reason why I threw myself into numerous projects. This was all well and good for me, but I needed to remember that I also had a business to take care of and a lady who needed me as well. For the time being it worked okay. The only band I was doing any extensive kind of travelling with was with RESISTANCE 77. The other two bands were doing sporadic local gigs and one was just getting off the ground. I learned a large proportion of the MARCH TO THE GRAVE's songs in a couple of months and started doing gigs which, to be honest, were real fun, and for the most part, just a good reason for the band and their local following to have a good singalong and get pissed. I'm sure they knew it themselves, but they were actually another one of those bands that were massive underachievers. Great, catchy songs, with a charismatic front man who knew how to do his job. I just liked playing that kind of stuff, but underneath I knew that I wouldn't be doing it for long. There was talk of writing some new stuff with a view to recording, and that instantly pricked my ears up as I love getting involved with the writing of new stuff, and recording is something I've always relished. We worked on four new songs, and after a matter of weeks we went into a studio and got them down. A few weeks later we met up in Stamford and did a photo shoot. We all got dressed up in suits and basically the look we were hoping to achieve was to come across like a punk rock version of the RESERVOIR DOGS. The results were great and the look we wanted was achieved. The recordings were released on CD and picture disc vinyl, the only picture disc I've ever done, as it happens. And there we are, four suspect-looking dudes in black and white emblazoned across the disc. A nice touch. A similar thing was going on with the new outfit, the MOONTHINGS. We'd now got enough material to go out and do the odd gig or two. We played in our hometown and then played Leicester and Nottingham. We did, however, come across a bit of a stumbling block as DIK, keyboard player, was a DJ, and he had to work every weekend. This wasn't good for a band that wanted to gig, and so we ended up playing the few gigs we were doing in the week, which didn't make for good turnouts. It was definitely going to be an issue if the band were going to progress. That didn't stop us from wanting to record our songs, and so after going to another studio in Leicester, we put down a number of songs over a couple of days. The results were good although completely different to what I was doing with RESISTANCE 77 or MARCH TO THE GRAVE. After more meetings at my practice room and more working on new songs, and with more gigs which again were hard work due to them being played midweek, the MOONTHINGS once again went back to Leicester to record our efforts. The songs and the quality of the recordings were definitely getting better. Having the two batches of songs recorded we decided to put them all on one CD and release them as an LP. We got rid of them locally, but we really were in a quandary due to not being able to play gigs at weekends. We'd been doing this thing for well over a year now, and it didn't really look like we could go any further with it. For me, it would turn out to be a good thing as my circumstances were about to change anyway. A change that would ultimately mean that sacrifices would have to be made. I got an offer, which after telling the MOONTHINGS about, made it quite clear that I needed to move on and take advantage of the opportunity that was being put to me. They understood completely my desire to get out there doing proper gigs to proper audiences, and so with that in mind there was no animosity whatsoever. We all still get along fine and the guitarist, RITCHIE MOONTHING, is one of the best friends I have.

3. HELLO ARTHUR. AND JELLO, HAVE YOU HEARD OF RESISTANCE 77?

I got a call from a gent sometime in mid-2013. A gent I feel I owe a huge sense of gratitude to, the reason being that because of him getting in touch it set me on a path that would see me achieve some of the things I felt had definitely passed me by. That gent, that geezer, is one ARTURO BASSICK, otherwise known as ARTHUR from THE LURKERS. Unbeknown to me he'd been living in Lincoln for a few years and an associate of mine came to see me, saying that Arthur wanted to have a chat. I got his number and gave him a ring. In short, he asked me if I want to play for the LURKERS. I was honoured that he had even thought of me in the first place. I said, 'Yes of course I would love to join the LURKERS.' Now, playing music is Arthur's main source of income, and so it's imperative for him that he is out gigging regularly and earning a crust. He relayed to me how much he was willing to pay me per gig and the talk then turned to rehearsals. Now, I knew a vast majority of the classic LURKERS songs, having first heard them when I was about twelve or thirteen. I told him that we could use the practice room above my shop, which made things very easy. The guitarist, DAVE, also lived in Lincoln and so Arthur and Dave would come over to mine and I could get acquainted with the songs as soon as possible. I told Arthur that I had some gigs abroad coming up with RESISTANCE 77. Once back from these I could focus 100 per cent on getting myself ready. Arthur sent me a list of the songs and I immediately set about learning them. A rehearsal was set up for the following week, a couple of days after I'd done my pre-arranged gigs. RESISTANCE 77 had undergone a line-up change in recent times, that being because Ellis the outstanding guitar player had joined a band called FEROCIOUS DOG. His new gigging schedule meant that he couldn't commit to both bands, and to be honest we couldn't blame him for sacrificing RESISTANCE 77 in favour of FEROCIOUS DOG as they were rising very quickly, and no doubt he was earning good money playing his mandolin for them. They were getting some great gigs too. And so with his departure we set about finding a replacement. That replacement came in the form of a hell of a big fella called JOHNNY MARCH, otherwise known as JOHNNY LOUDPANTS. He came into the band at rather an awkward time because, for one, we had to get him up to scratch with the quite vast repertoire of songs we had, but we were also in the throes of writing new songs for a prospective new album. To the lad's credit he really knuckled down, as did we all, because we also had gigs coming up, namely one in the Czech Republic, and another two in Italy. After a couple of warm-up gigs at a small venue in Nottingham, we flew out to the festival in the Czech Republic. This was Johnny's first major gig for the band and I remember the trip being memorable for a couple of reasons. One, it was very hot indeed, which under usual circumstances isn't a problem, but playing in extreme heat can be quite taxing, especially as we were playing at about four in the afternoon and facing the sun. The festival over there is a very popular one and we'd played it before. It was called the 'POD PAROU' festival, and some of the biggest names in punk played it. Now, Johnny and myself have always been big fans of the DEAD KENNEDYS and we noticed that JELLO BIAFRA'S latest band, THE GUANTANAMO SCHOOL OF MEDICINE, were also appearing, alongside a vast array of other bands. We noticed that they were playing a couple of hours after us. Well, knowing that we were going to be able to watch their set from the side of the stage was good enough for us, but we were in for an extra little treat. We'd got to the festival site nice and early, and as always these festivals abroad run like clockwork and everything is in order, just as it should be. We'd been designated a makeshift dressing room, as had all of the bands. Myself and Johnny clocked that Jello's band also had a room to themselves. With that we were discussing how cool it would be to meet the man himself. Within a few minutes we noticed a car pulling up with MR DEAD KENNEDY himself in the passenger seat. We couldn't believe it, and started jumping around like excited kids. We didn't want to impose so we chose our opportunity carefully. We were just about to go and introduce ourselves when to our amazement he made a beeline for us and came and said 'Hello'. He'd heard of RESISTANCE 77 and was happy to give us a bit of his time. We had photos taken with him and the like, and he said he'd come and check us out when we played. The man was true to his word too. When we went on, there he was watching from the back of the stage, no more than a few feet from myself. Like I say, it was fucking hot but we played a good set and good old Johnny had made his foreign debut gig with RESISTANCE 77. Later on we returned the compliment and went off and watched Jello's band from the backstage area, and his band were brilliant, even including a couple of DEAD KENNEDYS tracks. Johnny proceeded to get very drunk for the rest of the night, not quite believing that he'd actually got to meet one of his musical heroes. Going abroad has always been an absolute pleasure for me, even more so when going with the lads from RESISTANCE 77. We were out there and put on a good gig, but aside from that, for the most part there's this healthy atmosphere of camaraderie, coupled with the need to make it fun. To have a laugh I think is one of the most important things in life, and the times I've had with those boys are some of the best I've ever had. No egos, no backbiting and no bullshit. This is rare for a bunch of blokes who had worked in close confinement for as long as we have. On returning to England I had my first rehearsals with the LURKERS. I'd been revising the songs that I'd been told to learn. Arthur and Dave turned up and, fortunately for them, they didn't have to bring much in the way of equipment as I pretty much had everything in the practice room above my shop. Arthur gave me certain instructions with regards to some of the songs, especially the ones that ran into each other, and off we went. I'd be counting the songs in, RAMONES' style, 'one, two, three, four' and it was great to play some of the songs that had ingratiated me into punk rock many years before. *I Don't Need To Tell Her, I'm On Heat, Freakshow, Jenny, New Guitar In Town, Cyanide, Then I Kicked Her* are all songs from my youth. Add to that some of Arthur's later compositions like *Go Ahead Punk, Too Late To Change And Come And Reminisce*, and you had a pretty frenetic classic 77-style set. Gigs were on the horizon and I wanted it to be bang on. It didn't take long for the set to come together, and if Arthur and Dave were happy then so was I. I was quite impressed with Dave as a guitarist too. He came from a heavy rock way of doing things, so playing this style of punk rock was easy for him.

Before my first gig with the LURKERS I had a trip to Italy with RESISTANCE 77 to fulfil. We played Milan and Turin, and once again Mr Loudpants had proved himself to be the right man to replace Ellis, who had moved on to pastures new.

After the gigs were done, the band's said intention was to make good on our ambitions to write and record the new album. For the time being rehearsals were fully committed to that goal. My first gig with the LURKERS took place at an all-dayer in Leamington Spa Assembly Hall. From joining the band my experience of playing gigs was about to change quite drastically. No more doing gigs sporadically as such, but an itinerary that was mapped out until the end of the year. Gigs would be played over weekends, taking in Friday and a Saturday or a Thursday, and Sunday too. That bumped up the earning potential for us all, especially Arthur, who needed to be constantly gigging to make a living. Arthur owned the band van and, within a brief time of offering to drive, I was put on the insurance, and from then on I would do a lot of the driving. I didn't mind, I actually enjoyed it. Arthur appreciated it as it meant that he could have a good drink, and it worked for me as it kept me occupied. Soon I was driving all over the country from one weekend to the next. With the increasing gig schedule the LURKERS' live show got better and better. From Penzance to Kilmarnock, and everywhere in between, we played festivals and one-off gigs. Some gigs were better or worse than others, but that goes with the territory as every gig is different. One thing I loved about being on the road with Arthur is that, what with the guy being one of the original first wave punks, he has a fantastic memory for recalling a lot of the stuff that went on in the late seventies, when I was too young to be involved. He's been involved with, or pretty much has come into contact with, all of the main players in punk rock. I'm always fascinated with what he has to tell me about certain incidents and people from that era. First and foremost Arthur's a good musician, and he also has a great voice that isn't always put to best use just singing punk rock songs. He can croon and sing in a Country and Western style. We soon found that we shared the same warped sense of humour as each other and, for the most part, we get on well. Arthur is a very burly fellow, and if you didn't know him and his loud demeanour one could be mistaken for thinking that he could be a bit of a handful. In fact, nothing could be further from the truth. He likes a good drink and is a true raconteur, and aside from getting a little eaten up sometimes when things don't go smoothly, there is no malice in Arthur whatsoever and, to be honest, he's a gentle giant most of the time.

I'd been doing a few gigs with those Stamford cowboys, MARCH TO THE GRAVE, for a good year or so, but with my new-found gigging schedule, and writing sessions with RESISTANCE 77, I was finding myself a little too busy, and I was thinking of calling it a day with them. One of the last gigs I did with them was in Berlin, at the well-known WILD AT HEART club. We were there to support the band DRAGSTER, and so, what with the band not gigging out of the country ever, took a sizeable entourage . Now MTTG and their followers were well-known for liking the odd bevy or two, and getting into Berlin a good day before the gig, the lads went on their adventures into the city. Andy the singer stayed with me, knowing that drinking wasn't an option for me. This was really charitable of him, so we decided to indulge in a pastime that wasn't going to get us arrested, but at the same time we both enjoyed. Now I love my food, and what with having to curtail a lot of my former vices, I always am partial to some good grub to make up for it. Myself and Andy ventured out in the hope of finding somewhere that dealt up top- notch tucker and we chanced upon a Chinese restaurant. We set about gorging ourselves on the vast array of dishes that were on offer. Like I've mentioned, I can eat when the need arises, and I can eat a lot if I so desire, but on this night it seems that I'd met my match. After I'd had more than my fair share of fine Chinese cuisine I was starting to feel a little bit uncomfortable. Well, it seemed to me that Andy probably hadn't eaten for a week because the amount of food he was putting away was a sight to behold. He just kept eating and eating, he's a big lad anyway but I was absolutely gobsmacked at the guy's appetite. It still makes me chuckle to this day.

4. 999 EMERGENCY. THERE'S 'NO ESCAPE' WITH RESISTANCE 77, AND IT'S TIME TO STOP 'LURKING ABOUT'

The day after our gorge-fest, all the MTTG boys met up outside the Wild at Heart club and looked forward to a somewhat different night of revelry. The club is a legendary little venue and it was great to play there. DRAGSTER were midway through a tour and so when they came on you could tell that they were gig-hardened because they sounded tight as hell. Fronted by one of the best female vocalists I've ever seen, FI, as she's known, was down to earth, as were the rest of the band, and everybody had a really good night. The next morning I caught an early flight back to England while the rest of the lads stayed on to enjoy an extra couple of days partying. My second to last gig with MTTG took place in their home town of Stamford. For this particular gig we were supporting the legendary first wave punk band 999. I'd done this on a number of occasions in the past as RESISTANCE 77 had supported them before in London and various other places. MAMA LIZ'S had become the main venue in Stamford and throughout my tenure with MTTG I'd performed there on a number of occasions. Andy the vocalist is quite a well-known face in punk rock circles and through him a few of the well-known punk bands have played at the venue, namely UK SUBS, GBH, VICE SQUAD and of course 999. Mama Liz's is a basement venue that only holds about 120 people, but it's ideal for a little punk rock gig. MTTG provided most of the amplification and the drum kit and as I remember it we sound-checked and afterwards just chilled out until gig time. Most of you will know, but for the benefit of those who don't, Arthur from the LURKERS is also a full-time member of 999, albeit playing bass. Seeing him on the night was just a formality, being already well acquainted, but I'd never really conversed with the rest of 999. We'd had the odd word, but to be honest they didn't seem to be as outgoing as Arthur was. Our stage tenure drew close and the place was quite busy. We started our set, which was to last for about 45 minutes. We were entertaining and warming up the audience quite nicely when I noticed to my right, at the side of the stage, Nick Cash the vocalist from 999 watching me play. He was manning 999's merch stall and glimpsing him watching me drove me to really focus on what I was doing. In a moment or two's time I'd forgotten he was there and just got on with the rest of the songs. We finished our set, which went down well, as it always did on home turf, and got off stage so that 999 could get on with the business in hand. I made some idle chitchat with PABLO LA BRITTAIN/drummer and GUY DAYS/guitarist and then they went off and played their set. I can't recall catching much of 999, and I may even have left early due to having to be up early the next morning. A couple of days later I got a phone call from Arthur. I answered, half expecting a conversation that would be LURKERS-related, but instead he proceeded to tell me that NICK CASH had been impressed with my playing and he wanted to know how I would feel about doing some gigs as a replacement drummer for Pablo. I was being asked to play for 999! I couldn't believe my ears. I didn't need asking twice and I immediately said yes. Arthur said that he would give my reply back to Nick and we would go from there. I got off the phone, and to say that I was joyous is an understatement. It seemed that what my old friend had said to me about 'good things happening to good people' was really coming true. At last I was starting to fulfil my true worth. For me this was a gift of recovery, a lost dream that was reawakened. Staying sober and free from drugs was really paying off, and for the first time in my adult life I was getting to right where I wanted to be. Arthur forwarded me the 999 song list shortly thereafter, and for the next month I revised and revised until I knew most of the songs off by heart. Through my involvement with the ENGLISH DOGS and RESISTANCE 77, I'd developed a somewhat healthy reputation as a drummer on the punk rock scene, and my new involvement with the LURKERS just added to my profile, and a lot of that was down to the amount of gigs we were doing. One week we'd be playing Nottingham and Northampton and the next week I could be in Billingham and Carlisle. My diary started to fill up quite drastically and as time progressed I would be out for at least two weekends of each month. We played the famous 100 CLUB on Oxford Street in London, and we also played the now sadly closed down 12 BAR CLUB on Denmark Street. These were joyous occasions to me as the PISTOLS had kick-started things down at the 100 Club in 1976, and Denmark Street is where they initially rehearsed. Being a bit of a romanticist, and not short of an imagination, it was great to tread where my influences had once trod. It wasn't long before I was travelling to places that I'd never been. We did some gigs in Germany, Sweden and a little island off the northern tip called Heligoland. We'd also make regular trips up to Scotland playing Edinburgh, Glasgow, Kilmarnock and Aberdeen. You could pretty much point to a spot on a map of the UK and we'd more than likely have played at the nearest point of call. I was in my element and loved being out on the road. Don't get me wrong, being a full-time musician isn't for everybody. The days are long, its arduous and sometimes rather boring, but for me and for the most part I enjoy it. It's an escape from the everyday humdrum and makes for a life less ordinary. That doesn't take away from the fact that it can be tiring with the amount of waiting around you have to do, when sometimes all you just want to be doing is to be at home curled up on the settee with your lady, watching a bit of telly. For me though, the feeling I get from playing in a band is still the main reason for me doing it now. For the buzz. Add to that playing in front of an appreciative audience, and as I sit here writing this I know that I was blessed with the gift of playing an instrument, and that's something a lot of people can only dream of doing. In August 2014 I played the Rebellion festival with the LURKERS and RESISTANCE 77 on the arena stage on the same day. Two frenetic sets and I loved it. I really felt like I'd done a good workout on that day.

A LURKERS set is always very hard-hitting with a lot of drive. And aside from the more dynamic songs like PILLS, NEW GUITAR IN TOWN and I'LL GO SANE, the rest of the songs were heads-down, no nonsense, 77-style punk rock. From Bath to Norwich to Southampton and then Telford, we played everywhere. More tours abroad were arranged. An uneventful thirteen-date tour of Germany had to be curtailed because of health problems after only five days, which was a tad disappointing as I was really looking forward to taking in parts of Germany I'd never been to. A fantastic five-day trip into Switzerland. What a beautiful, untouched country that is. Being with Arthur and Dave on the road was on the whole a good experience, but I was in a position where I was working with a couple of chaps who really liked to let their hair down once we'd finished a gig. Now, that was all well and good and I couldn't blame them one bit, but it was muggins here who was driving us to wherever we were staying that night. Say we finished our set at 11 in the evening, we would then have to pack up all the gear and get it into the van. That could take an hour to an hour and a half, which means getting out of the club at around 12.30 or 1.00 in the morning. I would then drive to wherever we were staying. After two or three nights of this, I'd be getting more and more fatigued, which didn't always leave me feeling in such a great mood, especially when those two were having a good natter and a drink. It wasn't that I was being anti-social, it just used to grate on me every now and then. Getting people who are pissed to get a move on is not the easiest sometimes, and aside from a few instances where my lack of patience got the better of me and minor differences of opinion were noticeable, most of the time things ran quite smoothly. I started to broach the subject of perhaps writing some new material with Arthur, but after nearly 40 years of playing and writing stuff he wasn't enthused by the idea at all. We did, however, bring in some tracks that hadn't been in the set for a long time, which I always think is good. It was noticeable to me that we were playing the same set month in, month out, and so bringing in other songs I always relished. One song that we reintroduced was an old B-side called *Mass Media Believer*, an absolutely brilliant song which I loved playing. *Too Late To Change*, which I've already mentioned, was another song that was written by Arthur, with its autobiographical subject matter which pretty much anyone could relate to. Sadly though, we'd bring these new inclusions into the set only for them to be dropped in favour of the songs that had been part of the set for ever and a day.

Any creativity that I was lacking from playing with the LURKERS was certainly being made up for in other quarters. For months now, whilst out gigging at weekends, in the week I was making the hour or so journey over to Alfreton to meet up with the lads from RESISTANCE 77. Our song-writing sessions were starting to pay off and with each passing week we inched that little bit closer towards having an album's worth of material ready. Writing an album in this day and age is not an easy thing to do and, if any decent band is worth its salt, then it surely has to mean that the band should at its heart be intent on bettering its previous efforts, whether it be live or in a studio. The band's last album, SONGS FOR A NANNY STATE, wasn't a bad effort in my opinion, and as much as I was proud and quite pleased with it on the whole, it was lacking that little something. There's hardly any albums that I've ever listened to, and I've listened to a few, that are perfect from start to finish. Three punk rock examples for me that achieve that are: NEVER MIND THE BOLLOCKS by the SEX PISTOLS, THE CRACK by THE RUTS and FRESH FRUIT FOR ROTTING VEGETABLES by the DEAD KENNEDYS. Don't get me wrong, there's hundreds of other albums that I love just as much, but as examples these three flow brilliantly from start to finish. As a band, when you're in the throes of writing stuff you don't really know how good it is until it's all finished and recorded. This gives you a bit of an idea of our mindset. We wanted this to be the best album RESISTANCE 77 had ever done. We'd written eleven new songs and learned a cover of the SHAM 69 song, *I Don't Wanna.* Oddy and Kieron would predominantly work on lyrics with Kieron coming up with some great tunes. By his own admission he's not the greatest bassist in the world, but to his credit he's one hell of a songwriter, hence the band's vast array of different songs. With the basics down, that's when we all worked on the material. It really is a labour of love, but with everyone involved working together, after nearly a year we were finally ready to go and record the new material. We booked the by now very familiar Zoo studios in Nuneaton, and in March and April 2015 recording commenced. As was always the case, my parts went down first and then everything else was layered over the top. It took me two days to get everything down, and with that done I could now relax while the lads did all their individual parts. Everybody worked hard, and from start to finish the whole recording progress took about ten full days with a couple of days mixing on top. I have to say that full credit has to go to Johnny Loudpants as he hadn't been in the band that long, and he'd been thrown in at the deep end, but having taken it all in his stride, I think that some of his guitar work is fantastic on that record. With the recording done the next stage was getting the artwork, photos and the rest of the package together. This took another month or two to arrange, but eventually with everything in place we decided to call the album NO ESCAPE. The album would be self-released, which when looking back I stated would be a mistake. The fifth and unknown member of the group, GREN, took charge of that side of things as he did all of the band's merchandise. The concept for the album cover was brilliant. A double gatefold sleeve with a picture of the band greeted the listener when it was opened. A picture of Johnny's tattooed arm adorned the front, but of course it was what was inside that was the important thing. The music. Now I'm going to be biased, but in all fairness I think a lot of the credit has to go to Karl at Zoo studios, who in my mind did a grand job of engineering the recording sessions. So much so that in all of the times I'd recorded at his place I honestly feel that this stands as probably the best recording session I'd ever done up to that point. With the master tapes at the record printers, I couldn't wait to receive my test pressing and play it on my own record player, and thankfully it sounded just as good as I'd hoped it would. Within weeks we had our first batch of CDs and albums and with that we arranged an album release gig in Nottingham at The Maze. I can remember that gig very well because we played in the middle of June and it was one of those freakishly hot days; inside the venue it was like a sauna. The place was packed, which only made matters worse, but that aside, it was an absolutely amazing gig. The interest in the new album was apparent as they were flying out like hot cakes and the positive turnout for the gig just added weight to the fact that the band still had something to offer. For me I saw it as another one of those 'gifts of recovery' moments. I'm sure I wasn't the only one in the band who was proud to have pulled off this little victory. A cracking new album that could sit comfortably with a lot of the other bands that were releasing stuff at the same time as we were. Personally my only gripe was the fact that we hadn't had it released through a proper record company so that it could have had wider coverage and reached a lot more people. I would like to have had it distributed abroad, where the punk rock fraternity are still ardent vinyl collectors, and that would have raised the band's profile. It wasn't particularly anybody's fault that we didn't get it out there, but in hindsight I feel that it's a shame as we could have reached a wider audience. I think it really is an album that deserved recognition.

If you haven't heard it, do yourself a favour and you'll hear what I mean. That being said, at the time it was a buzz having a new record out and it felt better than having done nothing at all and becoming just another stale punk band.

At the tail end of 2014, having been asked to play for 999, and learning all the songs, I got word that my first gigs were to be a slot of three in Scotland. In an ideal situation some rehearsals with the full band beforehand would have been deemed appropriate, but this wasn't to be the case, which did make me a little anxious and just a tad nervous. On the days running up to the gigs I listened over and over again to the songs at the shop. The closest thing to a rehearsal I was going to get was a couple of hours run-through with Nick Cash once we were at the first venue in Glasgow. Underneath the IVORY BLACKS venue in the dressing room with Nick and an acoustic guitar and myself drumming on my knees. We went through the songs one by one. A couple of hours later I was playing them for real to an audience. I wasn't overly enthralled with my first performance, but I knew that this would take some time to get right. It was quite a nerve-wracking experience and so I just did the best I could. Now, I'd been called up to do these gigs, but at the time Pablo the original drummer was still playing for the band. He did, however, have things going on that meant he couldn't always commit to the band's hectic gigging schedule. Firstly, Pablo had quite an important job. Not many know this but over the years he'd become an authority on antique watches and timepieces. His knowledge had gained him a position as curator of the Watch Department at the British Museum. Not bad for an old punk rocker, is it? Anyway, his job often waylaid him, which meant that he wasn't always available for gigs, especially as he had to attend seminars and the like at the museum. Secondly, as a younger man Pablo was very fit but in more recent times he'd developed a few health issues which made drumming quite difficult for him. With myself coming in as stand-in we divided the band's gigs up between ourselves, with him doing half and myself doing the other half. I can't overstate enough how much of an honour it was and is for me to be held in the same regard as someone like Pablo and the rest of the chaps from 999, and from the outset of me being asked to join, I was treated as an equal. This was proven to me straight away because for every gig we played I'd be given an equal share in wages as the rest of the band. Pablo, whose real name is PAUL BUCK, is a lovely down-to-earth fella who I respect hugely, and him giving me his blessing was a huge compliment.

These first three gigs seemed to go by without a glitch, and it seemed the 999 boys were happy with my contribution. As a young snotty-nosed punk, I'd cut my teeth on songs like *I'm Alive, My Street Stinks, Boys In The Gang, Feeling Alright With The Crew* and *Nasty Nasty*. The list goes on and on. All of the singles and the early albums were essential little nuggets which made the band one of the iconic punk bands worldwide. The 999 logo was just another thing that made the band instantly recognisable to all genres of the scene, whether it be from the later hardcore crowd to the original late-70s first wave fanatics. The song HOMICIDE is one of the all-time great punk singles, and here I was playing them all. The truth is that if someone had told me a few years earlier that after getting myself clean I'd not only be playing with the LURKERS but 999 too, I'd have told them they needed to get their head testing. I was a busy boy, playing in three bands and running a business. I was in a really good place for the first time in many years. I felt very happy with my life. This was made all the better due to having recently become five years clean and sober. The 'one day at a time' routine had paid off and it was my longest dose of sobriety since I started using, many years prior. I felt lucky to have a great relationship with my mother and father, my daughter and my girlfriend, and in general with everything seemingly in place, life was good. Myself and my good lady were both working really hard, and with me being away gigging, it was only fair that we made some time to spend with each other, and set about planning a couple of holidays a year. With myself being a history buff we made sure that we got to see some of the things that interested me. Aside from the usual beach and sun breaks like Tunisia and Tenerife, we started going to places like Egypt, where we took in the pyramids, the Valley of the Kings, and the Karnak temples at Luxor. The pyramids I found were incredible, and for only a tenner each we went right into the heart of the great pyramid of Khufu and into his burial chamber. At the Valley of the Kings we visited the tombs of some of the great pharaohs, as well as the tomb of Tutankhamen. His body lies at the foot of the stairwell in a specially designed glass coffin. We also went to the Cairo Museum, with its abundant collection of artefacts, including all the treasures from King Tut's tomb. It fascinates me no end and I still make sure I get to watch any new documentaries on the subject. We went to Italy specifically to visit Pompeii, Herculaneum and Rome. Again all very interesting. Holidays to Crete and Rhodes, which satisfied my need to soak up the ancient history, and for us to enjoy good food and even better sun and beaches. We even went to South Africa for two weeks to visit my Dad and his wife and stay with my old friend who I'd met in rehab years before. Doing this kind of thing seemed completely off limits a few years before. For one I couldn't afford it, and two, I was always running around in circles and trying to feed my addictions, and although I didn't have a completely normal life - not that I'd have wanted that anyway - I was free to do some of the normal things that normal people do. Going out for meals or going to the cinema. For me this had all been made possible by staying clean. It would be so easy for someone such as myself, someone with a bit of clean time, to think that I could just have that one drink or take a tug on a spliff, but that's not how I view it. That would be like trying to fix something that isn't even broken, and so I choose just for today not to use anything mood altering. For me the addictive part of me is still there just beneath the skin, and to let any form of complacency in would be disastrous. I did that before a few years back and the after-effects were huge, and it took me a long time to get back on track. As an addict it's still quite natural for me to still think about using, and I don't think those feelings will ever diminish, but today I'm very aware of where it could all lead. And besides, I'm happy as I am.

In 2016 things were hotting up on the gigging front. I went to Antwerp in Belgium with RESISTANCE 77 to play a festival. PETER AND THE TEST TUBE BABIES, as well as a few other UK bands, were also there. I was playing full-time for the LURKERS, taking in Lincoln, London, Wakefield, Welwyn Garden City and a fair number of other towns and cities. My itinerary with 999 was growing slowly too. We played Hull, York, Trowbridge, Bristol, Wolverhampton and back up to Scotland. I can't remember all of the gigs I was doing, but in short, I was travelling all over the fucking country and enjoying myself immensely. With August coming up, and the Rebellion festival fast approaching, it looked like I would be making two appearances once again, one with RESISTANCE 77, the other with 999 in the Empress Ballroom. I didn't mind at all. In fact, I was over the moon. I loved going up there and playing. It was the one gig whereby I was assured of being treated really well when it came to gig time. And the crowd of people who were up there to see the bands, or just to get pissed, made the whole event one massive great punk rock party.

I'd played a few big stages before, and I'd played the Rebellion festival on more than a few occasions. But the Empress Ballroom venue had always eluded me. I'd watched some great bands on that stage and had always hoped that I would one day get the chance to do the same. 999 always had pretty much the same time slot every year on a Saturday afternoon between four and five, and this was an arrangement Nick had with the organisers for years, and it seems to have served them well. I'd been playing for the band for a while now, and although Pablo was still doing gigs, it was quite noticeable that I was slowly doing more and more. I never wanted to tread on Pablo's toes as he was the main man and I was the new boy on the block. That being said, I was eager to do as many gigs as I could, and when the opportunity to do the Rebellion gig with 999 came through I was really pleased. With the amount of gigs I'd done already I was more than ready to deliver the goods in a 4,000-capacity venue on a Saturday afternoon. To me it was a big deal. I'd come a long way in the last five years and this was the culmination of all the hard work I'd put in. Saturday came, and when it was time for us to get on stage and get ourselves ready I can remember getting onto the drum riser to prepare myself, and I looked out in front of me. The hall really does look huge from up there and I can remember thinking to myself, 'Don't fucking worry what's going on out front, just get on with what you've got to do.' Arthur, Nick and Guy were busying themselves whilst I prepared my drums. Once we were all happy and we were ready to play, we ambled off of to the side of the stage and waited for a couple of minutes until it was time for us to go on. I had feelings of nervousness and excitement, and to be honest, I was really hyped up. A bit like speed but without the speed. It was time to go on, and so I went on first. I couldn't help myself from going up to Nick's microphone and greeting the crowd in front me with a raucous, 'Are you ready for 999?' With that, a huge roar went out, and as I looked out the ballroom was packed all the way to the back. I went straight over to the drum riser, hopped up and got behind the kit. The others came on and I immediately started a military drum roll as a cue that we were about to start. Nick got behind his microphone and greeted the crowd and said, 'Get a load of this.' With that I hit the snare drum in a 'one, two, three, four' fashion and we went into the first song, *Black Flowers For The Bride*. From then on it was classic 999 song after classic 999 song. I had to calm myself down as I was that pent up and I didn't want to play the songs too fast. We seemed to be going down really well and eventually came to the last song of the set. Nick introduced the song and with that we went into the band's most popular song, *Homicide*. The feeling of playing that track in front of so many people was indescribable. I'd been waiting all of my musical life for a moment like this. The chance to play in front of an audience that was all bopping to the beat I was putting out was literally a dream come true. It was as good as any drug rush and just for that brief couple of minutes I felt on top of the world. After the gig I remained in the dressing room for some time until I'd cooled down. The rest of the band seemed happy with our performance, and after a while I returned to the festival. Loads of people came up and said hello and credited us with putting on a great gig. It was the icing on the cake as far as I was concerned, and for the rest of the day I relaxed with the knowledge that we'd pulled it off.

5. COZ WE'LL SING WHAT WE WANT AND PLAY WHAT WE WANT

The next day I played the arena stage with RESISTANCE 77, and after having a sufficient enough rest from the day before, I was just as eager to play a blinder as I had with 999. RESISTANCE 77 are always ready for the Rebellion fest and have always pulled in a great crowd. The number of people I see walking around with the band's shirts on is always pleasing to me, as I know it is for the rest of the band. The nice thing about this year's gig was the fact that we were still pushing the NO ESCAPE album, and before the gig I manned the merch stall and loads of people were wanting signed copies of the CD and vinyl. Thankfully we'd signed loads before we went up to the festival. We were also looking forward to playing some of the stuff from the album, and by now, with doing a few gigs playing some of it, a few of the songs were pretty much in the set, no matter what. *Religion Today*, which speaks for itself, and *Fear On The Street*, which again is quite self-explanatory, and the hardcore style track *No Escape* were becoming well-known new songs that we aired at nearly all gigs since the album had been released.

As a band, we would always end up in deep discussion about a certain song that we played which had courted a little bit of controversy from certain quarters of the punk community. The song in question is *The Spirit Of St George*. Now, this song had become a crowd favourite. For one, it's a very catchy tune with its trademark catchy RESISTANCE 77 chorus. Very singalong. And two, Oddy's lyrics take a nod towards being proud of where one comes from, and that one shouldn't be misled into thinking that that's negative or a bad thing. It's as plain and simple as that, nothing more and nothing less. The song, however, had drawn some attention from a select minority of the 'punk police', as we like to call them, who misconstrued the song's subject matter, implying that it may be in some way promoting racist undertones. In fact the lyrics promote exactly the opposite. It amazes me how certain people hear what they want to hear but without actually realising how cloth-eared and ignorant they really come across. Oddy's words inform everybody that we should be proud of where we come from, and that there is nothing wrong with being proud of one's heritage.

I don't wish to dwell on the topic because at the end of the day it's just a song. But those that choose to judge the band, and judge us for that song, would do well to remember the ANGELIC UPSTARTS made a fantastic song called *England* and COCK SPARRER also wrote an absolute gem called *England Belongs To Me*. *The Spirit Of St George* was written with the same feeling in mind and with no malice intended, but sadly that doesn't stop the keyboard warriors and the snowflakes from having a dig. Anyway, at Rebellion 2016 we played the song, and as is more often the case, we played it as the last song of the set and it went down great. In recent times I've learnt the best policy is not to rise to these people or react to the negativity that they project. Punk rock is about unity, not division, it's all inclusive and is for everybody. In recent times the ANTI NOWHERE LEAGUE got some flak, which was unbelievable. If the LEAGUE had released their debut album WE ARE THE LEAGUE with its inflammatory lyrics today, can you imagine the snowflakes' reaction? Or just imagine THE CLASH releasing *White Riot* in 2020. My God, they'd have to go into hiding. It's punk rock you fucking idiots.

Rebellion 2016 was great for me, and from then on it became my gigging weekend of the year. One, for the people who attended and two, the bands and the music. The week after Rebellion 999 travelled up to Edinburgh to play with THE DICKIES. It was great to be in the presence of another of the bands from my youth. THE DICKIES though, bless them, were having a spot of bother. The band were midway through a European tour and LEONARD, the singer, had taken ill and had to fly back to the States. With his blessing, the rest of the band pressed on and chose to complete the tour, taking in guest vocalists at each stop they made. We did wonder what would transpire but with us being in Edinburgh, it soon became apparent that a couple of obvious choices for guest vocalists would make an appearance. I was upstairs having a chat with THE DICKIES' guitar player when in walked EUGENE REYNOLDS from THE REZILLOS. Now, I'd seen the band before but had never met any of them. I engaged with the two of them and had a nice chat before excusing myself and heading off down to the venue. As I got to the bottom of the stairs I bumped into WATTIE from THE

EXPLOITED, who was with his wife. We greeted each other and exchanged a few words. But to be perfectly honest I couldn't understand a fucking word he said. We went on and played a mediocre set, but in all honesty I was waiting to see what would transpire with THE DICKIES. They came on and as always, musically they were brilliant. Various band members sang some of the songs and then the guests came on. The REZILLOS' front man did a few and didn't sound too bad. And then Wattie came on and did one. Let's just say that it was interesting. All in all, THE DICKIES had made the best of a bad lot, and it just went to show that when the chips are down, other people from the same scene come out and support each other. A show of unity, which was great. After this it was more gigging up and down the country. As well as the smaller town gigs, a few of the bigger one-day festivals came up as well as further treks abroad. I played Doncaster, York, Blackburn, Birkenhead, Stoke, Dundee, Aberdeen, the MIDLANDS CALLING all-dayer in Wolverhampton, Coventry and Corby. In November I went with THE LURKERS to do three gigs in Germany. With the three bands I was playing with I was busier than ever, and I felt like I'd hit a new peak with my playing. What was really nice, too was the fact that I'd be seeing the same faces at some of the gigs, and slowly but surely we'd recognise each other instantly, and it was great that my social standing was growing in the best way that I'd hoped it would. All of this activity certainly meant that I had to take care of myself. My health and ongoing sobriety had to come first, otherwise all of what I was doing could become undone. It has to be said that I got the full backing from all of my bandmates, and through them all and their support it definitely helped me with my desire to remain on the right track.

Most of the people that know me are well aware of my passion for the SEX PISTOLS. I've been collecting the band's memorabilia for years. I'd amassed a right hefty collection. From posters to flyers, tickets, and all the records that came in different covers and foreign imports etc. It got to a point where a lot of the stuff I had was just hidden away and gathering dust. My real passion is for posters, and having collected and framed a lot of the iconic posters that the PISTOLS had released to promote their records, I felt the urge to start collecting other bands' memorabilia too. After doing some research, the punk rock era of

1976 to, say, 1983 had a huge wealth of bands that had used posters and flyers to either promote records or gigs. So I started selling some of my PISTOLS collection and started investing in other bands' material. All of the first wave bands from THE DAMNED, THE CLASH, THE JAM, SIOUXSIE AND THE BANSHEES, X RAY SPEX AND THE VIBRATORS, just to mention a few, had some great promotional posters designed when releasing their early records. As I looked into it, the more I became immersed in collecting the stuff. My barber shop became a platform for me to air this stuff, which in turn gave my place of work that unique and distinctive feel. I had no problem at all getting rid of some of my PISTOLS stuff and started to enjoy the wheeling and dealing side of things. I would purchase a new acquisition at first via Ebay and then slowly but surely I started to come into contact with other collectors and dealers. I would use my Facebook page to promote nearly all of my band work, and so started to do the same with my passion for collecting punk memorabilia. When a new poster came in I'd show it off on various punk-related groups, and in a short space of time I became quite well known as one of those collecting-type nut jobs, and every now and then my playing gigs on the circuit would also connect me with the collecting of memorabilia side of things. Members of the audience would recognise me when I was mingling and ask me whether I was the guy who collected all of the memorabilia. I would confirm that I was and immediately ask if they had anything and if they wanted to sell. It also made for good conversation a lot of the time, as most people aren't always interested in selling stuff because for them it's their memories, and I got that straight away and wouldn't press the matter, but every now and then this would be a good point of contact a bit further down the line. My passion for buying and selling has also brought me into contact with some rather interesting people. I came into contact with a gentleman via one of my Facebook posts. I was showing off a very rare Sid Vicious poster and shortly received contact from this gent who wished to own it. A deal was struck and I moved it on. It turns out that the gentleman in question was an Italian fellow called MARIO, who was the sole owner of a punk museum in Venice. I did some research online and it transpires that he collected only punk rock posters from the period of 1976 to 1979. There is a collection of all that he has and it is the most impressive collection I've ever seen. Over time I struck up a conversation with Mario, and in turn he requested that I help him with regards to finding stuff that he hadn't already got. Being from England I was in the perfect place where a lot of the stuff originates from. Through my contacts and with my uncanny ability of somehow finding this stuff, I managed to secure items for him by the likes of THE JAM, ADAM AND THE ANTS AND THE BUZZCOCKS. Eventually Mario invited me over to Venice with a view to visiting the museum. I didn't need asking twice and, wanting to go to Venice with my girlfriend anyway, we took a trip over there for a few days and arranged a meeting with the man himself. The collection defies description, and for a collector such as myself what he has got together over the years is very impressive. I would still find a few bits for him after our meeting, and if anything comes my way that I feel will be of interest to the museum, I get straight in touch.

On another occasion I came into contact with a certain lady and gent who were more close to home, but still no less interesting, at the Rebellion festival in 2017. I chanced upon a distinctive-looking chap who happened to be the owner of the infamous ROXY CLUB in 1977. He was there with the same woman who he'd been with back then all those years ago. I'm talking about ANDREW CZEZOWSKI and SUSAN CARRINGTON. I saw this pair milling about and, myself being the ever inquisitive type, I couldn't help myself from going up to them and introducing myself. I was very polite and they were the same back to me. I was very interested in talking to them about something that they had started, something I was too young to have witnessed, but something that held a lot of fascination to me. We had a brief chat and I told Andrew about my musical aspirations, but also about my hobby of collecting punk rock related items. He informed me that he still had all of the artwork designs that were done when he ran the famous club. This piqued my interest even more, and after talking some more we parted company, having arranged a possible meeting in a different setting. I contacted Andrew a few weeks after our initial meeting and informed him that I was doing a gig down in London, and so it would be an ideal time for us to meet up. With that he invited me to his and Susan's house. I bid him farewell and told him that I looked forward to spending a little bit of time with them both. On the day in question I got to their address, which happened to be on the other side of Brixton. I was invited in, and for the next couple of hours I had the most pleasant chat with them both. I wanted to know all about their time as club owners and what it was like to be around when punk was just exploding in the late seventies. Susan went and made tea and came back into the room with her best china. It was all very civilised. The house was bedecked in an array of different styles of artwork with the odd SEX PISTOLS design mingled in, which would inform any observer that it was part of their past. Andrew informed me that the Roxy Club was financially a disaster, but culturally it was a success, due in part to the fact that historically it was and still is something that people wanted to know about. The discussion got on to memorabilia and the like, and with that he took me to an outhouse which was basically his office. From there he proceeded to show me ultra-rare artefacts of that time. He'd managed GENERATION X and THE DAMNED briefly, and had rare artwork for flyers and posters for both bands, as well as the original designs used to promote the gigs that took place at the club. It was a real pleasure for me to see this stuff, and I came away from this visit with an original gig poster for WAYNE COUNTY AND THE ELECTRIC CHAIRS, and a book, *100 NIGHTS AT THE ROXY*, signed by them both.

A few months later, I bought some signed prints of THE DAMNED. They were individual shots of the band taken to be used for the front cover of the band's debut album. Each print displayed an individual member and they came with the original photographer's signature at the bottom. The photographer's name was PETER GRAVELLE. Now, I knew who he was regards him being a photographer, but little did I know that if I'd delved a little deeper, I'd have found that he was more of an interesting person than I'd initially realised. Back in the late seventies he'd used the surname KODICK rather than Gravelle, and that's when the penny dropped. This chap had a SEX PISTOLS connection; I knew that I'd seen him before in a documentary or something similar but I couldn't recall when. It transpires that this gentleman had been acquainted with MR VICIOUS during his last days in New York in '78. This is the kind of person I like to talk to, someone who was there in the thick of things. With that I pressed him online, and lo and behold he was quite willing to recall the memories of his time with

Sid all those years ago. A pleasure to hear it from the horse's mouth, so to speak. I did also end up buying a couple of other items from him as well. So yes, my deep interest in the collecting of memorabilia has put me in touch with some interesting folk and, needless to say, I can't see that interest dissipating anytime soon as I just love the artwork and the colourfulness of all the designs that came out of that era. In fact collecting the stuff, if anything, is a sound investment as being on the cusp of things, I noticed that certain bands' material just keeps going up in price, and one day when I'm old and doddery, I may just cash it all in. Let's be honest, I can't take it all with me.

My first gig of 2017 took place with RESISTANCE 77 at Rock City in Nottingham. We were good friends with the band HUNG LIKE HANRATTY, who have always supported us through thick and thin. AL SATION and JEZ PAYNE are great blokes who love everything punk rock-related. So as a joint venture we decided to put a New Year's gig on in early January. A few other bands were involved too, and with both bands being pretty local to the area, tickets sold well in advance. HUNG LIKE HANRATTY were only formed a couple of years before, and with their fantastic live performances their stature was growing with every gig. The whole way that Al Sation puts across what he says, I'm sure, has the PC brigade frothing at the mouth. He doesn't bat an eyelid and refuses to be browbeaten by anyone, and for that I salute him. They have a healthy fan base now, and no doubt they'll be making certain people laugh and annoying the snowflakes for a good few years to come with their tongue-in-cheek and 'if you don't like us then just fuck off' brazenness. The gig at Rock City went really well with a great atmosphere and we pledged to do the same again the next year.

For me personally something had been nagging me for a while. I knew that I'd only been playing for the LURKERS for a few years now, but I was already yearning for a change. It always comes back to that same old thing with me. If I feel that I've seen something through to its logical conclusion, or if I feel that I've achieved as much as I can from something, with nothing more to be done, I quickly lose interest and want to move on to something new. I'd done countless gigs in the UK and abroad and enjoyed pretty much everything we'd done, and being involved with Arthur and Dave was great, but I'd gotten to a point where there wasn't enough to keep my interest levels raised. For one, I'd liked to have written some new songs with the possibility of recording a new album, something to keep the creative juices flowing. I'd broached this with Arthur on a couple of occasions and for a brief time he expressed a little interest in probably writing something new, but the idea just fell by the wayside. The truth was that he didn't really want to, or didn't see the point in writing new stuff due to the fact that, in his mind, the punters or the record-buying public aren't interested in such things. His reasoning was, and I do somewhat tend to agree with him, that the punk rock fraternity seem to be only interested in their little bit of nostalgia, and that beyond a band's initial flurry of early releases people soon lose interest and are only interested in hearing the so-called classic tunes from the band's heyday. To Arthur it was a waste of time making new records as they hardly sold. He'd pretty much resigned himself to the fact that he was happy to just keep playing gigs until the time came that he couldn't, or didn't want to do it anymore. As I've said, I partly agreed with his analogy, but for myself I felt that I was in a somewhat different position to him. Arthur had been playing and recording for nigh on 40 years and had seen how these things go. Me, I'm quite a lot younger and still feel the urge to do stuff that was in line with being creative. So with this avenue seemingly looking like it wasn't going to happen, my mind started veering towards doing something else. For the time being we just got on with the gigs as per usual, and I wasn't going to drop the lads in the shit, but my brain was definitely ticking.

At this stage of the game everything in my life was just as I wanted it to be. In short, I couldn't be happier. Any insecurities that I'd had about almost anything had gone and I was in a position where I thought that almost anything was possible. This was especially true with regard to my drumming. I'd been playing solidly again for the last six years and although I was already committed to three bands I felt the urge to push myself that little further. So, with the attitude of 'nothing ventured nothing gained' leading the way, and after keeping my eye on what some of my favourite other bands were doing, I decided to be really pushy and get in touch with the lead man of a particular band that I'd loved since I was about 16. That man was COLIN JERWOOD, vocalist of the anarchist punk band

CONFLICT. I left him a private message stating that I'd been a lifelong fan of the band and what it stood for, and that if he ever needed a drummer for whatever reason, then I'd love the opportunity to be involved. I know I was being pushy here but, like I say, if you don't ask you don't get. As a youngster I'd embraced everything to do with punk rock and what I loved were all the different styles that went under that banner. Discovering bands like CRASS, RUDIMENTARY PENI, SUBHUMANS and, of course, CONFLICT was just another extension of that. The way that they presented themselves and what they sang about, if you can call it that, influenced me hugely. I'd never witnessed CRASS live, which I regret, but I got to see CONFLICT at two of their early pivotal gigs. One was at Leeds Polytechnic in 1986, and the other was at the now legendary GATHERING OF THE 5000 at the Brixton Academy in 1987. At both gigs I experienced things that I'd never witnessed before. For a start there was the police. Both gigs are etched in my brain for the sheer ferocity of the performance, and the reaction they got due to their unwillingness to compromise and Colin's insistence on attacking everything to do with the establishment. Along with CRASS and SUBHUMANS, these three bands informed me more about the world than all the other bands put together. Forget whether you like the music or not, what they were saying was so powerful that a lot of what these bands told me and their view of the world has remained with me to this day.

I got a reply from Mr Jerwood thanking me for my offer, and that he would get in touch if I was ever needed. We had some infrequent contact for a short time, culminating with myself heading down to a gig the band were playing in London. I wanted to let him know that I was serious, so I went down there and introduced myself. We had a brief chat which, to be honest, I was a bit nervous about. Afterwards I thought I'd made my point. For all I knew he probably thought I was a bit of a cunt because, after going to the gig that night, I hardly heard from him again. The reason I was so keen was because CONFLICT's original drummer had passed a few years before. PACO, as he was known, was a fantastic drummer who'd been with the band from its inception and had played on all the band's recorded output. Now I'd met Paco a few years earlier when I was playing for the ENGLISH DOGS and he was there with his other band,

THE INNER TERRESTRIALS. He was a very nice chap and he kindly offered to let me use his industrial fan so that I could keep as cool as could be whilst playing. I was saddened to hear of his passing, but still followed CONFLICT and kept myself up to date with what they were doing. On attending that London gig and meeting Colin, then watching them play that night, I was interested in seeing what their new boy was like and to see if they were as good as I thought they might be. Whoever was having to fill Paco's shoes would have to be good and within moments of the band kicking in there was no mistaking that they'd got hold of someone who was very capable, and as a result of that the band as a whole were still very tight indeed. I did, however, sense little bit of disharmony when I initially contacted Colin a couple of months prior, which accounts for my being a little pushy. Needless to say, after the gig and with contact dwindling down to nothing, I heard nothing again so I just got on with my own business.

My gigging schedule continued, and I was keeping myself as fit as a fiddle. I was active with all three bands, taking in towns and cities all over the country. I was now using a wall planner to plan all of the dates that were coming my way. 999 played the SCOTLAND CALLING all-dayer in Glasgow as well as NORTHWEST CALLING in Manchester. It was with 999 that I was the busiest, followed by the LURKERS and then RESISTANCE 77. The odd gig here and there I would even play with both 999 and the LURKERS on the same bill. We were always going up to Scotland as well, which I didn't mind as I tended to find the Jocks some of the most amiable people I've ever met. RESISTANCE 77 went off to Belgium to play a festival with SHAM 69 and PETER AND THE TEST TUBE BABIES, and a few weeks later we also did two gigs in Slovakia, which was another first as we'd never played there before. A beautiful country and a trip that had a bit of a holiday feel about it, due to the amazing weather we experienced out there. 999 received some good news in the form of a request to write and record a new song for an up-and-coming release. CLEOPATRA RECORDS, an American label, were investing in a Halloween-themed project and had approached a number of bands to contribute. I was wondering how this was going to work for us as I'd never had one full band rehearsal with the 999 chaps at all, and to get a new song together would mean that we would have to do just that. Well, it seemed that a bit of fortune was on our side because just around the corner we had a three-gig trip out to Ireland and there the opportunity to get our heads round the table, so to speak, would present itself. We were booked to play Belfast, Dublin and Dundalk. In Belfast the band had a great ally in the form of Thomas Murdock, otherwise known as BUCK from the band THE DEFECTS. He'd partly arranged our trip over there and we were to be staying at his and his good lady's place for the first night. Buck and his lady SHARON are great hosts and for me it was good to finally meet Buck. When I was a young punk I'd acquired THE DEFECTS' debut album and absolutely loved it and played it non-stop. Buck and Sharon have their own place with another fair-sized building next to their house which is predominantly Buck's studio-cum-rehearsal room. Buck had picked us up from the airport and had taken us back to his place. After having chilled out for a couple of hours, Nick and I asked Buck if we could use his facilities to work on a new idea that Nick had come up with. He didn't mind at all, and so we both got set up and immediately started working on this new song. I was pleased that we were doing something new and fresh at last. Within an hour or so Arthur and Guy joined us and by the end of this little session we had the workings of this brand new song. With a working title and in keeping with the album subject matter, the song was going to be called EVERYDAY IS LIKE HALLOWEEN. After that first little writing session, the first the band had done in a long time, we got on with the business of doing the Irish dates. When we got back to England, we would work on the song with a view of making it ready to record. The Irish trip was great, and after the first gig in Belfast we stayed with a friend of Buck's who took time to show us round some of the beautiful parts of the Irish coastline near where he lived.

When we got back to England, studio time was secured as we were on a deadline to get the track done and sent off to the record company. On a Sunday morning I got up really early and headed up to Newcastle, and on finding the place, I was informed that the studio was owned and run by the band PENETRATION. The band's bass player ROBERT was engineering the session and, as per usual, I was expected to do my parts first and then everything else would be layered over the top. With there just being one song it didn't take me long at all, and it was just a case of me playing the song as good as I could all the way through. It wasn't a difficult song at all to play and after only a couple of attempts I had it down. In all honesty, when everything had been recorded, and we got the chance to listen back, I wasn't that impressed with the results. The song was a bit weak and I didn't feel that the production was that good. However, what did come out of that day that would prove to be very positive indeed, was that after I had laid down my drum track, leaving Guy and Arthur to do their bits, myself and Nick went off to another room, and with him playing an acoustic guitar, he showed me some more of his ideas for new songs. He'd run through an idea and I would tap into the rhythm and drum along on my knees. We'd then record it on my phone so that the bare bones of the idea was down. Nick had been working on stuff for a while at home and he had some great guitar riffs with lyrics to go over the top. In just over an hour or so we'd gone through six or seven of his new compositions and I'd recorded them on my phone. To me this was great, as it seemed that getting this one new song down was going to set in motion the possibility of recording more new stuff a bit further down the line. My thoughts were that, if I'm involved with this fresh batch of writing right from the beginning, then there would be a good chance that I'd make it onto the recordings. Pablo was still the main man but unfortunately he'd been doing less and less these days due to his other commitments and health restrictions. If it turned out that he would be recording the new stuff in the future then that would have been fine by me, but just to show my eagerness at wanting to be involved, I approached the possibility of writing new material with my full enthusiasm.

6. A CONFLICT OF INTERESTS

It was midweek and I was back at the shop when my phone went off. I'd gotten a friend request from a gent called GAVIN KING. So I look at his profile and I'm instantly made aware of the fact that he is the guitarist from CONFLICT. I thought I recognised him as I'd seen him play only a few months before down in London. I accepted his request and within a couple of minutes I received a private message. It said, 'Are you still interested in playing for CONFLICT?', and that was it. My heart skipped a beat and I immediately messaged back saying, 'Of course I am.' I was instantly buzzing at the prospect and wanted to see what would happen next. After a brief conversation I found out that Gav lived just up the road in Peterborough, which was great as it meant that we could get together and see how things went. If all went well, the rest of the band would join us later after we'd worked on some of the songs. We agreed that we'd rehearse above my shop as I had everything in place. All I needed now was a list of the songs to learn. This was another great opportunity for me and I had no intention of wasting it. I started to hear from Colin after this, and I just naturally assumed that the disharmony I'd felt within the band had come to the fore and matey boy on the drums had moved on. HODDY the bass player got in touch and with the first rehearsals set, I set about doing my homework. After being sent a full set list, I plugged them into my computer via Spotify and set about revising the songs. It soon became apparent to me that this was going to be quite different to anything I'd done before.

A lot of the music in CONFLICT is not as straightforward as one would think, and a lot of it was not written in the traditional sense of the word. Most rock'n'roll, and that includes punk, has a format that has been replicated over and over again and is only really made to sound different from band to band due to the way the different members play. CONFLICT's music bends the rules by not always repeating itself where it would seem natural to do so. In short, some of the stuff I was having to learn was very difficult, and I had to really dig deep and get to grips with the changes, the stops and starts and especially the speed at which the songs were played. The original drummer, Paco, was very good indeed and I wanted to emulate him as much as I could, but I knew that I had my work cut out. To prepare myself before my first meeting with Gav I played the songs over and over again, even to the point where I would use my headphones and play along to the songs on my kit. How I did on the first rehearsal would decide whether I was going to be the man for the job or not. It was already quite daunting, but that was made more so due to the fact that I would be playing the songs without the accompaniment of any vocals.

With just Gav and myself meeting up first, I prepared the first ten or so songs in my head and I'd just give it my best shot. Gav came over and met me at the shop. After we'd introduced ourselves to each other for the first time in person, we got to work. We went through songs from the INCREASE THE PRESSURE, THE UNGOVERNABLE FORCE and the THERE IS NO POWER WITHOUT CONTROL albums, and it went rather well. Of course, being the self-critical individual that I am, I felt that I could have done better, but Gav seemed happy enough. He'd recorded a couple of our efforts to send to the other chaps and after we'd finished, I definitely felt confident that this could be an ongoing thing. The initial flush of hard work had paid off for Colin was happy with what he heard and urged us to press on. And so for the next month we worked on songs, culminating with Hoddy finally coming over to add his basslines over the top. Again, we'd never spoken but that didn't matter. We soon got on and I could tell straight away that he was happy with the way we all gelled and played. The real test would be when we all got to play together as a full band. Colin hated rehearsing, which I found a little confusing at first, but just accepted it and realised that's just the way things were. It made my job harder but it made me try that little bit harder. The fact that we were all from different parts of the country didn't help matters, but with the quite intensive rehearsals I was getting close to being gig-ready. The fact that I loved playing this stuff helped me learn it that little quicker. It was certainly a lot different than playing the songs that I played with RESISTANCE 77, 999 and the LURKERS. It's by far the hardest set of songs I've ever had to learn and the big test was just around the corner. My first gig with CONFLICT took place in Derby at an all-weekend PUNKS FOR CANCER charity festival. I hadn't seen Colin since our meeting a few months back when I went down to London, so it was good to finally be together as a full unit. I have to say that I was a little nervous although I wasn't unused to being in this situation. I had a similar experience when I joined 999. No rehearsals with the band whatsoever, and then Boom! - straight in at the deep end and on with the show. With CONFLICT at least the two other musicians and myself had had the chance to gel. I just approached this gig like I did any other, but with it being something completely new, I did feel a little anxious beforehand. Before I knew it though, it was time to go on, get my kit ready and do the gig. We played for nearly an hour and I really enjoyed it. I'd asked my RESISTANCE 77 workmate Gren (merch man), to come and film the gig, just so that I could view it afterwards and assess what parts I needed to work on.

We went down very well and I felt that I'd done my best, taking into consideration that it was my first gig. I knew that it could be better but I was also aware that through more gigging, the songs would improve the more times I played them. Colin, Gav and Hoddy seemed to be content with the set we'd just played, and for me getting to play *The Serenade Is Dead, Increase The Pressure, Mighty And Superior* and all the rest of the iconic tunes that are CONFLICT's was great. Playing songs with a real meaning to them was inspiring, and to top it off, getting some healthy and positive feedback from a lot of the Derby punks was nice. I knew a lot of them from my POUNDAFLESH and ENGLISH DOGS days, and don't mind saying that playing this gig was rather special. On my way home that night, Colin got in touch and said I'd done a good job and he looked forward to the next lot of gigs with myself on board. Just what I wanted to hear.

Having ingratiated myself into the ranks of CONFLICT, something was definitely going to have to be sacrificed. Playing in three bands was enough, although a few relished informing me that three was too many. So, weighing up my options, I informed Arthur that I would fulfil my gig duties for the next couple of months, but those would be my last dates as a LURKER. Arthur was cool with my decision and besides, he always had a couple of backup drummers ready to step in for the LURKERS or 999. One in particular is a lovely chap known as CASS. I'd replaced him to play in the LURKERS a couple of years back, but he was back on the scene and he often filled in for me if I ended up being double-booked. I still had a few gigs to do though, and with this in mind

I informed Arthur and Dave that my last gig would be at the up-and-coming Rebellion festival. We ended up doing a couple of small club dates, and one really great gig at the Assembly Rooms in Leamington Spa with the likes of VICE SQUAD, THE MEMBERS and PETER AND THE TEST TUBE BABIES. Blackpool was fast approaching and I found myself in the enviable position of playing with three bands, THE LURKERS, RESISTANCE 77 and 999. I was well chuffed to be playing three gigs up there. What I wasn't overly enamoured with was the prospect of having to play all three sets on the same day. It would have been perfect to do consecutive days, which would allow me to at least be gig-ready for each set. But no, all three sets fell on the Saturday. Not an easy task, but not impossible either. It wasn't an ideal situation, but I just thought, 'Sod it, it is what it is.' I got up to Blackpool on the Friday night, and whilst milling about and chatting to a lot of people, I spent most of my time on the RESISTANCE 77 merch stall doing a bit of business while Gren went off to get a drink or do some filming. Rebellion is an endurance test for everyone involved, especially if you are there for the duration. I have a 'stepometer' app on my phone and I couldn't believe how many steps I'd done by the end of the festival. I'd walked about seventeen or eighteen miles over three days and, on top of the playing, that's some amount of exercise. Obviously most folks are exercising their vocal chords and enjoying the time to have a good drink. Four to five days of that and people start looking a bit frayed around the edges. Saturday came and thankfully I'd had a decent enough night's sleep to deal with the day's activities. I was with 999 in the Empress Ballroom at 3.15, THE LURKERS in the Opera House at 6.35 and RESISTANCE 77 on the Arena stage at 9.55.

Thankfully there were a few hours in between sets and I was only playing 45-minute slots. Starting with 999 mid-afternoon was great, and as per usual we played to a full ballroom and played a blinder. Next up, THE LURKERS. I'd never played the Opera House venue before and, to be honest, as much as it's an amazing venue, I found it hard work. The stage is too big and the venue is exactly what it says it is. It was fairly full in there but it seemed like we were miles away from the audience. We still went down really well though, and this being my last gig with the band, it was a fitting way for me to bow out. I was knackered after this one, and I can remember having a quick word with Dave, thanking him for the opportunity to play with a great guitar player, and he returned the compliment. I bid him farewell and said I'd no doubt see him again soon. I had one more set to do and to be honest I wasn't really looking forward to it. I felt that I'd expelled enough energy for the day. Saying that, I didn't want to let the RESISTANCE 77 boys down, so I dug deep and got myself ready. I met everyone backstage at around 9.00. It was time to go on and get ready. We had a full house all raring to go, and this helped me. We kicked into the set and it sounded great, but I have to admit I really had to pace myself as I was struggling a little. I'm not just tapping the drums here. It's punk rock and has to be approached with some fervour. I'm afraid when I hear those guitars kick in I feel like I'm ready to go to war, but right now I was starting to feel a little sluggish and my poor hands were feeling a little tender too. We did the gig and as always with RESISTANCE 77 the chaps put on a brilliant performance, and that was shown by the reception we got when we'd finished. I'd like to think that I hadn't short-changed anyone, but to be fair, I was glad when we were done. I'd done my duty and God knows how many calories I'd burned off that day. The day was a success, but not one I'd like to go through again. The mixture of adrenalin and the energy I'd used left me feeling absolutely cream-crackered. Let's just say I'd earned my wages that day.

Which brings me to the incident that put a dampener on the whole thing. My girlfriend was with me, but with me being busy going from one place to the next, we just arranged to meet each other backstage at the three different venues. I'd been paid for all of my slots and was wearing black bondage trousers which had limited space for keeping money in. I always carry my own money but on this occasion I asked Michele to look after it for me. Five minutes before I'm due to go on with RESISTANCE 77 she appears and comes up to me and tells me that she's been robbed. She looked distraught, and in a flash I wasn't feeling best pleased either. Everything I'd earned that day was gone. I didn't really have time to be angry as I was just about to go and play. For a brief moment though, I was absolutely seething, but all I could do was shrug my shoulders and get on with the business at hand. I couldn't be angry with my other half, as it wasn't her fault. She may have let her guard down, so to speak, but that's not the point. Some bastard had decided to take advantage. So much for the punk rock family spirit eh! Needless to say, Michele was that upset about it, she didn't come out of the hotel room until it was time to leave for home. Alas, she hasn't been back to the festival since. Yep, that year's festival will remain in my mind for years to come. I wonder if anybody else has done three gigs in one day up there.

With that out of the way things were rolling along rather rapidly. It was back to business with CONFLICT, with a gig in Poland and another in the Czech Republic. I'd never been to Poland before and so what with this new venture being new and fresh to me, I was raring to go. The first gig was at a festival near Gdansk. Whoever was putting us on meant business because we had a really nice van with all mod cons, with a driver taking us wherever we needed to be. It was still the height of summer and so I can remember it being very humid. Now this was only my second gig with CONFLICT and so I'm still a long way from feeling the way the band played the songs as a full unit. To be honest, it was the speed that the songs were played at that was bothering me. I was playing them too fast. It's a drummer thing. With CONFLICT, Colin packs in a lot of lyrics and so if the music is being played too fast he can't fit all of the words in. This is where I came to realise that CONFLICT were totally different to a band like DISCHARGE, for instance. With a band like DISCHARGE the music is played at breakneck speed, whilst only a very few words or lyrics are put over the top. CONFLICT is totally different. Loads of lyrics on top of the music, which Colin had obviously thought a lot about when writing them. This is what makes them different to a lot of the other similar-sounding bands. And so, with that in mind, the music has to be played at just the right pace that suits Colin, otherwise it tends to throw him right out. We played the gig and that night I met a big fan of the band, an American called SCOOTER who had travelled from the US just to see us. A lovely fella. Anyway, he'd filmed some of the gig and sent me the footage the next day, and I realised I was playing the songs far too fast. My aim was to play along with Colin's vocals, and not so much the music. That way Colin could deliver his lines in a time that suited him. As I found though, this wasn't always going to be easy, as from night to night the tempo could change depending on how he was feeling. The next gig was in the former Czech Republic at the very popular Pod Parou festival which I'd played a couple of years earlier with RESISTANCE 77. For this we had a very long ten-hour drive, which wasn't made easy as it rained non-stop all the way there. This festival is very popular over there, and with bands like THE COCKNEY REJECTS, THE VIBRATORS, THE REAL MCKENZIES, as well as ANTI FLAG, THE CASUALTIES and THE STREET DOGS from the US all putting on sets, it's easy to see why. We played the main stage and it went well, but on a personal note I still knew that I was cutting my teeth with the band. The CONFLICT set is definitely the hardest set of songs that I've ever had to perfect. There was a bit of mischief going on after we'd played, which made for some mild amusement. After we'd done our bit, Colin had imbibed a drink or two, and with THE COCKNEY REJECTS being in attendance, he wanted to go and say hello in his own inimitable way. To everyone involved, this meant that the meeting probably wouldn't end well. Hoddy, who's been the mainstay of the band since the mid-eighties, knows only too well how Colin ticks, and so thankfully he took it upon himself to quell the situation. Needless to say, Colin never went up and said hello to the REJECTS and we all breathed a sigh of relief. The other incident was altogether different, and although it was rather cruel, it ended up being rather funny. The American band TOTAL CHAOS were at the festival, and being fans of CONFLICT they came over to say hello. Being the typical 'Yankee Doodle Dandy' types, they were a little over the top, but very friendly, I must add. Well, the conversation got onto the band DISCHARGE. Now Hoddy loves DISCHARGE and even had the fortune of playing a few gigs with them many years before. He was also an original member of BROKEN BONES. The TOTAL CHAOS boys just so happen to be DISCHARGE fans too, and so Hoddy as a bit of a wind-up decides to tell the guitarist that DISCHARGE are reforming with the original line-up. Now this wasn't true at all, but on hearing this matey boy from TOTAL CHAOS pretty much started doing back flips and couldn't contain his excitement. Like I say, a little over the top. With that he said he had to go and tell the rest of his band the wonderful news, and so off he went. Oh, how we laughed.

So I'd done three gigs with CONFLICT, and as much as they'd gone OK, I wasn't entirely happy with my playing. I did, however, come to the conclusion that it would only get better the more gigs we were doing, and I had nothing to worry about there as the band had bookings coming in left, right and centre. Without realising it at the time, this was an area which I would be playing a part in very soon. I offered to the lads my help in arranging some of the gigs that were coming up as well as taking on new bookings. I'd picked up a lot of tips from the way that Arthur from the LURKERS and 999 did things, what with him being the one who booked all the band's gigs. I just took it upon myself to do the same with CONFLICT. CONFLICT had gained a reputation for not showing up to gigs, and I thought that this needed to be rectified. Being an ardent fan of the band before I joined, and now being a full-time member only made my allegiance to what the band stood for even more solid. Not an easy thing to do, cleaning up a tarnished reputation, but I faced the task ahead, and with the full blessing of the others, started securing gigs from all over the country and even Europe.

With an itinerary fuller than ever, all gigs were booked months in advance so that everything could be put in place i.e. venue, fee, promotion, support slots and the like. As a rule I didn't have a lot to do at all really, and once the gigs were booked it was then left to the promoter or club owners to do their job. I could just turn up, play and collect the money. I'd now got it sorted so as not having to take a full drum kit with me anymore, which makes life a lot easier. In-house kits were always provided at the bigger festival-type gigs, and support bands provided one for the smaller ones. I always take my own snare drum, cymbals and stands just in case. But everything else was, and is, provided. As a rule I've always used a five-piece kit, but most other punk rock drummers only use a four-piece. So, without wanting to cause any more fuss than is necessary, I've just learned to adapt to using a four-piece. It's not a problem but if a five-piece is on hand then I really get the chance to let rip. As busy as I was, it was all too obvious that I would get tired. Drumming being as strenuous as it is, is all well and good, but I was playing week in and week out, and with all the driving involved I was constantly having to be vigilant and rest when I could. My mother and girlfriend had both expressed some concern with some of the distances I was driving after doing gigs, and after one particular night and a long drive home, I very nearly came unstuck. 999 were booked to play a one-off gig in Middlesbrough and so I needed to make my own way up there, and decided to drive back pretty much as soon I'd played. For company I took a mate with me, someone to talk to on the long drive home. Of the gig all I can remember is how hot it was inside and out. We didn't hang about, knowing the length of time it was going to take to get home. It was a good three and a half hours' journey, but I didn't think that it would be a problem. My mate was well pissed, and so at least I had him jabbering away in my earhole. We set off but after an hour or so I started to feel a bit knackered. I soldiered on and didn't feel too concerned. But after a couple of hours my companion had pretty much burnt himself out and was falling asleep. With that, every now and then I'd wind the windows down and take in some fresh air, but I have to admit I was flagging. I'd driven nearly 120 miles when I must have nodded off for the briefest of times, because all of a sudden there was a huge bang. With that I immediately came to, and so did my passenger. Within seconds we realised that I had hit the kerb on the passenger side at nearly 80 miles an hour. I obviously slowed right down and regained my composure, and rest assured we were both wide awake now. Almost as soon as I'd hit the kerb I also realised I had done some damage because within a minute or so I had to stop the car, as I could tell that one of the tyres was completely fucked. We were only a few miles away from home but we weren't going anywhere - well, not in my car anyway. It was 3 o'clock in the morning and we were stranded. Thankfully my mate came to the rescue. He rang his missus, told her what had happened and where we were, and she came and picked us up. We'd just had the closest of shaves, and to be perfectly honest, we were lucky to be alive. The fact that there was no other traffic on the road was a godsend, the flipside being that we could have ended up in a field upside down, and nobody would have known that we were there. Alternatively we could have hit the kerb and lost control of the car and that would have been another nightmare scenario. Late the next morning we headed out to my motor to assess the damage. There was no way I could drive the car so I called the AA, and they came out and told me the true extent of the damage. In short, the complete passenger side suspension was knackered, and both wheels were ruined. After this I vowed to never again drive for longer than two hours after a gig. It just isn't worth it. Let's just say that I got the swiftest of reprimands from the senior females in my life.

With that out of the way, and another one of my nine lives used up, it was back to business. RESISTANCE 77 had been invited to play at the GREAT ALTERNATIVE MUSIC WEEKEND at BUTLINS in Skegness. We were booked to play the introducing stage, which I found a bit odd, as we are not a new band; quite the opposite in fact. I suppose it was a thing whereby we were being introduced to the festival as a whole. Anyway, this is how it works. Four bands play on each consecutive day and at the end of each day's sets, the audience are invited to vote for the band that they enjoyed the most. The band with the largest amount of votes wins the day and is then promoted to play one of the main stages the following year. As is always the case in the RESISTANCE 77 camp, we aim to be as tight and energetic as possible, and this here event gave us the impetus to really dig deep and give it some welly. I'd never played one of these do's before and I was a little apprehensive. I'd never really shared the view that punk rock and the like would sit well in such a setting as Butlins. I travelled up to the gig not knowing what to expect really, so I approached it like any other gig and looked forward to it. On getting to the site and being granted entry and getting backstage, it was obvious that this was another one of those well-organised events. After meeting up with the lads and sussing out the venue we were playing, we went and soaked up the atmosphere, then went and checked out the other stages. I was surprised how big they were and did relish the opportunity of playing on one of them if we were lucky enough to win on our respective stage. Come show time we were ready to give it our best shot, and blasted into our half-hour set. We didn't hang about, and rest assured we were firing on all cylinders. To be honest, when RESISTANCE 77 are on form there aren't many bands who could touch us live, and that's including the top-notch bands. We give them all a run for their money and this here set was no different. We all played like demons, and as much as the setting was a little alien to us, we played a blinder. I can't remember the names of the other bands we were up against and I wasn't totally into the idea of the competitive element, but that's what it was. We finished our set knowing we'd given it our all. A couple of hours after we'd finished, and all the bands had played, we found out that we'd got the most votes and would be playing on the main stage the following year. Well-deserved, I thought. Good luck hasn't always followed the band around, so for all of us this, was a nice bit of karma. We'd be back the next year with the same attitude, playing what I think are some of the best songs on the punk rock scene.

7. HOW DO YOU FEEL ABOUT PLAYING IN THE STATES? I DON'T THINK THEY'LL LET ME IN

Back in 2007 when the re-formed ENGLISH DOGS were back and firing on all cylinders, there was talk of the band going to America to play some gigs. For everyone involved, this seemed like a really exciting proposition, but there happened to be one major snag. My prison record and list of former offences was going to be a problem. For someone such as myself, with a fairly extensive criminal record, it wasn't just a case of booking a flight to the States and just turning up willy-nilly and expecting a welcoming party to greet me on the other side. Everybody has to apply for a visa to enter the States and so this entails going online and answering relevant questions. If one has no police record whatsoever, then gaining a visa is pretty much straightforward and is most probably likely to be granted immediately. Not quite so straightforward when it comes to somebody like me. The ENGLISH DOGS knew of my chequered past, and with that in mind I informed them I would make the application but told them not to build their hopes up. I went online and started the process. Now, it had been some years since I'd been in trouble with the law, but with good advice from another party I was told that honesty was the best policy to proceed with such a thing, so that's what I decided to do. To answer the questions as honestly and as accurately as I could. Various questions came up with regards to criminal offences, and the nature of the offences incurred. Well, after finishing the questions and answering them I was told I would not be granted a visa but there was another option available to me if I wished to pursue the matter further. If I made a request to the relevant department I could apply for an interview at the American Embassy down in London in the hope of being granted a visa that way. Thinking ahead I felt I had nothing to lose, as this was definitely up there with one of the things I wished to do. Who wouldn't want to go and play in the States? With that I pressed forward and got a date to go down to the embassy and be interviewed. It was a long shot, but one I felt worth taking. Especially taking into consideration the time that had elapsed between my last run-in with the law and the present day. It wasn't just the criminal record that was going against me though, it was the nature of the offences and the seriousness of them.

Drugs are a big no-no over there, but having got this far I felt I had nothing to lose. I got a date for my interview and was keen to see this through and hopefully come out of it with a heads-up that I could travel to America. Come the day of the interview I travelled down to the Big Smoke and made my way to Grosvenor Square. There were loads of people down, all hoping to secure themselves the document that would allow them to travel. On arrival, and after giving the appropriate people some basic information, I was told to take a seat and wait to be called, and so that's what I did. I waited and waited. Dinner time came and went and I'd been there since nine already. The afternoon wore on and still I hadn't been called. Eventually I went to one of the empty interview booths to ask what the delay could possibly be. The person on the other side informed me that my documents may have gone to another department to be checked, but as soon as they were ready I would be called for. I went back to my seat and waited. Eventually after what seemed like an eternity, and after seeing people who had been way behind me in the queue getting their pink forms with permission to travel, at last I was called. I entered the booth and an American gent started the interview. All of a sudden I felt quite nervous and proceeded to answer his questions clearly and as honestly as I could. This fella had a computer in front of him and asked me questions with a look of stoic reservation on his face. After the formal questions he turned to my criminal activities and his line of questioning took on a more serious tone. I thought I was doing fine until he asked me when I was last arrested. Well, I had to think about this one as I needed to answer him as honestly as I could. It seems that I had answered his question incorrectly, because no sooner had I given him my answer than I was informed that according to the information on his computer the date that I gave him didn't correspond with his. This irritated me somewhat and I think it showed. My retort to him was that I couldn't remember everything from those days and, being possibly a little too forward, asked him what was the point in asking me a question that he already had the answer to. With that I think he'd made his decision. The interview ended and he informed me that on this occasion my application for a visa was being denied, and that I could apply again in another eight years. After the initial shock, I just wanted to get out of the place. I wanted out of London and to just get back home. I remember getting on the Underground and ringing the DOGS' guitar player and telling him the bad news. He assured me that it wasn't a problem and that there was still loads of other places in the world to go and do gigs. His response was reassuring, but I was still rather disappointed and couldn't stop myself from feeling that I'd shot myself in the foot. So I came home feeling a little despondent, thinking I was probably never going to have the opportunity of playing in the States.

Forward the clock to 2017 and once again I found myself in exactly the same position. All of the bands I was a member of had been to the States in the past and so the question of doing gigs over there came up again. RESISTANCE 77 had been invited to play at the now famous PUNK ROCK BOWLING festival in Las Vegas, and although they had started to press me about making a new application for an American visa, I had been avoiding the issue for a couple of reasons. One being the actual lengthy process involved, and two, the prospect of another disappointing refusal put paid to me wanting to go through with it all again. CONFLICT were also constant visitors over to the US and there was the mention of even 999 going back out there. It now seemed that the time was right to reapply. The eight years had elapsed and with the possibility that gigs over there were going to happen I once again started the process. The procedure to apply had changed somewhat, but in short the online approach was still in place. I knew I would get a rebuttal on my initial application, and would more than likely have to go through another interview down at the US embassy. Being a UK resident the document I was applying for to gain entry is called an ESTA form. Without that it's a non-starter. I logged on to the relevant site and proceeded to start my application, and as I knew it would, was initially refused an ESTA due to my past criminal record. But as in the past I was granted the right to an interview down in London. Once again I secured a date that would take place a few weeks down the line. In the meantime I had to get other pieces of documentation and information together for the embassy people to look over.

All the while I was taking bookings and doing more gigs with CONFLICT, which for me was great. I was now getting to grips with the way the songs were played. I started to put my own little spin on certain tracks due to the fact that my playing style is quite a lot different to Paco's. Colin didn't seem to mind as long as I didn't veer it too far off the original format, and even acknowledged that the way the songs were now being played updated them somewhat. With CONFLICT it's all about control. The songs don't have to be played at breakneck speed, thus allowing Colin to spit out his vocals in full and in time. It was great getting to know how Hoddy and Gavin, the two guitarists worked, and before too long we were one hell of a tight unit, with both of them being very good at what they do. We played one gig which turned out to be one hell of an experience. This being my fourth or fifth gig we travelled to Ferrara in Italy. CONFLICT were headlining this one-off gig, which could only mean one thing. Having played Italy before and from my past experience, for some bizarre reason, they like to do everything really late. This meant that we would more than likely be going on stage at around midnight to about 2.00 in the morning. Not ideal, but that's the way they do things and you just have to go along with it. True to form, that's exactly what happened. On this occasion though, there was an extra little surprise in store that would make this outing particularly gruelling. In short, we flew out to Italy and got picked up by a couple of females who then took us out for some food. I then chose to go to our hotel to get some rest while everybody else carried on drinking. The others came back for a couple of hours and chilled out until it was decided that we would head off to the venue around 7.30pm. It was at this point that we were informed that our flight back to England the next morning was at 6.30 am. With the late hour we were due to play our set, there would be no point in going back to the hotel as we needed to be at the airport at least two hours before we flew back, and the journey from the gig to the airport would take nearly two hours. We got to the venue and for the next five or so hours, it was a case of waiting till stage time, and it was a long wait indeed. Come 1.30am we hit the stage and played a really good set. We came off stage soaking wet, to a bunch of exuberant Italians who were very kind and responsive to the fact we'd made the effort. We couldn't hang about though, as we needed to get off to the airport to catch our flight. It was about 3.30 am and bloody freezing.

We got to the airport a couple of hours later, and after settling down to wait for our flight, we started to talk amongst ourselves about how insane we must be to put ourselves through this kind of thing. All for that hour or so on stage. We arrived back in England in the late morning and I was just so pleased to get home. I'd never done this before and I'd never want to do it again. I'd literally left the house to do a gig abroad, done the gig and come straight home. Unbelievable but true. Next up was a trip up to Scotland to do three gigs, two in Glasgow and one in Dundee. They went very smoothly indeed and they paid well too. We took our own van and driver, and aside from the one gig in Dundee, where Colin stated I played too fast, the band as a whole went down well. Also, just for the record, on the third and last gig at the AUDIO CLUB venue in Glasgow, Colin must have procured himself some serious Colombian marching powder, because I've never seen anybody put in such a manic performance in all my life. He very nearly took Hoddy and Gav's heads off on numerous occasions with his microphone stand antics. As punk rock a performance as I've ever seen and played. CONFLICT finished the year with a great gig in London just after Christmas at the NEW CROSS INN venue. I was enjoying myself with these chaps and couldn't wait for the oncoming New Year and the prospects it would bring. After RESISTANCE 77's great gig at Butlins we played three more gigs to see out the year. One in my hometown, another in Stamford, and a somewhat predominantly skinhead affair in Bruges, Belgium. The last six weeks of 2017 also saw me play a number of gigs with 999. That would make this year as being the busiest I'd ever had as a player. I was in great shape physically and mentally, and although a few people would quote that I was doing too much, I really felt I was making up for lost time. I was now achieving the goals that had passed me by when I was stuck in active addiction for all those years. I still had no desire to use and intended on keeping it that way. Why try and fix something when it's not broken? Life was good, the best it had ever been, in fact. All of my personal relationships were in good order, my business was ticking along nicely, and my musical adventures were reaching new heights. I didn't really see things being bettered with the New Year coming up, but I was on a roll and I wished for it all to continue. So I just approached the

New Year with the same enthusiasm that I'd approach all of the others since I'd gained my sobriety. 100 per cent focused.

As the New Year rolled in I had plenty on my plate to keep me focused to. Saying that, there was one thing that was occupying my headspace, and that was my imminent interview down at the new and upgraded US embassy in London. I definitely felt more confident that I may get the go-ahead on this application, but I didn't want to build my hopes up too much, so I went along with the attitude that there was probably a 50/50 chance of me being granted permission to go. With the New Year in I seemed to hit the ground running because I was out gigging with all three bands. RESISTANCE 77 played the annual Rock City/Nottingham gig with HUNG LIKE HANRATTY, DUNCAN REID AND THE BIGHEADS and THE FUCKWITS, and then the WATERLOO VENUS venue in Blackpool with NO THRILLS. CONFLICT played in Birmingham, Telford and the three Scottish dates mentioned earlier, and with 999 I played Stoke, Newcastle, Birkenhead and Blackpool. I also had gigs in Europe coming up, two in Germany with RESISTANCE 77, Holland, France and a festival in Germany with CONFLICT, and another three in Germany with 999.

Two of these gigs that are most memorable were playing at the famous Berlin venue, the SO36, firstly with CONFLICT and then shortly afterwards with 999. An amazing venue that's hosted loads of decent outfits including THE RAMONES and even DAVID BOWIE. These were little dreams come true for me, as I thought that these kinds of opportunities had passed me by. But here I was, soaking up Berlin and playing my arse off. Yes, I was a busy boy. One month I would play just a handful of gigs and then the next I would be out playing eight or nine. I was definitely out with 999 more though, and that's down to Arturo Bassick/Arthur block-booking gigs over whole weekends, and sometimes starting on a Thursday and then doing the customary Friday and Saturday, or every now and then, finishing with a Sunday night gig too. In all honesty, 999 were especially cheap when one thinks of them being one of the classic first wave bands. Hence the amount of gigs we were doing. It has to be said though, that I was always paid equally with it being a four-way split when it came to payment for playing. It also became very apparent to me at this point that all three bands

I was involved with all had different dynamics, and it is obviously down to different members and their differing personalities. I've always been an observer of people, and none more so than in my musical environment. Each musician or vocalist has their own character, with an abundance of assets and defects, which can sometimes make for a lot of hilarity or a lot of fucking drama. Ying and Yang, so to speak. At the end of the day we are musically minded, otherwise we wouldn't be doing what we do, and with that being said, all you lot see most of the time is the four or five individuals up on the stage doing their thing. What you don't often get to witness is some of the high drama that goes on behind the scenes. You can imagine, can't you, a band that's been on and off the road for two or three decades onwards doesn't always make for happy bedfellows when around each other all of the time. Saying that, there has to be a bit of mutual respect, otherwise we'd just go off on our separate ways and not even bother to turn up and play or rehearse. Oh, that's funny, 999 and CONFLICT barely rehearse anyway. Ha Ha.

A date came through for my embassy interview and I felt a sense of relief that I was going to find out once and for all whether I could go and perform in the States. I was really frustrated that this avenue was unavailable to me, as RESISTANCE 77 had just flown out to Las Vegas to play at the Punk Rock Bowling festival using a young drummer called ALEX, who plays for the band FEROCIOUS DOG. Also, CONFLICT flew out to play a couple of festivals using an American guy on the tubs. Personally I needed to get this sorted, and so was eager to get my interview out of the way, and hopefully get my visa. To show my commitment to the cause I felt that a change in appearance was necessary. I'd been sporting a half black and half white spiky hairdo for the last few years, so I thought that needed to go. So I cut my hair really short, getting rid of all the colour, so that my true hair colour was exposed. Then I bleached it white. In my mind this was a lot less radical than my former barnet incarnation. I didn't wish to come across as a musician type. Besides, I was a barber, so I thought my blonde look would be seen as somewhat job-related. In short, I wanted to set the right impression for my interview. I must have looked totally different, because when CONFLICT played in Leicester a few days before my interview, on meeting the chaps Colin didn't recognise me when he came into the venue. Armed with all the documentation that was being requested, and looking as dapper as one could, and with my good lady travelling with me as a bit of support, we took the train down to London and from there walked the good mile or so to the new embassy. Michele couldn't come in with me. So after wishing me luck she tootled off and found a coffee while I went in. I went through all of the security rigmarole and was eventually given a ticket with my number on it. It was just a case of waiting to be called, and I didn't have to wait too long, not like the last time. Within half an hour or so my number came up and so off I went. In short, the interview went as good as I could have expected, not nearly as terrifying as the one ten years previously. Although there was a glitch in the fact that I was missing a particular document concerning my police records. The interview didn't last long at all, and after asking me various questions, and looking over my documentation, the interviewer concluded by telling me that I wouldn't be granted a visa on that day as they would like some more information. By that they were requesting that I attend a full medical on another date, and for me to forward them the correct police records. This wasn't quite what I was expecting as they hadn't said yes, but they also hadn't said no. I left the building and proceeded to find my girlfriend and tell her the news. I felt disappointed as I was wanting an answer one way or the other, but as my lass pointed out, this was a good thing as I was still in with a chance, and I just had to be patient and see the process through. As soon as we got home that day I immediately got in touch with the relevant parties with regard booking the medical requested. These people only dealt with people like myself, people who were seeking to gain visas to the US. I got a date sorted, and then also requested the missing police document and sent it to the embassy. My medical was to take place, again in London at Bond Street. I got the impression that the medical was a test to see whether I was fit and healthy, but primarily to ascertain whether I was clean and free from any mood-altering substances. If this was to be the case then I had nothing to worry about. My conscience was clear and I knew I could attend the medical knowing that I would pass with flying colours. I did, however, feel that I was being given hoops to jump through here, and that my journey towards getting a visa wasn't being made easy for me.

Wishing to see this through to its logical conclusion and having already invested some time and money getting to this point, my determination in obtaining a visa remained steadfast.

And so once again, myself and Michele travelled to London and on to Bond Street. On finding the place, and being signed in, I had to supply a urine sample and go and wait to be called. I hadn't been waiting long when a lady came and called for me and took me into a room that looked not too dissimilar to a doctor's office. This did all feel a little strange, coming all this way for such a procedure, but hey ho, hopefully this would go some way to helping secure my dream. The medical began with the lady asking me some health questions, concluding with a chest X-ray. After that I was told to go back to the waiting room and once again wait to be called. Not long after this a young Asian guy called through and we then went into his office. His line of questioning was a lot more personal and specifically dealt with my drug-taking history. I answered all his questions honestly and relayed to him that I had now been clean and sober for a number of years. A couple of blood samples were required and so I happily obliged and let him take my blood. And with that he said my medical was done but that they required one final sample of urine, to which I duly obliged. It cost me over £500 for the medical, and after having paid my dues, I was informed that once the US embassy had gone over everything I would hear from them in due course. With that we left and spent the rest of the day in London. I had now done everything that the Americans asked of me, and paid quite handsomely for the privilege. Now I just had to wait. After getting back to town I heard back from the RESISTANCE 77 boys about their one-week stay in Las Vegas at the Punk Rock Bowling festival. I was most envious after hearing what they'd got up to, and who they'd met while over there. I just had to sit and wait now, and hopefully my chance to experience America would come through soon. CONFLICT too, headed out to Chicago leaving me behind, and this just added to my lack of patience with regard this matter. I knew that I was going to have to wait. I just didn't know for how long.

In the meantime it was down to business as usual. I'd finally honed my playing to complement the CONFLICT set list, with gigs in Derby, Sheffield, Stoke,

Leicester and Preston as well as appearances at the Leperfest in Belgium, where I also got to see one of my favourite hardcore bands from Brazil called RATOS DA PAROU. We also played three dates in Paris, Caen and Dijon in France, with the Paris gig at the famous LE GIBUS CLUB being particularly memorable. Another memorable gig with CONFLICT took place at THE EXCHANGE venue in Bristol. Bristol has always maintained a rather healthy punk scene since back in the day, and on this occasion they didn't let us down either. A mid-sized hall packed to the rafters, with people that seemed to be melting before my eyes because of the heat. They should have been up on stage where we were, it was almost unbearable. Thankfully the management decided to turn on the massive fans that were in there, which offered everybody inside a bit of relief. I was just as busy with the lads from 999 taking in gigs in Hull, Leeds and Doncaster, as well as trips over to Poland with PETER AND THE TEST TUBE BABIES, and Hamburg and Berlin in Germany. With RESISTANCE 77 back from their trip to the US without me, we reconnected and headed out to Germany to play two gigs in Dresden and Oranienburg. On a personal note, it was a real pleasure to visit Dresden, what with being a history buff. I was fascinated to walk around the city and see the evidence, still there, of the horrendous blanket bombing done by the British during the war. Saying that, we also ventured to parts of the city that hadn't suffered bomb damage, namely the palace area, and it was absolutely stunning to see some of that old architecture in all its glory and untouched. Very gothic indeed, and I liked it. As I've already stated earlier, with the chaps from RESISTANCE 77 there was always more of a holiday feel to our adventures abroad, which was great, whereas with 999 and CONFLICT it felt more like we were actually working, although there still had to be a fun element to it otherwise that defeats the whole object of doing this stuff. All of the bands have a slightly different approach to how we worked. With CONFLICT it was always a slightly more serious approach as the message of the band has always been direct and in your face, which is exactly as it should be. I was influenced by that message years earlier as well as the blistering music. All of the bands I play in offer a different message, one that appeals to the differing fans of each particular band.

With myself taking bookings for Conflict I was contacted by a promoter from Mexico who wanted us to play at a festival he was putting on. There was instantly a communication problem between us but I basically got the gist of what he was requesting. I mentioned this to the rest of the band and we all agreed that to do the gig would be great. We were, however, all of the opinion that to go over there just for the one gig seemed a bit pointless, so if there were other gigs to go with the festival, then we would be happy to do it. This started a very lengthy process between myself and the Mexican promoter to organise this trip - one that would take months to finally arrange and confirm. There were flights, accommodation, travel whilst over there, as well as payment to us to sort out. And what with the language barrier to sort things out, it became a bit of a headache toing and froing. Eventually everything was in place. We'd secured four gigs in Mexico to commence on 1 May 2019. This was great as none of us had ever been to Mexico, so it was new territory for all of us, and it was great to have somewhere uncharted to look forward to in the near future. Also, the great thing about going to Mexico was that I didn't need a visa to go and play there.

There was still loads to be getting on with this side before a trip like that would be undertaken. Playing a constant number of gigs from month to month often meant that set lists had to change. This was most noticeable in the 999 camp. The chaps had got so used to playing the same set list that I started to notice on social media that a few comments were being put forward about the band playing the same songs year in year out. This is all well and good if you're only doing sporadic gigs, but as this wasn't the case, we really did need to freshen things up a bit. So with that in mind old songs were suggested and brought back into the set. Songs like *Subterfuge, Brent Cross, Soldier* and *No Pity* were all worked on at sound checks and then reintroduced into the set. Some worked better than others and that tied in with how they went down in a live setting. *No Pity* I particularly relished as it's a very fast song and has to be played very tightly on the drums to make it work. It's also one of the very first punk songs I can remember hearing as a youngster. There's no denying that 999 over the years have written some fantastic songs. The same applied to CONFLICT, and this is something that I can certainly credit Colin with. He never wants the band to sound staid or get into a rut with playing the same old set repeatedly for years. He always wants the band to sound as anarchic and as relevant as it always has been. This band is a completely different animal to the other bands I play with. The set list is long, and with no idle chit-chat between songs, you can expect an aural assault from start to finish. As I've quoted, it's the most difficult and challenging set of songs I've ever had to learn, made all the more difficult due to Colin's reluctance to rehearse with the band. I found this to be the same with the lads from 999. They didn't like rehearsing. This was a revelation to me as I'd always been used to meeting up and practising, whether it be to get ready for a gig, or to write new stuff. With CONFLICT now embarking on a more vigorous schedule than had been known for some time, other songs were brought in. *Cruise, This Is Not Enough* and *From Protest To Resistance*, three awesome songs that again informed me as a youth were now included in what was already a lengthy and powerful set. You can imagine what it was like for me to get to grips with the different songs that 999 and CONFLICT had between them. With RESISTANCE 77 it was different again. There was always a desire to rehearse and that came primarily from Oddy, who is a stickler for detail. Being a bit OCD, he likes things to be just right. A good quality which for the most part guaranteed a sterling performance by the band when we did gigs. This was particularly evident when it came to the Rebellion festival appearance each year, and 2018 was no different. RESISTANCE 77 where nowhere near as prolific as 999 and CONFLICT when it came to gigging, but being one of the Rebellion festival's mainstays, and always pulling in a good crowd, we made sure that we were ready to deliver. With the festival just round the corner I was booked to play just twice with RESISTANCE 77 and 999. Sadly, CONFLICT were banned from the event due to an altercation between Colin and the event's security a few years earlier. It wasn't the festival organisers that were banning the group, but the firm who arranged the security. They weren't used to being threatened with extreme violence by maniacal punk rockers. And so with a ban being imposed, I suppose that was quite understandable. Saying that, it didn't stop us from making inroads into putting that behind us and trying to rectify the situation, in the hope of the ban being lifted and CONFLICT being once again allowed to participate. As per usual at Rebellion, 999 played in the Empress Ballroom. Now I do remember that we hadn't done a gig for a couple of months because of health issues within the ranks, and to be perfectly honest we could have done with a rehearsal before the gig. I thought we were a bit ropey, especially at the start of the set. Saying that, having got into our stride, the rest of the songs went well, and the reaction we got from the crowd belied the fact that we as a band knew our performance was a tad lacklustre. RESISTANCE 77, however, were on top form, and we played the next day on the newly revamped Casbah stage. The place was packed and we played really well to a packed venue of about 2,500 people and went down well. Again, the popularity of the band was evident due to the amount of merch we were selling, and the amount of shirts fellow punks and skins were wearing.

From the end of August, and for the next few months, I had a heavy schedule to contend with. 999 went off to Stockholm without me as I was already booked with CONFLICT. This was an ongoing problem, and so understandably 999 got themselves in a deputising drummer to take my place when I couldn't attend due to my other commitments. They didn't have to look far though, because Cass, who played for the LURKERS, filled in for me, and I'm sure he relished the opportunity to do so, what with him being a lifelong fan like myself. After that though, we played a steady stream of gigs, taking in York, Norwich, Northwich, Glasgow, Carlisle, Sunderland, Brighton and Portsmouth. It was also towards the tail end of the year that some serious discussions with regards recording a new album began. It definitely looked like it was going to happen, but at this stage the main topic of our conversations were about who was going to pay for it and who could we get to release it.

With a slight sense of loss about not being able to play the Rebellion festival, CONFLICT just cracked on regardless. Firstly we played at the Warehouse 23 venue in Wakefield, a fantastic venue, with GBH, which was a great night. We then went up to Scotland and played at Bannermans in Edinburgh and then the Krakatoa in Aberdeen, a great little venue that I'd played with 999 a year or so earlier. Myself, Gav and Hoddy had tried to rework the song *Berkshire Cunt* out for future use, but once again Mr Jerwood hadn't been there when we were practising it. So when we sound checked to it in Aberdeen he proclaimed that it was played far too fast, and so for the time being that one went back on the back burner, so to speak. We then went over to Poland and played Warsaw and Poznan. As it was approaching winter it was very cold, and so I made sure that I was well prepared for the trip. From past experience I've learned to adapt to the cold environments, especially after developing chest infections due to going into the cold after playing a frenetic set in a hot and sticky club. The gigs went well, and it was at this point that I had a fantastic new CONFLICT backdrop made up which would accompany us to all future gigs.

After Poland we played at the annual punk festival held in Chippenham, along with other like-minded bands, THE SUBHUMANS and ZOUNDS. After that we played at THE WITCHWOOD in Manchester. We took things right to the wire by playing in London on New Year's Eve, for which we were handsomely rewarded with a very enthusiastic crowd.

Resistance 77 finished off the New Year by also playing at the Warehouse 23 venue in Wakefield with BILLY CLUB and THE ANTI NOWHERE LEAGUE, and finally in Newcastle-under-Lyme with CONTROL, SNIDE REMARKS, KNOCK OFF and NO THRILLS. This was a memorable gig, but not for the reasons that I would have liked it to have been. After the gig, and whilst I was on my way home, I had a run-in with the law. I remember being absolutely knackered after the gig and just wanted to get off and on my way home. Well, I must have made a couple of dodgy moves in my motor due to being in unfamiliar territory, because before too long I had the coppers behind me with their lights flashing like fuck. I was on the motorway and I have to admit that I didn't know where to stop. I thought I would pull over at the first given opportunity. But no, the driver of the police car pulled alongside me and his female colleague was gesticulating frantically at me to pull over. I thought OK, right, I'll pull over straight away. After doing so I got straight out of my car before the officer did, so as to prove my compliance. He ordered me into the back of their car and proceeded to lay into me about not stopping when I should have done, and that he thought that I wasn't going to stop at all, and with that he was about to call for backup. I remained as calm as I could and stated that I was actually quite startled when they started up with the lights flashing right behind me and that

I'd never experienced anything like this before, and being on the motorway, I didn't actually know where a good place to stop would be. The cop ranted on for a while, but I didn't rise to his manner of speaking down to me, and with that his colleague started asking me all of my driver details and the like. As I say, I retained a level head and answered the questions clearly and calmly. He started to relax in his tone after a while, but not before informing me that I was going to be reported for not stopping, and driving without due care and attention. Amazingly I wasn't breathalysed. I thought that would have been a certainty. My details came through all above board, and with that I was allowed to go, but not before I was told I would be hearing from them in due course. What a bastard. A somewhat minor blemish on what had been an absolutely incredible year. Later, I received a rather hefty fine and some points added onto my licence. What could I do? Absolutely nothing except take it on the chin and crack on regardless. With a New Year on the horizon I had to be thankful for what I had. Life was good and I was ready and eager to see what adventures the New Year would have in store.

In 2014 I joined Facebook and soon found that it was a great and a positive way of reaching like-minded people. By that I mean people who are into their music. I'm not interested in food posts, politics or airing one's dirty linen in public, but I found it a great platform with regards to music promotion and networking, and finding out what other people are doing. Initially I searched out groups that dealt primarily in the SEX PISTOLS, and soon found hundreds of pages of pictures of the band that I'd never seen before. This was of great interest to me, what with them being the band that pushed me on and into my musical journey. From then on though, I started to use Facebook in a number of ways, to enhance my profile as a musician. A bit self-indulgent I hear you say, but let's be honest - no fucker else was going to do it for me. At first I'd promote the fact that I was doing gigs with RESISTANCE 77 and then the LURKERS, and then 999 and so on and so on. I'd hear from people that were either going to said gigs, or ones a bit further down the line, and slowly my social circle on social media was starting to grow. For me it's a positive avenue of communication as I've got to know hundreds of people this way, to the point whereby I actually have ended up meeting people at gigs primarily through our initial introduction

In my element and loving every moment of it

Stuck in some hotel somewhere, killing time. My hair's looking pretty hardcore.

It can be a tad frustrating being sat at the back sometimes. Time to get up and let my presence be known.

One of the most underrated bands on the scene. A kick-ass punk rock band.

Giving it some welly with Nick Cash

CONFLICT, somewhere in Poland. Myself, Gav, Colin and Hoddy

In mid-flight. Another small club gig in Poland. 100 degrees inside and minus 6 outside.

Monterrey in Mexico. At a street food vendor's at about 1.30 in the morning. 4 May, my birthday.

I feel that I now have a somewhat charmed life. During the day, I deal with one section of the general public. On the other I get to travel and play all over the world. Sometimes I just wish to take it easy, hence the motorbikes. Riding a bike is freedom from everything.

999 in Washington DC. This picture was taken on my phone. Also used as part of the sleeve work for the BISH BASH BOSH album.

Realising my lost dream at Joey Ramone St in New York.

Walking the Golden Gate bridge in San Francisco with Colin Jerwood and Kieron Egan.

I'm lucky to have these ladies in my life. Jade, my daughter and my good lady Michele, the one other being my mother. They all play a part in helping me keep my feet firmly on the ground. That's just what I need, especially now that I'm a grandpops.

via Facebook. This enables us all to communicate on different levels, but mainly through a love and passion for all things punk rock. As time went by, and aside from using my own profile page, I started to join other punk-related groups that opened up another whole new world of interest, communication, promotion and new contacts. Eventually, in more ways than I could have imagined, good things started to happen due to my weekly posts with regards my ongoing activities, and I soon had promoters and the like getting in touch with regards to putting us on for future events.

Another thing that I found rewarding was the opportunity to communicate with people who are more in the public domain than myself, as in the past the only way of being able to do this would have been to write to them directly. Now, almost everyone famous or not is in some way or other almost instantly contactable. I've got to know some great people on the music scene that I wouldn't have if it had not been through Facebook and social media. I also found that this was a great way to get across that I was a collector of somewhat rare and collectable memorabilia. My love of original punk posters and other sundry bits of ephemera is well known, and so through advertising my latest acquisitions I often come into contact with like-minded souls who cherish their own bits of ephemera and the like. I suppose one would call it networking, and eventually I would also come into contact with people who had stuff to get rid of. Now, I've always loved a bit of wheeling and dealing, as parts of my earlier story attest to. But back then I went to prison. This was completely different. I started buying stuff and then started to move the odd bit on here and there for a small profit. I stayed away from Ebay and found various Facebook punk rock memorabilia sites that allowed me to do just this. In the last few years I have obtained some amazing little artefacts, namely posters, flyers, fanzines, gig tickets, promo photos and various other items that I've enjoyed for a time and then moved on to a kindred spirit who will enjoy them for what they are. I'm predominately a collector, but some would say I'm a dealer too, which is fair enough, as I do like to make a few quid here and there if I can. Being the collector that I am has introduced me to other collectors too, and as much as I have a sizeable collection of my own it pales into comparison to some of the others out there. I suppose some would deem us collector types a bit odd, collecting bits of paper and stuff for what seems like large amounts of cash, but I don't care, I like it. At least the dealing side of things is legal and not going to get me put away. I've bought and sold from all over the world and will endeavour to do so, because I actually enjoy the momentary buzz of acquiring my next acquisition. Finally regards my Facebook experience, a few years ago I came across a particular group that I found attractive. It dealt with predominantly first wave punk, but to a lesser degree, all punk rock and everything it entails. The group is called PUNK'S NOT DEAD BUT I'M NOT FAR OFF and is run solely by a chap known as SPENNY.

I found myself being drawn to the group more and more and have become a regular participant over the years. Full credit has to go out to this chap who has brought people from the punk rock fraternity from all over the world together. By his own admission he claims that it's the members of the group, people like myself and countless others, that make the group what it is, but from my point of view it wouldn't be what it is if it wasn't for the time and effort that he puts in to make it constantly interesting enough for it to continue year in year out. Over time my band mates from RESISTANCE 77 also got on board, which in turn put us in touch with all of the people on the page, and this started to raise the band's profile. There's a lot of piss-taking, a lot of food posts, which as you know I abhor, and a great deal of camaraderie, but we're all involved through our mutual appreciation of all things punk rock. I can be out gigging somewhere and some random soul will come up to me, introduce themselves and tell me that we're friends through our connection via Spenny's PUNK'S NOT DEAD page. Spenny in particular champions RESISTANCE 77 and over time we'd all meet up at gigs, and in particular at the Rebellion festival, where a large number of members from the group would all congregate at the Churchills pub to talk rubbish, get pissed, reminisce about the good old days and just have a good laugh. Eventually RESISTANCE 77, at the behest of Kieron, wanted to show our gratitude and respect to all the people on the page, so we would write a song and release it as a single as a tribute, but I'll get to that in a little while. So yeah, I've taken advantage of Facebook. Some of you so-called real punks may think that's a cop out, but who cares? Best to move with the times otherwise we get left behind. All publicity is good in my book. OK, bad publicity is not so good in this day and age, there's the keyboard warriors and the snowflakes to deal with. But one can't please everybody all the time, and besides, I'm not really interested in doing that anyway.

8. THE STRAW THAT VERY NEARLY BROKE THE CAMEL'S BACK

I had a wall chart full of gigs to contend with, and from what I could see, I was about to embark on the busiest gigging schedule to date. Negotiations were now in motion with regards 999 doing an East Coast tour of the States. There was the likelihood that CONFLICT would be off over there at some point, and RESISTANCE 77 had also been invited to play a one-off gig at a festival in San Francisco. This all sounded rather grand, but to be honest, I was starting to feel a little anxious. For me everything relied on whether I could actually go to the States or not. I needed that visa to come through, and there was definitely a chance that I would be denied entry. My anxiety was constantly on the up as each week passed by and I wasn't hearing anything back from the US embassy. I just had to sit tight and wait. Closer to home there was the usual run of gigs to be getting on with. For the time being I was out constantly with one band or another, and over the next twelve months I would do 56 gigs, which was unprecedented for me. Looking back, as much as I enjoyed doing them all, it left me feeling a little bit jaded by the year's end.

I kicked off the New Year with my usual stint with RESISTANCE 77 at Rock City in Nottingham with DUNCAN REID AND THE BIG HEADS and THE REVERENDS. And then, as per usual, it was heads down for a flurry of gigs with 999. In January, on 24th we played TRILLIANS in Newcastle, the next day it was the ELEVEN CLUB in Stoke, the next day it was MOLLY'S CHAMBERS BAR in Birkenhead, and to finish off we played at the WATERLOO music bar in Blackpool.

Birkenhead was an important one, because while we were at our digs the next day, as is often the case, we had some time to kill before we headed off. And it was here that Nick Cash and I sat down to work on the nine or so new songs that he'd written. Armed with an acoustic guitar, he'd got the tunes and his vocals already worked out. After giving me a basic rendition of how the songs went, I'd film us both playing through them until they were all down in a basic form. We spent a good two to three hours getting them down with myself adding a basic beat, and by the end of our little session we had the bare bones of some of the songs that were hopefully going to be recorded for the prospective first 999 album in over thirteen years. I wasn't holding back with regards showing my enthusiasm for this because I really wanted to be the one to be included in the recording of anything new. Pablo had pretty much conceded that his playing days were over, and after getting his blessing he encouraged me to get on with it and be the man for the job. A golden opportunity was staring me in the face, and the rest of the 999 boys were right behind it too. A great way to get the New Year underway.

My first CONFLICT gig of the year took place in mid-January at the BRUDENELL SOCIAL CLUB in Leeds. I'd played here in the past with the LURKERS and 999, and this was one of those gigs where I'd got to know the promoter beforehand with a view to getting a CONFLICT gig secured. HOSPITAL FOOD and ANTI SYSTEM also put in appearances. On 2nd February CONFLICT played at the NO FUTURE FESTIVAL with DRONGOS FOR EUROPE, THE VARUKERS, THE MEMBERS, GBH and PENETRATION at THE FLEECE in Bristol. We then flew out to Greece to play at the VIVE LE PUNK festival in Athens. I found this date and place particularly appealing. Being into ancient history and having the whole of the day free before we played, I felt compelled to go in search of the famous Acropolis. It only cost a tenner to get in, and so myself and a couple of the others went in and had a look around. Pretty amazing really when one considers that it is 2000-plus years old. The modern day Athens I saw wasn't up to much, but saying that the country has been going through some shit in recent times and that was reflected with the way it looks today. Rather run-down, with graffiti daubed almost everywhere. Graffiti and street art has its place if it's done properly but it's just everywhere in downtown Athens, and I for one am glad that we don't have that in the UK. Later on that day we headed to the venue, and it was a great club. CONFLICT were on after PETER AND THE TEST TUBE BABIES but we were there early to sound check. The sound check went well, and it promised to be a great gig. We had hours to kill though, so I headed back to our hotel to chill out before stage time.

I headed back to the venue about an hour before we were due to go on, to find the place rammed with hardcore punks and the like of all ages having a good old time. I was really looking forward to this. Sadly, it wasn't to be. It came time for us to go on, and after us all getting ready and then coming off for a brief moment, we finally went on and after the first couple of songs, which went really well, we just seemed to fall apart, and the whole set became a struggle. Colin wasn't happy, which immediately affected his way of putting himself across, which in turn affected the way myself, Gav and Hoddy came across. Colin uses his microphone stand as a prop and for some reason his stand was playing up and so he proceeded to destroy the damn thing, which meant that he was without one completely. From the audience's point of view this must have looked either great or left them a bit confused, thinking that this is how CONFLICT present themselves these days. Things didn't get any better and in short, as a band, we played terribly and I felt it was one of the poorest gigs we'd played since I'd joined. We had one opportunity to win a fairly large crowd over and we blew it. You see dear reader, it ain't all glamour and everything running smoothly. We have to take the blows, dust ourselves off, and live to fight another day. I've been around long enough in this game to realise that's what happens sometimes. We flew back to England a little bloodied, but definitely unbowed. Next up was a gig with RESISTANCE 77 on the 23rd of February at THE STAR AND GARTER in Manchester for the annual PUNK FOR PAM charity gig with DRONGOS FOR EUROPE and GBH. In early March on 1st, 2nd and 3rd CONFLICT played at the MAZE in Nottingham, THE DUMBELLS GALLERY in Liverpool and THE TIVOLI in Buckley, North Wales. A week later I played with 999 at THE LEOPARD in Doncaster on the 8th and the DUBLIN CASTLE in London on the 9th. This was a great gig as I'd always wanted to play there, what with it being such a legendary little venue. Being right near Camden as well. Which is another great place that I like to visit every now and then. It was great to finally do a gig where the likes of MADNESS, AMY WINEHOUSE and various others had cut their teeth, so to speak. Being as small a venue as it is, the atmosphere was great and we played a great set in front of a very hot and sweaty audience. The next day, from London we drove down to Minehead to play the Great British

Alternative Music Weekend. I was on double duty at this event as I played on the Sunday with 999 on one of the main stages, and then the introducing stage with RESISTANCE 77 a couple of hours later. I was knackered after playing with RESISTANCE 77 but, saying that, both sets went well. I just don't know about these Butlins events. It all seems a bit weird that punk bands end up playing at these events, and especially the venues themselves. I personally don't feel that punk rock and these halls go hand in hand. Aside from the Rebellion festival and the odd big stage I've played abroad, I much prefer the smaller venues where one can feel the atmosphere that I would usually associate with a punk gig. The next morning I travelled home with Johnny, the guitarist from RESISTANCE 77, feeling a little bit frayed around the edges, having played four gigs in three days. I had a week off from gigging and spent some time working in my shop. The following week I flew out to Germany to play another three gigs with 999. On the 21st we played at MONKEY'S MUSIC CLUB in Hamburg, the HAUS DU JUGEND in Düsseldorf on the 22nd and the SO36 venue in Berlin on the 23rd. The trips we were taking out to Germany were some of the best that I had done in all my time, and that was partly down to the guy who promoted our trips out there. He had everything down to a tee, from picking us up, to the gear we used, our hotels and transportation. Everything ran very smoothly and he always looked after us to a standard which makes the trip comfortable for everyone involved. The main thing is also that the gigs are all promoted properly, which makes one relax in the knowledge of knowing that night's gig attendance will be half decent, which in turn enthuses us to put on as good a gig as possible. Playing the SO36 once again was fantastic. For this trip we had DIRTBOX DISCO'S side project, SPUNK VOLCANO AND THE ERUPTIONS along as support for all three gigs, and bloody good chaps they are too. A great rock'n'roll band and it was great to have them on board.

April was a relatively quiet month, which was just as well as the coming months were going to be busy ones. The Waterloo venue in Blackpool is a great up-and-coming hotspot for gigs, and I'd had the fortune of playing there a couple of times already. RESISTANCE 77 and CONFLICT were both invited to play at an all-weekend festival, so with more double duties in order I headed up to Blackpool for the weekend. CONFLICT played on Friday 19th and RESISTANCE 77 the next night on Saturday 20th. I was in my element for these gigs, especially for the fact that I was playing two days on the trot. The club owner was kind enough to let me stay in a room above the venue. And so, after doing the CONFLICT set, I waved goodbye to my bandmates as they set off on their journey, quite pleased with myself that I'd be doing it all again the next day. I went off and socialised a little with the pissed and the proud punters, and not too long after that I went and got my head down. I got up the next morning, got myself ready, and headed off into Blackpool to get some breakfast. After that I went and met Spenny from the Punks Not Dead Facebook group and spent a few hours round at his gaff until it was time to head back to the festival. By early evening the RESISTANCE 77 mob had turned up and it was good to see them all.

The band got interviewed a bit later by a magazine called *The Eighth Day*, which really put us in the mood for the gig we played an hour or so later. We played a blinder and went down really well. As much as it was apparent to me that all three of the bands that I play in are different from one another, it's at festival-type events that I really notice that difference. Each band that I play for has its own crowd. I feel very lucky to be able to dip my toes in, so to speak, when it comes to playing with the bands that I do. To the everyday music lover the bands I play for all probably sound the same, but to the trained ear there is no doubt that RESISTANCE 77 are completely different to CONFLICT, as 999 are to the other two. CONFLICT definitely has by far its own distinctive audience, whereas 999 and RESISTANCE 77 appeal to an audience that is in keeping and associated with the punk sound of the late seventies. This particular weekend of gigs I really enjoyed, and that was down to a great venue and a great audience of people who appreciated the music. The only other gig I played in April was at GLASGOW ACADEMY for the great SCOTLAND CALLING all-dayer with CONFLICT. PETER AND THE TEST TUBE BABIES, The EXPLOITED and SLAUGHTER AND THE DOGS were also in attendance. What was also good to see and hear was that Wattie from The EXPLOITED and Colin had buried the hatchet after years of bad-mouthing each other. Whilst we were playing, I observed Wattie sneak onto the side of the stage to come and watch us play. I had a brief chat with him later on as we both ended up watching a little bit of SLAUGHTER AND THE DOGS playing their set. The Calling gigs have become quite a thing over the last few years, and the promoter is a true gent who knows how to look after the bands. I just wish that RESISTANCE 77 were given the chance to play at a couple of these events as I know we would go down a storm.

Next up was the eagerly awaited Mexico trip with CONFLICT. I'd worked really hard to get this outing arranged, and so after months of negotiating and making sure everything was in place, all concerned were looking forward to breaking new ground and giving it some to the Mexicans. On 1 May CONFLICT flew out from Heathrow on a direct flight to Mexico. Now, the guy that I had been doing all the arranging with had initially booked the band to play at one big outdoor festival. But, at the behest of myself and the others, he was encouraged to get us other gigs. Taking into consideration that we were flying all the way out there to do just the one gig seemed a little pointless. So another three gigs were arranged as well as the festival slot. We were going to be in the country for nearly a week and so the prospect of doing four gigs seemed easily doable. The flight over there was long but it wasn't uncomfortable as we had plenty of space to stretch out as the flight wasn't full by any means. Now, I'd done some travelling in my time but I have to say that when we touched down in Mexico City I was a little disorientated as I was now in a completely different time zone. We landed at about 9.00 in the evening local time, but my body was telling me it was four in the morning. We eventually got to our first port of call which was a hostel-type place, and we couldn't wait to get our heads down. It was here that we met the guy that I'd been liaising with to get the trip arranged. He was a small, dumpy Mexican punk called LOKO and he seemed pleasant enough. But things weren't going to be easy as he barely spoke English and my Mexican is not the best. He got us booked into the hostel after what seemed like an eternity, and as far as we knew he would be meeting us at some time the next morning. With that we all went and slept. Again not easy, because by the time I hit the sack, my body was telling me that it was time to get up. My body clock is so strict these days that any deviation from my normal routine knocks me right up. Well, I knew that this was probably going to happen and so I just got on with it and tried to get some shut-eye. I found that Colin, however, had no such problem. That bastard could sleep anytime and anywhere. Hoddy wasn't far behind and Gav's a little younger than the rest of us so he could recover a little quicker. Old muggins here would often be the last to get to sleep and the first to wake up. Since I got into recovery my sleep pattern is fine-tuned. I cannot sleep like I did when I was in my twenties. I have to get by on about five to six hours a night. Anyway, I got some sleep but lo and behold, about three or four hours later I'm awake, and once I'm awake I can rarely ever get back to sleep. So I got up and so as not to disturb the others I put some shorts on and went out of our dormitory and into the kitchen area, where I observed a spiral stairway that led up to the roof. Taking into consideration that it was still only the middle of the night I ventured up there and found myself on a roof top that doubled up as a social area with chairs and tables. I sat up there and chilled out. It was noticeably warm and I definitely felt that I was a long way from home. Knowing what time it would be in the UK, I messaged a few of my significant others, including my girlfriend and daughter, informing them that I was safe and sound in Mexico City. I was knackered but I was pleased to be there. A few hours later the rest of the lads started to stir. By the time we were all up we were getting a bit peckish, but we didn't have a clue where we were, so with that we waited for our host Loko to turn up and hopefully provide us with some grub, or at least point us in the right direction. It was from here on in that we found that this wasn't going to be as smooth and relaxing a trip as we were hoping. If the word mañana is a term used to indicate that something will get done when it gets done, over the next few days we would find ourselves becoming rather exasperated with the way things got done over there. Loko turned up eventually and, with the language barrier being such as it was, we finally got it through to him that we needed food and water, so to speak.

By the early afternoon we'd finally been fed and decided to take in some of the atmosphere of downtown Mexico City. It was a beautiful day and we were in for a treat as we happened to chance upon the longest carnival-type event I have ever witnessed. The procession went on for some considerable time and everybody seemed to be in good spirits. It was a nice way to ingratiate ourselves with the place. I soon noticed that the locals seemed to be enjoying themselves.

As a rule they were all rather short in height compared to us westerners. After a few hours we had to head back to our digs and get ready for our first gig that night. We got picked up by a typical punk mobile-type van and made the hour or so journey across the city to the venue. As we progressed I noticed a prevailing and not necessarily pleasant smell emanating over the place, and from what I could gather this was due in part to the city's sewerage system having to deal with its nine million or so residents. It wasn't overpowering but it was definitely noticeable. I love being driven around a completely different country to my own. However, on seeing the different surroundings on the way to that first gig, it was definitely noticeable to observe that we were in a place that would be considered third world by comparison to all of the countries I'd played in Europe. On parking up outside the venue I don't think that any of us expected the reception we got when we stepped out of the van. There was already a large crowd outside the club, but we must have looked like creatures from another planet, because as soon as all of these hardcore Mexican punks saw us, they flocked around us like flies, with requests for photos and stuff. Now, this is not the kind of thing an anarchist band like CONFLICT would normally associate themselves with, but in truth I got the feeling that these punks were quite overwhelmed that we were actually there to bring a bit of real English punk rock to brighten up their lives. I'd never experienced this kind of welcome and later on, once it had died down a little, Colin and Hoddy admitted the same too. In short, we were mobbed by hundreds of these punks but sadly we could only gesticulate with our hands as a source of communication, as none of them spoke English. To be honest it was very nice, and we all dutifully complied with the incessant requests to have pictures taken with them all. We stuck out like sore thumbs! Eventually we got to our little place of seclusion under the stage. The place was absolutely jam-packed, and personally I couldn't wait to go on and play. I observed over the next couple of hours a couple of the home-grown type bands and I have to say that I wasn't overly impressed. As much as these Mexicans certainly looked the part, the style of punk music they were playing was what I would call very generic. One speed, breakneck, and each song sounding very much like the one they had just finished. That aside, one couldn't fault them for their enthusiasm, and to be fair, the atmosphere was electric inside the club. It was time for us to go on and so, as per usual, Hoddy, myself and Gav went on to set our gear up and get the onstage sound right in readiness for when we went on. The venue was packed downstairs at stage level and upstairs on the balcony and, as I looked out just before we were about to start, before me was a heaving mass of Mohicans, spiky hair in multi-coloured style, which in all honesty reminded me of a modern-day city Indian congregation of punk rock. On cue I started the bass drum intro to the song *The Positive Junk* and then, as Gav came in with guitar, I looked down and I couldn't believe what I was seeing. I kicked into the beat and then Colin came in with his first lines. I looked down and the whole crowd of about 400 people kicked off. To me, it looked like a battle had just commenced. It was truly awe-inspiring and, dare I say it, delightfully terrifying. I was screaming out loud as this was happening. This was fantastic. I was witnessing a punk rock version of the battle of Agincourt, and these crazy Mexican fuckers were battling it out whilst I provided the beat. As a punk musician this was heaven. The last time I had witnessed anything like this was way back when I'd witnessed ENGLISH DOGS gigs when I was sixteen and seventeen. In short, this was by far the wildest audience I've ever played in front of and for the rest of the set I enjoyed watching the throng of people heaving and swaying from one side of the room to the other. Colin had a few problems with the stage monitors, but aside from that, for me this was a brilliant and classic punk rock gig. We were eager to get out of the venue and back to our place of residence. One, because we were all still pretty knackered, and two, we had a flight to catch the next morning. The people who were taking care of us though, had other ideas, and after what seemed like an eternity, they finally got their shit together and drove us back so that we could try and get some rest. Personally, I was jet lagged to fuck and I remember getting some semblance of rest, but as per usual I was one of the first up. We had a mid-morning flight to catch.

We were off to Monterrey and we were supposed to be getting picked up around 8 o'clock. Well, 8 o'clock came and went, and so once again we all started to feel on tenterhooks wondering where the fuck our transport to the airport was. We waited and waited, and a woman who was taking care of things arrived and was making phone calls in order to ascertain where the band van was, and how long it was going to be before it arrived. Myself and the band were getting concerned because if we missed the flight that meant we miss the gig, which in turn means no money. With the tiredness we were all feeling everyone was already a little edgy, and so this just made things worse. Everyone that is except Colin, who just thought that this was all rather amusing. Eventually the van turned up and we finally set off for the airport. The only thing was, we were now in a race against the clock to get there on time. We were a little stressed, to say the least, but our Mexican hosts didn't seem to be too concerned at all. We arrived at the airport and flew out of our carriage and told the organisers that we would see them in a couple of days. After some more confusion, whereby it became apparent that we'd been dropped off at the wrong terminal, we finally - and after some considerable rushing around - arrived at the right point of call, just in the nick of time for us to board our flight to Monterrey. It soon became apparent to us that these fuckers over in Mexico were far too laid-back. More laid-back than we were used to anyway, but at this point we were just happy to be on our flight out of Mexico City. We landed in Monterrey in good time. People were waiting for us when we came through and immediately took us to a hotel in the city. We arrived mid-afternoon and it was as hot as hell and so, after being allocated our rooms, once again we all retired for a couple of hours to get some rest. I was feeling rough, I have to admit. The combination of hardly any sleep coupled with the intense heat only added to this. I was still happy to be there, and besides, we had another gig to do in a few hours. Later on we were called to the venue to do the sound check, and we were pleasantly surprised. We were playing at a great venue, whereby everything was provided, and after being amply fed and watered, we sound checked and just chilled out. Someone had taken the time to get a massive CONFLICT backdrop together and I expressed the desire to obtain it after the gig and to bring it home with me. Later, however, I gave up on that idea, realising that it was far too big and cumbersome for me to drag around Mexico and back to the UK. Eventually the punters started turning up and, once again, they were the friendliest bunch one could ever meet and we all duly obliged when it came to group photo requests. Not as many turned up for this gig, but we went on and played our socks off. Afterwards we again mingled with the locals who were really kind and complimentary, or that's how it came across to us, as once again both parties couldn't understand each other at all. I do remember speaking to a young punk who was there to photograph the gig and he spoke relatively good English. I remember leaving the gig earlier than the others as it was only a short walk to the hotel, as I was eager to try and get myself some rest. The jet lag was hitting me quite hard as we'd been on the go pretty much since we'd got there. We were being picked up quite early the next morning for our next flight to a place called Mexicali, and I wanted to try and keep myself mentally and physically in check. The next morning we found ourselves once again heading towards another airport, and thankfully everything was running smoothly. We flew right up the country and ended up on the border with America. It was even hotter up there, and when we arrived two punks met us and we travelled in two separate vehicles to a house where we were treated really well and shown some nice hospitality. After we'd been there a couple of hours I ventured outside and the heat hit me like a ton of bricks. Whilst outside I noticed that all of the houses, which were very basic and humble in comparison to regular homes I was used to seeing in the UK and Europe, all had really big motors that didn't really match the quality of the somewhat basic houses. It seemed to me that flashy motors took precedence over people's homes.

Eventually we were informed that we were going to be taken to where we would be staying for the night. Once again the two punks took us all in the two different motors. After a relatively short journey we pulled up outside this building to be greeted by Colin, who had gotten there first in one of the other motors. On getting out the car he said to me, 'We're not fucking staying here. It's a fucking shithole.' We went and took a look, and Colin wasn't wrong. It was a shithole. In short there were two floors, upstairs was a practice room with these three old boys banging out some dirge on substandard equipment. I said hello and then wandered downstairs. To be honest, downstairs resembled a crack den and the garden area was adorned with what looked like flea-infested chairs, and dog shit was everywhere. Colin was right, we weren't staying there. I immediately set about trying to tell our driver that this wasn't acceptable, and that we weren't happy. We needed and deserved somewhere proper to get some rest and relax. On further observation I noticed that there didn't even seem to be anywhere for us to sleep. To his credit the driver got straight on the blower, and before we knew it we were being driven to another location, one that was more suitable for five blokes to get some rest and recuperation. We ended up in a complex-type facility where there were hotel rooms next to each other. Very similar to what you see in American films. Courtyard to park in, then the rooms up a stairway with numbered doors running along a landing. It was a little run-down but that was becoming a familiar theme here. Everywhere in Mexico we were experiencing seemed to be run-down. At the time though, we were just happy to have somewhere to regroup and relax. We had the night off, so with Colin and Hoddy in one room and myself, Gav and Tony (our merch guy) in another, we kicked back and tried to acclimatise ourselves a little more. If this trip was proving to be a little taxing, little did we realise that it wasn't going to get any easier over the coming days.

The next day was my birthday, and at this point I was still quite happy to be in Mexico. As far as I was concerned the two gigs we had done had been great. The flip side was the way things were being arranged and the organisational skills seemed to be really lacking. Between myself and the rest of the band it was the main topic of conversation. What with us being in the country for at least another two to three days, and with another two gigs to do, we just had to grin and bear it. There was no food available from where we were staying and so on that morning, and with a few hours to kill, I decided to venture out with the intention of finding somewhere that did decent food. I wanted somewhere to sit down and take in the atmosphere. Tony, our erstwhile number one follower and general merch guy, and Gav joined me. We set off out of the apartment complex to find such a place. For some reason most places were closed, but I do recall someone mentioning a national holiday or something along those lines. Eventually we found a traditional Mexican cafe restaurant that dealt with all the usual stuff - fajitas, enchiladas, burritos and tacos. We managed to get through a mix of much of everything, and I even treated myself to a massive dollop of chocolate cake, and for the first time in the last few days, I felt like I'd eaten something half-decent. We left the place quite fulfilled in the truest sense of the word and out into the full-on Mexican heat. It was bloody hot, and so we decided to head back to our place of stay by flagging down a taxi. Tony had our hotel coordinates on his phone, and gave them to the taxi driver, who then proceeded to take the route he had been given, only to find that he couldn't find where we were staying. This was just another thing to add to our growing frustrations and exasperation. Eventually, through the driver's patience and wherewithal, he managed to find our place. After paying the man we bid him farewell and went off to find Colin and Hoddy. Those two are pretty adept at just chilling out and doing fuck all until gig time, something I wish I could do. Sadly, I just can't do it. I've even witnessed them both crashed out at a venue while a manic and raucous gig's going on all around them. But as soon as it gets to stage time, up they rise and on with the show they go. Later on in the early evening our two punk rock drivers turned up to take us to the gig. Now for the purpose of you, the reader, I'm going to briefly explain because I don't want to bore you with all the details, and because to be honest, I fucking hated it. So here goes. We turn up at the venue. Venue is upstairs on a large open air veranda-type setting. Makeshift stage, very rickety. After observing the equipment we are supposed to be using we ascertain that it's shit. There are five bands on before us, which means we won't be on until God knows when. Aaaagh. Nobody seems to know who CONFLICT are. Hardly anybody has turned up.

With that aside there were three things that I remember about that night that were all different but all connected, due to all taking place within a few hours of each other. As is often the case, I sometimes go off on my own for a walk. I don't know why, I just do. On this particular night I left the venue and proceeded to walk into what I can only loosely describe as an old west saloon bar-type area. It was dark and I remember walking down the street, and as I'm walking I realise I'm approaching what looks like a heavily made-up and scantily clad female who is, in actual fact, a prostitute. And how do I know this? Well, as I approach she steps out from the building and gesticulates to me with her hand and says something to me. From a distance, and as I was approaching, she didn't look too bad. But it didn't take long at all for me to realise that she was actually a he. I spurned his advances and moved on. Next, with the venue being shit, the equipment being shit, and the fact that hardly anybody was there, CONFLICT played the fastest set I had ever played with them. We got ourselves out there as quickly as possible, just to get the whole experience out the way pronto. And thirdly, and this was the nicest memory of the day, after the gig, our drivers took us to a traditional open-air street food vending joint. About five or six folk all cooking food to order with an array of vegetables and sauces, firing food out in a conveyor belt style. It was here that we all sat down as a band about one in the morning and all the lads wished me a happy birthday. This was a nice touch from our drivers, who probably felt that we needed a reward after the very weird gig we had just done. Eventually we got back to our digs and got our heads down. The next morning everyone rose slowly but we were all eager to get ourselves out of Mexicali and back to Mexico City for what was to be the primary gig of our trip. Our drivers turned up and we ended up driving along and adjacent to what is the massive high red metal border wall that divides Mexico from the United States. As we drove along you could see just wasteland through the fence and apparently that wasteland went on for many miles until any form of human habitation and civilisation could be reached. This was all to deter the Mexicans from even thinking about scaling the wall and escaping to America. After being in the real Mexico for only a few days and witnessing the frail infrastructure and how downtrodden they are as a country and as people, I can understand completely why certain numbers would feel the need to try and escape for a better way of life. America doesn't want them, hence the wall. The Mexicans, bless them, without the money or the ability to speak English, even if they could get over the wall and beyond no-man's-land, wouldn't stand a chance. As we were being driven to the airport we all came to the realisation that we were, in fact, in a third world country, and that good old Blighty isn't such a bad place after all. We flew back to Mexico City and after being picked up we were informed that we would be staying on-site where the festival was taking place. We weren't playing until the next day, and so with that in mind we were once again eager to just get ourselves into our rooms and to get some rest and chill out. I can remember that while we were on the journey from Mexico City airport to the festival I heard from my 999 bandmate Arturo that the proposed tour of America was now confirmed for November and that if my visa application didn't come through soon then another drummer would be going in my place. This made me feel rather anxious for a few minutes, but I kept it to myself. There was nothing I could do except hope that it would come through in time. Also, I didn't really have time to think about that. I was on the other side of the world and I had business to attend to here.

We got to the festival at around nine in the evening and after getting through the main gates, the familiar sounds that one would associate with a festival were in full swing. I was a little disorientated due to it being dark but eventually Loko, the main man who I'd arranged everything with, appeared with his brother and they showed us to our place of stay. We found out that the festival site was an old disused holiday camp from the seventies and early eighties. After being shown to our chalets, this soon became apparent to us because like everything else we had witnessed, the place was very run-down. At that time this didn't bother us. Our main concern was that we needed a couple of essentials, towels and lots of bottled water. Both for obvious reasons, but on further investigation, neither were present in our rooms. We requested both of these from Loko who, after showing us to our rooms, said he'd be back, or he'd send someone with them to us shortly. Needless to say neither turned up that night. We slept and the next morning, myself being the early riser was up early and out looking for the necessities that we needed. It was also apparent that we didn't have any loo roll, so after what seemed like ages I managed to find someone in charge who showed me to a place where I was given all three of the essentials that we needed. I handed them out to the lads and got myself cleaned up and went for a wander to take in the surroundings. It was a beautiful morning and not too hot yet. We were situated in a chalet complex adjacent to another row of rooms, and everybody else was rising too. It was then that I recognised a couple of the lads from THE SUBHUMANS, so I went over and said hello. They'd flown over to Mexico the day after us, and they'd had some similar experiences as us also with regards to late pickups, one shit gig, and a general lack of communication from their organisers.

After a brief chat I said I'd see them later, and with that I made my way into the main field where all the punters would congregate. It was still about nine or ten in the morning and it was going to be a long day. I spent the next few hours just chilling and drinking coffee, only to be joined by a few of the others from the band. Groups of Mexican punks would come up to us, say hello and want photos with us. Being as friendly as they were, it was definitely a good way to kill the time. I spent most of the day like this and eventually the bands started up. There was a main stage we would be playing on later, and a smaller stage away from the main area that was well within earshot of our chalet. Every now and then I'd go back to my room to see what was going on and have a chat with the boys, but all I could hear is what I can only describe as the sound of hell coming from the second stage. You really had to be there to realise what it sounded like and to witness it. The Mexicans are the most brutal and hardcore bunch I've ever come across. The style of music, or whatever you wish to call it, makes the likes of bands like DISCHARGE sound like THE OSMONDS in comparison. After a few hours of this I started to feel like it was wearing me down. Eventually I thought I'd go and take a look and see what all the commotion was about, so I made my way over there and, being Mr pale skin among the throng, a lot of them greeted me in their native tongue, and as I say they are very friendly indeed while not being overbearing with it. And there they were, some indigenous band really giving it some and the crowd around them having a wild old time. Needless to say it still didn't sound any better close up. I didn't hang about for long and by this time I was now getting impatient. I wanted to get on and get this trip over and done with. Thankfully, day turned into night. Colin and Hoddy, true to form, had been asleep all day, and with everybody all together we were all of the same opinion. Let's get this gig over with and get the fuck out of here. This was the gig we had originally been booked for. One big festival date, but me in my infinite wisdom and at the request of the rest of the band had got Loko, the promoter, to book us the other three dates. This trip had been really hard and taxing for all the reasons I have explained. We'd not expected it to be so hard, but here we were at the final furlong, so to speak. We all made our way to the stage, and at around 10.30 we hit the stage to a couple of thousand Mexican punks.

We pulled a rabbit out the hat, everybody did their job and we went down really well. Afterwards Colin went back to the chalet and the rest of us went over to the merch stall in the main area. And everybody, except myself, had a good drink and a smoke. We were done and could relax in the knowledge that we would be flying home the next day.

There was just one final thing to sort out and that was the money. We were owed money for each of the four gigs. Before we went out to Mexico, it was myself who had arranged with Loko the amount we would be getting for all four gigs. Loko and his brother met us at our chalet, and as if things couldn't get any worse and with his brother doing his best to translate, there was a considerable shortfall with our money. After a lot of toing and froing, with Loko explaining in Spanish the reasons for the shortfall, and his brother trying to translate to us, Hoddy's patience had finally run out and he became really irate, relaying to them that they were taking the piss. Loco was explaining that he would get our money to us, but as you can imagine, not for a minute did we think that would happen. Once we'd left the country he could forget about us and there was nothing we could do about it. And so that's how it was left. Another reason why this trip had become a nightmare from start to finish. We got paid just over half of what we were owed and I vowed to myself that once we got back to England I would be on Loko's case for the remainder of our wages. The next morning we all got up and everyone was leaving the festival site. Just before we left in separate cars we had one final photo opportunity with a huge group of Mexican punks. And then we were thankfully on our way to the airport in preparation for a long flight home. We were in Mexico for just under a week, and aside from the very first gig we did in the capital, which for me was one of the best gigs I'd ever done, the rest of the trip I could have done without. And I think I speak for the rest of the band too. It had affected us all and, in short, I think all of us to a man would be quite happy to never step foot on Mexican soil again. On a personal note and aside from the musical aspect, I would love to have visited some of the ancient and historic Aztec ruins at Teotihuacan, and at one point it seemed a possibility, but what with the unreliability and chaotic organisational skills of our hosts it was never going to happen. I know that the SUBHUMANS got to visit, which pissed me off. Alas, for us it wasn't to be. We flew home with our tails between our legs and into another time zone. I couldn't wait to get home to my woman and the cats and spend a couple of days recovering. One final note on the Mexican debacle which did come as a big surprise for us all. A couple of months after we'd been back Loko, true to his word, kept in touch and paid into my account the money he owed CONFLICT in full. We'd called him a cunt to a dog, but bless the little Mexican fucker, he was a man of his word, and for that I hope he's doing OK. I certainly won't be going back there to thank him.

I had a couple of weeks off, which was a good job as getting over the jet lag and the flight back from Mexico took a little longer than anticipated. I returned to my day job in order to make sure that everything was in order there. I was very lucky as the two chaps who made up the team with myself were doing a great job of seeing to the day-to-day running of the shop. With that in mind I knew I could relax in the knowledge that I could get on with the second half of the years gigging schedule. No sooner had I got back from Mexico than I was getting a lot of information from Guy Days/999 guitarist with regard to the recording of the proposed new album. The American label, CLEOPATRA RECORDS, had approached the band with a view to financing and releasing a new album, and Guy was taking care of all the arrangements. The intricacies of such an arrangement were to be done in a professional manner whereby 999, meaning all four members, would sign a contract agreeing to provide a certain number of songs, all of which being original and new compositions. Thereby, once having done so, Cleopatra would then pay for recording sessions, the artwork and everything else in readiness for a worldwide release sometime in the not too distant future. I received my copy of the contract through the post, to which I had to add my signature and then send it straight back with all of our signatures down: those being Nick Cash, Guy Days, Arthur Billingsley (Arturo Bassick) and myself. The realisation that this was really going to happen finally dawned on me. The hard work was finally paying off and I was in the position of facing the prospect of recording a full-length record with one of the classic punk rock bands from the 70s. With the contract signed things started to gather pace. We had a series of gigs coming up, and so rehearsal studios were booked for daytime sessions in the particular cities we were playing that day. Cleopatra records were paying the band $15,000 to create the new album, and so with that it was decided that three intense sessions would be needed in order to make ourselves ready for the recording process, which would take up most of July. I still had business to take care of elsewhere first. On 1st June I travelled up to The Ritz in Manchester to play at the annual NORTHWEST CALLING all-dayer with CONFLICT alongside DISCHARGE, THE SUBHUMANS, PETER AND THE TEST TUBE BABIES, DIRT BOX DISCO, THE ANTI NOWHERE LEAGUE, UK SUBS and SLAUGHTER AND THE DOGS. A week later on the 7th we played a headlining gig at The Underground venue in Stoke. The gig was OK, but what I remember most is torrential rain before and after the gig. Also I can remember waving goodbye to Hoddy, his wife and Colin, who was staying at Hoddy's house that night, only to find out the next morning that whilst on their way home they were involved in an accident whereby their car was hit quite seriously by another, only for the driver of the other vehicle to drive off in order to avoid taking responsibility for his reckless driving. Thankfully, my people were shaken up but OK. Their car, however, was a complete write-off.

From here on in anything to do with CONFLICT or RESISTANCE 77 was put on hold. I now had to immerse myself fully into the up-and-coming recording sessions with regard to the new 999 album. Various studios had been approached, and after some care and attention CRASH STUDIOS in Newcastle was picked as the place most suitable to provide what we needed. Guy and myself had even paid the place a visit a few months prior when we played at the TRILLIONS venue. It had looked impressive and we both came away and had relayed to Nick and Arthur that it would most definitely be the right place for us to record. The month of June was taken up with five gigs. On the 14th, and after some arranging from Guy, we met at a rehearsal studio in Leeds in the early afternoon. And so began the first full band session with regards the new material to be recorded. Everyone was prepared for what lay ahead and, taking into consideration that the band hadn't done this for over ten years, everyone was on board and committed to the task ahead. We were all thinking along the same lines and the job of getting the songs down and ready for the studio would hopefully run smoothly. There was a lot of work to be done, but this first session was rather encouraging. After that first get-together, which lasted about three or four hours, we headed up to that night's gig at the WHARF CHAMBERS venue. The next day, which was a Saturday, we travelled to Bedford early and got ourselves into another pre-booked rehearsal room where work reconvened on the new songs. This place was a sweat box, what with summer kicking in big time. We didn't look a pretty sight. All practising shirtless, but that didn't matter, we were going in the right direction. Once again though, and as much as it was just to get a basic idea, I used the camera on my phone to record what we were doing. We'd work on a particular song until we were happy with the format and what we were all doing individually, and then record the results. We knew that the songs were in their embryonic stage, but at least we had something to go back to and use as a reference. After another lengthy session of stopping and starting and discussing what needed to go where and when, we were another step closer to being ready. And so once again, and after getting out of the sweat box, we moved on to the ESQUIRES venue to play that night's gig. Now Nick and Guy were writing all of the songs for the record, and for the most part we had been working on Nick's compositions. Myself and Nick had already worked on some of his stuff a couple of months back, and so we were partly ready for the work that needed to be done. In the meantime Guy had been at home working on his stuff in his home-built studio with his guitar and a drum machine. A few weeks before we had started these preparatory rehearsals, I had stipulated to them both that whatever they wanted from a drumming point of view they would get, and I would endeavour to give them exactly what they needed. From them both came the same retort, 'keep it simple'. Guy was very strict with regard to this as he was writing his songs with the aid of a drum machine. And so after recording them on to his computer and sending them to me he was quite adamant that I should not deviate from what he had recorded. This would prove to be quite a challenge for me, as I like to be quite flamboyant with my playing, putting in fills, accents and complicated bass drum beats. I rose to the challenge though, and in order to give Guy what he wanted I changed my style of playing. On more than one occasion, and as we progressed, Guy would stop me and tell me that I was still making the song too busy. I dug deep and disciplined myself in order to give him exactly what he wanted. A back beat driving all the way through from start to finish. In short, I was playing along a simple beat just like a drum machine does. With Nick's songs it was a little different. The two brothers have differing styles and this now became quite apparent, and Nick allowed me a bit more scope to let the listener know when changes were about to occur. I still had to keep things tight and basic, and primarily keep the bass drum beat on a constant. This was fine by me, and to be honest, I was rather enjoying being coaxed in the direction that they wanted. I was willing to do whatever it took to make them happy. Arthur was also most compliant, and eager to get his bass parts down as good as he could. We were all singing from the same hymn sheet and after a week's break we had more gigs booked, with two more sessions of daytime rehearsals in place. In the last weekend of June we had gigs booked for the Thursday, Friday and Saturday. We played at the MARRS BAR in Worcester on the Thursday, and the next morning we were up and off to Bournemouth. We checked ourselves into another pre-booked rehearsal studio, and once again got cracking on with the new material. We would be staying in Bournemouth after that night's gig, and the next morning we would be back at the rehearsal studios to finish off the final touches in preparation for the beginning of recording which would begin in early July. For these particular sessions I came armed with an app that I'd downloaded onto my phone which allowed me to get the songs down live. Having only these last two sessions to get everything done we really worked hard and put in a lot of effort. The first session we got the majority of Nick's songs down, went and played at the ANVIL ROCK CLUB and then the next morning went back to the studio and worked on Guy's songs. After another intensive session we had them all in the can, and I had them all on my phone to distribute to the others at a later date. After we'd finished we then made our way on the long journey to Corby to play our last gig of the weekend at THE KINGFISHER. I was particularly knackered after what we'd done over the last few days. That aside, I was really happy with our efforts. We were now as ready as we were ever going to be to go in and start recording the new 999 album.

Whilst completing these last sessions, and unbeknown to the rest of the 999 boys, I was in the middle of negotiating some final details with regard to three gigs CONFLICT were doing in Scotland. I was in contact with a promoter that I'd never dealt with before, and after confirming all the details a few months prior, I felt the need to get in touch with him to make sure that everything was in order and ready for our up and coming trek up there. Now, as a rule fees for us playing are always confirmed at the time of finalising the dates. Well, I was glad I got in touch with the promoter because he immediately came back to me with concerns about not being able to pay us our agreed fees for the three gigs. As a rule, and without fail, I always get in touch with Colin to let him know what's going on as it happens. Well, this promoter wasn't necessarily reneging on the deal that we'd arranged, but he was definitely backtracking enough for me to think that we would end up out of pocket. After informing Colin of the situation his response was simple and to the point. 'Tell him to fuck himself and that we ain't coming.' Myself, wanting to remain as diplomatic as one could be, and as is often the case, found myself being the middleman. I tried to quell the situation by informing the promoter that, with our original arrangement being in place, the only way that CONFLICT would turn up was if that arrangement was honoured. He came back to me with promises of paying us such and such after one gig and then paying us such and such after we'd done all three gigs. And so there we were, going back and forth for some time. All the time I'm keeping Colin in the loop. I couldn't seem to find some common ground whereby all three of us could agree that we could go up there, do the gigs, and come away with everybody happy with the new agreement that the promoter was putting to us. Colin wasn't happy about the situation, and I wasn't totally confident that the promoter wasn't going to come up short, thus leaving us short. All I was trying to do was to make sure that we didn't cancel the gigs, as I knew that people were waiting for us to go up there and play. At the same time I was really struggling to make the two sides meet. Then to make things worse, Colin started having a go at me. This caught me on the hop, as I was used to him telling me to slow the fuck down at gigs, but he'd never had a go at me about the business side of things. I let it lie and just tried to quell the situation, but it seemed that I wasn't getting anywhere. The promoter wasn't going to be able to pay us all of the money, as originally agreed, but he was offering to pay us shortly after we'd played the gigs. Colin was having none of it and was adamant that I tell the bloke to fuck off and that we wouldn't be travelling up to play, whilst at the same time giving me abuse about the situation. My worst fears were about to be realised. We were now going to cancel three gigs, which in turn would once again make the band look bad, and the reputation as a no-show band come true. I'd been working really hard since I joined to ensure this didn't happen, but now with this out of my control, and myself getting aggro from the promoter and the singer from the band, I snapped. I was just in the throes of finishing my practice session with 999 when I got one final abusive message from Colin. I excused myself for a moment, went outside, and said to myself out loud that I'd had enough. With that I sent him a WhatsApp message informing him that I was fucking tired of him giving me abuse when all I was trying to do was the right thing by his fucking band. My parting shot was that he should go and fuck himself. I was really angry and I'd let that be known. I didn't have to put up with it, and so I did my best to put that across. I really didn't want to fall out with the bloke, but I'd been backed into a corner, and so I said my piece. As soon as I'd done that I then got in touch with the Scottish promoter, informing him that the situation was unworkable and so we wouldn't be playing the gigs, and that he had best cancel them. With that done I then went back to the rehearsal studio to finish my business with the 999 chaps. I got some abuse from the promoter, which I expected, but I wasn't bothered about that at all. My attitude was 'fuck him', I was more bothered about my clash with Colin and what my position in CONFLICT would now be. I didn't hear from Colin again until I got home after that weekend's activities, and to be perfectly honest I was quite gobsmacked when he got back in touch. He was totally apologetic and admitted that he had been out of order and didn't mean to take what I was doing for granted, and hoped that we could put this incident to bed and move forward with what CONFLICT needed to do. I got straight back to him and said that everything was good between us once again. I was relieved that my shock tactics had worked. I love CONFLICT, and by that I mean I respect Colin, Hoddy and Gav and wished to remain the man who carries on where Paco left off.

9. ALL GOOD THINGS COME TO THOSE WHO WORK FOR THEM. AMERICA and BISH BASH BOSH

After being home for a few days, and midway through a working day at the shop, I received the best news I could wish to hear in a long time. Through an email from the US embassy I was informed that my application for a travel visa was being processed. I couldn't quite believe it. After over a year of jumping through hoops, and with my patience being tested to the max, it looked like I'd finally done it. I had to keep asking people what they thought after showing them the email, and all agreed that the wording pretty much confirmed that I'd been successful. I was elated as it now seemed that all my efforts had paid off. The next day I received another email instructing me to send my passport to Nottingham, whereby it would be stamped with my US visa installed within it. I was on the cusp of being able to realise a dream that I thought had passed me by for good. I could now go and play in America, and at the same time experience a little bit of the good old US of A. I informed all of my family and girlfriend of the good news, and they were all pleased for me, knowing how much it meant to me. Then I got straight in touch with everybody in the bands. The news couldn't have come at a better time as both RESISTANCE 77 and 999 had dates booked in the States, and if I hadn't heard anything or if my application had failed, then replacement drummers would be going in my place. Not now though, I was all set to go. My first trip over the pond would take place at the end of August, whereby I would fly over to San Francisco to play at a festival with RESISTANCE 77. Then at the end of October, along with the lads from 999, I would embark on a two-week tour of the East Coast. All l was waiting for now was word from the processing company in Nottingham informing me that my passport was ready to be picked up. A week later that's exactly what happened. I didn't hang about, I drove straight over to Nottingham and, after having some trouble finding the place, I finally ended up on an industrial estate and at a rather nondescript office block. They let me in and I handed over my phone with my details on it. A few minutes later I was handed my passport which now had a new red page added with the words American visa at the top. That was it, I was now free to go to the States.

When I'd been on one of my stints in rehab a few years back, I can remember being given a promise that if I kept myself clean and sober for a long enough period of time, that lost dreams would be reawakened. It seemed that promise was about to come true and that the dreams I had as a much younger person were finally coming to fruition. I didn't get too ahead of myself though, because before I could do anything that was concerned with going to the States, I had another lost dream to take care of, and that was to go into the studio and record the new 999 album.

I love going into the studio. I like the feel of the place. The fact that there are no windows and everything is soundproofed. It makes me feel like I've escaped from the outside world, even if it's only for a short time. While all the hustle and bustle goes on around us it seems that we are in our own little cocoon, concocting little masterpieces that will at some point be inflicted on to the people who are interested in what we've done. I always like to be well prepared in advance of entering this little underworld, because at the end of the day, whilst the clock is ticking it's costing us money to get the stuff down. And although it's not a process that can be rushed, wasting time is not a good thing. After paying the studio a brief visit a few months prior, I was really yearning to get in there and get things under way. With an album's worth of songs to get down, the first two days would be all about the drums. I drove up to Newcastle and was happy to see Nick, Guy and Arthur already there. I immediately set about formulating a bond with the engineer as he would be the one who would hopefully give me the best possible sound. Besides, we were all going to be working on this thing and the last thing an engineer wants, or needs, is a bunch of dickheads that come across as prima donnas and the like. I had fifteen songs to record, and also a reworking of the band's most iconic track, *Homicide*, which would make it sixteen. Firstly, I got the studio drum kit set up to my specification, and once that was ready the engineer's helper set up a number of microphones all around the kit, which would capture whatever I played. The main part of the studio comprised of two rooms one where the engineer would operate the recording and mixing desk, and the second room where I would be operating from. Dividing the two rooms was a huge glass wall or partition, which enabled everybody to see what the other was doing. The engineer would also speak to me via headphones that I would be wearing throughout the recording process. This enabled me to hear his instructions with regard to stopping and starting, or anything else for that matter. Primarily I would be hearing the other instruments and vocals through the headphones too. As I've stated earlier, this process is almost akin to layering a cake. First the drums, then the bass, then the guitars, and finally the vocals. With everything ready we began recording. As soon as I started, I immediately started enjoying myself, which in turn brings out the best in me. Now these songs weren't all about 'crash bang wallop', and although a fair few were of a similar style, there were a lot of subtle differences that had to be adhered to in order for Nick and Guy to be happy with what I was doing. The main body of songs, which were Nick's, were all very mid-paced, even verging on slow, but both Nick and Guy had both written two of the more punky tracks, Nick's track, called *Shoot,* and Guy's track called *Addicted*. Guy requested that I come up with a tight and snappy drum intro to his song, and so that's what I did. During the song *Shoot* there's a part where everything drops out and just the drums keep the momentum going, and once again I came up with something. Both of these improvisations I had never done before, and for as much as the basic beats had to be kept very simple, I was still breaking new ground in ways I hadn't before. On the track called *I Hate It All*, my efforts as an old military player even came to the fore whereby I didn't play a standard beat at all, but military rolls all the way through. On a few of Guy's songs namely, *"Crazy Tuesday World", "Psycho Man" and "Statue"*, the strict metronome style of drumming that he insisted I play came into good use, which I have to say worked to good effect, as it definitely helps with making the songs come across as catchy and solid. One of his songs which was rather taxing to remain focused on was the very slow *Timebomb*. It was difficult not to speed up, and with it once again remaining very solid and straightforward on the beat, this tested me somewhat. On Nick's song *The Midnight Express* I even incorporated a different style again with more of a percussive feel on the verses and then the usual beat on the chorus. The only song where I was given free rein to rock out, so to speak, was the Nick-penned song *The Pit And The Pentagon*. For me this is my least favourite song I recorded on these sessions, as I feel that it's just a standard punky rock'n'roll song played with a bit more gusto. An album filler, so to speak. That being said I recorded the song, putting in a lot of energy, and since the album's release I've noticed that a fair few people have stated it as being one of the better songs of the bunch. I recorded a large proportion of the tracks on that first day, but with still a fair amount to do the following day, it was only natural that I'd stay in Newcastle with Nick and Guy, with Arthur going home that night, and us all returning for the next day's session. We were staying at a Premier Inn within eyeshot of the River Tyne and the bridge of the same name. After parking up at the inn I ventured out and took a long stroll along the river. I was well pleased with the day's efforts, and rang home and told my girlfriend how well it was going. The next morning, and as per usual being up early, I ventured out and parked myself up at some cafe for an hour or so in preparation for the day's proceedings. I like these brief interludes of solitude as it allows me to take stock and get myself geared up for whatever lay ahead. Back to the studio and more recording, and slowly but surely I was getting through the tracks. I would have a break after doing one or two as it's nigh on impossible to play a track perfectly the first time round. I'd pretty much get the track down on the third attempt, which was all well and good, but sometimes very frustrating. Especially if I was on a near-perfect take only to fuck it up right near the end. Then it would be me saying, 'Sorry Mr Engineer, let's take it from the top.' Being as well prepared and well-rehearsed as I was, by the mid-afternoon I'd finished all 15 songs to the best of my ability. There was just one remaining song to record, and that was the iconic *Homicide* track. Now the record company wanted the track to be as close to the original recording as we could get. Our efforts were to be rewarded with an extra couple of thousand dollars for a real and true representation of the original song. I played along to the original 1977 recording, and after having played the song loads of times at gigs, and with just a couple of minor adjustments, on the second take I had it down. This particular recording wasn't going to be part of the new album, but was going to be used by the record company due to the fact that the original recording didn't belong to the band anymore. Something to do with publishing rights, and the music business side of things. Something I know very little about. My work here was done and the rest of the band could now start to put their individual parts over the top of my drumming. For the next month or so that's exactly what happened. I left them and returned back home. Arthur didn't take long at all to get his bass lines down, but Nick and Guy would be holed up for some time, and really went to town on making the songs sound full and complete. This wasn't going to be an all-out punk album. This was a 999 record and, like a lot of the band's output, it would have some songs on it that made it stand out from the rest of the so-called punk fraternity. I would venture back up to Newcastle on a further three occasions, to add some bits of percussion on a couple of songs, and even a couple of piano notes on the song *I Hate It All* and to take part in the final mixing of the songs. With the whole of July being taken up recording the album, I would have been off up to Scotland to fulfil the three dates with CONFLICT. But with that debacle out the way, and with myself being quite thankful that it was, I now had something else on the horizon to look forward to.

I had good reason to be looking forward to the Rebellion festival of 2019. CONFLICT had been banned from the event due to an altercation between Colin and members of the security team. Now, it is not for me to divulge all of the details, but let's just say it had got rather messy, with Colin being escorted out of the Winter Gardens by a considerable amount of security people, with the sole intention of never letting him or the band near the festival again. Now this wasn't down to Darren Russell, as he, from what I can gather, has always championed the band. The decision was made by the people who oversaw the security arrangements and who were a totally separate organisation altogether. After a seven-year ban that had held fast, it was lifted with strict instructions that there wouldn't be a repeat performance and that CONFLICT would show a commitment of reconciliation as a sure sign that the incident was definitely in the past. Colin came up with the idea that any money the band were to be paid would be put to good use and donated to a respectable charity for the homeless. With all of that in place, and all of us agreeing that it would be the right thing to do, the ban was lifted and we were booked to play the Casbah stage on the

Sunday. Everyone was stoked and raring to go, especially considering that none of us thought that this would happen. This was great news to me because it meant that for the second time I'd be playing with all three of my bands. On this occasion though, I wouldn't have to play all three sets on one day. All three slots were on separate days, which was a huge relief. And what a relief it turned out to be. If there's anything to be said about Rebellion 2019, aside from the fact that it was another great festival, it was the heat. For some reason it was so hot in the venues that for a lot of people it was unbearable, to the point where people were leaving the venues after half an hour or so. This was a shame, especially when bands were playing 45-minute sets only for the punters to leave the building in search of fresh air outside. Don't get me wrong, it's always great to be up in Blackpool at the greatest punk festival in the world, with good weather adding to the overall atmosphere, but this year was particularly hot for everyone involved, and hence my relief at having my sets over consecutive days. A first for me was the fact that I would be up in Blackpool for the duration of the festival, due to playing my first slot on the Thursday with RESISTANCE 77 in the Casbah. I had the Friday off and then played on the Saturday afternoon with 999 in the Empress Ballroom. On the Sunday I did my final slot once again in the Casbah with CONFLICT.

After having played the festival repeatedly over the years, and playing in all the different venues, I can honestly say that the Casbah stage was by far the best to play. After having a facelift and the acoustics getting sorted, I think that a lot of you out there who have attended Rebellion would probably say the same too. On a personal level, to play to a packed house in the Empress Ballroom is a real buzz, and I love it every time I play in there. But the sound is always a bit of an issue, and I think it is for the punters too, depending on where they are standing. The Casbah however, is quite different and for me a great experience.

Like I say, in 2019 it was just too hot, but I feel that I need to mention that for the first time in many years, I actually had a bit of a wobble, and I put that down to a number of things. Having played with Resistance 77 on the Thursday, which was a great way to start the weekend as loads of people turned out and we put on a great gig. The next day and, with having nothing to do. After spending all of the day milling about, as the day wore on, and with a little tiredness kicking in, I starting to feel uncomfortable. People were getting more lubricated, which was fine by me, but for once I felt my guard starting to slip and felt a desire to have an alcoholic drink. Thankfully I recognised this trigger and removed myself from temptation, called it an early night, and returned to my hotel early to put myself out of harm's way. It would have been easy for me to think, 'Oh, just one drink won't hurt,' but with someone like me that's not how it works, hence the urgency of removing myself from danger. The next morning I felt loads better, and that was partly due to knowing that I was playing that day with 999. I'd recognised the trigger and thankfully had done the right thing to keep myself safe. Having just recently recorded the album, morale in the 999 camp was as high as it had ever been, and this performance was the best we'd played at the festival since I'd joined the band. The next and final day was the climax for me as it would point to the return of CONFLICT to the festival. I was so looking forward to the gig, as was the rest of the band. Everyone had travelled up under their own steam, with Gav and Hoddy planning on getting to the gig, performing, and then heading straight back home afterwards. Colin made his way up from London on the train and requested that I meet him at the station. I headed up to meet him and didn't have to wait too long for him to turn up. We started to walk towards the festival site, and as we did so, Colin was in good spirits as people recognised him and myself. We had a couple of hours till stage time and so this allowed him to mill about and soak up the atmosphere. Within an hour of our slot we all met each other and commented on how hot it was in there. With minutes to go I made my way to our dressing room and was greeted by the band, but with JEFF JANIAK from DISCHARGE and Pinch from the DAMNED also in attendance. It was good to see them and for the first time in a long while, I actually felt a little nervous.

Pinch is one of the best drummers out there, and I had replaced him a few years earlier by filling his shoes with the ENGLISH DOGS when he went off and joined the DAMNED. Now, I've always had a lot of respect for Pinch as a player, and knowing that he was going to watch us play only added to my nervousness. I had no time for that though, as it was time to get ready. Jesus, it was hot. I'd made sure that I had brought along the massive backdrop that we'd had made up, so that we looked the dog's bollocks as a band. And then before I knew it we went and started. The Casbah was rammed and for the next fifty minutes we played a lot of the classic CONFLICT songs, with all of us giving it 100 per cent. The sound on stage was brilliant, which made my job easier and really enjoyable. CONFLICT are a different entity than a lot of the other bands. For one, the songs aren't riddled with catchy choruses and the like, but they do have something else. For me it's the way the music has been written, and of course, a lot has to do with what Colin is saying. His words resonate as powerfully today as they did years ago when I first heard them. My nerves soon dwindled once we were headlong into the first couple of songs, and so with that I went into full-on attack on the drums. One of the highlights of the set was when Jeff from DISCHARGE came on stage and shouted along with Colin on the song *The Serenade is Dead*. Before we knew it the set was over and we had played a great gig, and I could tell that Colin was really pleased with himself, and for want of a better word, had put to rest the ghost of the past. After we'd finished I couldn't wait to get outside and get some fresh air. After doing so I knew that we'd done a good job, as loads of people came up to Colin and myself and commended us on the set. My work was done, and on a personal level this was my best year ever at Rebellion. A pinnacle achievement - three sets with three different bands. I returned home the next day feeling rather satisfied.

A few days later, CONFLICT were booked to fly out to Berlin, but for some reason or other it didn't happen. To be honest, I was quite glad that we didn't go as I was still recuperating from the hectic Rebellion weekend. I didn't have long to be called up again though, as towards the end of August I went and played a gig on the other side of the world. For years this territory had been off limits to me because of my past, but now with all my paperwork in order, and an American visa installed into my passport, I was heading off to the good old US of A and the city of San Francisco, to play a festival with RESISTANCE 77.

At this juncture in my story, it's quite plain for the reader to see that I was on a roll here. Only a matter of years earlier I had been at one of my many rock bottoms, only to once again pull myself up and get back on the road to recovery. If someone had told me the things I would see, and the things I would do since getting clean would happen, I would have told them that they were dreaming. But here I was, pretty much living that dream, only now that dream was to be extended even further with the realisation that I was finally heading to the States to play. In the last week of August I met the lads from RESISTANCE 77 at Heathrow and boarded the flight to San Francisco. The flight was a grueller, taking eleven hours. I wasn't too fussed about the journey as I knew that was a given when flying around the world. What was causing me a little anxiety however, was what may happen once I got to America. By that I mean the question of immigration. For a lot of musicians from the UK going to the States, especially from the punk scene, mentioning that you're a musician can open a whole completely different can of worms. If you're a tourist then you're fine, but if it looks like to them that you're over there to earn money, it can be a nightmare, with all sorts of uncomfortable questions being asked. With us all in the band having our reasons for being there agreed upon before we travelled, I was still feeling anxious due to the fact that my lot had done this before and I just didn't know what to expect. The fact that we were only going to be over there for four days made me feel a bit better as it showed that we weren't likely to be earning so-called bucks over there. With that in mind it was agreed that if any of us were pulled aside and questioned, then we were over there to celebrate a birthday. Which in actual fact did happen to be the case. After the extensive flight we landed at Frisco International and in a different time zone. With an eight-hour time difference I did feel a little strange, especially with not having a proper sleep on the flight. My greatest fear proved to be founded because, after disembarking the flight and getting into the customs block, there happened to be a fucking great long queue. I joined it along with the rest of my crew, then waited to be called for my passport to be checked. Lo and behold, after checking my visa I was asked to accompany a customs officer to another area. As I looked back at the queue I saw my bandmates fade away, and for the next 30 to 45 minutes I was left with a massive feeling of anxiety while I waited in a secluded room to be interviewed. I was facing a stoic-looking bunch of officers in their blue uniforms and nothing but loads of possible questions that they may ask me bouncing around in my head. I kept calm and thought to myself, 'What will be will be.' At long last I was called by a gentlemen of colour to come forward, so I grabbed my rucksack and braced myself. He proceeded to ask me the purpose of my visit, to which I replied, 'I'm here to celebrate a friend's birthday.' He asked me how long I was planning on staying and I told him for a few days. Now, I'd made sure that I wasn't overdressed for the journey, but I was really hoping that this guy wasn't going to want to search my bag, the reason being that I had punk T-shirts and a couple of studded belts in there. I didn't want to give away the fact that I may be a musician. I didn't have to worry as no sooner had he finished his line of questioning than he stamped my passport, wished me a pleasant stay, and sent me on my way. I was in, and with that I breathed a sigh of relief and went off to find the others. I couldn't help but laugh when I greeted the others as they all looked rather concerned, as it had taken me so long to get through. They all knew the hassle I had to go through to do this, and so with us all together we made our way to meet the organisers of the festival. We met our driver and he was a punk rock dude called RANDY. The DRONGOS FOR EUROPE from Birmingham had flown over as well, and after having a brief sit down and a drink it was time to go. We all piled into the van and headed towards Oakland, just outside San Francisco, where the festival was taking place. I started to realise that I was actually in America because as we headed down the motorway, or freeway as they like to call it, the San Francisco skyline came into view and the city looked really impressive.

As we passed over the bridge leading into the city, to my right I caught a glimpse of the Rock, otherwise known as Alcatraz, with a hazy view of the Golden Gate bridge a little further in the distance. We got to the hotel in Oakland, which thankfully was within earshot of the festival site, and after getting checked in with the rest of the band I flopped on my bed, thankful that I had finally made it. We were booked to have a rehearsal the next day so it was important to try and get some rest. This wouldn't normally be an issue, but as in the time I went to Mexico, my body clock was all over the place. I didn't get much sleep, which I pretty much expected, and the next morning I ventured out in a search of breakfast. Adjacent to our hotel I found the archetypal and generic-type all-American diner. I parked myself down at the bar right opposite where all the food was being prepared. People of all denominations were entering for their main meal of the day. Truckers, bikers, everyday people and obviously other punks who were there for the festival were situated in the booths around the place. Varying different-looking ladies, Hispanic, Mexican and white American, were taking orders and constantly filling people's cups with coffee. I was in a prime position to take in what for me was a new experience. Two Mexican dudes were cooking all of the food, and the portions that were coming out were huge. The girls looked great in their uniforms and I was now getting my first taste of America. It may not sound like much to you, the reader, but I was really enjoying this, listening to the hustle and bustle, and watching food go out in all directions, while listening to yank ladies with their drawling American accents. One of the waitresses who served me kept coming up to me every now and then, asking me, 'Is everything OK, baby?' which I found most amusing. She looked like a really glammed-up version of Amy Winehouse, and she left an impression on me. Not in a sexual way or anything like that. But just her demeanour, and the way she conducted herself. Eventually a couple of the band came in and joined me. We drank more coffee and chewed the fat. We got picked up later on and headed to the rehearsal studios. I was told that a lot of the Frisco area punk bands, including the DEAD KENNEDYS, had used the practice rooms, and it was good to be doing the same thing. Saying that, I was struggling as I was completely washed out, having only arrived the day before. That aside, we got on and practised the set that we were going to play. It was still the height of summer over there and it was hot, which was great. After we'd finished we headed back and I went on walkabout with Grenville, the RESISTANCE 77 merch and cameraman. The next day I felt loads better and after another visit to the diner we headed into San Francisco. Randy, our driver, was really accommodating and was willing to take us wherever we wanted to go. We ended up taking in some of the city and enjoyed visiting the site of the 'On Broadway' venue that put on loads of my old favourite yank punk bands back in the day, and the Golden Gate bridge. A visit to Alcatraz was on the cards but that didn't happen due to it being all booked up, which was a shame. Personally I was hoping to go to the WINTERLAND BALLROOM and visit the last venue that the SEX PISTOLS had performed at in 1978, but was duly informed that it had been knocked down some years prior.

We headed back to Oakland as we were playing that night. CHRIS, our rhythm guitarist, was one of the organisers of the festival and requested that we sound check the PA rig, which we didn't mind doing at all. We met a few of the fellas who had been at the rehearsal studios earlier in the day and it turned out they were also working as stage hands at the festival and they couldn't do enough for us. We were playing the OAKLAND METRO OPERA HOUSE with some great bands from all over the world, namely AGENT ORANGE, FANG, THE VARUKERS, THE GENERATORS, THE ADOLESCENTS, POISON IDEA, WONK UNIT, and a great band from Rotterdam called DISTURBANCE.

Loads of other bands were also on the bill but these were the ones I can remember. Come show time, and as always we were ready to roll. There was a fair-sized crowd in, but a lot of them didn't know our songs. As is often the case, Oddy with his stage antics and his natural ability to win over a crowd soon had a number of the audience jigging and bouncing about. I gave it everything I'd got and as a whole the band played well. We'd come all this way to play a good gig and we delivered the goods. Job done. I'd played my first gig in the States and I felt a sense of accomplishment at having done so. The rest of the night I spent chilling out and taking in some of the other bands.

The next day was spent with another tour around parts of San Francisco, taking in some of the hillier parts which very much reminded me of watching old American films like STEVE MCQUEEN'S *Bullitt* and CLINT'S, *Dirty Harry* films when I was a kid. We ended up in the Haight Ashbury part of town, which reminded me somewhat of Camden in London. We went into the biggest record shop I'd ever seen and took in the hippy vibe of the place. A little later on, after being dropped back off at the hotel, I was sat in the reception area when all the boys from the band POISON IDEA turned up. Well, I don't know any of the other musicians in the band but I'd met JERRY A, the singer, a few times in the past at gigs, and we'd struck up a somewhat infrequent bit of correspondence via the internet. We recognised each other, and after having a brief chat, I told him I looked forward to catching the band play later on. A few hours later I made my way to the festival and ended up having a great discussion with a couple of people who were like myself, recovering addicts who had set up an organisation that helps punks, and other people involved in the music scene, who are struggling with, and are recovering from drug addiction. I was pleasantly surprised and somewhat impressed that there was such a help group and that sort of camaraderie within the music scene, and thought how positive and beneficial it would be to have such an organisation in the UK.

I was really looking forward to watching POISON IDEA, a band I'd been into since the early 90s. And, after another brief chat with Jerry A, they went on and I had the perfect vantage point to watch them from the side of the stage. I didn't watch the whole set as I was knackered and decided to make my way back to the hotel. One thing I did notice about the Oakland and San Francisco area was that there was a pervasive aroma of cannabis nearly everywhere I went. I can smell it now, just thinking about it. What with the laws being loosened in certain states, and shops being opened to cater for the demand, I suppose it will just become the norm. These things definitely left an impression on me, and that impression spreads to the trip as a whole. If I never get to visit the place again, along with the lads from RESISTANCE 77, and all the people that I met on that short four-day trip, the waitresses at the diner, the people who helped me at the festival, the other bands and the punters I met at the gig, I'll never forget my first foray into the US of A and everything it entailed. The next morning Randy the driver came and picked us up and took us all back to the airport and we promised to see him the next year. Little did we realise that events would interfere with those future plans. We thanked him for being a great host and driving us everywhere, and he replied by saying he'd had a blast spending time with us. We were all really tired and couldn't wait to get back home. The flight home was long and seemed to take forever, but I'd had a great time and was pleased that I could finally tick off another thing on the to-do list.

After getting back to England and realigning my body clock back to UK time, which took nearly a week, in the first weekend of October I played with 999 at the Great British Alternative Music Festival in Skegness. Now, I'd played a couple of times at these events, and as much as I'd like to say that I enjoyed playing them, I'd often found them to be quite hard work. It was the whole setup that seemed to make it so. In my mind, these venues weren't really designed for punk rock bands per se, and as much as the stage crew and the sound people were always very friendly and very professional, I get the impression that they're used to working with artists of a somewhat different ilk, artists who are used to wanting a somewhat different sound than that usually associated with punk rock-type bands. I'd often struggled playing a gig in such an alien kind of environment. However, on this occasion it was to be a completely different experience. What made all the difference was the fact that for once we had as long as we wanted to get things right on stage in preparation for the gig. The event had started on the Friday and we were booked to play on the Sunday. We were the first band on at around just after midday. This meant that we could get our sound and setup just right without having to rush. With it being just a one- off gig, Guy, our guitarist, came down to mine on the Saturday, and on the Sunday we would meet Nick Cash and Arturo at the venue at around 10.30. It was great getting into the venue early with all of the stage hands and sound crew waiting for us to set up the sound, which would be not only for us, but that would also set the stage for all the other bands that followed. We were able to take our time and get things just right. The sound check would prove to be a little different than usual because, as well as playing the song *Homicide*, which we always did to get the sound of everything just right, having ample time on our hands, we proceeded to play and practice unrehearsed songs like *Boiler* and *English Wipeout*, that were to be new additions to the set for the up and coming East Coast American tour. When we felt that we'd done enough, and with about an hour to go to show time, I went and met a couple of mates, knowing that we were on top form and ready. That was specifically down to the fact that we hadn't had to rush like we usually do. A fifteen to twenty-minute turnover is usually all we get, and then before you know it's straight into the set, and before you know it is time for the next band to go on. The place filled up from midday, and by the time we went on the venue was near enough full. There's a few things for me that made the gig memorable. One was that we played really well, and that was partly down to the great sound we had on stage. I can remember that during the song *Feeling Alright With The Crew*, in the middle part of the song we brought everything right down, with Nick Cash paying homage to the recently deceased BARRY MASTERS, singer of EDDIE AND THE HOT RODS.

After our slot I then had to meet up with a guy I'd recently sold some memorabilia to. His name is GRAHAM 'BEANO' HEENAN, and he's a very popular face on the punk scene. Now, he's been battling a condition that is known as motor neuron disease. Well, we'd arranged to meet as he'd already paid for these items and so it was just left for me to put them in his hands. We meet up and on greeting the guy he looks the dog's bollocks, with his own punk look down to a tee. But he was struggling to communicate with me, and I just thought how brave he was, not letting his illness hold him back from doing the things that he wanted to do. I got someone to take a picture of the pair of us for posterity, and later paid a dedication to him via the social media, out of respect for him and his attitude towards his ongoing battle. A true warrior, in my mind. We parted company and he was the happier for it as he'd just taken delivery of his bits of punk rock nostalgia. After that I went and met some of my old punk friends from my home town who'd all gone to the festival, and we sat down, ate some grub and had a laugh for about an hour. This was great, as I hardly ever had the opportunity of my home crowd coming to see me play, as I was more often than not playing a long way from home. So yeah, playing the festival on that occasion happened to be the best one yet for all the right reasons. After my meet up with my fellow Granthamians I headed back into the venue just to soak up a bit of the atmosphere before finding Guy and then heading off back home. It had been a good day. If I had been busy up to this point, and this year being the busiest I'd ever had, then I was about to reach the high point. In a matter of days I was about to fly off once more to America, to commence on what would be 999's first US tour in many years. Arthur had sorted everything out with the Americans and all was in place. I was going to be in the country for two weeks with these boys and I sincerely hoped it would be an adventure rather than an ordeal, and I knew I had to prepare myself. There was going to be a lot to take into consideration, the first being the temptations that go hand in hand with being on tour and being a long way from home. A relapse didn't need to happen, and it couldn't happen. The long drives, the tiredness, the Americans and their exuberance, a whole list of factors played around in my head. I approached the tour with an open mind, but with a positive outlook, as this is what I'd wanted to do all my life. Inside I was buzzing and couldn't wait to go over there and face what was coming. This was going to be an adventure.

On 21 October I caught a train from Grantham and made my way down to Heathrow Airport. Arthur had flown over a couple of days before the rest of us. Nick and Guy were catching their own flight and I was making my own way over. A little bit daunting, as you can imagine, travelling on one's own, but I'd done this before and I think it was the fact that I was going to America that put me slightly on edge. I needn't have worried though, I knew that I had to be alert and ready for any obstacle that might present itself. All I needed to do was make sure I made it to the flight on time, which I did. The flight was great as I had a row of seats all to myself so I could at least stretch out and get some semblance of rest, which for the most part made the flight a pleasurable one. A number of hours later I landed in Philadelphia and, with the memory of immigration in San Francisco still etched in my mind, I wasn't overly surprised when once again I had the rigmarole of being taken aside and being questioned by the US immigration people before being allowed to enter. I put this down to the nature of the visa in my passport, and I can only imagine that on checking the nature of it, that it must bring up a red flag, so to speak, that requires a little further investigation when letting people through. Once through, I made my way to the airport reception and for a few moments I felt totally alone and isolated. The airport was near-enough empty and for the time being all I could do was wait until someone came to pick me up. Eventually a gent appeared who looked a little alternative and made a beeline for me, and asked me if my name was Stoo. I said it was and he introduced himself as JOHN. Little did I know it at the time but this guy was the one who had arranged the whole tour. But he also happened to be the front man and bass player in the band that would support 999 on all dates of the tour. His band are called THE CLAP and they were providing pretty much everything for the tour - a van and all of the equipment for both bands to play each night for the next two weeks. And so it began, and as each night progressed, 999 along with THE CLAP worked and lived together. They would prove to be good friends who seemed to relish being on tour with an original seventies punk band, and they showed that by making sure that if we had any problems, they were there to help us sort them out. We played gigs in Philadelphia, New York twice, Pennsylvania, Massachusetts, New Jersey twice, Washington DC, Pittsburgh, Cincinnati, Chicago and Cleveland. All in all, we played thirteen gigs in twelve days, which seemed like it may be a tall order to complete, but to be honest it seemed to get easier with each gig we did. As a band we definitely got tighter and tighter after each night. And that showed with the audience response at each gig. Of course some gigs were better than others, which is always the case. And some gigs were better attended than others. But we knew that we were doing something right as thousands of dollars' worth of 999 T-shirts had been sold, to the point that we had others made while we were on the road and delivered to us when we arrived at another of the venues. As I write this down the tour conjures up a large array of memories that make me realise how far I had come since those days, years back, when I was in a dark place and could only dream of doing exactly what I was doing right now. To put it plainly, I was now living the dream, and I intended on enjoying it as much as I could.

I informed all of those who were with us on the tour that I didn't drink or use drugs anymore. It wasn't that I felt awkward, or anything like that. It just cleared the topic up straight away without me having to repeat myself over and over again. It was just that at every gig we would turn up to, the people who were in charge of that night's venue would always make sure that the bands had an ample supply of booze of all denominations in stock ready. The boys from THE CLAP were all pretty much about getting loaded, as they say over there, and there was a fair amount of weed and stimulants flying about. All good fun, but deep down I knew I had to keep my awareness on high alert. Living in the moment was great, but I also had to think of the greater good. By that, what I'm saying is that having a slip-up in America would probably mean still suffering the consequences now. As it happened, it didn't turn out to be a problem, as my resolve was solid and I didn't buckle, although I have to admit that whilst over there I did get offered crystal meth one night, and angel dust on another. On both times my inner demon pricked up his ears in interest, having tried neither of those two very interesting-sounding substances in the past. For a brief moment I was tempted. Thankfully, the invisible wall of steel I had built around myself held fast, and I kindly declined. As I say, I was living in the moment and I was enjoying myself without that shit. The first gig in Philadelphia was touch and go as Nick and Guy's flight was delayed by nearly seven hours. So, rather than getting into the States late the night before, we picked them up from the airport mid-afternoon, and by the time they got through customs we had to go straight to the venue and sound check. I felt a bit sorry for them having to get straight off a flight without a break and head straight to work, so to speak. To their credit though, they didn't let it bother them and just got on with it as if it was just business as usual. We played the gig and afterwards, when It had calmed down, a woman wanted to interview myself and Guy for some radio station. Anyway, she had a companion with her, a black guy who was introduced to me as one of the original members of the all-black punk band from the late seventies called PURE HELL. I couldn't quite believe it as I instantly remembered that the band in question had hung out with Sid Vicious in 1978. With that, the interview went out the window for me as a wanted to quiz Mr PURE HELL about his time with Sid. To be honest, he was a lovely fellow and it was great to hear him recall his memories of being involved with punk's Mr Anti-Hero. And he didn't look too bad either for 62 years of age. The next day we travelled to New York, which I was really looking forward to, and as we approached, the iconic skyline of the city came into view and it really is an amazing sight. Of course, one is instantly drawn to where the twin towers once stood. As we got closer I looked to my right and caught a glimpse of the Statue of Liberty. As we got closer still we spotted the Empire State Building. We were playing at a venue called the BOWERY ELECTRIC, and to my great surprise it was literally 100 metres from where the famous punk club CBGB's was. Of course, as soon as I got out of the van a couple of us went and took a look at the place. Sadly it's long gone, and what with it now being a posh clothes shop, the only things that give away its past are some iconic pictures in the windows and some graffiti on the pavement. I was really buzzing to be in New York. The venue we were playing was underground and that night the place was packed. I even met a couple of people who I'd met at the Rebellion festival only a couple of months before. The atmosphere that night in the Bowery was electric and we put on a great show. Things were hotting up. As we came out of the venue later that night, I got a great view of the Empire State Building lit up in all its glory.

What a lot of people fail to realise is that doing this kind of thing takes up a lot of time on the road travelling, and we were certainly going to be racking up some miles in the van. A lot of people who would relish touring would probably buckle at having to do so much travelling, and I completely understand if people would just rather stay at home and watch TV or go out down the pub. Not for me though. I'd sampled a little bit of the touring experience, albeit on a lot smaller scale, and I kind of got used to long journeys. So with the amount of mileage we were going to notch up, it was just best to go with the flow. With pit stops every hour and a half to two hours it soon breaks the journey up. And before you know it you're at the next venue. Next up was Pennsylvania, where we played an American Legion club. This gig would turn out to be a big surprise to me because we were playing in a town called Catasauqua, which is a native American word. I wasn't expecting that many people to turn up. The hall was big and I thought the gig may be a bit of a let-down. After sound checking I can remember going out to the van just to get a bit of solitude, as jet lag was starting to kick in big time. I was sat there with Guy and loads of people started to appear from everywhere. Needless to say, this would be the best attended gig of the tour, and when we went on after THE CLAP the place exploded, and once again a good night was had by all. A superb gig. Next up was another gig in New York at a very small venue, which ended up being quite hard work, as the place was too small for the number of people who turned up. People who'd seen us a couple of nights before came once again to see us, and after each night, I would be in touch with people who'd come to the gigs via Facebook and private message, who wanted to follow our progress on the East Coast. I also hooked up with a fellow Englishman who took some great photos of the second New York gig and sent them to me the next day. As much as I didn't fully enjoy the gig, the highlight for me that day was being dropped off outside the infamous CHELSEA HOTEL, where Sid and Nancy had resided 40 years before. I got some photos of myself outside the place, let my imagination run wild for several minutes, and then jumped back in the van and we pressed on. Next was Massachusetts, at the HAWKS AND REEDS PERFORMING ARTS CENTRE, which turned out to be what I can only describe as a theatre. It was a seated venue, which was a novelty for us. A very professional setup and a great sound. I remember them giving us some amazing food, and after the sound check I went for a walk into the town with Guy. The towns certainly look different than they do in England, but after a few days, everywhere looked pretty much the same as everywhere else, only on a much larger scale and with bigger distances in between. New Jersey was next, and once again we seemed to end up at a town that one wouldn't associate with punk rock. But people came out and had a good time. We were still in New Jersey the next day to play a gig for a very wealthy long-time fan who wanted us to play in his record shop. On meeting him and a few of his friends he took us all to a bar across the street, where we were all treated to a 'no holds barred' food fest before playing a weird gig in this gent's very cool record shop.

Another long drive the next day and we landed in Washington DC to play at the BLACK CAT. A fantastic venue which I hoped would be a great gig, but was sadly marred by poor attendance due to some American football game where Washington were hoping to secure some sort of historic victory. All wasn't lost though, because while we were playing I noticed a gentleman to my right stood at the side of the stage, and I instantly recognised him as being MR IAN MACKAYE from the bands MINOR THREAT and FUGAZI. I was hoping to say hello and have a chat with him after the gig, but by the time I went looking for him he'd gone. I did however have a brief chat with his brother Alex and his friend whose name I can't remember. He'd been the vocalist in another legendary DC band called the TEEN IDLES. It has to be said, the band that came on the road with us were a really good bunch and they were pretty nifty on stage too. John, the main man who had arranged everything, had certainly come up trumps with the hotels he'd booked us into. There was no slumming it whatsoever, as he'd done his homework well in advance and for the most part we were made to feel most comfortable and everything ran like clockwork. After Washington we went to Pittsburgh, and after that it was Cincinnati. I went on walkabout in Pittsburgh and, after coming across a bar with mini US flags on holders stuck into pots filled with sand, I couldn't help myself and nicked one for posterity. Later I tucked it away in my suitcase and brought it home with me, where it now resides as part of my window display in the shop. From Cincinnati we travelled to the penultimate gig of the tour in Chicago at REGGIE'S ROCK ROOM. The venue was split into two halves, with a smaller venue which 999 and THE CLAP were playing in, and next door was a bigger venue which happened to have a guitarist known as JOHN 5 and his band playing. After sound checking and filling our bellies, Guy and myself decided to go and check this John 5 geezer out. Turns out he was the one-time guitar player for MARILYN MANSON. Thankfully we didn't have to pay to get in as we were performing next door. I was impressed on witnessing him and his band. He was one of those virtuoso types who really knew how to play. It was very busy in there, but after about twenty minutes I'd had enough of his twiddly diddly fret board trickery and headed back to my own gig. We had plenty in too, and another gig was done. Last gig of the tour and we headed to Cleveland. In all honesty it felt to me like this one was just to make up the numbers, as with it being a Sunday night it was a relatively low-key affair. However, with 999 and THE CLAP having been on the road solidly for the last two weeks, we all had a good time and put on a good show for all who attended. This was the gig where a very pleasant, but very large lady introduced herself to me and said 'Hey honey, d'ya wanna try some crystal meth?' As I say, I kindly declined her invitation and moved on. After all the gear had been packed away after the gig, me being the sentimental old sod that I am, requested everyone from both bands get on the stage so that we could get one final photo opportunity of us all together. It would be the last that I would see most of these boys, and thankfully I got a couple of great pictures of us all giving the thumbs up. A great memory and the culmination of all those miles and all of the effort that had been put in by us all. When it was time to go, and after we'd said our final farewell to the boys from THE CLAP, John THE CLAP main man and ourselves headed to our final hotel stop. Early next morning we started the longest journey of the tour back to Philadelphia airport. I'd had an absolutely amazing time, met some very warm and kind people, and played my heart out. I can't put into words how grateful I am to 999 for giving me the opportunity to do something I really had thought had passed me by. An old friend of mine had once told me that good things happen to good people, and for me this was real evidence that through being good, I was getting good things back. Also, whilst we'd been on the road, back in England the guys who were mixing all of the new 999 album were sending us the mixed album and finished songs. This had given us lots of time to discuss the songs and album while we were on those long journeys in between gigs. By the time we'd finished the tour I had all of the album down on my phone. The tour had also rewarded me with the largest amount of money I'd ever earned in a band capacity. So when I got to the airport I intended on getting some shit-hot headphones, soak up the new songs and kill the time of hanging about. We got dropped off at the airport and we all bid farewell to John and commended him on a super tour. We then headed into the airport and from there I had to say goodbye to my band mates as they were flying back on a different flight to me. All of a sudden I was on my own for the first time in a few weeks. It felt a little strange for a couple of hours, but before too long I was fully focused and thought to myself, 'Right, let's get the fuck home.' Twelve hours later and I landed back at Heathrow, caught a train, and before too long I was back home in Lincolnshire. I was bloody knackered but felt really proud of what we'd done.

All was not well in the CONFLICT camp. Although we'd just completed the busiest couple of years in a long time, culminating in the band being able to perform at the Rebellion festival after what looked like a lifetime ban, little did any of us realise that the Rebellion festival would be the last gig that Hoddy would play with the band. Ever since I joined he was never the most upbeat bloke in the world. He always faced everything in a very relaxed and matter-of-fact fashion. It wasn't that he moaned about everything, or anything like that. I think it was just basically a case of him being a veteran of travelling, of playing and sometimes staying in insalubrious dives that had slowly worn him down over the years. That doesn't mean that he was miserable or didn't look like he was having fun. I just got the impression that he'd gotten somewhat disillusioned with being on the road. I had to remind myself that he'd been playing gigs before he was even in CONFLICT, as a member of BROKEN BONES which formed in 1982. Hoddy's attitude was admirable and quite unique in the fact that nearly everything that CONFLICT stood for, Hoddy had remained true to the cause. Still a strict vegan, and often making me still question why I ate meat. I respect Hoddy for having his own point of view, although I did find it funny when we were on the road. Because he couldn't, and wouldn't, eat most of the stuff that I would, he used to eat crisps and other shit that wasn't doing him any favours at all. But hey ho, fair play to him for sticking to his guns. His disenchantment after the Mexico jaunt had finally put him in a position where he felt that he'd rather stay at home at weekends and spend the time relaxing with his wife, rather than playing in some venue in front of a load of anarchist punks. He'd been threatening to pack it in for a while, and after mulling it over since the Rebellion festival he let us know that he didn't want to play anymore. This was a bitter blow as I have a lot of respect for him as a person, and also as a player. He is a fantastic bass guitarist and a great band member. He was an integral part of the band, and so with him gone there was a massive hole to fill. I honestly don't think Colin expected him to leave either, but to his credit he bounced back and immediately set about getting someone to fill Hoddy's shoes. And that wasn't going to be easy.

10. RESISTING NO MORE AND RELISHING THE GIFTS OF RECOVERY

In the meantime it was back to business as usual. On 15 November I played with RESISTANCE 77 where we supported the ANTI NOWHERE LEAGUE with another band called HOSPITAL FOOD at the fantastic Warehouse 23 venue in Wakefield. I'd now been fortunate enough to have played there with THE LURKERS, 999, CONFLICT and now finally with RESISTANCE 77. There were plenty of punters in that night, and as always I came away with a large poster, courtesy of the venue for that night's gig.

All was not well in the RESISTANCE 77 camp either. And this was pretty much down to me and my lack of availability to play gigs. I'd gotten so busy with 999 and CONFLICT that when it came to RESISTANCE 77 getting bookings, more often than not I was already booked to play with one of my other bands. RESISTANCE 77 weren't about doing loads of gigs, but the fact that I wasn't available a lot of the time was becoming a problem. For the previous year or two I'd actually stated that it would be a good idea for the lads to find a replacement for me on more than one occasion. They'd done gigs with somebody else before, but Kieron had stated that he was willing to plan gigs around my other commitments so that this line-up stayed as it was. The thing is, I could tell that this wasn't necessarily the opinion of the others, and if I'm really honest I can understand their frustration. I was holding them back from fulfilling the things that they wanted and needed to do as a band. And so, just as I could feel a little bit of dissension coming from a couple of the lads, I made the decision to leave. It wasn't an easy thing for me to do as I consider all of the RESISTANCE 77 chaps as friends, and I didn't wish for there to be any major bad feeling. I also didn't wish to be kicked out of the band, as that would have really hurt. Although, saying that, I could completely understand if they had made that decision. After informing them that it was time for me to step down so that they could find a replacement, all were in favour of the next gig that the band were booked to play being my last. And so on 13 November I travelled to Northampton with

Johnny the guitarist to play at the ROADMENDERS venue where we supported the MACC LADS. There was a slightly sombre mood in the ranks, but we all knew it was for the best. I fucking love that band, and so that night, although we only played for about 40 minutes, I played with every ounce of energy I could muster. STUART PEARCE was also in attendance that night. After we had won over most of the audience, who had obviously come to see the main attraction, right at the end of our set and before I played the song *True Punk And Oi* for the last time, Oddy gave a little bit of a speech about me moving on, culminating with him getting the whole crowd to tell me to fuck off in unison at the top of their voices. A nice touch I thought, and a fitting way to bow out. When I got home that night I knew I'd sacrificed something, but it was definitely for the greater good. Oddy, Kieron and the rest of RESISTANCE 77 had supported me through thick and thin, and for that I will always be very grateful. We had some great times, and took the piss out of each other something rotten, but there was never any malice there. We parted company as friends and that's how it should be. I offered my services if they ever needed them, but as it was they could now go off and do what they needed to do, unimpeded by me.

With year's end coming into view I had a wallchart in my shop that was filling up nicely for gigs in the New Year. Pencilled in already were a steady roster of gigs, not only in the UK, but also tours of Canada and the US and one-offs in Italy and Germany with CONFLICT, as well as another array of gigs that stretched out over the year with 999. Add to that the release of the new 999 album and the possibility of starting work on a new CONFLICT record, the coming year promised to be as productive as the one I was about to see out. So in the final month of 2019 I played seven gigs, all with 999. These took place over the first two weekends of that month. We played THE SALTY DOG in Northwich, THE CONTINENTAL in Preston, the WESTGARTH SOCIAL CLUB in Middlesbrough and EPIC STUDIOS in Norwich. All back-to-back in the first week.

In Preston I got double bubble also playing with THE LURKERS that night, and in Norwich we played a double headliner with the UK SUBS. We were still on fire from the States tour and pretty much gave the SUBS a run for their money that night in Norwich. Finally, my last gigs of the year took place at THE READYPOP venue in Reading, THE BOSTON ARMS in London and THE CRICKETERS in Southend. The gig in London I remember as being particularly memorable for the fact that after playing a blinding set we went off for a couple of minutes, with the intention of coming back on, as we always do, only on this occasion the management turned the PA off, and then the house lights on. Well, the audience weren't best pleased that we couldn't do an encore, and neither was Nick Cash, who went into a frenzy and proceeded in trying to tear the massive stage curtains down in a fit of rage. Also in attendance that night was the band MENACE and NOEL MARTIN, who is a lovely chap. Knowing that I collect punk memorabilia he gave me a nice original flyer from 1977. A real gent, who is still a good drummer even in his mid-sixties. To finish off my year, the last two weeks were spent dealing with the Christmas trade at my shop, and it rounded things off nicely. For me the year had been very much a roller-coaster of one. If anything, I took a bit too much on. Fifty-six gigs, bouts of rehearsals, lots of travelling, recording the new album as well as running a business. Sounds quite exhausting just writing it down. But on a personal level it had been the most productive year to date. It also has to be said that whilst all of this was going on, I had the full support of my girlfriend, whose patience no doubt had been tested, taking into consideration the fact that I was hardly at home throughout the year. With that I vowed to ease off a little, and make sure that I balanced my time so that we spent quality time together. And just to prove it, we had a trip to New York coming up. The trip did involve music, but it was a trip too good to miss. And so for once myself and Michele went off to New York with all expenses paid.

Going back to the 80s, when the ENGLISH DOGS had pretty much ruled over my hometown, at the same time there was a slightly lesser-known band who were part of the new wave of British heavy metal scene, and they were called OVERDRIVE. Well, in more recent times, going back ten or twelve years, I'd got together with a couple of the original members and we would meet up, and after a while we composed some songs. A far cry from the stuff that I usually played, which made it all the more enjoyable, as it meant stretching myself as a player. For a long time, myself, TRACEY (guitarist) and IAN (bassist) had just toyed around playing instrumentals, but eventually Ian started adding a few lyrics here and there, and before long we had entire songs down. We didn't really intend on doing that much with the stuff in the way of gigs, etc., as we were all busy playing in our respective bands. Eventually these guys came up with the idea of using the songs that we'd written and getting the vocalist from the original OVERDRIVE back onboard, reinstating some of the original material, and going out to do a few gigs, using the OVERDRIVE name. Back in their heyday they'd released a couple of singles on independent labels and these records had become quite collectable and valuable in places such as Greece, where the metal scene had really taken off.

That's when a call from New York came through. A promoter got in touch and invited us over for just the one gig at some legendary old metal venue and was willing to pay for all our flights and accommodation. Turns out that we'd be in New York for four days and nights, and that's when we decided amongst ourselves that it would be an ideal opportunity to tie in the gig with having a short break in the city for next to nothing. All of our wives and girlfriends were invited. And so when I told my lady that she was coming to New York she was over the moon. Now, I'd been to New York recently with 999, but this trip would be a different kettle of fish, for as much as I still had a gig to do, and with that taking place the first night we were there, the remaining three days could be spent enjoying New York city. So in the first week of January 2020 myself and Michele made our way down to Heathrow. The rest of our entourage had flown out the day before. Ten hours later we landed in New York in the middle of the night. Once again I had to go through some hassle with passport control, which was wearing a little thin by now. My missus though, waltzed through no problem. We were hoping that somebody would be on hand to meet us, but after being in the airport for some time and with it now almost deserted, I was getting a little anxious. We were tired and a little disorientated and so I had to resort to ringing one of the band. I got through and, bless him, he can't have been best pleased as it was the middle of the fucking night. He got it sorted though, and before too long, some crazy rock chick met us and drove us to our hotel. I needed to get some rest as we were playing the next day. Needless to say, I didn't get a lot of what I would consider good sleep, but I didn't care too much because when I got up and pulled open the curtains, I was greeted with an amazing view of the bridge that takes one into the city, with a great view of all the skyscrapers beyond it. Welcome back to New York.

It felt great to once again be in one of the most iconic cities in the world, and even better to have Michele with me for a change. We were situated on Long Island, and after getting some breakfast and catching up with the rest of the crew, Michele and I headed into the city where we caught one of the distinctive yellow cabs and headed towards Times Square. Walking along the main stretch one couldn't fail to be amazed at the sight of the place with all the very colourful digital advertisements that adorn the very tall buildings. We spent a couple of hours walking round and vowed to inform the others, with a view to coming back when it was dark to really take in the brightness and atmosphere. We headed back to Long Island as we were both still reeling from our journey over the day before. My lady can sleep anytime and anywhere, which as you've now gathered isn't always the case for me. Come late evening and my lady was happily catching up on her rest, but I had to get motivated. She decided to stay in bed and I went off to play the gig. We all met in the lobby and got picked up by some of the gig organisers and headed off to Brooklyn. We turned up at the venue, which was called the SAINT VITUS and duly got down to sound checking. Everything was provided for us, which was great, and now all we needed was some punters. Slowly the place started to fill up, and it was then I started to realise that I was attending a somewhat different gig than I'd normally do. These weren't punk rockers, these were heavy rockers man. Saying that though, I then noticed some punks turning up, which was a pleasant surprise. For the most part these dudes were predominantly of the long-haired variety. Eventually the other band playing with us went on. They were called OVERDOSE, and I thought that was quite cool. OVERDRIVE and OVERDOSE on the same bill. Within a few songs it was really obvious that these chaps were very much influenced by MOTORHEAD, which is no bad thing as personally I'm a huge fan of LEMMY and Co, RIP. It was getting late and I was fucked, and now it was time for us to go on. We plugged in and kicked off, and for the next hour or so we had a great time, made all the better with a rapturous response from a roomful of punks and rockers punching their fists in the air. Who would have thought that possible years ago, eh? But here we were in Brooklyn 2020 and it was happening. Around about two in the morning we got back to Long Island and got our heads down for some shut-eye, knowing we'd done what we came over to do. The next couple of days were ours to kick back and take in New York City.

Of the things that we did in New York, there's a couple that will remain etched in all our memories. We went to the top of the Empire State Building and looked out over the city. The views were absolutely staggering. I was automatically drawn, as were we all, to where the Twin Towers had once stood. And we ended up talking about what it must have been like watching the events of 9/11 play out from the vantage point we were at. I have to say it's one of the most impressive sights I've ever witnessed. We took a ferry from Manhattan and sailed right past the Statue of Liberty. A more sombre outing, but still as impressive, was a visit to what has become known as the National September 11th Memorial and Museum. We got a taxi and pulled up right outside the new World Trade Centre and made our way to two 30-feet deep reflecting pools that create footprints where the Twin Towers once stood. Now, these things are absolutely huge and it immediately brings home how enormous these buildings actually were. The names of the 2,983 people whose lives were lost are etched across bronze panels surrounding the two pools. Let's just say for the next couple of hours, while we were there at the museum, we were all very quiet, taking into consideration the magnitude of what had happened. Moving on, the next day we all went to Times Square to experience it by night, and it was fantastic. Very futuristic, and even more impressive than in the daytime. On the day of our flight home Michele and I decided to go to Central Park. Myself being a bit of a sentimental old soul, I felt that one couldn't come to New York without visiting where JOHN LENNON had lived and died. So we caught a cab and asked the driver to drop us as close as he could to the Dakota Hotel, where we made our way and paid a little tribute. The outside of the building is just as it was when he was shot and killed outside. And by that I mean that the golden bell boy's booth is still right outside the hotel gates. From there we headed across to the park where the entrance is still bedecked with tributes to Mr Lennon. For the next couple of hours we walked around the park, taking in its various bridges, underground caverns and landmarks. It was a really nice way to end our few days in the city. We headed back to Long Island and met up with the others in preparation for heading to the airport. A bedraggled punk rock dude picked us up in his somewhat clapped-out bandwagon, which made the ladies in our party wince a little, as they weren't used to travelling around in such vehicles. I thought it was quite funny. We got dropped off and twelve hours later we were back at home after what I can only describe as an absolutely fabulous trip away. If we'd have had to pay for such a trip in a normal situation, then I can only imagine how much it would have cost us. But there you go. Playing rock and roll can sometimes gift sweet fruit, so to speak, and this just so happened to be another one of those instances where it did exactly that.

No sooner had I got back to England that there was still plenty of stuff going on to keep me occupied. I was back at the shop, taking care of business. It's always very important that I reconnect with the very thing that allows me to travel everywhere and lead the kind of life that is less ordinary. For as much as I have very able people to run the business, at the end of the day I am the face of the business and I suppose it's vital that I seem to be still playing an active part as the head of the team. One, for the lads who help me run it, and two, for the loyal customers who have put bread on the table for the last twenty-odd years. Like I say, I was back at work, but was still able to perform duties to do with my musical ventures. For now my attention was focused on the new 999 album. Now that all of the music was down and recorded we needed to take care of creating the artwork for the album and compact disc design. While we had been in the studio recording we had all been in discussion about the title of the record. It needed to be something snappy and obviously something memorable. Well, ever since I'd joined the band, at the beginning of almost every set Nick would bring us in with a shout of 'Get a load of this', and so I made a suggestion that this could be a possible title for the album. It stuck for a while, along with a few other titles, but not everyone could agree on one that we all felt fitted. I remember us taking a break during recording and Nick came out with the suggestion of BISH BASH BOSH, and for the first time we all seemed to like it. The next thing was to get a graphic designer, or someone who knew what they were doing to create some artwork for the cover. So I posted an ad on Facebook requesting all designers to get in touch with regard designing a cover. Luckily I had a great response, not just in the UK but from America too. So I answered a couple of people and set them on after giving them some pointers as to what we were looking for. Within a few days I started to receive various designs, and as much as they were really good, once again getting everyone to agree on one was proving to be difficult. Eventually I asked one guy to use a full band photo that had been taken a few months earlier at the Rebellion festival, and voilà, everyone liked it. A gent called PAUL DAVIES who had designed loads of stuff for other punk bands came on board with some very encouraging ideas, and he was now encouraged to complete the artwork for both the album and the CD. Front sleeves, back sleeves, inner sleeves, lyric sheets and labels for the track listings; all had to be designed and completed, taking into consideration that every time he'd completed something he would send it to me, and then I would have to share it with the others and get the heads-up from them and instruct him to make little alterations here and there, so that we all felt it was just right. Slowly but surely it all came together, with one final detail to finish it off, and that was the running order from side one to side two. The lads gave me the duty of coming up with the running order, and so I sat down for ages getting what I thought would be a continuous flow to the songs. I went back to the lads with the order, and after a couple of adjustments it seemed we had everything in the bag. Everything was now ready for the record company to work their magic, and get the new record ready and printed up in order for a release in April or May time. The next few months dragged real slowly as I wanted to see the album in its entirety now, now, now. Mr Impatient here would just have to hold his horses though, as there's obviously a process with regards to these things. Thankfully I still had other stuff that kept me distracted while the album was being made up.

11. IS IT A GOOD THING TO REALLY KNOW WHAT'S ROUND THE CORNER? I THINK NOT

CONFLICT's last gig had taken place at the Rebellion festival a few months prior, and so with Hoddy the bass player gone, Colin had put some feelers out, as had myself and Gav, with regards replacing him. Once again I'd used social media to hopefully procure a possible candidate, but this was going to be a tall order. As I've mentioned already, Hoddy's shoes were big shoes to fill. Luckily some good news came from Colin who had found this youth who sounded just like the person we needed, A lovely lad called FRAN had started making visits to Colin's in London, and had been making good progress with learning the songs. As well as having to bring a new player on board, in Colin's mind he thought it time to have a complete shuffle, and so with that he came up with the idea of bringing in a female vocalist too, which in turn would mean that when we started up again CONFLICT would be back with an almost new and revitalised line-up. The lucky lass who had been invited on board to perform some vocal duties was none other than FI from the band DRAGSTER. A striking-looking woman and a great singer. For a brief time Colin was tutoring them both, and before too long it was just time for us, the musicians, meaning myself, Gav and Fran to get together and get to grips with the songs. We had some gigs on the horizon in March, and so I secured a practice room in town, and for the first few weeks Fran, myself and Gav worked on the set, and by all accounts the new boy had done his homework and was coming on really well. The chances of Colin rehearsing were made clear, meaning they were probably never going to happen, knowing his history of hating rehearsals. So we just cracked on regardless. While we were doing exactly that, Fi in the meantime was making herself ready and rehearsals with her were in the pipeline. It was looking like CONFLICT would be back on track very soon, and so with everything falling into place our next gig was to be down in Southend at the same venue I'd recently played at with 999.

It wasn't totally unexpected but I got a call from my old mates RESISTANCE

77, asking whether I'd be up for playing a gig. Now I hadn't been out of the band for long, and they'd not had a chance to break in a new boy on drums. So when they asked me to play at The Fleece in Bristol at one of the many all-dayers down there I was happy to oblige. The NO FUTURE all-dayer is one of those events put on by a couple of promoters who put on great gigs all year round. For this outing we were playing alongside GBH, THE ANTI NOWHERE LEAGUE and THE COCKNEY REJECTS. For me it was going to be a good day out with my mates, have a laugh, play a gig and mix it up with some of the punters. And that's exactly what it turned out to be. I had a great time and RESISTANCE 77, as always, played a great gig. I can remember watching THE REJECTS that night too, who had recently acquired a new boy on drums. I thought they were brilliant, made all the better with the new lad on the tubs. Very tight, polished and just a great live band. I stipulated to the RESISTANCE boys that I would always be willing to help them out if they needed me. But at that time in Bristol, and with another 45 to 50 gigs to play throughout the coming year, little did I realise that something very weird and strange was just around the corner.

The following couple of weeks would be dedicated to more quite intense rehearsals with CONFLICT before I went on a holiday to Egypt with my lady. When I got back we would be doing our first gig with the new line-up, and the first CONFLICT gig since the Rebellion festival in August a few months prior. In the first week of March, CONFLICT were to have a full band rehearsal in Grantham. Colin had some personal issues to sort out, which meant he couldn't make it, but myself, Gav, Fi and Fran all met up and played through the set. Fi sounded great, showing that she was really serious by honing her vocals perfectly. Fran was nervous but focused. We were as ready as we were ever going to be. It would have been so good if Colin could have turned up, but hey ho, we were used to playing the songs without him. In my mind I had no doubt that when we hit the stage in Southend, this was going to be the start of possibly a great last chapter in the history of one of the most infamous but influential anarcho-punk bands ever. With the possibility of lots of gigs worldwide and on home soil, and talk of work commencing on a brand new CONFLICT single and album, everything seemed to be slotting into place perfectly. I intended on having a good break first and then when I got back, it would be full steam ahead.

We were about to set off on a well-deserved holiday, but we knew something was afoot, what with the news reports coming through about some new virus that had seemingly started in China. The reports that we were getting seemed to show that it was quite serious, as parts of China were being shut down. At that time I didn't really give it much thought as I was too concerned with getting myself and my other half over to Egypt. Watching this thing evolve though, did raise concerns, what with travelling abroad. I needed to know that everything was OK for us to travel. So I got some advice from my travel agent who stated that there wouldn't be any problems and that we were fit to go. We got to Egypt and the only thing that gave away the fact that events were moving into something different was the fact that on entering the airport everybody who had been on the flight was tested with a thermometer-type device pressed against the forehead. From then on we were moved on through, and we got on with enjoying some rest and recuperation. Weather, good. Food, good. Everything was fine and we were having a great time, with a few excursions arranged for the coming days.

We were six days in and then the shit hit the fan. I was stretched out by the pool when one of the representatives of the resort came and informed everybody that we had to go back to our rooms immediately until further notice. Little did we realise it, but at that moment our holiday was over, and we wouldn't be allowed to leave our hotel room again until it was time to leave and return home. For the next four days all we had for company was each other and the television that was showing blanket coverage of the onset of the Corona virus spreading worldwide. Someone on the resort had gone down with virus-like symptoms. With that the place was shut down, and all holidaymakers, including ourselves, were confined and shipped out accordingly. Thinking back it was a fucking nightmare. Food was delivered to us morning, noon and night, and what with us being at the far end of the resort, it got to us eventually, but not hot as one would expect. It turned into a surreal and strange experience. To add insult to injury, on either side of our room were two families, both from the Czech Republic, who seemed to be having as good a time as possible, ordering loads of alcohol which, to the resort's credit, they duly delivered. We were trying to communicate with each other, but it was no good, and after some attempts at hand signs and trying to explain things, we just gave up and smiled at each other in resignation at the predicament we found ourselves in. I ended up getting a bollocking from some of the hotel workforce because there wasn't a decent wi-fi signal in our room so I clambered from our balcony on to a wall to obtain a signal. Now we were quite high up, and so when these workmen saw me sitting precariously in just my shorts on a long wall they started ranting and raving at me in Egyptian to get fucking back into my room. Not wanting to cause a fuss I obliged and climbed my way back into the hotel room, which now seemed to serve as a short-term prison cell.

What concerned us was the issue of getting back home. Would we be allowed to fly home, as the news was telling us that all flights round the world were being affected because of the virus? We knew things were happening because throughout the final days of us being there we noticed people leaving. Thankfully, we were informed that we would be leaving as originally planned, and that ours would be one of the last flights to leave Egypt. On our day of departure we couldn't wait to leave. And as we made our way from our room to get picked up, we walked through the resort and it was eerily quiet and desolate. A complete contrast to a few days before when the place was a hive of activity. We just wanted out of there, and shortly thereafter we were on our way to the airport. We were uncertain as to what kind of reception we would get on arrival in England. Everything, it seemed, was so up in the air. As we approached England I have to admit to being a little nervous. We flew back into Birmingham and amazingly we went straight through the customary passport checks, picked up our luggage and headed for a hotel nearby to get our heads down. I'd had visions of as being carted away somewhere and put into quarantine, but no, we were back on home soil and thankful that we were back safely. The next morning we had breakfast and the hotel was very quiet. From there we went to pick up my motor, and after doing so we headed home. The roads were quiet, but a couple of hours later we stepped into the house, and grateful for the fact. That had not been the holiday experience we wanted, nor expected, but that being said we were both just happy to be back at home.

Over the next 48 hours everything began to unravel. I was set to regroup with the new line-up of CONFLICT and play our first gig in Southend. It promised to be the start of a new and healthy chapter of creativity, with Colin pledging that a new album could now be worked on and recorded later in the year. It wasn't to be though, because, at the eleventh hour, the gig got cancelled, and over the next couple of days I noticed all gigs that were being advertised over social media were also being postponed or cancelled because of the Corona virus. I'd also only just got back into the shop when it was announced that the whole country was to go into a full lockdown. It was a strange feeling indeed. Everyone's life was now going to be affected as if being in some strange sci-fi film. This was tough for me, as I'm sure it was tough for everybody. No work, no gigs. Thankfully in mid-March, when the first lockdown was imposed, the onset of summer made life a little easier and so I took full advantage of the situation.

Living right on the edge of town, and having the countryside literally a stone's throw away, I have to admit that I flouted the 'not leaving the house' rule and went out on the quiet country roads on my motorcycles. I have a Yamaha DragStar that looks just like a chopper, and a Triumph Trident that I had personally modified. These brief outings broke up my day and thankfully diluted the overwhelming feeling that I was under house arrest, so to speak. That, coupled with spending time in my garden and chatting to people on the phone, definitely made the early part of lockdown bearable. And it was also during this period that Michele came up with the idea of me writing this book. I now had the time and could focus on getting it down. I wished to prove to myself that I could produce something positive from a seemingly negative situation. To be honest, writing became a great source of therapy for me as it gave me focus. Without a goal to achieve, or something constructive to strive towards, I start to feel like I'm sailing aimlessly in a large ocean with no sense of direction in sight. And for me that is a dangerous place to be, as my head starts veering towards thoughts of negativity, and I get feelings of worthlessness and unease. So, in a roundabout way, writing all of this has been the perfect antidote to all of those negative feelings that would have no doubt challenged me during the three-and-half months I was in the first lockdown.

12. STAY CLEAN, MR MEADOWS, AND ALL WILL BE WELL, SIR

Talking of which, a few days after the lockdown was implemented, I reached another personal milestone by achieving nine years clean and sober, and as I faced going into a tenth year of sobriety, having the time on my hands, it gave me time to reflect and realise how far I'd actually come in those nine years. I ask myself this question quite a lot. How did I get to this point?, and to be honest I can never give myself a full answer. For years I was a junkie who couldn't, and wouldn't, stop using drugs. It has to be said that the fellowship of Narcotics Anonymous has played a huge part in helping me obtain the tools an addict such as myself needs to live as normal a life as a recovering addict can. You notice that I still refer to myself as an addict, and that's because I am. I am under no illusion that the addict is still inside of me, just beneath the skin. The difference today is that I don't allow that part of my character to evolve and become fully active. Narcotics Anonymous gave me a few basic tools that I've held on to ever since. To not have that first drink, or in my case a drug, no matter what. To do that one day at a time. To look after myself, and surround myself with positive people. To be honest, I have come unstuck sometimes, as do we all. I possess countless character defects, and every now and then the devil I have inside shows its face. As long as I don't pick up, then pretty much everything will be fine. In early recovery I was promised that lost dreams would be reawakened, and today I can honestly say that promise has come to bear sweet fruit. The last decade of my life has seen me achieve personal highs I thought had well and truly passed me by. And as much as there are a number of factors that have made that attainable, the one single thing that has glued everything together has been my ongoing quest to remain clean and sober. I honestly think that without that mindset put firmly in place I wouldn't have what I have today, and I wouldn't have achieved some of those lost dreams that seemed so distant from me all those years ago, when I couldn't seem to get out of that dark hole I'd dug for myself. Every now and then I do give myself a little pat on the back, and why the fuck not? It hasn't always been that way. I always knew that deep down inside, even when I was at my heroin-induced worst, I had something to offer. And I think that's what gave me the strength to repeatedly keep picking myself up, and to try and forge myself a life without the use of drugs. I certainly wouldn't have been able to write about it as I'd probably be brown bread (dead), in prison or still living in that nightmare.

But hang on, I still haven't quite finished. The culmination of all the hard work, I still had one final thing, one final reward to prove that I had chosen the right path. Midway through the first lockdown the new 999 album BISH BASH BOSH was released worldwide on Cleopatra records. For me this single event is the icing on the cake to this whole colourful story. The gigging all over the world, and the people I've met, have been absolutely amazing. The bands I've played with, and all of the various people I've been involved with. I feel blessed, and underneath I have a respect for each and every one of them, even though at times we didn't see eye to eye. To have that album released with myself playing on it with such an iconic band has made everything I've done in my music ventures all worthwhile, and the single thing I'm most proud of. It's important to me because it's something that's solid and something that will be out there forever, and it ties me in with the legacy of a band I first heard when I was about twelve years old. There's one person who is worthy of mention here and that's Arturo Bassick/Arthur. I will be forever grateful to Arthur who initially roped me in with the LURKERS, but through that opportunity it put me into the path of 999, who asked me to come on board. So yeah, 'Thanks, Arthur.'

I'd like to think that there's loads more yet to come, but who knows? The Corona virus has ensured that all fun is cancelled. It's controlling us all in one way or another. It's definitely kicked the performing arts and the live music industry between the legs. To be fair, I don't know when we're all going to be able to get back out there and get into venues and enjoy this thing we call rock'n'roll. I honestly think that a lot of the older bands may even call it a day. The days of gigging seem like a distant memory already to me. It must be so hard and frustrating for the younger bands and musicians, who too can do almost nothing to further their own ambitions and pursue a life less ordinary in music. And it's when I think about them, I realise again how lucky I am. At least I've had a fair crack of the whip and been out there and done it. Hopefully by the time you read this book some sense of normality will have returned, and we can all laugh and smile at each other, knowing that we got through it. Rest assured I'll be one of the first out of the traps when it comes to going out and playing some maximum rock'n'roll to a room full of crazy, but lovely people. We must remain positive.

On 13 July 2020 I became a punk rock grandpops to a beautiful little boy called HUGO FRANCIS MEADOWS WHITE. A gift, I'm sure, that over time will just keep giving. And so the journey continues.

Enjoy Yours

Cheers

STOO – June 2021

ACKNOWLEDGEMENTS

Some people need to be given the credit they deserve, as my colourful journey as you all now know hasn't been the smoothest one. So, just to wipe the slate clean. First off I want to make an apology to everybody out there who has had to put up with me when I was at my worst. If I ever pissed you off or if I drove you to distraction, I apologise. It was never intentional. For as much as I was never fully responsible for some of the things I did or said, I am at least accountable for my actions, and I am here to accept the fact that I was wrong. These days I focus on trying to be a good HUMAN BEING, and that's the best I can do. Thank you.

I want to thank my Mum first and foremost as she's been there for me right from the beginning. Michele, for sticking with me for however many years and for however many years more. My one and only child, Jade, for showing that in more ways than one, she's a chip off the old block. Matt Thompson, for remaining steadfast and loyal to me, and with regards the shop. Trevor Parkinson, the only one of my old using friends I'm still associated with. Ritchie Moonthing, for possessing the same sick sense of humour as myself. My brother James, who took on a punk rock journey of his own. Raymond Gill RIP, Jim Kershaw RIP. All of my band mates past and present, but special thanks to Arturo Bassick/Arthur, whose path I'm glad I crossed. Ian 'oddy' Hodson and Kieron Egan for supporting me through thick and thin (good and bad). Nick Cash and Guy Days for treating me as an equal. Kevin Boyce, a true gent for helping me get this book together and for looking after some of the finer details (he played drums on SUBURBAN REBELS, the definitive album by THE BUSINESS, ya know?). Paul Davies, for his artistic input. Thanks to anyone who's sold me punk memorabilia over the years and thanks to anyone who's bought memorabilia from me (I know, we're all a bit crazy). Thanks to you for taking the time to read this book and those of you out there who still get your arses out to punk gigs all over the world. Our scene is like no other, so let's enjoy it while it lasts because nothing lasts forever.

Finally, a big thank you to the fellowship of NARCOTICS ANONYMOUS for giving me the tools to enjoy a life less ordinary and for helping me do something I couldn't do on my own.